SOVIET UNION

• Rostov

Caspian Sea

Aral Sea

Tbilisi

Baku •

Yerevan •

Tashkent •

Alma Ata •

CHINA

Dushanbee •

YRIA   IRAQ   • Tehrān

Damascus   Baghdad

Shatt al-Arab

Basra   Al Basrah

Amman

JORDAN

Iraq-Saudi Arabia
Neutral Zone

SAUDI
ARABIA

IRAN

AFGHANISTAN

Kābul •

Islāmābād •

PAKISTAN

New Delhi •

Persian Gulf

UNITED ARAB
EMERATES

• Muscat

Masirah Island

INDIA

BANGLADESH

Red Sea

• Sanaa   PDRY*

YAR*

Djibouti

Aden

ddis
baba •

Berbera

ETHOPIA

OMAN

Arabian Sea

SRI LANKA

Colombo •

SOMALIA

Nairobi   • Mogadishu

KENYA

• Mombassa

Fao Peninsula

Bubiyan Island

Warbah Island

Kuwait

KUWAIT Persian Gulf

Manama

BAHRAIN

QATAR

Tunbs I.

Abu Musa

STRAIT OF
HORMUZ

Abu Dhabi

Indian Ocean

Diego Garcia
Island
British Indian
Ocean Territory
U.K.

*United in 1992 as Yemen

TWIN PILLARS
TO DESERT STORM

TWIN PILLARS

— TO —

DESERT STORM

America's Flawed Vision in the Middle East from Nixon to Bush

Howard Teicher
and
Gayle Radley Teicher

William Morrow and Company, Inc.

New York

To our parents
and to our sons,
Samuel Alexander and Seth Benjamin

It is the policy of William Morrow and Company, Inc., and its imprints and affiliates, recognizing the importance of preserving what has been written, to print the books we publish on acid-free paper, and we exert our best efforts to that end.

Library of Congress Cataloging-in-Publication Data

Teicher, Howard.
    Twin pillars to Desert Storm : America's flawed vision in the
Middle East from Nixon to Bush / Howard Teicher and Gayle Radley
Teicher.
        p.   cm.
    Includes bibliographical references and index.
    ISBN 0-688-11254-4
    1. Middle East—Foreign relations—United States.   2. United
States—Foreign relations—Middle East.   3. United States—Foreign
relations—1945–   4. Teicher, Howard.   I. Teicher, Gayle Radley.
II. Title.
DS63.2.U5T45   1993
327.73056—dc20   92-34560
                                                                        CIP

Printed in the United States of America

First Edition

1   2   3   4   5   6   7   8   9   10

BOOK DESIGN BY MICHAEL MENDELSOHN

ACKNOWLEDGMENTS

The authors gratefully acknowledge the assistance and contributions of many individuals who helped make this book possible. From Howard Kaminsky's first telephone call during the Gulf War through Lisa Drew's careful editing, the people of William Morrow and Company have been a pleasure to work with.

The George Kemp Keiser Library at the Middle East Institute in Washington, D.C., was an important research resource, as was the Library of Congress. The librarians at the Middle East Institute, Christine Rourke and Betsy Folkins, were gracious, helpful and especially patient. Lucinda Conger of the State Department Library provided invaluable assistance during the early research stage of the book. We are very grateful for the diligent efforts of Donna Dillon of the Ronald Reagan Library in Simi Valley, California, and Nancy Menan of the NSC staff in Washington, D.C., in support of our research. We also want to thank Congressman Howard Berman and Lise Hartman, staff director for the House Subcommittee on International Operations, for their assistance in helping us understand the congressional perspective on the U.S. tilt toward Iraq.

A special word of appreciation goes to those friends and family members who read the manuscript and gave us detailed comments, criticism and suggestions. Francis Luban, Claude Salem, Ken Simonson, Jan Solomon, Robert C. McFarlane, Tim Kilbourn, Steven Emerson, Juan Blazquez, Charlotte and Harry Teicher, Sandra Caskie, Robert Booth and Nancy Bard provided invaluable assistance and encouragement.

The past six years have been bittersweet, filled with lessons and struggle, hope and joy. To those friends and family members who stood beside us and believed in us, you have our profound gratitude. You know who you are and what your support has meant to us. We especially thank Cristina Conte for her dedication and hard work in helping to care for our family and home.

To our children, Samuel Alexander and Seth Benjamin, we thank you for your love and good humor, cooperation and understanding while this book was being written.

To our parents, Harry and Charlotte Teicher and Herbert and Charlene Radley, we couldn't have done it without you.

HOWARD AND GAYLE TEICHER
Washington, D.C.

CONTENTS

GLOSSARY

Airborne Warning and Control System Aircraft (AWACS)

Aircraft Carrier Battle Group (CVBG)

AK-47 Assault Rifles (AK-47)

American University of Beirut (AUB)

Arab Cooperation Council (ACC)

Armenian Terrorist Organization (ASALA)

Armored Personnel Carrier (APC)

Bachelor Officers' Quarters (BOQ)

Cables—Overseas telegraphic communications between and among U.S. government agencies and their representatives

Central Command (CENTCOM)—The joint U.S. military service command responsible for the Persian Gulf and Middle East, exclusive of Israel

Central Intelligence Agency (CIA)

Chief of Naval Operations (CNO)

Commodity Credit Corporation (CCC)

Crisis Pre-Planning Group (CPPG)—An interagency body comprised of senior-level officials from National Security Council member agencies, which manages crises

Date/Time/Group (DTG)—The time-stamp automatically assigned to a cable according to the date, place and exact minute the cable is transmitted

Defense Intelligence Agency (DIA)

Defense Security Assistance Agency (DSAA)

Department of Defense (DOD)

Deputy Assistant Secretary (DAS)

Deputy Chief of Mission (DCM)

Deputy Director for Intelligence (DDI)

Deputy Director of Central Intelligence (DDCI)

Director of Central Intelligence (DCI)

European Command (EUCOM)

Executive Secretariat—State Department office that controls the distribution of cables throughout the national security bureaucracy and to the White House

13

Foreign Broadcast Information Service (FBIS)—A U.S. government agency that translates and disseminates foreign media of potential interest

Foreign Military Sales (FMS)

Foreign Service Officer (FSO)

Freedom of Navigation (FON)

Government of Lebanon (GOL)

Government of National Unity (GNU)

Gulf Cooperation Council (GCC)

Hard Points—A connection on an aircraft for fuel tanks, bombs, missiles and other payloads

International Emergency Economic Powers Act (IEEPA)

International Security Affairs (ISA)—The division within the OSD responsible for coordinating foreign affairs issues

Iranian Revolutionary Guards (Pasdaran)

Israeli Defense Forces (IDF)

Israeli Air Force (IAF)

Joint Chiefs of Staff (JCS)

Joint Logistics Planning (JLP)

Joint Military Commission (JMC)

Joint Political-Military Group (JPMG)

Joint Special Operations Command (JSOC)

Landing Zone (LZ)

Lebanese Armed Forces (LAF)

Marine Amphibious Unit (MAU)

Memorandum of Understanding (MOU)

Middle East Force (MIDEASTFOR)—Small group of U.S. Navy ships deployed permanently to the Persian Gulf

Military Airlift Command (MAC)

Ministry of Defense (MOD)

Multinational Force and Observers in Sinai (MFO)

Multinational Force in Lebanon (MNF)

Multiple Ejection Racks (MER)

National Intelligence Estimate (NIE)

National Intelligence Officer (NIO)

National Military Command Center (NMCC)—The Pentagon War Room

National Military Intelligence Center (NMIC)

National Salvation Front (NSF)

National Security Agency (NSA)

National Security Council (NSC)

National Security Decision Directive (NSDD)

National Security Directive (NSD)

National Security Planning Group (NSPG)—A decision-making body comprised of the president, vice president, secretaries of state and defense, national security advisor, DCI and chairman of the JCS

National Security Study Directive (NSSD)

Near East, Africa and South Asia Division of ISA within the Department of Defense (NEASA)

No Distribution Cable (NODIS)—Very sensitive State Department cable the distribution of which is at the discretion of the State Department executive secretary

Non-Aligned Movement (NAM)

North Atlantic Treaty Organization (NATO)

Office of Management and Budget (OMB)

Office of the Secretary of Defense (OSD)

Old Executive Office Building (OEOB)

Operational Security (OPSEC)

Palestine Liberation Organization (PLO)

People's Democratic Republic of Yemen (PDRY; now Yemen)

Rapid Deployment Force (RDF)

Rocket Propelled Grenade Launchers (RPG-7s)

Rules of Engagement (ROE)

Senate Select Committee on Intelligence (SSCI)

Senior Interdepartmental Group (SIG)

Southwest Asia—A geographic region stretching from Marrakech in the west to Bangladesh in the east, comprising Pakistan, Afghanistan, India, the former Soviet Central Asian republics, Iran, Iraq, Turkey, Syria, Jordan, Israel, Lebanon, Saudi Arabia, Oman, YAR, PDRY (now Yemen), UAE, Qatar, Bahrain, Kuwait, Egypt, Sudan, Ethiopia, Kenya, Somalia, Libya, Tunisia, Algeria, Morocco

Special Compartmented Intelligence (SCI)

Special National Intelligence Estimate (SNIE)

Special Situation Group (SSG)—Interagency crisis management body chaired by the vice president

State Department Bureau of European Affairs (EUR)

State Department Bureau of Humanitarian Affairs (HA)

State Department Bureau of Intelligence and Research (INR)

State Department Bureau of International Organizations (IO)

State Department Bureau of Near East and South Asia (NEA)

State Department Bureau of Policy Planning (S/P)

State Department Bureau of Politico-Military Affairs (PM)

State Department Office of the Legal Advisor (L)

State Distribution Only Cable (STADIS)—A highly sensitive cable which an ambassador believes should not be distributed outside of the State Department

Strategic Air Command (SAC)

Surface-to-Air Missile (SAM)

Surface-to-Surface Ballistic Missile (SCUD)

Tactical Aerial Reconnaissance Pod System (TARPS)

Tactical Satellite Communications (TACSATCOM)

Tube-Fired, Optically Tracked, Wire-Guided Anti-Tank Missile (TOW)

United Arab Emirates (UAE)

United Arab Republic (UAR)

Yemen Arab Republic (YAR; now Yemen)

INTRODUCTION

As a guest on the *Larry King Live* show on January 15, 1991, I* was asked to speculate about the prospects for war between the forces of the U.S.-led coalition and Iraq.

During a meeting between Secretary of State James Baker and Tariq Aziz, the Iraqi foreign minister, on January 9, 1991, Foreign Minister Aziz refused to accept a letter for President Saddam Hussein from President George Bush which warned that Iraq "will pay a terrible price" if it refused to comply with U.N. Security Council resolutions demanding that Iraq withdraw its army of conquest from the Emirate of Kuwait. I recalled an earlier statement by Aziz, in 1984, that "Saddam will execute me on the spot" if Aziz even considered accepting a secret message for the Iraqi president from the prime minister of Israel. There was no doubt in my mind that Saddam Hussein would not back down, and I predicted that the war would begin by the end of the week. Broadcast live throughout the world by CNN, Operation Desert Storm began less than nineteen hours later.

From 1977 through 1987, I had served in the United States government as a member of the national security bureaucracy. My government career spanned the administrations of Jimmy Carter and Ronald Reagan, during which I participated in the development and implementation of U.S. policy in the Middle East. This tumultous decade was marked by revolutionary upheaval in Iran and the rise of Islamic fundamentalism, the conclusion of a treaty of peace between Egypt and Israel, the Soviet invasion of Afghanistan, the Iran-Iraq War, the Israeli invasion of Lebanon, the renewal of international terrorism, the bombing of Libya and the Iran Affair. Two vital interests dominated American strategy for the Middle East during this period: assuring access to Persian Gulf oil, while avoiding a U.S.-Soviet military confrontation.

The assumption of responsibility by Washington for the security of the Persian Gulf was a recent phenomenon, although competition between the United States and the Soviet Union for influence in the Middle East dated back to the end of the Second World War. During the administra-

---

* The pronoun "I" is used throughout the book to refer to Howard Teicher, although the book was written jointly with Gayle Radley Teicher.

17

tion of President Richard Nixon, Secretary of State Henry Kissinger devised a security strategy which became known as the "Twin Pillars" policy. This policy relied upon two regional powers, Iran and Saudi Arabia, to protect important American interests in the Persian Gulf. Following the collapse of the Iranian pillar, the U.S. government began to tilt toward Iraq, as the underlying doctrine of reliance on regional powers continued to guide U.S. strategy through the Bush administration. Operation Desert Storm was the inevitable result of America's flawed vision in the Middle East.

The evolution of many of the region's conflicts can be traced to the strategies which supported the British Empire. The British established a presence in the Persian Gulf in the early eighteenth century. The Middle East was the pathway to India, and Britain's policies in the region were designed to protect its Indian empire. Imperial Russia had long sought direct access to the warm-water ports of the Indian Ocean. Throughout the eighteenth century, Great Britain and Russia vied for supremacy throughout the region, most notably in Afghanistan, Iran and India, where the two powers competed for influence in the "Great Game." After oil was discovered, the Middle East began to assume economic value to other nations, including the United States.

During the Second World War, the Indian Ocean was an important route to the Soviet Union for the delivery of Lend-Lease supplies. Great Britain and the Soviet Union moved troops into Iran to ensure that the strategically located, oil-rich country did not fall under Axis control, agreeing to withdraw their forces after the termination of hostilities. Together, London and Moscow connived to depose Reza Shah and place his son, Mohammed Reza Pahlavi, on the Peacock Throne in Tehran. As American needs for imported oil started to grow and the political alignments engendered by World War II ebbed and flowed, U.S. interests in the Middle East began to take root.

By the close of World War II, the global balance of power had fundamentally changed and the United States emerged as the most powerful and prosperous country in the world. Europe was exhausted and virtually bankrupt, as Great Britain and the United States found themselves confronting their wartime ally, the Soviet Union. While consolidating its hold over eastern Europe, Moscow resumed its historical competition with the British in Iran, causing the first confrontation of the Cold War, when it refused to withdraw Soviet forces from Iran's Azerbaijan Province in 1946. This crisis was brought before the new United Nations Security

Council, where Moscow was forced to back down and reluctantly agreed to withdraw its troops.

This was a period of rapid decolonization and dynamic change throughout Asia and Africa. Churchill had hoped to convert the British position in the Middle East to an Anglo-American one, but America regarded both the British and the French as colonialists and chose instead to support emerging Arab and Jewish nationalism. Despite conflicting political goals, the United States wanted the British and French to continue to maintain a strong enough presence in the Middle East to protect mutual interests and provide America with access to their military bases.

Churchill's Iron Curtain speech and the enunciation of the Truman Doctrine ended the period in which the United States was able to rely on other Western powers to take care of America's interests in the Middle East. With the Berlin Blockade and formation of NATO, Britain assumed a military commitment to help defend the European continent, rather than its contracting empire. In this environment, the United States developed a set of regional strategies which enabled NATO allies to cooperate with newly emerging states collectively to counter Soviet inroads and protect Western access to Middle Eastern oil. The strategies of the historic "Great Game" were absorbed by the Truman Doctrine.

Despite President Truman's strong support for the establishment of the state of Israel, the Departments of State and Defense, as well as U.S. oil companies, argued that U.S. backing for Israel would pose unnecessary risks to Western access to Middle Eastern oil, which was needed to help rebuild Europe. They also claimed that U.S. cooperation with Israel would increase the likelihood that Arab nationalist movements would become vulnerable to Communist subversion and allow Soviet inroads in the Middle East. Israel was therefore excluded by the United States and Britain from multilateral defense pacts, modeled on NATO, which were formed to defend the northern tier from Soviet aggression. Turkey, Iran, Iraq and Pakistan became increasingly important, due to their proximity to the Soviet Union.

But Moscow found a way to leapfrog the barrier of the northern tier, taking advantage of the latent hostility of Arab nationalists toward the Western powers. Gamal Abdel Nasser of Egypt was a charismatic leader who breathed fire into the heart of the Arab world in its struggle against residual colonialism and imperialism. Nasser rallied Arab nationalists, including a young firebrand from Iraq named Saddam Hussein, and turned Egypt away from the West and toward the Soviet Union. For its part, the

Soviet Union sought to enhance its position in the Middle East and advance its interests in the region by exploiting Arab nationalism and establishing a political base in Egypt.

In return for wide-ranging political and military cooperation, the Soviet Union concluded a historic arms transaction with Egypt which upset the regional balance of power. Emboldened by Egypt's new relationship with the Soviet Union and his growing mass appeal throughout the Arab world, Nasser nationalized the Suez Canal Company in 1956. Fearful of the consequences for their strategic interests, France and England collaborated with Israel to seize the Sinai Peninsula in an attempt to regain control of the Suez Canal and depose Nasser. During the course of the Suez Crisis, President Eisenhower forced Britain and France, who had been working with Israel, to abandon their plans to seize the Suez Canal.

Eisenhower's unilateral action engendered considerable anger and mistrust in Great Britain and France. By the end of 1956, the United States found itself the self-proclaimed primary defender of Western interests in the region. Fearing that Moscow would exploit the region's conflicts and install Communist regimes in key Arab capitals in the wake of the Suez Crisis, the Eisenhower Doctrine of 1957 stated that the United States would use force to defend the sovereignty and territorial integrity of any Middle Eastern country requesting American assistance against overt armed aggression from any nation controlled by international communism. Washington was especially concerned about the situation in Damascus, where Baathist nationalists and Communists had gained control and concluded a major arms deal with the Soviet Union.

In 1958, Egypt and Syria merged to form the United Arab Republic (UAR), a development which threatened the conservative governments of Lebanon, Iraq and Jordan. In Lebanon, a coalition of Moslem Sunnis, Druze and other forces rose in rebellion against the Christian president, calling for his resignation and political reforms. The UAR supported the overthrow of the Republic of Lebanon, and Syria began to provide military assistance to the rebels. The president of Lebanon asked the Eisenhower administration for help against Syria's aggression. At the same time, a coup d'état took place in Iraq by a pro-Nasser military junta, ousting the pro-Western monarchy and calling for nationalist forces to overthrow other Arab monarchs. These radical nationalist threats to conservative Arab regimes led to calls for Western intervention to help stabilize the situation. Recalling the earlier situation in Greece after World War II, and fearing the potential elimination of Western influence in the Middle

East, Eisenhower sent U.S. Marines into Lebanon. The mission of the Marines was to protect U.S. citizens and lend assistance to the legal Lebanese government.

The shah of Iran's hold on power had been tenuous since he was put on the throne by the British and Russians during World War II. He was finally able to consolidate his control in Iran with the help of the British and the Americans (including General Norman Schwarzkopf's father), who helped overthrow Prime Minister Mohammed Mossadegh in 1953. Mossadegh had challenged the authority of the shah by nationalizing the Anglo-Iranian Oil Company. The United States supported Britain and the shah out of fear that Mossadegh's challenge would create an opportunity for the Soviet Union to expand its influence in Iran at the expense of the West. Concerned that U.S. troops might have to intervene, together with other NATO forces, to deter a Soviet invasion of Iran, the United States increased its military support to the shah, providing $1.3 billion worth of weapons by 1963. Dissatisfied with this level of assistance, the shah played Moscow off against Washington by concluding a major arms deal with the Soviet Union and further developing commercial relations between the two neighbors. The shah's gambit paid off in 1967 when the United States, fearful of growing Soviet inroads in the Middle East, agreed to sell Iran a squadron of F-4 jets.

Despite an evolving military relationship with Iran, the United States continued to rely on Great Britain to protect American interests in the Gulf through London's longstanding ties with the Gulf's sheikhdoms. One of the important roles Britain had performed earlier in the century was to assist in the demarcation of modern boundaries. Unfortunately, even after World War II, boundary disputes, involving territorial and maritime claims, continued to be a principal source of regional tension and conflict among Gulf neighbors. For example, Iran reasserted claims, dating back to the eighteenth century, to the island nation of Bahrain, and to several strategic islands in the Gulf. Border disputes between Iraq and Iran often erupted into hostilities. When Kuwait was granted independence in 1961, Iraq immediately claimed Kuwait as Iraqi territory. The British government sent troops to deter an Iraqi invasion and help ensure Kuwaiti independence. Iraq officially recognized the independence of Kuwait only in 1963, agreeing to the demarcation of the international boundary in return for Kuwaiti "economic assistance." Ever fearful of Baghdad's intentions, Kuwait became the only Gulf state to establish diplomatic relations with the Soviet Union, hoping that Moscow's influence might temper

Iraqi designs on Kuwait. (No other Gulf state established diplomatic relations with Moscow until 1987, owing to Soviet support of radical regimes that sought to subvert Saudi Arabia and the others.) But Baghdad continued to renew its historic claims to Kuwait, eventually justifying its 1990 invasion of Kuwait, in part, on these grounds.

The June 1967 Arab-Israeli war ushered in a new era in the Middle East, as the United States and the Soviet Union tried to compensate for their apparent loss of control over the situation. The Soviet Union proved relatively adept at exploiting widespread Arab discontent in the wake of Israel's victory and enhanced its political position throughout the region. Moscow immediately rearmed the Egyptian forces, receiving in return such strategic concessions as fleet storage and repair facilities—equivalent to naval base rights—at Alexandria and Port Said. Soviet pilots also began to fly Egyptian aircraft on missions in the Mediterranean.

While Egypt's strategic importance was growing in the eastern Mediterranean, Iraq became the Soviet Union's main staging area for projecting power into the Persian Gulf. The principal supply line to Baghdad flowed through the Syrian port of Latakia, despite the constant political tensions which marred the relations between the Syrian and Iraqi leaders. Moscow invested huge sums of money in both countries to outflank NATO's eastern flank in Turkey and to develop a counterweight to the growing power of the U.S.-equipped Iranian armed forces.

After the June 1967 War, the United States also attempted to strengthen its position in the region. In order to preempt a Soviet move into Jordan, the United States replaced Jordan's losses after the war, even though Amman had broken its promise not to deploy U.S.-made M-48 tanks into the West Bank. The United States agreed to sell Israel F-4 jets in 1968 and instituted a supply relationship that soon provided military equipment for every branch of the Israeli Defense Forces (IDF). The United States eventually replaced Europe as the primary supplier of military equipment to Israel. At the strategic level, however, the United States politely, but firmly, rejected Israeli offers of access to its military facilities, owing to concern over Arab reaction.

The U.S. Strategic Air Command (SAC) had access to bases in Saudi Arabia, Libya and Morocco, although the giant Wheelus Air Force Base in Libya was lost in 1970, following the coup which brought Colonel Muammar Qadhafi to power. Qadhafi was an Arab nationalist who saw himself as a charismatic leader in the mold of Nasser of Egypt. By 1972, not only had Qadhafi abrogated the U.S. access rights to Wheelus, but he had extracted severe commercial and financial concessions from the foreign oil companies operating in Libya. Moreover, he became a major ally of Moscow, purchasing billions of dollars' worth of advanced armaments, while offering training facilities and logistics assistance for Soviet-sponsored radical groups and international terrorists.

On January 16, 1968, Great Britain announced that it would withdraw its forces from the Far East and Persian Gulf by the end of 1971. Having already established a foothold in the former British protectorate of Aden, where Marxists had seized power and expelled British forces, Moscow wasted no time trying to fill the emerging power vacuum and began deploying the Soviet fleet to the Indian Ocean on a regular basis. U.S.-Soviet strategic competition in the Gulf and Arabian Sea intensified.

The most pressing concern of the U.S. government was to bring an end to the Vietnam War. Thus, in 1969, President Richard Nixon enunciated the Guam Doctrine, later known as the Nixon Doctrine. This doctrine called for the United States to provide key regional powers with all the means necessary to protect American interests, without requiring the United States to station American troops. Faced with the prospect of a power vacuum in the Persian Gulf in the wake of the announced British withdrawal, and reluctant to commit U.S. troops, the Nixon administration formulated a strategy that became known as the Twin Pillars policy, whereby Iran and Saudi Arabia were anointed as the protectors of U.S. interests in the Gulf. The Twin Pillars policy was designed to preserve access to oil and the stability of pro-Western regimes, while reducing opportunities for the Soviet Union to expand its influence.

In May 1972 on a visit to Iran, President Nixon and Henry Kissinger concluded a series of agreements with the shah. Of greatest significance was the decision to increase the level of the U.S. military advisory presence in Iran and to accede to most of the shah's requests for arms purchases, in return for Iranian political support and the protection of U.S. interests.

Important American interests were dramatically threatened by the Arab-Israeli war of October 1973. With Israel poised to annihilate the Egyptian Third Army, Moscow prepared to deploy combat forces to Egypt in order to prevent the destruction of its ally's armed forces and the potential collapse of the government of Egypt. To deter this Soviet move, Washington increased the alert posture of American conventional and nuclear forces, creating the potential for a direct U.S.-Soviet military confrontation.

Separately, America's Saudi pillar unsheathed its oil weapon, embargoing the sale of oil in order to bring about a change in U.S. policy toward

Israel. The goal of Saudi Arabia and the Arab world was explicit and unambiguous: the Arab oil embargo would not be lifted until Israel withdrew from all Arab territories occupied during the June 1967 War. With supply and demand for oil suddenly out of balance, America's Iranian pillar, seeking to boost its revenues, led OPEC's price hawks to use the crisis to quadruple the price of oil, although the shah continued to sell oil to the United States and Israel. The U.S. position in the Gulf eroded further when the emir of Bahrain demanded that the Middle East Force withdraw from the port of Manama, thereby depriving the United States of naval access rights inside the Gulf.

Contrary to American expectations, our twin pillars, Saudi Arabia and Iran, acted in their own self-interests, rather than to protect American interests in the Gulf. The consequences for the United States and the world economy were severe and long-lasting. By failing to respond decisively to the oil supply and price war, the United States encouraged more pressure from the Middle East oil producers; the failure helped convince Middle East leaders and others that the United States would not act forcefully to defend important interests.

On the political level, Kissinger's adroit shuttle diplomacy brought about the "Kilometer 101 Agreement" to end the fighting in the Sinai, a U.S.-Soviet international peace conference in Geneva (which produced no results) and disengagement-of-forces agreements between Israel and Egypt and between Israel and Syria. Of greatest long-term significance was the ability of Kissinger's diplomacy to deliver president of Egypt Anwar el-Sadat a political victory from the jaws of military defeat. As the Egyptian and Israeli forces disengaged, Egypt retained control of both sides of the Suez Canal, a dramatic achievement that laid the groundwork for the future peace treaty between Egypt and Israel.

Although U.S.-Soviet tensions in the eastern Mediterranean subsided, the dramatic increase in the price of oil and lingering questions of the willingness of Arab states to resume reliable supply relationships led policymakers to conclude that the United States was in a very vulnerable position. American interests were threatened and the United States seemed to be in no position to protect them. The contradictions inherent in the Twin Pillars policy were becoming manifest. By December 1974, Kissinger warned that the United States was prepared to use force, if necessary, to prevent the economic strangulation of the West.

The United States deployed a carrier task force into the Arabian Sea from its home port in the Philippines. In order to maintain a long-term naval presence in the Indian Ocean, the administration requested emergency appropriations to upgrade the airfield and mooring facilities at the British Indian Ocean territory of Diego Garcia, a coral atoll located over 2,500 miles from the head of the Gulf. In March 1975, President Gerald Ford declared that Diego Garcia had become essential to the national interest of the United States. In June, Bahrain permitted the United States to resume its use of air and port facilities, although at a substantially increased cost.

About the same time, the Soviet Union doubled its warship presence in the Indian Ocean and constructed the longest runway in the world at Berbera, Somalia, in the Horn of Africa. Moscow began to improve its air and naval facilities on the island of Socotra, located off the coast of its ally, the People's Democratic Republic of Yemen (PDRY), astride the sea-lanes carrying oil from the Gulf to Europe and America. In 1975 Soviet ground-based maritime aircraft were deployed, enabling Soviet reconnaissance planes to overfly and track U.S. naval forces in the Indian Ocean.

France established an Indian Ocean Command in 1973, and the British continued to "second" officers to the military services of various Gulf states, periodically deploying naval forces to conduct "presence missions" in the Gulf. But by the mid-1970s, only the United States possessed the resources to protect Western interests and compete with the Soviet Union in this suddenly vital, but distant, area of the world.

In March 1975, Iraq and Iran issued a communiqué, known as the Algiers Accords, to end a protracted, violent border war. Fought primarily in adjacent Iraqi and Iranian Kurdish provinces, Iran had exploited the burning desire for independence of Iraqi Kurds in order to weaken the Iraqi government. U.S. and Israeli covert military support had fueled the forces of Kurdish resistance. As a result of the Algiers Accords, the Kurds were left to the mercy of Iraq. Baghdad began a ruthless campaign to systematically uproot the Kurds from their mountain villages, butchering tens of thousands of men, women and children and relocating others to newly constructed towns where they could be controlled by Iraqi authorities. In exchange for ending Iran's support for the Kurds, Iraq agreed to demarcate the vital Shatt-al-Arab waterway down the middle, forfeiting riparian rights, which had previously extended to the Iranian bank of the waterway.

The long and debilitating struggle with Iran over, and the will of the Kurdish rebellion seemingly broken, Baghdad launched a multipronged economic and military development program to rapidly increase Iraqi power and reduce its dependence on the Soviet Union. In July 1975, Iraq and Saudi Arabia reached a boundary settlement on the division of the oil-rich neutral zone that both countries claimed. Unsure of the willingness of Washington to come to its aid following the oil embargo, Saudi Arabia had negotiated its own compromise with Iraq to avoid the possibility of a military confrontation over the disputed territory. Sharing Iran's hawkish pricing policies in OPEC, Iraq rapidly developed its oil production capacity to earn the hard currency it needed to purchase French, Italian and German manufacturing technology and military hardware.

Iraq had learned several bitter political and military lessons in the early 1970s at the hands of the Israelis and the Iranians. Saddam Hussein, the secretive strongman of Baathist Iraq, was determined to avoid repeating Iraq's earlier mistakes as he sought to build up Iraq's power and independence.

President Jimmy Carter was inaugurated on the east side of the Capitol Building on a cold and blustery winter day in 1977. As a graduate student in international relations in Washington, D.C., I attended the ceremony with my close friend Tim Kilbourn. We wanted to experience the moment when Jimmy Carter would become the new president and set forth his vision of a new role for the United States in world affairs. During the Carter administration, the United States went on to take a different course in the Arab-Israeli peace process, but the basic strategy to rely on Iran and Saudi Arabia for Gulf security remained the same. In less than a year, however, U.S. policies in the Middle East were turned upside down as Egyptian, Israeli and Iranian leaders took fate into their own hands and left American policymakers grasping the tails of two very different and unpredictable tigers.

CHAPTER 1

TWIN PILLARS

There Is *No* Internal Instability in Iran

My career in government began in June 1977 and coincided with a period of dynamic change, violence and instability in the Middle East. For the United States it was a time of uncertainty—uncertainty that continues today. America was still trying to recover from the oil shock of 1973, and fears that the unsettled Arab-Israeli conflict could escalate to a superpower confrontation dominated the prism of policymakers. Peace between Israel and its Arab neighbors seemed as remote as ever. In May 1977, the Likud bloc in Israel emerged as the dominant force in a rightist government and Menachem Begin jolted the world to attention by assuming leadership of a new Israeli government in June, thus ending thirty years of Labor party rule. Neither Israeli politics nor U.S.-Israeli relations would ever be the same.

The shah of Iran ruled his vast country from the Peacock Throne seemingly without serious opposition and confident in the strong support of the United States, its military hardware and the presence of some forty thousand American advisors and their dependents. Outside of a small circle of concerned scholars, few considered Islamic fundamentalism, or a particular religious leader, to pose a serious threat to the stability of Iran. The Algiers Accords in 1975 had ended for a time the long, simmering fight between Iraq and Iran, yet Iraq under Saddam Hussein remained poised, intent on building its power to challenge Iran, reassert its honor and become the hegemonic power in the Persian Gulf and the arbiter of the supply and price of oil.

Although détente was supposed to have reduced the potential for superpower confrontation, by mid-1977 the Soviet Union under Leonid Brezhnev had stepped up its competition for influence with the United States throughout the Middle East, Indian Ocean, Horn of Africa, Arabian Peninsula and southwest Asia regions. By increasing the strength of the Soviet naval presence, by its support of indigenous Communist parties and international terrorism, by dispatching Cuban expeditionary forces to bolster pro-Soviet regimes and by selling large amounts of increasingly sophisticated military hardware, the Soviet Union worked diligently to undermine Western interests wherever possible.

At the end of my first year as a graduate student in international relations focusing on the Middle East at the Johns Hopkins School of Advanced International Studies (SAIS), I obtained a nonpaying summer internship in the Bureau of Politico-Military Affairs (PM) at the State Department. The director of the bureau, Leslie Gelb, was a former Pentagon official and national security affairs correspondent for *The New York Times*. Gelb was keenly interested in reducing the sales of conventional weapons systems by the United States, and made arms sales policy his top priority.

On my first day in the office, Arnold Kantor, a young academic–turned–bureaucratic wizard, briefed me on the *modus operandi* of PM's International Security Policy office (PM/ISP): pursue every possible means of reducing the sale of American arms. This policy structure had been formalized in May 1977 by President Jimmy Carter through Presidential Directive 13 (PD-13), which directed the U.S. government to reduce substantially the sale of U.S. weapons to all countries except for NATO allies, Japan, Australia and New Zealand. Carter strongly maintained that a U.S. policy of reduced arms sales represented a moral good that would advance American interests throughout the world. The bureaucratic spearhead of this zealous initiative was to be the State Department's Bureau of Politico-Military Affairs.

To President Carter's dismay, numerous bureaucratic, congressional, domestic and foreign interests immediately sought to undermine this policy. Arms sales were big business. This industry had created self-sustaining interests in and out of government and overseas, interests which waged an unrelenting battle against PD-13.

Carter's preoccupation with the principle of conventional arms control led him to discount the central role played by arms sales in ongoing U.S. national security strategy. The reduction of arms sales, however intrinsically good and moral a goal, contravened the basic tenet of U.S. foreign policy as articulated by the Nixon Doctrine. As long as the basic foreign policy of the United States continued to be reliance on regional powers to protect important U.S. interests, a self-imposed arms control policy, which limited America's ability to give regional powers the ability to act on our behalf, was destructive and self-defeating.

Since the enunciation of the Nixon Doctrine and the Twin Pillars policy for the Persian Gulf, arms sales had become the basic military ingredient of American security policy for protecting American interests in Third World regions. Some reduction of arms sales might have been achieved, at least in the Persian Gulf, had it been coupled with an overt military strategy, or some other security structure, to protect important U.S. interests. However, in the wake of Vietnam and given President Carter's very strong desire to promote human rights while reducing arms sales and avoiding the use of force, there were no serious attempts to develop a political consensus to support such a strategy.

Within the government, arms sales administration, training missions, security assistance requirements assessments, logistics support, and numerous other arms sales–related activities kept hundreds of U.S. government bureaucrats employed. Few, if any, career military officers, civil servants, or foreign service officers wanted to see these activities diminished. Bureaucratic success for many careerists could best be achieved by successive assignments in the arms sales bureaucracy, not in agencies or commands which once advocated U.S. military interventions to protect American interests.

Although I was only an intern in PM, I quickly found myself centrally involved, at the working level, in several high-profile arms sales to Iran, Saudi Arabia, Israel, Egypt and Lebanon. Of greatest significance was the sale of arms to Iran.

The Twin Pillars policy relied on Iran and Saudi Arabia to serve as the two key protectors of U.S. interests in the Persian Gulf. Although the policy statement suggested that the two were to be treated equally, it was apparent that Iran was the more important partner. This importance resulted primarily from Iran's geostrategic location adjacent to the Soviet Union, Iraq, Pakistan and Afghanistan; its physical control of the Strait of Hormuz; its proven oil reserves, daily production and Organization of Petroleum Exporting Countries (OPEC) leadership; its large population; and the stated willingness of the shah to act aggressively on behalf of American interests whenever they might be threatened.

None of the states of the Gulf were prepared to acquiesce to Iranian hegemony, although they welcomed the shah's willingness to confront radical elements while keeping the Persian Gulf sea-lanes open for the shipment of oil. Through his intervention in the Dhofar Province to help the sultan of Oman defeat the Communist-backed Dhofari rebels and his seizure of Gulf islands belonging to Dubai and Abu Dhabi, the shah exploited his military capabilities and relations with American presidents to dominate the Persian Gulf. Iran was our pillar of strength.

For some time the shah had been politely but firmly pressing for approval of additional purchases of advanced weaponry. Upon learning of Carter's new policy, he grew alarmed over the implications of PD-13 for his regional ambitions and ability to compete with the Soviet buildup of Iraq. Although Iran had dramatically increased the size and armament of its military, the shah wanted more advanced fighter aircraft, tanks, self-propelled artillery, armored personnel carriers and Airborne Warning and Control System (AWACS) aircraft.

Critics of the shah and U.S. policy seized on this request to draw attention to the growing and potentially destabilizing nature of the U.S.-Iranian relationship and the creation of what appeared to be a Persian Gulf superpower. Nearly forty thousand U.S. military personnel and their dependents, along with technical representatives from U.S. defense contractors, had relocated to Iran to train the Iranians in the use of these ultramodern weapons systems and to help maintain the equipment. Legitimate doubts regarding the dangers of overarming the Iranians with equipment that they could not afford, absorb or use, however, were discounted, as the sale of additional sophisticated equipment became the litmus test of U.S.-Iranian relations.

Within the U.S. government, three offices fought for control of the shah's request for more arms: one, known as International Security Affairs (ISA), belonging to the Office of the Secretary of Defense (OSD) of the Department of Defense (DOD), and two—the Near East Asia Bureau (NEA) and PM—at the Department of State. In the past, ISA and NEA had managed most, if not all, arms sales to Iran (as well as to other Middle East recipients). Thus, the intervention by PM was viewed as a bureaucratic power grab, notwithstanding PM's legitimate role in the formulation and implementation of PD-13. In order to sort out the bureaucratic responsibilities, Secretary of State Cyrus Vance and Secretary of Defense Harold Brown directed that PM assume the lead in analyzing Iran's requirements for the very substantial and costly additional weaponry it sought. ISA and NEA were to play secondary roles during the analysis phase, but would then become jointly responsible for implementation.

I had a very exciting summer working at the State Department. Most of the men and women I got to know were skilled professionals, the subject matter was fascinating, and I was learning so much I could hardly believe my good fortune. I was actually a part of the process; I was helping to make national security and foreign policy. This is what I had dreamed of doing and the reason I had decided to attend graduate school in Washington. As the summer internship drew to a close, David Gompert, my supervisor in PM, asked me whether I wanted to continue working in the office after my internship ended. I wanted to accept but simply could not afford to work for course credit alone. I needed a paying job. Gompert seemed pleased I wanted to stay and told me to go and talk with Pat Hayes, PM's administrative director. "If anyone could find a way to hire you it would be Pat."

I explained my situation to Pat, who shook his head and told me that State did not hire anyone to work part-time on substantive matters. Pausing and reflecting for a few moments, he looked at me and asked, "Do you know how to type?" I wondered what my typing skills had to do with my analytical skills as Hayes, ever the creative bureaucrat, went on. "If you can pass the civil service clerk-typist exam, we can hire you as a part-time clerk-typist. You'll keep doing the same work, but we can pay you $4.20 per hour." Fortunately, as a senior at Horton Watkins High School in St. Louis County, Missouri, I had the foresight to have taken a one-semester typing course. "No problem, Pat," I said. "When I'm really cooking I can type nearly sixty-five words per minute." Within one week I had registered for and passed the exam. Thus I began my paying career in the U.S. government as a very proud, part-time clerk-typist at the Department of State.

The Iran arms sale study began in the fall of 1977. The shah had requested 160 F-16 and 80 F-14 aircraft, 400 M-60 tanks, 200 self-propelled artillery pieces and 7 AWACS aircraft. PM was directed to review these requirements on their own merits, without regard to PD-13 and the limits on sales. After all, the administration might decide to sell the shah everything he wanted, but might want to schedule deliveries over a period of years in order to skew the annual arms sales totals. Taking advantage of operations analysis techniques, PM determined the range and scope of legitimate threats to Iran which might justify the sale. We tried to gauge the current and future capabilities of the Soviet military in areas contiguous to Iran and analyze the Iraqi threat, with and without Soviet intervention.

After months of systematic study, the results of the operations analysis justified the sale of nearly everything the shah requested. It is important to note that an analysis of intentions played a minimal role in the study. It was assumed that Moscow retained its historic warm-water ambitions.

Given the Soviet Army's military capabilities in areas contiguous to Iran and its ability to mobilize significant additional forces, the sale was justified on the basis of Soviet or Iraqi capabilities. Iraqi territorial and hegemonic ambitions were always of concern to Iran and the Arab states of the Gulf. Since Iraq was a client state of the Soviet Union, it was also of concern to the United States. Nonetheless, doubts about the ability of the Iranian military to absorb the equipment or to use it effectively and the concomitant need to detail tens of thousands of additional U.S. military personnel and contractor support to Iran raised concerns over the validity of the sales justifications.

Throughout the study process, ISA maneuvered to undermine PM's analysis. While on the surface it took issue with PM's scope and methods of analysis, and despite its agreement with the study's basic conclusions, ISA was dismayed that its primary role as the U.S. government arms sales agency was being eroded. Ad hominem criticism of the PM personnel involved in the study was frequent, along with the general comment that the State Department had no role or experience in the analysis of military requirements.

As the study moved toward completion, I was directed by Bill Barnett, who later replaced Dave Gompert as office director, to draft realistic "conflict scenarios" involving the Iranian military to illustrate the validity of the conclusions. I drew up five potential scenarios. The first had the Soviet Union, historically in search of a corridor to the warm waters of the Persian Gulf, invading Iran, unseating the shah and installing a Communist regime in Tehran. In the second, Iraq reneges on its 1975 Shatt-al-Arab agreement and invades Iran in order to regain territory and rights Baghdad claimed to have surrendered only under duress. In the third, Iranian forces are invited into the Arabian Peninsula in order to assist friendly states in defeating Communist-backed insurgent forces. For the fourth, the shah would renew historic Iranian claims to Bahrain, crossing the Gulf to seize the island nation.

In the fifth and final scenario, I wrote of internal rebellion developing in Iran, fueled primarily by radical exploitation of economic unrest and Iranian resentment of the large foreign presence throughout Iran. The paper emphasized that this last scenario was the most likely one in the near term and one in which U.S.-supplied military equipment would not play a significant role.

What I did not realize at the time, but which became abundantly clear in the days which followed the submission of my paper, was that I had written what should not have been written and had stated, all too bluntly, that the emperor might not be wearing any clothes.

It did not take a genius to recognize that Iran was in for a period of economic instability with potentially serious political consequences, even if regional experts in the national security bureaucracy were unwilling to so state. I created the scenarios after a serious review of readily available facts and materials, several State Department telegrams (cables), intelligence reports and European press pieces, which increasingly painted an alarming picture of growing economic disarray, intellectual ferment, a pattern of human rights abuses, and the anger of the religious leaders (mullahs) over the shah's secular, antireligious policies. In the United States, Iranian students were becoming increasingly brazen in their opposition to the shah and outspoken about the deteriorating social, economic and security conditions within Iran. I did not believe that stating the obvious in my analysis would prove to be so controversial with my colleagues or superiors in the State Department or the DOD.

Papers for the study were circulated within PM for comment before adding them to the text for final clearance by NEA and ISA. Few, if any, objections were raised by my colleagues in PM, as everyone strove to finish the study as quickly as possible for Secretary of State Cyrus Vance and Secretary of Defense Harold Brown. National security and foreign policy papers are routinely sent through the system for comment and clearance and are regularly changed for substantive reasons or simply to be rewritten. Given the bureaucratic rivalry between PM and NEA, negative comments were expected. But what happened next was an amazing learning experience for a young graduate student in the reality of how national security and foreign policy decisions are actually made.

The director of the Iran desk, Henry Precht, called Barnett to his office soon after receiving the PM draft and advised him, in no uncertain terms, that unless the fifth scenario describing internal unrest in Iran was deleted, in its entirety, NEA would "nonconcur" in the entire study and do whatever was necessary to prevent it from being sent forward to Secretary Vance. Taken aback by Precht's strong opposition, Barnett, a retired U.S. Army captain, asked him to explain NEA's opposition to the scenario.

Precht, a career foreign service officer, did not hesitate. "There is *no* internal instability in Iran!" he said, "And no chance that if there was real opposition that the shah would not act decisively against it. NEA will not agree to send any studies to Vance that suggest there might be potential unrest in Iran, let alone a scenario which PM describes as the most likely course of events in Iran. We have no problem with PM's analytical conclusions about the shah's military needs. We agree that the U.S. should sell the shah what he wants. But there are no internal problems in Iran or meaningful opposition to the shah. Nor are more outsiders going to cause internal instability."

Our team met later in the day for a debrief. Barnett told us what had occurred and that in the interests of moving the study forward he had decided to acquiesce to NEA and delete the fifth scenario. I took issue with Barnett's decision, pointing out the obvious political, economic and social trends which led me to conclude that the shah was in trouble and that the Iranian army was not going to be of much use against the Iranian people. "You may be right," Barnett replied, "but we need to get the study out the door. It's not about the domestic situation in Iran. I'm not going to fight with Precht. He's fallen on his sword over this." Just as the sale had become a litmus test for the shah, so had completing the study and carving out bureaucratic turf become the touchstone of PM's role in the arms sales bureaucracy. The fifth scenario was duly deleted and the study went forward.

Although other sources of information and analysis on the internal situation in Iran were available to the secretaries of state and defense and to the president, in this context, at least, the analysis was filtered to eliminate any consideration of the issue of whether there was internal instability in Iran and whether the United States should be selling arms to the shah. Consistent with the Twin Pillars policy, the United States continued to rely on Iran for protection of American interests in the region and to sell the shah enormous quantities of advanced weapons, hoping that somehow the situation would stabilize and our pillar would remain intact.

The shah's request did not take place in a vacuum. The Soviets were displaying increasingly aggressive behavior around the Middle East, the Horn of Africa, and Central America. This included the sale of virtually unlimited quantities of modern military hardware to the Iraqis, in part to counter Washington's Twin Pillars policy. Following Anwar Sadat's historic visit to Israel in November 1977, the Middle East balance of power and alliance system was in turmoil. Within Iran, the first signs of what was to become the Iranian revolution were starting to appear. The Iranian economy entered its third year of recession, leaving more Iranians unemployed and with little hope of improving their economic lot. Additionally, the first killings of Shia clergy and large numbers of their followers were reported in January 1978. Soon a pattern of violence and unrest became apparent, based around the forty-day period of Shia mourning. From the outset, the leadership of the rebellion came from the mosques.

F-15s for Saudi Arabia

The second pillar for the United States in the Gulf was Saudi Arabia. Although anointed a pillar, Saudi Arabia did not perform overt proxy roles on behalf of the United States, as did Iran. Saudi Arabia's oil was vital to the United States and its potential political significance in the Arab world was very important, but there was a fundamental weakness in Saudi support for American interests. Saudi Arabia employed a very cautious political and economic strategy to protect its own vital interests, a strategy that often confounded its friends in the West. American expectations of Saudi Arabia's ability and willingness to act on behalf of U.S. interests were greatly exaggerated. Nevertheless, long after the limitations of the relationship should have become obvious—given the use of the oil weapon after the October 1973 Arab-Israeli war—and despite vigorous congressional efforts throughout the mid-1970s to present objective analyses of Saudi interests and capabilities, representatives of the State and Defense departments regularly testified before Congress that Riyadh was a strong and reliable partner that could be counted upon to support the United States in the region.

Indeed, the Saudis did act discreetly to support American interests where there was no Israeli dimension and when U.S. interests coincided with Riyadh's own regional and inter-Arab goals. "Riyal diplomacy," whereby Saudi Arabia used its economic wealth to advance its political goals, increasingly came to reflect Saudi Arabia's core method for protecting convergent U.S. and Saudi interests. Saudi largesse toward Syria, the Palestine Liberation Organization (PLO), Jordan, Yemen and Egypt typified Riyadh's methods of buying influence and protection, as well as its tactics for dealing with crises.

As with its relationship with Iran and other countries, the United States needed to ignore many Saudi practices which "offended" American sensibilities and values. The most conservative of traditional monarchies, Saudi Arabia imposed severe limitations on those living in Saudi Arabia and upon those seeking to do business with the Saudis, such as restrictions on all women and the requirement that business affairs be conducted through members of the royal family. Saudi policy within the country and throughout the Arabian Peninsula was far from enlightened, despite the image Saudi friends and benefactors sought to project.

The Saudis wanted to preserve the conservative regimes of the smaller states throughout the Gulf, as long as Riyadh was able to assert its own hegemony in the area. In the early twentieth century, Ibn Saud, the founder of the House of Saud, sought to unify all the tribes of the Arabian Peninsula under his tribal dominion. Having failed to achieve that objective, his successors consistently sought to assert hegemony over the tribes that had maintained their independence. Boundary disputes between Saudi Arabia and its neighbors were a constant problem in the Arabian Peninsula. Saudi Arabia's aggrandizing tactics throughout the years in its border disputes received little attention from Western governments eager to preserve access to Middle Eastern oil, to maintain business relationships and to counter Soviet-backed Iraq after the Iraqi monarchy was overthrown. As with Iran, and despite its inherent limitations, Saudi Arabia was the regional Arab power the United States would count upon to advance and protect its interests in the Persian Gulf.

Because of Riyadh's relationship to the Arab-Israeli conflict, and its relative demographic weakness and inadequate economic infrastructure, the growth of the Saudi military took place at a much slower and more deliberate pace than its Iranian counterpart. Nonetheless, the Twin Pillars policy mandated that Saudi Arabia was to be made militarily strong. And so it was.

In the early 1970s, a series of formal analyses were undertaken by the U.S. military to determine the needs of the Saudi armed forces. Not unlike the threat-assessment and security-assistance-requirements studies performed to address Iran's arms requests, the analyses concluded that all of Saudi Arabia's neighbors, including Iran, Iraq, Israel, Egypt, Ethiopia and the PDRY, possessed military capabilities far in excess of those of the Saudi armed forces. The solution to these potential threats was to sell Saudi Arabia advanced weaponry—army matériel; air-defense and air force hardware; command, control, communications and intelligence packages; and naval systems—to enable Riyadh to meet its defense needs. Because of the very limited size of the existing Saudi military in the early 1970s and the absence of the necessary resources and infrastructure for supporting the enormous pattern of military growth that was envisioned by the analyses, the pace and scope of arms sales to Saudi Arabia recommended by the analyses tended to be much more limited than those recommended for Iran.

Within the national security bureaucracy, there was a powerful group that favored sales to the Saudis. Some of those favoring sales regularly released the analysis results, or briefed the Saudis on the analysis results, before the reports were circulated for the requisite bureaucratic clearance, clearance needed to avoid political issues related to the Saudi role in the Arab-Israeli conflict. Outmaneuvering the bureaucracy by this tactic of preemptive release enabled the group that favored sales to unilaterally strengthen the Saudis' bargaining position and undermine the influence of nonmilitary considerations.

Use of the tactic of premature release, among other effective tactics, resulted naturally from the personal relationships that developed between the American military officers conducting the surveys, training missions and other types of liaison over many years and their Saudi hosts and counterparts. Notwithstanding the political problems in U.S.-Saudi relations caused by fundamental disagreements over how to resolve the Arab-Israeli conflict, the Saudi government has always placed great confidence in American security commitments. This trust has been most manifest in the close personal relations which have been established between individual U.S. and Saudi officers. On the policy level, this has contributed to the creation of an important cadre of American military professionals who have mirrored the State Department's Arabists in their tendency to place Saudi interests at the top of America's Middle East priorities, regardless of other factors and the domestic political climate in the United States.

One of the key lessons I learned in my early days in government about policy and decision making was never taught in school: it was the human dimension of policy-making. I had always conceived of policy decisions somehow being developed by experts who would work together to weigh the facts and the pros and cons of issues that affect the country. In fact, decisions, however weighty, are more often shaped by the individuals involved in the process. Who occupies which position; what comes through which office for clearance; who worked previously with someone else and has maintained a good personal relationship; who decides which office gets a piece of the bureaucratic pie; who "signs off" on a paper. It is not simply a matter of the president or cabinet secretary making a policy decision and ordering that it be implemented. Most of the time, one needs to manage the system carefully in order to see a particular policy translated into action. This is one reason why leaders and their staff sometimes deliberately circumvent the experts, the bureaucracy and the system.

The domestic political dimension of arms sales to the Saudis in the United States has been and continues to be more formidable an issue than the absorption by the Saudis of modern weaponry. Unlike Iran, which maintained a full range of political, economic and security relations with

Israel until the Iranian revolution, the Saudis publicly maintained their enmity toward Israel. Saudi Arabia confronted Israel on every level, including contributing troops to the Arab-Israeli wars of 1948, 1967 and 1973, using the oil weapon against the West in the 1970s, leading the Arab boycott against Israel and financing Palestinian terrorism. Thus, arms sales to the Saudis, regardless of their military justification or Saudi Arabia's preeminent role as a pillar for protecting U.S. interests in the Persian Gulf, are inextricably entwined with the politics of the Arab-Israeli conflict.

The reality is that basic American interests in the Middle East conflict with and contradict one another. Yet access to Middle Eastern oil and America's interests in preventing Saudi Arabia and the Gulf sheikhdoms from falling prey to Soviet and radical elements convinced U.S. officials to accommodate the contradictions with arms sales and other significant manifestations of political and economic support. The challenge inherent in advancing the contradictory policy interests was to convince Israel, a democracy, Western-oriented and a close friend of the United States, that such assistance did not threaten Israel, but rather contributed to greater Arab support for a political solution to the Arab-Israeli conflict. Israel and its supporters in the United States, not surprisingly, found this argument to be extremely thin and not reassuring. This was, however, the argument which proved decisive in Carter's decision to proceed with the sale of F-15s to Saudi Arabia in 1978.

On the one hand, President Carter was intent on cutting the volume of arms transfers, particularly to the Middle East. On the other hand, the U.S. military had already conducted the systematic analysis of the threats facing Saudi Arabia which justified the proposed sale of sixty F-15 air-superiority fighters. Moreover, the Saudis were well-informed of the justification and had been promised the F-15s by the administration of President Gerald Ford. Riyadh made it clear to the Carter administration that it would purchase comparable or superior fighters elsewhere, perhaps the MRCA Tornado from Great Britain, if the U.S. government proved unable to fulfill its commitments.

Unlike the Iranian situation, however, Carter had already made the decision to sell the planes to Saudi Arabia. State's task was to demonstrate why the F-15s posed little or no threat to Israel. Working with the same team that had produced the justification for arms sales to Iran, PM prepared an analysis of the threats to Saudi Arabia as well as the implications of the F-15 sale for the Arab threat to Israel. A classified version of this paper was to be provided to the Congress, while the unclassified version was to be released to the public.

Saudi weakness, whether compared to Iraq, Iran, Israel or the Soviet-backed PDRY, was palpable. The paper explained why sixty F-15s would significantly increase Saudi Arabia's ability to defend itself without fundamentally affecting the regional balance of power. From a military point of view, the sixty F-15s which Washington proposed to sell to Saudi Arabia were to be configured and equipped for air-superiority missions that would provide a modest air-defense capability against a determined attack from any of Saudi Arabia's would-be adversaries. Such a defensive capability might deter aggression against Saudi Arabia. Although the Saudis could theoretically use the F-15s for ground-attack missions by replacing the airplane's external fuel tanks with a total of three 2,000-pound bombs, it was difficult to draw up realistic scenarios in which the Saudi leadership would decide to attack Israel with the F-15s or other, less capable, aircraft. Given the threats to Saudi Arabia, its importance to the United States and the low probability that these aircraft would be used to attack Israel, the sale of the F-15s appeared to serve the interests of the United States.

The government of Israel and its allies in Washington took harsh exception to the administration's analysis and justification. Israel's congressional and domestic supporters opposed the sale for a number of legitimate reasons: the deployment of most Saudi forces in the north, regardless of their air-defense configuration, would strengthen Saudi Arabia's ability to participate in a combined Arab confrontation with Israel with significant, if not decisive, consequences. Moreover, the Israelis argued convincingly that if Saudi Arabia did attack Israel, the United States would assuredly pressure Israel to refrain from retaliating, because of American interests in Saudi Arabia. A third major concern involved the compromise of Israeli qualitative and tactical advantages that derived from the Israeli military's operation of advanced U.S. weapons. The qualitative advantages enjoyed by Israel would be eroded once these systems entered Arab inventories.

Despite their rationality, these arguments were totally rejected within the U.S. national security bureaucracy, where there was near-unanimous support for the sale. Since the Israeli victory in the October 1973 War, annual U.S. National Intelligence Estimates (NIEs) repeatedly had concluded that the Israeli Defense Forces (IDF) maintained the capability to defeat any combination of Arab adversaries. The inherent contradictions for the goals of PD-13 and the implications for the nearly $1.5 billion sale were overshadowed by the political confrontation between opponents and proponents of the sale. At the conclusion of the debate between the executive branch and the Congress, the sale was justified based on the threat to Saudi Arabia, the Twin Pillars policy, U.S. oil interests and the argument that arms sales to Saudi Arabia would contribute to greater Saudi support for the Arab-Israeli peace process.

Moreover, when juxtaposed against the increasingly unstable situation in Iran (although the experts at the State Department continued to maintain there was no internal instability in that country), President Carter's human rights approach to foreign policy, the decline of U.S. military strength and ability to project power and the concomitant increase in military power by the Soviet Union, there was a growing perception by world leaders that Washington might no longer be a reliable security partner.

The F-15 debate was fierce. As Israel and opponents of the sale in the United States mounted a campaign to defeat the F-15 sale for posing a dire threat to Israel's basic security, the Saudis mounted a campaign of their own. Saudi Arabia was supported by oil, aerospace and construction companies. High-profile lobbyists and public relations firms were retained in the United States to influence Congress to approve the sale. Against this debate was the backdrop of the Egyptian-Israeli peace process and the deteriorating situation in Iran. Taking advantage of the acknowledged American commitment to Saudi security and the radical threat, the Saudis sought to undermine the pro-Israel forces' arguments that the weapons were destabilizing. Riyadh offered, tantalizingly, its tacit support of the peace process between Egypt and Israel and indicated it would take an even more active role once the sale was approved. As the debate over congressional approval intensified, continued U.S. access to Saudi oil supplies as well as the important role of recycled Saudi petrodollars were also suggested by Saudi spokesmen as interests that might be at risk, should the U.S. government prove unable to fulfill its commitments to Riyadh.

Recognizing that the sale was clearly in jeopardy, President Carter tried to trump the opposition and pressure the Israelis by explicitly linking the F-15 sale to aircraft sales to Egypt and Israel. In February 1978, Carter linked the sales together into a package with F-5s for Egypt and F-16s for Israel. The putative logic was to secure the Arab portion of the deal in Congress by combining the sales in an "all or none" package. But President Carter went further, sending a clear message that two Arab countries, one making peace with and the other a self-avowed enemy of Israel, would now receive the same treatment as Israel. This was a fundamental change in the Arab-Israeli political calculus.

From Jerusalem's perspective, linking Israeli arms purchases to Arab purchases of equally sophisticated weaponry, in the context of strong U.S. pressure on Prime Minister Begin to freeze Israeli settlement activity in the occupied territories, represented a watershed in U.S.-Israeli relations. This American tactic led Israel to argue strenuously that Saudi Arabia, while not itself a declared confrontation state, maintained close military cooperation with the confrontation states, including liaison relations with those states and financial support for the Syrian purchase of Soviet weaponry and Palestinian-sponsored terrorism. Emphasizing the geostrategic danger the F-15s would pose from Saudi air bases at Tabuk in northwestern Saudi Arabia, the Israelis also played hardball, going so far at one point as to suggest that Israel might seek to renegotiate its agreement with Egypt to withdraw from the Sinai desert.

Menachem Begin stated categorically that he did not trust American assurances regarding the deployment of the F-15s in a nonthreatening manner. As if to support Begin's denunciations, the Saudis, insulted that Carter had bundled the Saudi arms with Israel's, made it plain that they would brook no limitations on how the F-15s were deployed, casting further doubt on the credibility of U.S. assurances.

In the end, the final parameters of the sale were dictated by politics. To assuage the concerns of pro-Israel forces on Capitol Hill, Secretary of Defense Harold Brown sent a letter to Congress which promised significant restrictions on the F-15s' potential long-range ground-attack capability. First, the aircraft would not be deployed at Tabuk, the Saudi air base closest to Israel. Second, the range of the F-15s would be limited because the United States would not sell the Saudis refueling systems, additional hard points for external fuel tanks, or conformal fuel tanks that fit along the body of the aircraft. Third, the administration agreed that it would not sell multiple ejection racks (MERs), racks that would significantly increase the tonnage of bombs, from six thousand to sixteen thousand pounds, an F-15 could carry for ground attack. The Saudis were furious and their corporate supporters and lobbyists were vocal in their outrage at limitations they considered to infringe on Saudi sovereignty, but the Saudis nevertheless chose to acquiesce.

Despite the political struggles which accompanied its arms sales requests, the government of Saudi Arabia regularly requested billions of dollars in additional armaments throughout the 1980s. In 1981, the

Reagan administration succumbed to continued Saudi pressure and the pressure of their political supporters and lifted the limitations on the range of the F-15s, by approving the sale of conformal fuel tanks and equipment necessary for aerial refueling. As part of the later AWACS package deal, the administration found a logical argument for enhancing Saudi Arabia's air-defense capabilities, given the Iran-Iraq War and the potential spillover into Saudi Arabia. Other advanced defensive systems were also approved, such as the AIM-9L air-to-air missile, the most sophisticated missile of its type then in service with the U.S. Air Force. In contrast to these defensive enhancements, the revived Saudi request for MERs was denied, as the Reagan administration refused to concur in the logic that enhanced ground-strike capability would deter Iranian ground strikes.

Over the course of ten years, Saudi Arabia and its supporters, Israel and its supporters, the executive branch, and the Congress repeatedly struggled over tens of billions of dollars' worth of arms sales requests. Bureaucratic intrigue, corporate influence, domestic political considerations and individual biases all contributed to this process. From the perspective of Saudi Arabia and its powerful supporters, Riyadh was America's best friend in the Arab world, by 1978, assuring ample supplies of oil at market prices while purportedly using its political influence to support U.S. policies discreetly in the Arab-Israeli conflict. Arms requests were justified on military as well as political grounds. The administration generally agreed with Saudi arguments on the basis that arms sales had become the litmus test of U.S. credibility in Riyadh and that influential American corporations supported such sales. But political reality forced the administration to compromise, delay or deny Saudi requests in order to cope with the skepticism of Israel's strong supporters on Capitol Hill. Congress retained the right to veto arms sales which it believed did not serve the national interest.

Arms sales to America's Saudi pillar thus came to represent one of the fundamental contradictions of U.S. strategy in the Middle East. On the one hand, the Saudis needed to demonstrate that they could defend themselves, as well as U.S. oil interests, and they required advanced arms to achieve this objective. But weaponry which the Saudis needed for self-defense could also be used to threaten Israel or, as in Iran, contribute to internal instability, which would also threaten America's vital interests. Failure to supply Saudi Arabia with arms would lead Riyadh to turn elsewhere for assistance, while reducing the likelihood that it would turn to the United States in a crisis.

As a result of regional conflicts in the 1970s, including the Arab-Israeli conflict, Soviet expansionism and the Twin Pillars policy for the Persian Gulf, arms sales became the primary mechanism for competing for influence and wielding power in the Middle East. Despite PD-13 and the best intentions of President Carter, a Middle East arms race continued to spiral out of control.

CHAPTER 2

THE IRANIAN PILLAR CRUMBLES

The Skonk Works

The State Department agreed to let me stay on as a clerk-typist through the end of October 1978. I had received a master's degree in international affairs from SAIS in May, but because I was not a foreign service officer (FSO), there were no professional opportunities for me at State. I had a number of job offers from several think tanks (known as "beltway bandits"), which would have enabled me to stay on the margins of policy-making, but I wanted to work for the U.S. government. I was confident that if I remained patient and determined, I would secure an entry-level government job working on Middle East policy. My patience paid off by the end of September.

Across the Potomac River from the Foggy Bottom locale of the State Department, a new deputy assistant secretary of defense for ISA, Robert J. Murray, was organizing an Office of Policy Analysis for the Near East, Africa and South Asia region (NEASA). Headed by Nancy Bearg, a former staff member to Senator John Stennis, the mission of Policy Analysis was to provide analytical support to the country desk officers responsible for most of the work performed by the NEASA division.

Dubbed the "Skonk Works" by the Israel desk officer, Army colonel Paul Forester, Policy Analysis was supposed to produce think pieces that would contribute to evolving and future U.S. defense and foreign policy. In theory, analysts in Policy Analysis were supposed to devise creative, long-range analyses and not be "distracted" by routine arms sales and administration, bilateral military coordination activities, and congressional and public affairs, functions which were assigned to the regional desk officers. In practice, the scope of the Arab-Israeli peace process, particularly its political-military components, the Iranian revolution, crises in the Arabian Peninsula and Horn of Africa and the overall decline in the ability of the U.S. government to cope with the deteriorating situation in the Middle East led Policy Analysis to play an ever-expanding role in the day-to-day formulation of U.S. defense policy in the region. Murray offered me a job in Policy Analysis as a full-time policy analyst, and by mid-October 1978, my security clearances had been transferred. I was immediately enmeshed in the DOD's support for the Egyptian-Israeli negotiations and the intellectual hand-wringing over the plight of the shah of Iran.

Often referred to as the Pentagon's State Department, ISA was an exciting place to work. The majority of the staff were military officers with combat experience and/or regional backgrounds as defense attachés, weapons systems program managers or trainers. Most had advanced degrees in international relations or management and viewed a tour in ISA as a career highlight. An assignment in ISA was therefore a perfect place to continue my involvement in Middle East policy-making while gaining a hands-on education about the role of military power and security assistance programs in national security and foreign policy.

Policy Analysis was a relatively small office within ISA. In addition to Bearg, there was a deputy director, Army captain Christopher C. Shoemaker, Africa expert and humorist Vincent Kern, international affairs specialist Renee Joyner and me. The regional offices had ten to twelve desk officers in addition to a director and deputy director. The intimacy of the Policy Analysis office enabled our group to evolve into a well-motivated team, able to respond quickly to an ever-increasing pace of assignments with great humor in spite of long hours and the collapse of American policy in the Persian Gulf. In what proved to be the final two years of the Carter administration, Policy Analysis found itself heavily involved in the political-military dimension of the Arab-Israeli peace process, the Iranian revolution and hostage crisis, the first inkling of a U.S. tilt to Iraq, the Soviet invasion of Afghanistan, the creation of the Rapid Deployment Force (RDF) and the Iran-Iraq War.

While ISA certainly had its share of bureaucratic turf-fights, the intramural struggles of the OSD paled in comparison to the constant and vicious turf-fights typical of national security and foreign policy making at the Department of State. Policy formulation and implementation at OSD involved far fewer individuals than it did at State and often led directly to the creation of programs and the expenditure of funds. In contrast, the State Department managed words in order to affect bureaucratic and international political activity. There were no programs to implement or manage. Policy-making at State usually involved legions of individuals laboring to draft, comment on or clear endless memoranda and cables. It was an FSO's skill in playing by the rules of the foreign service that counted at State. Careers were made or lost based on intelligence, loyalty to the service, readiness to progress steadily up the bureaucratic ladder, one rung at a time, and skill in drafting cables. I found the dynamism at OSD more suited to my tastes and ambitions than a career in the foreign service. ISA turned out to be a perfect stepping stone to achieving my dream of serving as a member of the staff of the National Security Council (NSC), working on Middle East policy.

The summer of 1978 ended with a ferocious bang as events in the Middle East began to spin out of control, with adverse implications for American interests and the Twin Pillars policy. Engaging in his own version of Arab-Israeli brinkmanship, President Carter concluded the Camp David Accords in September. With considerable skill, he broke the deadlock in Egyptian-Israeli negotiations by laying the foundation for peace between the two belligerents and codifying a process that was supposed to lead to autonomy for the Palestinians of the occupied territories. To the east, the unrest and violence in Iran grew bolder and more widespread by the day as internal opponents of the regime intensified their increasingly well organized campaigns to destabilize the Iranian economy, mobilize mass protests and bring down the shah.

Neither the U.S. government, preoccupied with the Egyptian-Israeli peace talks, nor the regime of the shah proved capable of engaging in more than wishful thinking over ways to halt the rebellion in Iran and the collapse of the U.S. security system in the Persian Gulf. In these circumstances of violent and radical change in Iran and sharp divisions in the Arab world over the direction of the Arab-Israeli peace process, the other pillar of American policy, Saudi Arabia, found itself whipsawed by the opposing interests of Riyadh's American and Arab allies and the spread of militant Islam.

The Saudis had good reason to worry. Vulnerable to charges of supporting Egypt's "sellout" of Arab rights while they witnessed the collapse of U.S. security policy in the face of a radical Islamic onslaught, Riyadh was unsure how to protect the kingdom. Of immediate concern was the potential for hostile action against the flow of oil through the Strait of Hormuz or in the Shia-dominated, oil-rich eastern province of Saudi Arabia, and the instability of international supply due to the striking workers in Iranian oil fields. With the evaporation of the Iranian military deterrent, there was no power strong enough to check Soviet-backed Iraq's growing military capabilities and historic hegemonic aspirations on the peninsula. Fear spread throughout the Gulf over Iraqi intentions and possible aggression. To the south, the pro-Soviet regime in the PDRY provided greater access to the Soviet Navy and East German intelligence services while permitting its training facilities to be used by Arab and international terrorists. With the Soviet buildup in Ethiopia and the crushing defeat of the Somali Army by Cuban-led Ethiopian forces across the Red Sea, the Saudis found themselves surrounded by radical forces bent on overturning traditional, pro-American regimes.

The Carter administration pursued mutually contradictory foreign policies which undermined American allies and interests in the Middle East. In Iran, the United States tried to promote human rights while continuing to rely on the shah as a regional pillar. However, by linking the supply of military hardware to the shah's domestic policies, Carter created the impression that Iran's strategic importance to the United States had declined. This perception convinced many Iranian dissidents and revolutionaries that Washington no longer stood behind the shah, thereby increasing his vulnerability to domestic unrest and impairing Iran's ability to serve as America's pillar. Moreover, despite the importance of a pro-American Iran to the protection of U.S. interests, the failure of the United States to intervene in the Iranian revolution convinced most world leaders that the United States had lost its nerve to use force to protect important interests.

In Egypt, Israel and Saudi Arabia, the administration exacerbated regional tensions through arms sales that it claimed would promote the peace process. The one democratic state in the region, Israel, was under constant pressure from the administration to curb its settlement activity in the West Bank. Despite the volatility of events throughout southwest Asia, the Carter administration viewed settlements as the principal cause of instability in the Middle East, virtually ignoring, at least rhetorically, the myriad of other problems confronting the United States in the region. Carter effectively replaced strategy with rhetoric in the face of Soviet expansionism, as Washington appeared more inclined to punish American friends and reward its enemies by backing away from prior commitments. The United States increasingly came to be viewed as an unreliable security partner that had lost the will to act in defense of its own vital interests.

During the late summer and early fall of 1978, it became obvious, even to those experts who would not before acknowledge the vulnerability of the shah, that the U.S.-Iranian relationship was in serious trouble. In my new job barely one week, I was assigned by Bob Murray to analyze the implications for the United States of a hostile, anti-American Iran. I produced an information memorandum for Secretary of Defense Brown. The memorandum described such negative consequences as (1) the compromise of military secrets associated with sensitive U.S. military technology that might come into the possession of the Soviet Union; (2) the loss of secret listening posts on the Iranian-Soviet border; (3) implications of the loss of Iranian oil for the international economy; and (4) the spread of Islamic fundamentalism throughout the Middle East. In the concluding portion of the memo, I argued that with the loss of Iran, the Twin Pillars policy was dead. There no longer was a security structure capable of protecting America's vital interests or ensuring even a modicum of stability in the Persian Gulf.

Indeed, a case could clearly be made that the contradictions inherent in our policy, arming the shah while undermining his authority through criticism of his human rights records, had helped to provoke the very instability our policies had sought to deter. A precondition to the reconstruction of a stable order in the Gulf was a sustained demonstration of American power that left no ambiguity over America's intentions, capability and will to protect U.S. interests. I argued that the sooner the United States undertook decisive military action the better.

Before sending this memo forward to Murray, I sought the comments and concurrence of my colleagues in ISA, primarily U.S. Navy commander James Kelly, the Iran desk officer. Kelly, a hardworking, genial officer who had distinguished himself as a navy logistician, was being overwhelmed by the Iranian revolution. A prestigious assignment, Kelly had begun his tour as the Iran desk officer with the brief to manage arms sales to and the defense relationship with Tehran. Almost every defense-related matter between the United States and Iran required the active involvement of ISA's Iran desk officer. Diplomats, bureaucrats, defense contractors, Capitol Hill staff and journalists all sought him out. But the Iranian revolution turned Kelly's dream job into a nightmare. Anything that conceivably might go wrong in U.S.-Iranian relations was going wrong. It fell to Kelly to somehow cope with the deluge of bad news and provide instant answers to the host of questions that were asked of the Pentagon. (Kelly's brother John would later serve as the assistant secretary of state for NEA when Iraq invaded Kuwait in August 1990.)

Notwithstanding a truly onerous work load, Kelly went right to work on my paper. He came by my office about an hour later to inform me that I was "living in a dreamworld" if I thought there was any chance that the United States would use force in the Persian Gulf. While he was not ready to concede that the shah was doomed, he did agree with most of the projected consequences for U.S. interests, should the shah fall and should his regime be replaced by a radical, Islamic state. However, Kelly continued, "There is absolutely no chance that the United States will intervene militarily in this crisis. No one in this administration supports the use of force to protect our interests. Nobody around here thinks strategically about the use of American military power. That's why we adopted the Twin Pillars policy in the first place. Do yourself a favor, be creative, without a role for the American military, and I will concur in your analysis." When I tried to argue the point, Kelly looked up at the ceiling, shook his head and said, "Howard, don't you get it? We gave the shah everything he asked for so he could protect our interests. Now it turns out he can't even protect his own. What good will it do to bail him out now?"

"But we still need Gulf oil. Who is going to protect it?" I asked. "What power will deter Soviet advances, Iraqi designs on the sheikhdoms, or the possible spread of other anti-Western forces?" Kelly shrugged his shoulders and without uttering another word, left me alone to contemplate the worst-case scenario that seemed quite realistic to me.

His silent shrug spoke volumes about his confidence in the extent of forward-looking strategic thinking in the Pentagon. Despite the 1973 Arab oil embargo, America took its stable access to Persian Gulf oil for granted. Inevitably, policy-making toward Iran was based on a bizarre bureaucratic logic which, I soon came to recognize, cut across many issues and different parts of the world: policymakers, particularly careerists with a stake in the status quo, did not want to be confused by facts and analysis. In the case of the Iranian revolution, these individuals genuinely hoped the shah would overcome his troubles, muddle through and survive. To argue to the contrary, as I did, was to risk bureaucratic disdain. Kelly was right. Neither President Carter, Secretary Vance, nor most of the national security bureaucracy was willing even to contemplate a role for U.S. military power in the Iranian crisis, other than to assist in the evacuation of Americans.

A Toothless Gesture

In January 1979, the shah appointed Shahpour Bakhtiar as head of state in accordance with constitutional procedures. President Carter threw U.S. support behind Bakhtiar in the hope that an orderly, post-shah political process could take hold in Iran that would end the violence and preserve a measure of American influence. To demonstrate his commitment to Iran's political process and continued opposition to military intervention, the president dispatched General Robert E. Huyser of the U.S. Air Force to Tehran to urge the Iranian military to support Bakhtiar, avoid needless bloodshed and thereby count on the continued backing of the United States. While many pundits at the time mistakenly assumed that Huyser's mission was to promote a military crackdown, his mission was precisely the opposite.

Huyser reported back to the Pentagon from Tehran on a daily basis during his three-week stay. On two occasions I accompanied Murray to Secretary Brown's office while he took notes of the "secure" calls. Huyser consistently reported that the Iranian generals had the situation under control and President Carter could be reassured that the military would back Bakhtiar. His reports made no sense and did not agree with the objective facts. Diplomatic cables, intelligence reports and the open press painted a clear picture that the central authorities were quickly losing control to the newly formed Pasdaran (Iranian Revolutionary Guards) and growing mobs.

In these strange circumstances, the Joint Chiefs of Staff (JCS) argued that some "show of spine" by the U.S. military was necessary to back up Huyser and demonstrate that the United States was prepared to use force if events warranted. How to square the circle of Carter's self-imposed restraint was a genuine conundrum: what means would convince friends and adversaries that the United States remained a reliable security partner that was willing to use force while at the same time denying its legitimacy?

In January 1979, a squadron of F-15 aircraft was deployed to the Saudi capital of Riyadh as a symbol of America's commitment to the security of Saudi Arabia. Having expended so much domestic political capital on behalf of the Saudi F-15 sale less than one year earlier, Carter was convinced that this gesture would help reinforce Riyadh's confidence in the United States, while demonstrating the ability of the United States to project military power to the Gulf on short notice. The initial symbolic value of the deployment quickly dissipated, however, when it was revealed that the F-15s had deployed without ammunition. Whatever the underlying rationale—whether it was the ramifications of the deployment of the F-15s to the War Powers Act (U.S. forces were not technically "armed" for combat), the administration's fear of congressional opposition or the possibility that the United States might actually be called upon to perform a combat mission—this neutered deployment was a humiliating demonstration of Washington's failure to understand the realpolitik of the Middle East.

The advocates of the unarmed F-15 deployment, primarily political appointees who shared President Carter's and Secretary Vance's views on the use of force, carried the day. They boasted that an unarmed deployment was a clever move; a show of force, without force. Congress could not interfere. No one could perceive this deployment of advanced fighter aircraft into the region as a hostile gesture or unwarranted U.S. intervention in the crisis. While one could not dispute that the F-15s were indeed unarmed combat aircraft, this toothless gesture served only to undermine further the dwindling confidence of America's friends and embolden those who opposed U.S. policies. It helped convince those who sought to bring down the Iranian government that the days of U.S. influence in Iran were numbered. In such circumstances, it made no sense to reach a compromise with Bakhtiar when total victory seemed to be within grasp. Indeed, only one week after the unarmed F-15s were deployed to Saudi Arabia, the Ayatollah Khomeini made his triumphant return to Iran. By the middle of February, Bakhtiar had resigned and the Khomeini reign of terror was initiated. The Iranian pillar had collapsed.

Those who advocated a demonstration of American power in the current crisis were mortified by the unarmed F-15 deployment. The image of the United States as a pitiful, helpless giant was vivid and stark. In every direction, Soviet military power and that of its surrogates grew stronger by the day. Radical forces were encouraged, while those whom the United States hoped would take risks on our behalf could only wonder how the United States would possibly fulfill its commitments if, when confronted with the collapse of such an important ally as the shah of Iran, we behaved with such timidity.

Can I Please Get My Tanks Back?

Juxtaposed to the dismal situation in Iran, in February 1979 yet another crisis developed involving America's other pillar. Reports had been received from Riyadh suggesting that the Soviet-backed PDRY had launched an armored assault into the Yemen Arab Republic (YAR), Saudi Arabia's ally and a country with which the United States maintained diplomatic and modest security assistance relations. Details of border battles were impossible to validate and the Saudis became increasingly alarmed over the prospect that the YAR might fall to the Soviet-backed PDRY forces and that those forces might threaten Saudi Arabia. Riyadh appealed to Washington to help defend Saudi Arabia and bolster the YAR. The United States responded to the Yemen crisis with a deployment of

AWACS aircraft intended to enhance the air-defense capability of southern Saudi Arabia and to signal that the United States would not stand idly by in the face of hostile threats to the territorial integrity of Saudi Arabia.

Bob Murray led a Pentagon delegation, including Major General Richard Lawrence of the U.S. Army to the YAR capital of Sanaa to survey the situation firsthand and determine what military assistance might enhance the defensive capabilities of the YAR. Based on the team's assessment, the United States agreed to rush in M-60 tanks, M-113 armored personnel carriers (APCs) and F-5 aircraft. Although the most populous country on the Arabian Peninsula, the YAR was also the poorest, and the Saudis agreed to pay for the equipment.

Successful in eliciting a prompt and substantial U.S. response, notwithstanding our failure to take effective action in Iran, the Saudis grew wary of the U.S. plan to go beyond the delivery of the equipment to the training and arming of the YAR forces. The Saudis did not want to see the YAR grow too independent of Riyadh's political or financial influence, fearing a renewal of the Yemeni threats of the early 1960s. To foreclose such a possibility, Riyadh advised Washington that it reserved the right to approve the delivery of ammunition, as well as the training programs necessary to operate and maintain the equipment. Decisions were delayed for several weeks, during which time the border crisis abated. The Saudis later refused to pay for either the ammunition or the training.

A month or so later, we learned that Sanaa had manufactured the story of the PDRY invasion. YAR forces had started the hostilities when they launched a military operation into the PDRY in support of a renegade PDRY battalion that appeared to be mounting a coup against the PDRY regime in the city of Aden. When the operation failed, PDRY forces chased the YAR forces back inside the YAR's border, enabling the YAR president, Lieutenant Colonel Ali Abdallah Salih, to foster the impression that he was the aggrieved party. The tanks, APCs and planes the United States had sent in were sitting idle outside of Sanaa. I informed Murray of the new information we had received. Shaking his head and letting out a pained groan, Murray exclaimed, "Can I please get my tanks back?"

I Gave at the Office

The other core Middle East issue gripping the national security bureaucracy during that dismal fall and winter was the negotiation of a peace treaty between Egypt and Israel. Prior to my arrival in ISA, Policy Analysis had played a valuable staff role during the Camp David negotiations, providing information and analysis to the American participants on the broad range of defense and security issues central to the Egyptian-Israeli settlement. Notwithstanding the genuine and courageous political gestures made by Sadat and the significance of Egypt's departure from the Arab rejectionists, Israel was being asked to take significant security risks by returning land in exchange for an intangible peace.

The financial price of Camp David turned out to be quite high. President Carter had promised a major infusion of security and economic assistance for Egypt and Israel. For Israel, the United States agreed to provide $1 billion in grant aid to pay for the construction of two new air bases in the Negev to replace facilities that would be turned over to the Egyptians. In November 1978, Israeli defense minister Ezer Weizman led an Israeli delegation to Washington to meet with Secretary Brown to work out the size and scope of this special aid package.

Israeli delegations for such bilateral discussions are typically quite large. This was no exception. Weizman was accompanied by twenty-five or more senior Israeli Defense Forces (IDF) officers and Ministry of Defense (MOD) civilian officials. Being both new and very junior, I had not been invited to participate in the meetings. Nevertheless, one of the key lessons I had learned in my first days in government was that the fundamental aim of any effective bureaucrat was to "get into the meeting," whether or not you are invited. I learned that the plenary meeting was to be held in a large conference room adjacent to Secretary Brown's office. I showed up early and walked into the room as nonchalantly as possible. American and Israeli flags dotted the center of the table, and large maps of the Sinai and Negev deserts were displayed prominently at both ends of the long conference table. In addition to the twenty or so chairs located around the table, another thirty lined the walls. Taking a seat against the back wall close to the center of the American side of the table, I was well-positioned to listen to the discussions and grab any crumb of work that might fall my way.

While the larger group assembled in the conference room, Brown, Weizman and a small group of Americans and Israelis, including Murray, had been meeting privately in Brown's office next door. Joining the plenary twenty minutes late, their moods appeared positive, even jovial, as Brown and Weizman each made introductory remarks before turning to the business at hand. The focus of the plenary was on the construction of the new air bases in the Negev. Weizman emphasized that Israel had built three of the most modern air bases in the world in the Sinai. Giving these up was a tremendous sacrifice for Israel and presented real risks. Replicating their capabilities, if not their geographic advantages, would be quite costly and time-consuming. In addition, the new bases had to be operational in order for Israel to be able to complete its withdrawal from Sinai. The central issue before the plenary was, Could the air bases be completed in time?

Brown adamantly reaffirmed the U.S. commitment to construct two new bases in the Negev that would provide Israel with as much capability as it was forfeiting. He then turned the balance of the meeting over to the U.S. Army Corps of Engineers, which would be responsible for the new air bases. The Corps briefed on its approach, particularly "fast-track" construction techniques that would permit certain elements of the construction to begin even before all the detailed planning and design work was completed. The fast-track approach would prove essential to the successful, on-time completion of the new bases. As important as construction of the air bases was to the successful implementation of the peace treaty, the detailed discussion made it increasingly difficult to stay awake.

At the conclusion of the morning session, the principals had a private lunch with Brown and Weizman while the remainder of the staffs ate in an adjacent dining room. Unlike getting into a meeting, it is much more difficult to insinuate oneself into an official lunch. To my delight and surprise, Paul Forester grabbed me by the arm and told me "not to worry," he had found an extra seat in the luncheon. While the luncheon cuisine turned out to be "ho-hum" (official Washington's kosher catering leaves much to be desired), the conversation was not. Over lunch, the Israelis began to express their misgivings about Egyptian intentions, American pressure in the peace talks and the fear that promises made today would not be fulfilled tomorrow. A number of Israelis asked pointed questions about the situation in Iran and what the United States was going to do to save the shah. Our canned assurances were as worthless as our policy, but all the Americans at my end of the table carefully expressed the official line. Nevertheless, no one on either side of the table was fooled by our policy statements.

The plenary was to resume after lunch. Once again the staffs arrived first, taking up positions along the back wall. However, neither Weizman nor Brown returned, apparently having gone to the White House for a meeting with Carter. David McGiffert, assistant secretary of defense for ISA, assumed the lead for the Americans. Murray turned around and waved at me to come over to him at the table. My initial thought was that my uninvited presence had been discovered and I was about to be ignominiously ejected from the conference. My heart was racing as I walked the four or five steps over to him. Murray gestured to me to lean over and said quietly, "We offered the Israelis an aid package of $2.5 billion during lunch. Weizman is trying to convince the president to increase the amount to $4 billion. Secretary Brown needs an options paper which analyzes how to increase the aid level from $2.5 to $4.0 billion with the least impact on the American taxpayer by five P.M. today. Get going!"

Amazed and barely able to conceal my shock at receiving such a crucial assignment in the middle of the plenary, I asked Murray who in ISA I should ask for the formulae for this analysis. "Go see Carl Groth," he said. "He's the expert."

I raced down the corridors and up one flight of stairs to my office, where I immediately tracked down and called Groth. I quickly filled him in on my assignment, its imminent deadline and that I knew very little about accounting rules for different types of security assistance programs. Groth told me to come by his office, where he would run through the formulae and provide me with copies of all the pertinent legislation. An Air force lieutenant colonel with several years of experience in the Defense Security Assistance Agency (DSAA), the division within ISA responsible for managing the Foreign Military Sales (FMS) programs, Groth gave me a crash course in the law affecting security assistance, accounting and the presentation of budgetary analyses.

Analyzing the budgetary impact of different categories of security assistance as rapidly as possible, by 4:45 P.M. I had drafted a four-page paper, complete with handwritten graphs, that depicted how to increase the aid package from $2.5 billion to $3.0 billion to $3.5 billion and to $4.0 billion with varying consequences for the U.S. budget. Typing the paper up myself (there were no personal computers, let alone spreadsheet programs, in 1978), I ran down the hall to Murray's office on the "E ring" (the outermost ring of the Pentagon) and delivered the paper shortly after five P.M. Murray reviewed the numbers, asked me a few questions about the assumptions underlying the analysis, put on his jacket and went to deliver the paper personally to Secretary Brown. The next morning the White House announced that the United States and Israel had agreed to increase the aid package from $2.5 billion to $3.0 billion. It was decided that $800 million would be in the form of grant aid, while $2.2 billion would be in the form of credits.

The NEASA staff was summoned unexpectedly to Murray's office the following afternoon. A career national security bureaucrat who had worked his way through the system (he later went on to become under secretary of the navy and Michael Dukakis's campaign national security advisor in the 1988 election), Murray knew people and understood the importance of high morale, particularly in a staff that was always working overtime on the myriad of problems confronting the United States in the Middle East. He had called his staff together to take a moment to savor the progress being made in the Egyptian-Israeli arena and to acknowledge the role being played by so many members of his staff. Then, to my utter and complete surprise, he singled me out. "Secretary Brown told me that he was convinced by Teicher's paper that he could justify increasing the level of Israeli aid from $2.5 billion to $3.0 billion. Well done." From then on, whenever I was approached by the United Jewish Appeal representatives, I would tell them that "I gave at the office."

A Historic Treaty of Peace

The ensuing months saw a continuing U.S. preoccupation with the Egyptian-Israeli efforts to conclude a peace treaty. Although the Camp David Accords provided the framework for the treaty, many vital details remained to be negotiated. Secretary Vance and key State Department personnel were engaged in this process on a daily basis, and were unable to spend much time on the deteriorating situation in Iran.

With the conclusion of the Camp David Accords, Prime Minister Begin and President Sadat agreed to sign a peace treaty before the end of 1978, within sixty days if possible. However, the ink of the accords was still damp when the euphoria of Camp David began to dissipate as both leaders sought to convince their respective constituencies that neither had made compromises which would adversely affect fundamental national interests. From Jerusalem's perspective, it was essential to demonstrate that peace with Egypt and autonomy for the Palestinians were separate, unrelated deals. Such rhetoric, however, only fueled the fires of the Egyptian radicals, who condemned Sadat for concluding a separate peace with Israel. In Cairo, Egyptians maintained that the accords did not affect Egypt's political and military obligations to the rest of the Arab world. This stance aroused the suspicions of many Israelis that Egypt would join with fellow Arabs against Israel, regardless of its treaty obligations. Mutual confidence quickly began to be replaced by suspicion and mistrust.

In October, Israeli fears that the United States wanted to expand the process beyond the parameters of the Camp David Accords with pressure for more Israeli concessions were reinforced by the administration's wooing of Jordan's King Hussein. The Jordanian monarch had requested an official clarification of the accords. The United States answered his questions, emphasizing that Arab-Israeli negotiations over the formation of a "self-governing authority" and Palestinian autonomy would lead to a reduction in Israel's presence in the occupied territories. Policymakers hoped that such ambiguous replies would provide Hussein with enough diplomatic leeway to join the process, without offending Begin. This approach backfired. King Hussein sought further clarity and assurances, while Prime Minister Begin began to suspect the United States of betraying Israel. To ensure that President Carter understood Israel's more limited interpretation of autonomy, Prime Minister Begin announced that Israeli settlements would be thickened. He then upped the ante by amplifying that Israel's settlements freeze would be limited to three months and not for the period of autonomy negotiations, to which President Carter claimed Begin had agreed at Camp David. Israeli settlements in the occupied territories came to symbolize one of the most important political obstacles contributing to mutual distrust between Washington and Jerusalem.

Within the bureaucracy, an increasingly bitter debate developed over the prospects for seeing the autonomy talks take root and yield fruit. As Arab rejection surged, Arabists within the administration, keen to prevent the appearance of an Egyptian "sellout" from taking hold, slowly but with determination, pressed for a change in the U.S. attitude toward the PLO. They argued that the United States needed to find a way to start a dialogue with the PLO, notwithstanding the organization's violent opposition to the Egyptian-Israeli peace process and Kissinger's earlier commitment that the United States would not meet with the PLO until it renounced terrorism and recognized Israel's right to exist. In 1979, the U.S. ambassador to the United Nations, Andrew Young, met secretly with the PLO's U.N. representative in violation of official U.S. policy and was forced to resign. It was an uncertain time for U.S. policy.

One of my colleagues, a political appointee and self-described intellectual who claimed to have received a master's degree in international politics from the London School of Economics, was a vocal proponent of changing U.S. policy to actively engage with the PLO. She maintained that recent PLO statements somehow demonstrated a pragmatic change in the organization which should be matched by a "reaching out" from the United States. Like many who believe that Zionism is a form of racism, she believed that Israel was a colonialist state which subjugated and exploited the Palestinian people. Proponents and opponents of this line in the national security bureaucracy regularly engaged in fierce debates over the wisdom and consequences of a shift in the American position. My colleague maintained that Arafat and Begin were no different. Neither were terrorists, both were merely freedom fighters. Only the Palestinians were the oppressed, however. The Jews had won their freedom but had become the oppressor. Like many others who were trying to find any means possible to encourage PLO support for the Camp David Accords, she never tired of arguing that the United States should reward its enemies and punish its friends in order for the Arab world to support the Camp David process. Proponents of this line of analysis, including my colleague, presented a distorted and revisionist view of Israel and of the Arab-Israeli conflict. Apart from the relative merits of engaging with the PLO, it was difficult to believe anyone with any knowledge of the Middle East, particularly a Pentagon analyst working on these issues on a daily basis, actually believed the simplistic, Third World liberation propaganda she and others articulated with great fervor. It was profoundly disturbing. Yet these views were shared by many in the Carter administration.

One night Kern and I were working late on a contingency plan for a resumption of hostilities between the YAR and the PDRY. Our colleague was also working late. During the course of the evening, while sitting at her typewriter, she asked us, "Offhand, do you know Arafat's first name?" That she was a self-proclaimed intellectual who constantly debated U.S. policy in the Arab-Israeli conflict and an analyst in the Middle East division of ISA led me to think she was pulling my leg. When I failed to answer, she went on to explain, "I'm analyzing how Arafat has met the U.S. conditions for a dialogue, but I can't find his first name in any of these reports." Without another moment's hesitation Kern told her, "Offhand, Arafat's first name is Menachem." She politely thanked him for his help and returned to her analysis.

While the gaps between the Camp David signatories widened, the perception of American unreliability grew, due to the declining situation in Iran, and our unwillingness to act effectively to protect our interests or our friends. King Hussein was dejected over the clarification matter. Yet the United States was counting on Jordan, Saudi Arabia and the other more moderate Arab states. These states found themselves cornered into attending a radical, rejectionist summit in Baghdad. Emerging from years of radical isolation, Iraq had convened an Arab summit conference which was to be held in November 1978. Under intense pressure from

Baghdad, Jordan, Saudi Arabia and the rest of the Arab world acquiesced to Iraqi threats and intimidation, and agreed to participate in the Arab summit without Egypt, the state that had invented Arab summit meetings in 1964. What eventually became known as Baghdad I turned into a typical example of Iraqi jurisprudence: a kangaroo court where the defendant, Egypt, was accused of betraying the entire Arab nation. Egypt was found guilty of having acted outside the framework of collective Arab responsibility. The Camp David Accords were totally rejected. Egypt was urged to abrogate Camp David and not to sign any reconciliation treaty with the enemy. Saudi Arabia's ultimate support for the summit's hostile resolutions was a major defeat for the United States: it guaranteed that the Palestinians would be unable to join autonomy negotiations without putting themselves in harm's way, and made inevitable Egypt's continued isolation throughout the Arab world.

Over the next three months, Secretary Vance and NEA Assistant Secretary of State Harold Saunders worked feverishly to try to resolve differences and complete the treaty negotiations. Numerous meetings were held in Israel, Egypt and the United States. However, by late February, Jerusalem and Washington were at an impasse over settlements in the occupied territories, interpretation of key provisions of the meaning of autonomy in the Camp David Accords and the adoption of American positions that were supportive of the Egyptian positions on a number of outstanding treaty issues. Misunderstandings between the parties so typified the process that in February President Carter described outstanding issues between Egypt and Israel as "insignificant" while Begin was calling them "grave."

Fearing a collapse of the Egyptian-Israeli peace process, President Carter decided to undertake his own shuttle diplomacy in March 1979 to try to wrap up the negotiations. After five days of intense discussions in Cairo and Jerusalem, the president completed his shuttle, with both Sadat and Begin in agreement on the final matters of the treaty. Thirteen days later, on March 26, the treaty of peace was signed.

Teicher al-Tikriti

In preparation for Carter's shuttle, Murray prepared a briefing book containing background papers on the military issues affecting Egyptian and Israeli security concerns and the status of U.S. defense relations with each country. The majority of these papers focused on specific arms sales programs or other aspects of bilateral defense cooperation and were prepared by the Israel and Egypt desk officers, Paul Forester and Colonel Edward Redican.

However, Murray also wanted a paper that analyzed the changing regional military balance. The collapse of the Iranian military and the apparent strength of Iraq, particularly its leadership of the rejection of Camp David, were worrisome. Murray was concerned that the National Intelligence Estimate (NIE) on the Arab-Israeli military balance, an annual publication produced by multiple intelligence agencies, might have become overly sanguine and dated.

The NIE, like a scratched record, kept repeating the same thing; year in and year out it said that Israel could defeat any combination of Arab enemies on the battlefield. Backed up by reams of classified information, this NIE was the "bible" of the intelligence community when it came to American confidence in Israel's self-defense capabilities. But the region was undergoing dramatic, radical change. Murray believed it was vital to challenge old assumptions and test new theories. He gave me an assignment: analyze and contrast the current and projected military capabilities of Israel, Syria, Jordan, Iraq and Saudi Arabia on the assumption that Egypt stayed out of a new Arab-Israeli war.

This modest and fairly typical assignment would prove to be one of the most influential of my career. The paper illustrated the emergence of Iraq as a dynamic, dangerous and growing military power. Its stark analysis raised many questions about Iraqi goals, intentions, strategies, tactics, strengths and weaknesses, questions that were not under review anywhere else within the U.S. government. Although the intelligence agencies were collecting information about Iraq, monitoring Soviet-Iraqi relations, Iraq's military order of battle, and oil production and potential, I could not locate any analysis, in or out of government, which pulled this information together to assess the implications for American interests of evolving Iraqi power. There seemed to be almost a universal lack of interest in Iraqi intentions and capabilities, which was very troubling.

Soviet-backed Iraq's significance in the regional balance of power was obvious. Baghdad had become the most important Arab opponent of the peace process, the leading rejectionist, radicalizing the Arab world through blandishments and intimidation. Iraq had seized the initiative within the Arab world to try to prevent the conclusion of the peace treaty between Egypt and Israel. A confrontation state since the creation of Israel, Iraq had dispatched troops to fight in 1948, 1956, 1967 and 1973. The collapse of the shah and his replacement by a hostile, anti-American, anti-Israel regime, coupled with the perception of a dramatic erosion in

Iranian conventional military power (a perception which later proved false), the Iraqi military might be less constrained to keep large numbers of forces poised on its eastern border. A militarily weakened Iran would enable the Iraqis to join an eastern-front coalition against Israel. Greater numbers of Iraqi military formations armed with modern Soviet and French hardware could be deployed against Israel than had been in the past. Iraq threatened the new balance of power which the United States, Israel and Egypt hoped would eliminate the threat of another Arab-Israeli war by removing Egypt from the confrontation. Moreover, even Syria and Iraq, longtime competitors for Baathist supremacy and the title of the leader of radical Arab nationalism, used the occasion of Baghdad I to patch up their differences, at least temporarily. Although the reconciliation between the two radical states proved to be superficial and short-lived, it demonstrated how Sadat's boldness had galvanized unexpected and dangerous changes in the regional balance of power.

The clear threat which Iraq posed to the American-sponsored peace process did not forestall a second disturbing trend: the emergence in Washington of a notion that the United States should tilt toward Iraq to counterbalance America's lost influence in Iran. The progenitor of this concept was Assistant to the President for National Security Affairs (NSC Advisor) Zbigniew Brzezinski. As early as January 1979, in interagency meetings and private discussions among ISA, State and the NSC staff, Brzezinski was discreetly floating the idea that perhaps Washington should reconsider its "nonrelationship" with Iraq.

Within ISA, there was relatively little interest in Iraq, except for one other analyst, Richard Haass, who served during this time as a special assistant in the Planning and Requirements Directorate. This office had the principal responsibility within ISA for working with the JCS and the military services on the analysis, review, development and implementation of military programs, strategies, exercises and operational plans for various contingencies throughout the world. In 1989, Haass became the senior director for Middle East affairs at the NSC under President Bush.

Haass was a supporter of the Brzezinski view that the United States needed to compensate for the loss of its Iranian pillar by tilting toward Iraq. Although Haass and I were friends and shared a number of common positions on other issues, he consistently rejected my analysis of Iraq's intentions and capabilities. He regarded me as overly pessimistic and downplayed the significance I attached to Iraq's leadership of the rejectionist front. Haass was convinced that Iraq's emerging "moderation" should be reinforced by U.S. initiatives toward Baghdad. Although we engaged in regular and spirited debate over U.S. policy toward Iraq, neither was able to change the perspective of the other on this fundamental point.

Diplomatic relations between the United States and Iraq had been broken by Iraq after the 1967 Arab-Israeli war, when Iraq sought to seize the mantle of pan-Arab leadership from the defeated Gamal Abdel Nasser. Baghdad argued that because of U.S. support of Israel, Israel's occupation of Arab lands was tantamount to American occupation of those lands. Accordingly, the revolutionary regime in Baghdad broke relations with Washington. By 1972, Baghdad had consolidated its position within the Soviet orbit, concluding a treaty of friendship and cooperation with the Soviet Union, a treaty that guaranteed it a limitless supply of advanced military hardware, technical assistance and superpower support for its radical, anti-Western agencies. Iraq was not a Soviet puppet, however, and the Iraqi leadership defined its own interests, frequently acting independently of Moscow. Iraq also developed a significant trade and armament relationship with France.

With the 1975 Algiers Accords, Baghdad and Tehran resolved their outstanding border dispute. Iraq used the years of relative quiet between the Algiers Accords and the Iranian revolution to focus its energies on economic and military modernization. By the late 1970s, Iraq was seeking to break out of its isolation within the Arab world. The Iraqis were dissatisfied with their relationship with the Soviet Union. In 1978 at least fifty members of the Iraqi Communist party were executed as traitors to demonstrate Baghdad's unhappiness with the Soviet-inspired coup in Afghanistan, as well as to signal Moscow that Baghdad would brook no interference in its internal affairs by Iraqi advocates of its superpower patron.

Ignoring the overt, near-term danger to the peace process posed by Baghdad, however, Brzezinski maintained that with the right combination of blandishments, Iraq could be weaned away from Moscow. Encouraged by the suppression of the Iraqi Communist party, and perhaps believing that Iraq could, like Egypt after the October 1973 War, also be convinced to turn toward Washington, Brzezinski concluded that Iraq was poised to succeed Iran as the principal pillar of stability in the Persian Gulf.

Although this notion remained very discreet for nearly a year, by the spring of 1980 Brzezinski and others in government and the media began to suggest publicly that Iraq was the logical successor to Iran as the dominant military power in the Persian Gulf. The time had come for Washington and Baghdad to forge a new relationship. Indeed, in April,

Brzezinski stated on national television that he saw no fundamental incompatibility of interests between the United States and Iraq. Like the United States, Iraq also sought a secure Persian Gulf, and the United States did not wish to continue the anomalous state of relations, although the road to improving them would be a long one. The tilt toward Iraq, and the concomitant bureaucratic struggles over the implementation of this policy, can be traced directly to the tumultuous days of 1979. To the extent that the Carter administration had a vision for security in the Gulf, it was based on the Twin Pillars policy. The bureaucratic inertia established in 1979 was reinforced in the Reagan and Bush administrations, ultimately forcing the United States to face up to the contradictions inherent in this flawed vision for the Middle East in Operation Desert Storm.

The analysis was completed in early March 1979. Chris Shoemaker agreed that it was a mistake for the United States to tilt toward Iraq while simultaneously trying to help Egypt and Israel make peace. Although the analytical task at hand was finished, we agreed that I should undertake a more thorough analysis of Iraqi strategy and its implications for American interests. While we were unsure where the analysis would lead, there was no doubt that there was more to so-called Iraqi moderation than met the eye.

My study on Iraq was organized along the following lines: foreign policy, domestic affairs, oil policy, and military and economic development. I pursued the research for nearly a year, constantly uncovering new information, both classified and unclassified. My goal was to unravel the mystery that was Saddam Hussein. Had Saddam genuinely changed for the better, tempering his ruthless ambitions and his implacable hatred of the West in general and Israel in particular? Or was Saddam cleverly donning a mask to portray an image of moderation to help gain Iraq greater access to the technology of the West while pursuing his ambition to lead the Arab world and dominate the Persian Gulf?

I had begun my study of modern Iraq as a graduate student at SAIS in the spring of 1978 by comparing the minority dominance of the state instruments of coercion in Iraq, Syria, Burundi and Rwanda. I thought it was important to learn about Saddam Hussein al-Tikriti, then officially the number two man in Iraq. Even in the 1970s, one did not need access to classified information to understand the true nature of the Iraqi regime. The Arabic literature, and even the limited information available in English, left no uncertainty over what was going on inside Iraq. Under the rubric of the Baath party, Saddam's clique ruthlessly murdered opponents and stifled dissent in order to take and consolidate control over Iraq. Even the most casual observer of Iraq had to recognize Saddam's brutal nature.

As the months wore on, I invariably found myself trying to convince my colleagues throughout ISA of the reality of Iraqi politics and the direction in which Saddam was headed. It seemed I was constantly giving a seminar on ethnic politics, emphasizing the manner in which the minority Sunni Arab community (as distinct from the Kurdish Sunnis) had come to dominate the majority Shia community in Iraq. It was also necessary to describe the regional and clannish dimension of the ethnic mosaic of Iraq, particularly how Sunnis from Tikrit had managed to use the military as a path to escape from the drudgery of their rural existence in central Iraq. Organization charts of Saddam's security structure showed clearly that the Tikritis were in control. By the middle of the year, Vince Kern had dubbed me "Teicher al-Tikriti."

In July 1979, Saddam finally eliminated Ahmad Hassan al-Bakr, a relative by marriage and the titular head of state of Iraq, appointing himself president. By the end of the month, widespread reports were being picked up describing Saddam's purge of his rivals from the Baath party's Revolutionary Command Council. He had convened an extraordinary meeting in order to hear the confession of treason by one of the Baath leaders, Muhyi Abd al-Hussein al-Mashadi. By the time the confession was finished, al-Hussein had alleged that many others were traitors. They were arrested on the spot, and twenty-two were thereafter executed by Baath party officials. At first, I wanted to dismiss it as anti-Arab propaganda, too ghoulish to be true. However, wanting to ensure that the lesson was not lost on the Arab world, Saddam had taped the event and distributed copies to those whom he sought to impress.

After months of research and analyzing the data, I argued that Saddam's objectives were bold and clear. There had been no fundamental moderation of his intentions, only a crude effort to mask his behavior with a more tempered image in foreign policy. Within Iraq and the Arab world, the arena where he quite deliberately showed his true face, Saddam behaved with increasing cruelty and brutality. A new power balance was emerging in the Middle East in light of Egypt's isolation from the Arab world, the fall of the shah and the turmoil inside Iran set off by the Iranian revolution. In this environment Saddam seized the opportunity to cast himself as a latter-day Saladin and an enlightened, if necessarily authoritarian, modern man for the benefit of Westerners desperate for a pragmatic alternative to the medieval Islamic fundamentalism represented by the Ayatollah Khomeini.

Taking a leaf out of Arafat's book, Saddam and his spokesmen learned to speak out of both sides of their mouths, using language their listeners wanted to hear. Yet one had only to read the daily translations of Saddam's speeches, interviews or other Iraqi press pieces in the publications of the Foreign Broadcast Information Service (FBIS) to have a clear picture of his anti-Western vision of the Middle East. He boasted that he was destined to "cleanse" the Middle East of the political influence of the West by eventually bringing about the destruction of Israel, while promoting a renaissance of Arab culture. On the other hand, one could take the easier route of reading diplomatic reports or the occasional interview conducted by specially anointed Western journalists who effectively served as Saddam's propaganda instruments. In such interviews could be found the buzzwords "economic modernization," "emancipation of Iraqi women," "declining Iraqi infant-mortality rates," "improving literacy rates" and "importance of peaceful Western technology for Iraqi development." Even on the Arab-Israeli front, Saddam would demonstrate his "moderation" with an occasional reference to Israel by name, rather than the normal description of it as the Zionist entity.

Saddam understood that the fundamental step toward confrontation with Israel was to gain a controlling influence over the Persian Gulf's oil supplies by replacing the shah as the arbiter of oil supply and price. Not only would this give him the financial power necessary to buy, and eventually produce, whatever military hardware he wanted, but he understood that oil could command a high political price as well. Convinced of the West's cravenness, demonstrated by its weak behavior after the October 1973 War and the second oil shock (the latter accompanying the Iranian revolution in the winter of 1979), Saddam was confident that dominance of the free world oil supply would enable him to extract political concessions on key issues. His strategy called for investment in Iraq's petroleum sector, second only to investment in the military. Iraq took every possible step to increase its domestic oil production. It built pipelines across Turkey and Saudi Arabia and sought to use its influence as an OPEC price hawk to keep oil prices as high as possible.

By the time Iraq unilaterally abrogated the Algiers Accords and invaded Iran in September 1980, Iraqi oil production had reached nearly four million barrels per day, second only to the production of the Saudis. Had Iraq succeeded in seizing Khuzestan Province and Iran's Kharg Island oil terminal, Saddam would have had control of over eleven million barrels per day of oil production capacity, nearly one fifth of the world's global oil consumption at the time. As with Iraq's later invasion of Kuwait in August 1990, the fundamental rationale for Saddam's invasion of Iran in September 1980 was to take over Iran's oil and thereby wield the financial and political power that flowed from it.

But his ambitions were not limited to the region or even to the Arab world. Saddam wanted to assume the leadership of the Non-Aligned Movement (NAM) as well. Throughout 1978 and 1979, countless dignitaries from the Third World paraded in and out of Baghdad on a weekly basis. Heaping praise on the economic achievements of the Iraqi modernization program, these countries were paid off with economic assistance in return for good press and promises of support for Iraq's ascension to a leading role in the NAM. Saddam declared his ever-bolder ambitions to the international media with unambiguous alacrity.

The growth in Iraq's military did not slow down in 1979. Iraq possessed substantial offensive military capability. Indeed, in one area, armored warfare, Saddam's procurements demonstrated his clear intention to create the ability to project modern military power over great distances in any direction. Not only had the Iraqi tank force more than doubled since 1973, but Iraq was scouring international markets for tank transporters. By the end of 1979, it was estimated that Iraq had acquired over a thousand transporters, a mobility asset crucial to Baghdad's intentions to play a more active role in the confrontation with Israel or to invade Iran, Kuwait and/or Saudi Arabia. Tank transporters gave Baghdad the ability to project armor power over long distances, without wearing out its tanks. In support of the tanks, the Iraqi Armed Forces, organized into twelve divisions and three airborne brigades, was equipped with 2,000 modern, long-range artillery tubes, 3,500 APCs, 450 modern aircraft, SCUD and FROG surface-to-surface missiles, 12 torpedo boats, 14 missile boats and 250 attack and transport helicopters.

The area of unconventional weapons, while a potential concern, had not attracted much attention. Although several analysts in the intelligence community viewed Iraq realistically and were convinced that Iraq was, in fact, trying to develop a nuclear weapon, it was primarily Israel that argued vociferously that Iraq was not far from fielding such a device, however crude.

On this issue, there was only fragmentary evidence at best, and unlike Israel, Iraq was a signatory of the Nuclear Nonproliferation Treaty. Its facilities were safeguarded, and routinely received the International

Atomic Energy Agency (IAEA) seal of approval. Italy and France were in the forefront of international efforts to sell Iraq nuclear power facilities, research laboratories, fissionable material, and the technical expertise necessary to develop a comprehensive nuclear program. The reactor sold by France was extremely sophisticated, requiring several core loads of highly enriched uranium-235 each year. The by-product of used uranium-235 is plutonium, the ideal radioactive material for nuclear weapons.

A clear sign of Iraq's intention to stockpile plutonium came when Italy announced it had agreed to sell Iraq a "hot cell" technology that would enable Baghdad to reprocess its uranium by separating out the plutonium, which could not be used for power generation. Nor would Italy concur in harsh assessments of Iraq's intentions to use its growing arsenal to advance its avowed goals and ambitions. Soon after its invasion of Iran, in November 1980, Iraq unilaterally suspended the right of the IAEA to inspect the nuclear facilities. Yet for the most part, except American civilians with responsibility for promoting nuclear nonproliferation, most officials working on the Middle East did not want to believe that Iraq was developing a nuclear weapon.

The lack of realism throughout the U.S. government with regard to Iraq was staggering. Administration officials and most Arabists throughout the bureaucracy simply wanted to believe Iraq no longer posed a threat to American interests and indeed would eventually moderate into an acceptable security partner in place of Iran. They convinced themselves that Iraq could help advance U.S. interests in the region, and no one wanted to be confused by the facts. The tilt had become institutionalized.

Only at the CIA did a few analysts have a realistic appreciation for Saddam, his power and his intentions. One military analyst confided in me, however, that he had been told not to speculate about Iraqi intentions, just monitor the Iraqi military. The senior echelons of the agency clearly wanted to believe that Iraq had changed for the better. Although they might succeed in expressing their dissent internally, the voices of these skeptics were consistently stilled by the smothering bureaucracy of the interagency intelligence-production process.

Completed in November 1979, my study systematically outlined Saddam's (1) growing political influence in the Arab and Third worlds; (2) current and projected military capabilities, to include the creation of an arms industry and a nuclear weapons program; (3) current and projected oil production and export capability; and (4) support for various international terrorists that promoted Iraq's radical interests. In the latter case, Baghdad had begun in 1979 to place increasing emphasis on Iraqi-backed subversion, terror and support for the Arabistan Liberation Front in Iran's oil-rich Khuzestan Province, in addition to its traditional support for radical Palestinians such as Abu Nidal.

Bolstered by a comprehensive survey of Saddam's Arabic rhetoric and his violent suppression of any opposition elements within Iraq, I reached blunt, realistic conclusions about Saddam's intentions and the adverse consequences for the United States. The core conclusion was that Saddam was changing his image and nothing more. His steadily growing power, the collapse of the shah and the apparent indifference of the world community to his vicious tactics against his real and presumed enemies all combined to reinforce his conviction that the goals he had sought to achieve since the early 1950s were within reach.

In retrospect, my first prediction—that Saddam would invade Iran and seek to annex the oil-rich province of Khuzestan—turned out to be the most immediate. Such an act would have dangerous consequences for the United States, although some Middle East experts in and out of government would surely argue that an Iraqi victory would reduce, if not eliminate, the regional danger posed by Khomeini and the avowed desire of radical Iranians to export the revolution.

Despite the regional instability caused by the Iranian revolution, it was doubtful that the Iranians would roll over for the Iraqi military. Thus, the outcome of a war between Iraq and Iran could not be taken for granted. Because of Iraq's Arab ties with its neighbors, especially the Saudis, there was a reasonable chance that Iran might retaliate by lashing out at the Saudis or other Gulf states, thereby broadening the war and sending the international oil market into a panic. Still reeling from the effects of the 1978 Iranian oil field strikes, the market would have a difficult time coping with another major disruption without dramatic price increases. Finally, and most significantly, in the event of a successful Iraqi invasion, Saddam would emerge as the undisputed arbiter of the Persian Gulf, intent on dictating oil and security policy. Given America's interest in the free and uninterrupted flow of oil from the Persian Gulf, such an occurrence would further damage the international economy, weaken what was left of America's regional influence and enhance the potential for further Soviet advances throughout southwest Asia. In such a case, the United States would be forced either to acquiesce to Iraqi hegemony or confront Iraq directly.

I reached several other conclusions as well, none of which boded well for American interests. In addition to the invasion of Iran, Riyadh's declining confidence in America's security commitment and the strains in U.S.-Saudi relations caused by Saudi opposition to the peace process were sure to embolden Saddam to increase his pressure on Riyadh to cut back Saudi oil production as a means for coercing additional oil price hikes in OPEC. Baghdad's thirst for oil revenues was as insatiable as was the West's growing need for the oil. Saddam knew it and intended to squeeze every dollar possible out of the West to finance his grand designs. In addition to exercising traditional Iraqi claims against Iran's Khuzestan Province, I also asserted that a renewed Iraqi claim to Kuwait was inevitable. Moreover, since Iraq had forcibly occupied Kuwaiti territory in the past, to enhance its coastline, there was no reason not to expect that Saddam would be any less willing than his predecessors to undertake comparable action.

Saddam's popularity throughout the Arab world could be counted upon to grow in such circumstances, strengthening radical regimes in Syria, Libya, Algeria and the PDRY, while emboldening radical opposition elements in other Arab states. This would further damage the prospects for a Palestinian autonomy agreement or a general broadening of the peace process. Should Saddam turn his attention to the Arab-Israeli conflict, having procured tank transporters to carry thousands of modern tanks to the Israeli frontier, he could use these weapons and engage in brinkmanship, similar to that of Nasser in 1967, in order to stimulate American and Soviet intervention and extract concessions from Israel. Failing such an outcome, it seemed clear that Saddam had every intention of leading the Arab world into another war with Israel, most likely by organizing an eastern front composed of Syria, Jordan, Iraq and Saudi Arabia. Although it was likely that Israel would win the war on the ground, the political outcome of such a conflagration was totally unpredictable, particularly in light of the unsettled changes in the regional balance of power and the implications for East-West competition. One thing was clear: Saddam intended to use the power that Iraq was amassing. Even if Iraq could deter Iranian expansionism in the Gulf, one could not overlook the dangers that a resurgent, rejectionist and ever more powerful Iraq posed to long-term U.S. interests.

In mid-November 1979, I forwarded the paper, by now well over fifty single-spaced pages including tables and annexes, to Bob Murray with a cover memo proposing that it be sent through McGiffert to Secretary Brown. My views ran contrary to those of most of the national security bureaucracy, including other analysts in ISA. Murray concurred, however, that the findings in the paper were troubling and agreed to forward the study.

By now the administration was totally absorbed with the hostage crisis in Iran. My Iraq paper was returned to me a month or so later, clearly stamped "THE SECRETARY HAS SEEN," indicating that it had been personally reviewed by Secretary Brown. However, handwritten on the margin of the Executive Summary, Secretary Brown wrote, "I disagree. Iraq has changed. It has moderated its behavior." There was no other comment and nothing else to say.

With the administration desperate to end the hostage crisis, and wanting to believe that the situation could not get any worse, it was clear that Secretary Brown had already made up his mind about Iraq. Still hoping that the administration would reconsider its tilt toward Iraq, Shoemaker surreptitiously provided a copy to General William E. Odom on the NSC staff in February 1980, in the hope that Odom would suggest that Brzezinski read it. About a month later, Odom told Shoemaker that Brzezinski had reviewed the study and was surprised at the extent of Iraqi political, military and economic activism. He was not convinced by the analysis, however, to change his mind that Iraq was becoming more moderate. The tilt toward Iraq was now under way. Only its speed, scope and consequences remained to be determined.

I shared the paper with a number of other analysts throughout the government. Many disagreed with the conclusions, particularly my insistence that Saddam would invade Iran and use violence wherever necessary to attain his objectives. Others argued that Iraqi support of international terrorism was limited to anti-Israel activities, as if that was somehow less of a concern to the United States, justifying Iraqi power on the basis of past U.S. policies which enhanced Iranian power. Arabists at the State Department were particularly appalled, arguing that the paper read like "anti-Iraqi propaganda." The eventual resumption of relations with Iraq would mean another embassy added to the NEA domain. For these Arabists, it was clear that my forthright analysis was dangerous and unnerving. On the other hand, there were analysts, particularly at the CIA and the Defense Intelligence Agency (DIA), who were also concerned about Iraqi intentions and power. Unfortunately, their voices proved to be no more persuasive than mine.

With the signing of the peace treaty between Egypt and Israel in March 1979, those who worked on American Middle East policy took a deep breath in the hope that a new era was dawning. There appeared to be opportunities for American activism to expand the Arab-Israeli peace process, making it essential that the momentum generated by the treaty contribute to early progress in the autonomy negotiations. In the Persian

Gulf, President Carter hoped that the loss of American prestige and influence that accompanied the fall of the shah in January could be offset by Iraq's perceived moderation toward the West and the development and implementation of a new security policy that would protect important U.S. interests without destabilizing the conservative, pro-Western regimes. These hopes were dashed with the taking of the American hostages in Iran in November, and the December 1979 Soviet invasion of Afghanistan.

CHAPTER 3

OVER THE HORIZON

———◆———

Peacekeepers in Sinai

Immediately upon the signing of the Egypt-Israel peace treaty, a number of documents, "side letters" and other appendages to the treaty, were distributed to the bureaucracy and the public. One side letter from President Carter to Prime Minister Begin stated a U.S. commitment to work with the United Nations to create a peacekeeping operation for the Sinai. A U.N. force was to be positioned to act as a trip wire between Egypt and Israel to avert any hostile actions. This force was regarded by the parties as a vital "confidence-building" measure to help manage the security arrangements outlined in the treaty. President Carter wrote that if the United Nations did not agree to provide such a force, the United States took upon itself the obligation to organize an alternative, multinational peacekeeping force.

It seemed likely that the United States might well find itself forced to live up to this commitment, perhaps to include a contribution of American troops. Having been excluded from the peace process, the treaty had been harshly condemned by Moscow, and there was no apparent reason why the Soviet Union would cooperate in the U.N. Security Council. A Security Council resolution would be required to facilitate the formation of a U.N. peacekeeping force, and the logic of U.S.-Soviet relations suggested that Moscow would seize the opportunity to demonstrate its readiness to stand by its radical Arab friends and do its utmost to undermine the American-led peace process.

Who from the DOD had been involved in the decision to make this very significant offer? While the president certainly had the authority to agree to such a force on his own, it would be curious that such a commitment would be made without any staff work or analysis of the Soviet dimension. The offer, if it was to be implemented, raised many nettlesome legal, political and diplomatic questions. Moreover, because of its importance to the Israelis as an "international guarantee," the danger of failing

72

to fulfill the commitment might conceivably bring about a new crisis for Egypt, Israel and the United States. Surely consideration had been given to these matters.

I showed Bob Murray the side letter before he went to a daily ISA staff meeting with Assistant Secretary McGiffert. Murray read it, whistled quietly, looked up at me and said, "Howard, this is the first time I have seen this letter or heard about our commitment. Secretary Brown is probably aware of it, but I will make sure and bring the matter to his attention. Meanwhile, please check around with the folks at State and see what you can find out."

By nine-thirty A.M. I had spoken to various offices at State—PM, NEA and the Bureau of International Organizations (IO)—and to people who had direct responsibility within their offices for Middle East and/or peacekeeping activities. None were aware of the side letter. Just before lunch, someone in PM called me back. He told me that shortly after our early-morning discussion, he had spoken with NEA and IO to see what he could find out. Although no one had any information at the time he called, just before eleven-thirty IO invited him to attend a meeting on the subject of a "Sinai peacekeeping operation" later that afternoon. In the circumstances, he suggested that I should attend the meeting as well.

Based on my prior experience in the State Department, I had no expectation that Defense Department representatives would be formally invited to an IO meeting. Responsible for United Nations and other multilateral organizations, IO probably would not want any other bureaucracy participating in the creation of any structure that might be required for this peacekeeping requirement. State would see this as a diplomatic matter with no need for DOD input.

The meeting was chaired by Deputy Assistant Secretary (DAS) of State for International Organizations Gerald Helman. A career FSO, Helman was well versed in the intricacies of United Nations diplomacy, including political and procedural matters associated with U.N. peacekeeping operations. The small conference room was crowded, since every bureau in the State Department with a possible interest in this matter had sent representatives to the meeting. By the time Helman called us to order, there were over twenty people present and, other than me, all were State representatives.

Helman opened the meeting by circulating copies of President Carter's side letter to Prime Minister Begin. He advised the group that IO had only learned of this U.S. commitment earlier in the day following a telephone inquiry from PM. Given its potential significance, he had thought it wise to promptly convene a "State Department working group" to manage the issue. Helman expected that the U.S. delegation at the United Nations would need instructions for consultations with the permanent members of the Security Council right away. Additionally, press inquiries could be expected, making it necessary to produce several "Q's and A's" for the purposes of public diplomacy.

As far as Helman was aware, there had been no prior communications between the United States and the U.N. secretary general, Kurt Waldheim, or the Security Council regarding any U.S.-Egyptian-Israeli interest in inserting a United Nations peacekeeping force in the Sinai. Grousing about the lack of coordination and proper staff involvement, Helman concluded that the president was running a big risk by taking U.N. cooperation for granted. Given the general international climate of opposition to the peace treaty, most notably among the majority of the Arab states and the Soviet bloc, the United Nations could not be counted upon to cooperate with the United States. Indeed, there were any number of opportunities for the Soviet Union to oppose the U.S. agenda on several procedural and substantive grounds.

Morris Draper, DAS for Israel, Jordan, Egypt and Lebanon, was representing NEA. Draper was also a career FSO and had served throughout the Middle East and in the bureaucratic warrens of Washington. He was an excellent diplomat with a good sense of humor and was an individual genuinely dedicated to the cause of Arab-Israeli peace. Surprisingly, Draper told the group that NEA had not been aware of the preparation of the side letter, but its importance to the conclusion of the treaty negotiations was critical. While NEA hoped that the United Nations would cooperate, if it did not, it would be essential for the United States to form the alternative multinational force itself. To date, the subject had not come up in any of the Middle East capitals where U.S. diplomats were trying to persuade their Arab hosts to support the treaty and not automatically follow the radical line being promoted by Baghdad and Damascus. The European Bureau's (EUR) representative stated that no effort had been made as yet to communicate with Moscow on this issue, but in his opinion, the Soviets would likely oppose a U.N. force.

Following the opening remarks, the discussion focused on the questions of whether the United Nations would cooperate and what the presumed difficulty and disadvantages of forming an alternative American force would be. Most of the participants argued that Arab and Soviet pressure might make it impossible to form an alternative structure and expressed great apprehension about the possibility of deploying U.S. ground troops. Given America's defeat in the Vietnam War and the recent collapse of the Iranian pillar, and in light of growing anti-Western, militant Islamic fundamentalism, they argued that American military activism in the Middle East would be further destabilizing. The deployment of U.S. ground troops, even in the capacity of peacekeepers, would generate more anti-American sentiment by acting as a magnet for the radicals.

At this point, I entered the discussion as the DOD representative and argued that a U.S. led force that included American troops would not, by definition, be viewed as a negative element in the Middle East. Aside from the fundamental importance of America's commitment to fulfill treaty obligations, the presence of U.S. forces could help to achieve other goals. First, it would demonstrate that the U.S. military could play a direct role in the support of the peace process and help to restore some measure of confidence in American political-military commitments. Second, with the growing recognition that we lacked the capability of projecting military power rapidly to the Persian Gulf region in the wake of the Iranian revolution (a Rapid Deployment Force had only just become the subject of national debate), the predeployment of U.S. combat forces to the Sinai Peninsula would position U.S. forces only hours away from Saudi oil fields. Moreover, the troops would be able to exercise in a desert environment in which U.S. forces had only limited, noncombat experience.

While an American-led peacekeeping force was obviously not the ideal way to defend vital American interests in the Persian Gulf, I argued that this could be an opportunity for the United States to begin projecting modest amounts of U.S. military power from a base in the region. It would represent an important first step toward enhancing America's ability to defend its own interests and be less vulnerable in our reliance on other countries. Additionally, with the troops based in the Sinai desert, they would be virtually invisible, mitigating the argument of those who feared that their very presence in the region would attract anti-American elements. No one in the Gulf would be forced to see them unless the troops were actually deployed in a contingency. Comparisons to Iran or Vietnam were, therefore, totally inappropriate.

My comments were met with nearly universal disagreement. Helman concluded by saying that all the arguments I had raised for U.S. involvement in a multinational force only reinforced the need to find a way, however difficult, to convince the United Nations to cooperate. As the meeting started to break up, Helman closed the discussion by stating that for the time being, "State needs to keep this matter internal. Let's not let Defense get in on this."

In the circumstances, I interjected, "You're too late, Mr. Helman. I'm here from ISA and it was I who made the inquiries with your staff this morning. I hope we can find a way to cooperate in this matter." Looking sheepish, Helman replied that he had not meant to exclude Defense entirely, only with regard to the "diplomatic efforts." I thanked him for this clarification, but insisted that McGiffert be kept informed, noting that he would probably want to review and clear on any cables of instructions that could involve the formation of peacekeeping forces, whether U.S. troops participated or not. Helman agreed.

Later I recommended to Murray that he talk with Helman to ensure that ISA was not cut out and played a proper role in the evolution of the U.S. position on this matter. A few days later an interagency group was formed which included representatives from the Department of Defense. Not unexpectedly, the Soviets refused to cooperate, and a multinational peacekeeping force, led by American troops, was deployed in the Sinai, where they remain today, witness to the success of the U.S.-mediated peace between Egypt and Israel.

Out of Sight and Out of Mind

Aside from the wonderful moment when the peace treaty was signed on March 26, truly a tribute to the hard work of President Carter and to the dedication of many individuals throughout the national security bureaucracy, and the governments of Egypt and Israel, the situation in the Middle East progressed from bad to worse for U.S. interests through the end of 1979. The Iranian revolution entered an extremely violent, anti-Western phase that culminated in November with the seizure of the American embassy and the start of what would prove to be 444 days of captivity for American diplomats. The Arab world rallied around Baghdad, America's most implacable radical foe (even as the White House started to hint about tilting toward Iraq) in opposition to the peace process, while Israeli and Egyptian negotiators often talked past each other in the Palestinian autonomy negotiations. Soviet surrogates in Ethiopia and the PDRY consolidated their control, increasing their overt reliance on the props of power made available by Moscow, primarily Cuban expeditionary forces and massive infusions of advanced military hardware, posing threats to their neighbors that were without precedent in the region. The Christmas holidays brought a full-fledged Soviet invasion of Afghanistan.

As if operating from a textbook on the conduct of a Third World coup d'état, Soviet allies in Kabul seized power and asked Moscow for help in consolidating control over Afghanistan. Soviet airborne and ground forces and fixed-and rotary-wing aircraft conducted lightning operations the likes of which had not been seen since World War II. In a matter of days, over eighty-five thousand Soviet troops were in Afghanistan. Moscow had clearly calculated that Washington was immobilized by the hostage crisis, having done little, if anything, to protect its interests and shore up its vulnerabilities in the Gulf following the collapse of the Twin Pillars policy. Given the pattern of growing Soviet influence in and around the region, Moscow had good reason to believe that the tide of history in southwest Asia was flowing in its favor.

With the balance of power shifting in favor of the Soviets in the Middle East, Central America and Southeast Asia, Moscow correctly calculated that outside powers would not oppose the invasion. Cocky in his belief that the West was inexorably in decline, Brezhnev did not appreciate, until it was too late, that his brazen move into Afghanistan actually served as a wake-up call for President Carter and the American military. Any remaining illusions in the Carter administration over long-term Soviet intentions were shattered. There was no longer any doubt that Moscow could very well succeed in the modern "Great Game" and use force, whether Soviet or surrogate forces, to gain control over Persian Gulf oil resources. The central question became how the United States and its allies could design and implement a counterstrategy to thwart the Soviet Union—rhetoric alone would not be enough.

At the time of the invasion, and notwithstanding our important interests, the United States had no tangible policy and virtually no military capability in the region to counter additional Soviet advances toward the Persian Gulf. America's military posture was best described by the euphemism "over the horizon" capability.

Although the Gulf states clearly wanted Washington to provide for their security, their leaders were concerned that granting the United States bases or even "access rights" could provoke the very instability and aggression they sought to deter. There was great fear throughout the region of an Iranian determination to export its revolution and militant Islamic fundamentalism. The Gulf leaders wanted to keep the American military out of sight and out of mind in order to reduce the potential for radicals' fomenting antiregime unrest or for giving the Soviets a pretext for further aggressive behavior. In addition, they had virtually no confidence that the United States would effectively protect their interests and territorial integrity.

The administration could no longer expect either a different reality or an international standard of morality. President Carter was compelled by the circumstances to redress the military imbalance and to try to convince Moscow and the countries of the Middle East that the United States was determined to protect its important interests in the Gulf and roll back Soviet expansionism.

During the November leading up to the Soviet invasion, the national security and foreign policy bureaucracy was in a frenzied state, trying desperately to formulate diplomatic as well as military options to end the hostage crisis. At the staff level in ISA, there was overwhelming support for a rescue attempt and for harsh military retaliation if the hostages were harmed. The staff of the JCS made it clear that they believed there was little prospect for a successful rescue mission, given the lack of specialized forces and the practical problems associated with conducting a rescue mission over great distances into a hostile urban environment.

The hostage crisis created an instant operational requirement for some minimal infrastructure to support the projection of U.S. military power in the Persian Gulf. Yet such capability did not then exist. The Afghanistan invasion, however, provided President Carter with instant political support in Congress and from the American people in order to implement what became known as the "access strategy."

During this general time frame, the National Security Council (NSC) had been trying to mobilize the bureaucracy to create a new strategic framework for the Persian Gulf, including the notion of a tilt toward Iraq. By the time of the Soviet invasion of Afghanistan, planning had already gone into creating such a framework on such issues as the Rapid Deployment Force (RDF) and increasing U.S. military presence in the region, including the stationing there of an aircraft carrier and amphibious group, and the conduct of reconnaissance flights with B-52s.

In an effort to overcome universal skepticism about U.S. will and capabilities in the Middle East, President Carter used his State of the Union Address of January 1980 to declare what became known as the Carter Doctrine. He stated that any attempt by any outside force to gain control of the Persian Gulf region would be regarded as an assault on the "vital interests" of the United States of America, and such an assault would be repelled by any means necessary, including military force. Thus,

American oil interests in the Persian Gulf became vital. This was an important first step in the restoration of U.S. credibility.

The administration, unfortunately, was engaging in some significant measure of rhetorical bravado. In fact, the United States lacked sufficient capabilities for responding effectively, should a response actually become necessary. Although the Rapid Deployment Joint Task Force had been created and military exercises were being conducted, our existing ability to act was severely limited.

The Camels of Masirah Island

Reflecting bitter bureaucratic disputes between the NSC, State and Defense over what the political traffic in the Gulf could bear over the summer and fall, an interagency compromise had been reached to stop short of asking for the establishment of "permanent bases" and instead to seek "temporary access."

Gulf leaders were fearful that a visible U.S. military presence might provoke internal instability, and they were skeptical about the value and durability of American commitments in light of America's failure to come to the aid of the shah. Although consideration of the access strategy had been under way within Washington for months in response to the changing balance of power brought about by the Iranian revolution, regional leaders regarded American interest in access rights as little more than a limited, knee-jerk response to the hostage crisis.

Few believed that the United States was interested in the security of individual Gulf states, other than that of Saudi Arabia. They feared the United States would do no more for their countries than it had done for its Iranian pillar. Whether U.S. intervention could have saved the shah was, in any event, not really the issue. The fact that the United States had made almost no effort to assist such an important security partner left an indelible impression of American spinelessness, indecision and impotence. In such circumstances, Gulf leaders considered it more prudent to avoid the entreaties of the United States than to accept them. They were much more traumatized by the situation in Iran and the export of antimonarchical Islamic fundamentalism than by threats of further Soviet expansionism. Kuwait accused the United States of using the Soviet invasion of Afghanistan as a pretext for establishing bases in the region.

Galvanized by the seizure of American hostages and having little or no military means to effect a rescue, the United States quickened its efforts to build its regional power. The British were no longer there to help defend American interests. In late November, a high-level U.S. mission traveled to the Gulf region in order to negotiate agreements for temporary access for U.S. forces and use of concomitant facilities in the event that U.S. military intervention in the Gulf became necessary. The interagency delegation, comprising then PM director Reginald Bartholomew, Bob Murray, the JCS staff director of plans Lieutenant General Richard Lawson and Fritz Ermarth of the NSC, was able to secure agreement, in principle, for access to facilities in Oman, Kenya and Somalia. As noted above, these would not be U.S. bases: in each capital, the hosts agreed to grant U.S. forces "temporary access" to certain facilities on the conditions that the United States agree to consult the host country in advance of force deployments and that the United States upgrade the facilities to support the range of missions that it contemplated conducting in the region.

Although no agreement was reached (or attempted) with the Saudis, the access agreement with Oman carefully provided the United States with a lodgment on the Arabian Peninsula. This gave American forces direct physical access to an air and sea head directly astride the strategic Strait of Hormuz, the gateway out of the Persian Gulf through which passed nearly ten million barrels of oil a day. While access rights and an increased tempo of U.S. military activity in Kenya and Somalia were important in the global confrontation with the Soviets—primarily to counter the significant Soviet presence in Ethiopia—the agreement with Oman represented the major strategic enhancement of the U.S. military and naval position in the Persian Gulf and Indian Ocean.

After the Bartholomew mission returned, the DOD was designated the lead agency to implement the upgrading of the military facilities that U.S. forces might need to use. A decision had been made to send a military team to Oman to survey facilities and begin discussions with the government of Oman over the nature and type of improvements that the United States would want to implement. Although the Oman Facilities Survey Team would be composed primarily of operations, logistics and engineering officers, I was sent as the ISA representative on the team.

We left for the Sultanate of Oman just as the U.S. government was announcing the formation of the RDF. At the time, the U.S. Congress as well as American and foreign military specialists criticized this vacuous strategy by noting that the RDF was not rapid, was not able to deploy and did not exist as a real military force. The critics were right. But neither did the United States have any alternative than to try to convince friend and foe that we would fight, naked if necessary.

The RDF was hollow. No military units were dedicated to it. Instead, the Defense Department simply assigned additional missions to forces that were already designated to fight in any of several other areas of operations. Nor could these forces move rapidly. Air- and sea-lift capabilities were woefully inadequate for moving any units except the 82nd Airborne Division into the Arabian Peninsula, and even that mission would require nearly twenty-one days of continuous airlift by nearly every Military Airlift Command (MAC) C-5 and C-141 transport jet in the U.S. inventory. Tanks, APCs, artillery and other elements of heavy-armor divisions would take months to deploy and become combat-ready. Such a force could hardly be expected to deter a fast-moving ground assault. Nor could the forces deploy for combat once they arrived in the region. No preparations had been made in any of the countries that might logically serve as a staging area for U.S. forces. Runways were too short, aircraft parking space inadequate, oil and lubricants and the necessities of life were not stockpiled, housing for pilots, combatants, logisticians and headquarters staff did not exist. Aside from the U.S. Navy, U.S. forces had not conducted military exercises in the harsh, unfamiliar desert environments of the Persian Gulf.

The mission of our team was to ensure that the U.S. military fully appreciated the extent and nature of the Omani facilities that might support the RDF and assess what improvements were required. The two most critical shortfalls with regard to deploying American forces successfully were a staging area for ground operations and a secure air head to support fleet operations in the Indian Ocean. During the nearly two weeks the team was in Oman, we met with military and civilian officials, inspected every facility, surveyed runways and storage depots, assessed staging areas for division-sized units, identified strengths and vulnerabilities and developed a plan for rapid and long-term improvements.

Given the strategic location of Oman astride the Strait of Hormuz and opposite Iran to the north, the United Arab Emirates (UAE) and Saudi Arabia to the west, the Indian Ocean to the east and the PDRY to the south, it was critical that access rights be secured and improvements made as soon as possible. Critical to the emerging U.S. strategy were the air base at the Seeb International Airport outside the Omani capital of Muscat, the air base on the island of Masirah and the gravel runway in the remote village of Ghasab, strategically located at the tip of the forbidding Musandam, which jutted out into the Strait of Hormuz. Seeb was viewed as the ideal location for a ground and air forces rear staging area, while Masirah would best serve as the logistics hub for the Navy. Ghasab, because of its remote location in a most primitive and forbidding environment, provided an excellent location for launching and supporting "special operations," such as the ill-fated hostage rescue attempt.

Sultan Qaboos bin Said of Oman was a good friend to the United States and consistently supported Sadat's peace with Israel. While he was ready to make facilities available and cooperate militarily, he did not want the American military presence to get out of hand. Qaboos had come to power in 1971 aware that the reactionary policies of his father were deliberately preventing the Omani people from participating in the twentieth century. Since ascending to the throne, Qaboos had launched an enlightened program of social, economic and military modernization. He pushed his program of rapid change as hard as he dared, recognizing that antimodernization forces simmered beneath the surface of tranquillity. The Soviet-backed PDRY was constantly looking for opportunities to cause security problems for the sultanate. Qaboos was not willing to risk upsetting the delicate balance in his country by injecting an American military presence directly into the center of Omani modernization. Having survived cannily over the years with the help of the British and the shah, he did not now want to lose control.

Bartholomew returned to Oman just before Easter 1980 in order to conclude the access negotiations. His instructions emphasized the importance of securing Omani agreement to the construction of a rear staging area adjacent to Seeb International Airport that would support an army division. The Omanis balked, suggesting instead the island of Masirah, which our team had surveyed and the military had already begun to use in support of the fleet in the Indian Ocean. The United States and Oman were at an impasse. On Saturday, Bartholomew sent a cable back to Washington reporting this latest development and urgently requesting instructions for his Monday-morning meeting.

The NSC staff responded to his cable by scheduling a meeting in the White House Situation Room for two P.M. Easter Sunday. Early that morning, Vince Kern and I met with Air Force colonels Robert Lawrence and Sam Hall to devise a coordinated JCS-ISA position. Lawrence and Hall were a highly capable and genial duo of Air Force officers with special experience in the Middle East. We had served together in the Oman Facilities Survey Team the preceding December and had shared a number of amusing experiences.

One of the lighter moments of that trip took place in the middle of nowhere on Masirah Island, where we had chanced upon a herd of camels. Two of them were really enjoying themselves, notwithstanding the presence of an audience, and I had captured their moment of ecstasy in a 35-millimeter photograph. Everyone wanted a copy of the picture. For one reason or another, I had gotten around to giving copies to both Lawrence and Hall during our morning meeting.

When we finished our staff work, I called the principal deputy assistant secretary (DAS) of ISA, Frank Kramer, to advise him that a briefing paper was ready for McGiffert and him to take to the Situation Room meeting. After concurring with the position we proposed—which was to stand firm with the JCS and "hold the line" on Seeb for the rear staging area—Kramer said that Kern and I would represent ISA at the meeting. Heading out of the Pentagon's river entrance, Kern and I saw General Lawson and Vice Admiral James "Ace" Lyons, Jr., getting into their chauffeured car en route to the White House meeting. They graciously asked us to join them, pressing for ISA's support of the JCS position on Seeb.

The meeting, then called a "mini-special coordinating committee (SCC)," was chaired by Air Force general Jasper Welch, then a senior member of the NSC staff responsible for military issues. Also present were NSC staff member Gary Sick, DAS of State for Arabian Peninsula Affairs Joseph Twinam, other State representatives, Lawson, Lyons, Kern and me. The meeting quickly polarized into the State and DOD positions, with Twinam arguing in favor of conceding to the Omani demands, while the JCS insisted that Seeb was the only piece of real estate which made sense for a rear staging area. Lawson went up to the large map of the Gulf located at the front of the Situation Room and preceded to demonstrate why the distance from Masirah to the head of the Gulf made Masirah impractical, regardless of the diplomatic niceties.

In the heat of the debate, Lawson began to argue without watching to where he was pointing on the map and kept pointing to Aden, Britain's former seat in the Gulf and the capital city of the PDRY. Twinam seized upon this obvious mistake to renew his attack against the JCS position, arguing that Lawson was unfamiliar with the geography of the Arabian Peninsula. Twinam added that this lack of knowledge was probably on a par with Lawson's knowledge of the cultural environment into which the JCS sought to inject U.S. ground forces.

Seeing that his boss was in trouble, Ace Lyons suddenly interrupted Twinam by slamming his fist down onto the table. Succeeding in stopping Twinam's tirade cold, Lyons paused a moment for effect. Then with a glint in his eye he said, "We in the JCS want to show you a picture of what the Omanis are doing to us in this negotiation." Without further ado, Ace opened a folder marked SECRET sitting on the table in front of him and pulled out the camel photo I had taken on Masirah Island. First holding the photo up to show the group, he then proceeded to pass it around the table. I could actually feel the color drain from my face.

Lawson knew a perfect moment when he saw it and sat down. He placed his hands on the table in front of him and announced, "And the photographer is sitting right here at the table. Howard, that is really a great picture, the color, the composition, the expressions on the camel's faces." Before I could say anything, three other guys immediately asked me for copies. Joe Twinam shook his head and muttered under his breath about "those disgusting cretins at DOD."

The debate eventually resumed, with Twinam continuing to press for a compromise that Oman might accept—access to Seeb but no construction of a staging facility—while the DOD held out for agreement to build the facility at Seeb now. In the end, the mini-SCC concluded that the overall access agreement was too important to risk by insisting on Seeb. Twinam was directed to draft instructions to Bartholomew to concede, at least for now, on the issue of a rear staging area at Seeb, while preserving the option for such a facility at Masirah. Although the final document would not be completed and signed until June 1980, Bartholomew was able to use his instructions to clear away the major issues that stood in the way of this important agreement and made real progress in increasing regular U.S. military access.

Although most of the bureaucracy viewed this emerging regional access strategy as a response to the Soviet invasion of Afghanistan, the short-term requirement was actually to support a hostage rescue mission. Omani facilities were used for the unsuccessful attempt on April 24, 1980. Ghasab airstrip, in the Musandam, and the air base at Masirah were utilized by the C-130 transports and other aircraft, while crucial logistics support was provided to the fleet through Masirah. Lawrence and Hall were dispatched to Oman to provide communications liaison between the Omanis and U.S. forces; they likewise operated from Masirah.

Desert One failed for a variety of reasons, most notably the inability of sophisticated equipment to meet the extreme demands caused by distance and environment. This tragic failure demonstrated American vulnerabilities and why the United States needed access to facilities and bases near potential combat operations. While it was argued that this particular mission, due to its complex and secretive nature, was not really representative of the RDF's strategy and purpose, there was no reason to believe that a larger force could have fared better without adequate staging areas in the Gulf. Desert One, however flawed, at least demonstrated some willingness to use force to protect American interests. But the humiliating failure only reinforced the worst fears of Gulf leaders regarding America's intentions and capabilities.

Relations with Oman were severely strained and the crucial access agreement was almost not signed, owing to Sultan Qaboos's outrage that the United States had not consulted with Oman in advance of using Oman to support Desert One. In order to demonstrate to its neighbors that granting the United States military-access rights did not represent a violation of Omani sovereignty, the government of Oman had repeatedly and vigorously insisted that the agreement include a requirement that the United States government request Omani permission before using facilities, maintaining Oman's right to refuse the request. There was no ambiguity on this point. Iraq, Iran and the PDRY harshly criticized Oman for "giving the Americans bases." Baghdad Radio described the agreement as a "treacherous act, a dagger in the heart of the Arab nation."

The Omani foreign minister, Qais Zawawi, denied that Oman had granted the U.S. base rights. By pointing to the Omani right to accede to or deny American requests, the Omanis were confident that they could adequately deflect most criticism while avoiding any domestic instability. As a matter of principle and sovereignty, Oman would maintain its right to refuse the United States. It was quietly understood, however, that American requests would typically be approved on very short notice. The United States would not agree to such a condition, on the basis that it would create operational security (OPSEC) problems in the event of military action, and would create political problems with the Congress when it came to funding military construction and security assistance. Congressional opponents of the access strategy were especially prominent on the military construction subcommittees of the appropriations committees and argued that taxpayer dollars should not be spent to improve foreign military facilities without a guarantee that U.S. forces would be able to take advantage of the improvements paid for by Americans. Such improvements without guarantees were no more than foreign aid masquerading as military construction. Over a period of months, Bartholomew and his negotiating team had delicately managed to convince the government of Oman to agree to language which would require that the United States "consult" with the Omani government in place of "requesting" Omani permission. U.S. officials had assured the Omanis that "consult" really meant "request permission."

A dictionary definition of "consult" is "to consider jointly." As would later prove the case during the Reagan administration in its dealings with the Congress, "consult" does not mean the same thing to all people. For the executive branch of the U.S. government, "consult" usually means no more than "inform after" a decision has been made and implemented. The Omanis were mortified to learn that their facilities had been used for the unsuccessful rescue attempt only after the news had already become public early on the morning of April 25, 1980. The sultan demanded a high-level explanation, but the sultan's confidence in Bartholomew's word had been compromised by the way in which the mission had been conducted. To calm the situation, President Carter sent Ambassador-at-Large Philip Habib to Muscat to explain the extreme circumstances that had forced the United States to act militarily without consulting in advance with the government of Oman.

In protest over this limited use of American power, Secretary of State Cyrus Vance resigned while the national security bureaucracy watched with dismay as the rescue mission collapsed. Almost everyone had been trying to think of options. The hostages had been in Iran serving their country and America owed it to them to get them out, or at least launch a rescue that had some realistic chance of success. That Desert One was the best the United States could do was pathetic. How was it possible that so important an operation could be so badly botched?

No one doubted the courage of the American soldiers and airmen involved; they had tried their best and risked their lives to help save other Americans. Contributing to this tragic and humiliating miscalculation was the practice of operational planners to emphasize technological capabilities, while minimizing the tendency of the unexpected to undermine even the best-laid plans. The planners had simply allowed no margin for error. Instead of assembling a force of helicopters necessary to ensure the greatest probability of success, the operation was launched with the least number of helicopters necessary to have any prospect of success. Institutional depression and self-pity, however, quickly turned to outrage as the international media televised the Ayatollah Khalkali (known as Iran's "hanging ayatollah") desecrating the body of one of the dead American soldiers of Desert One by poking a stick into his burned remains.

Since early in 1980, it had become increasingly apparent that the

Ayatollah Khomeini was intent on bringing about the defeat of President Jimmy Carter in the forthcoming elections. A growing number of intelligence reports described Khomeini's determination to humiliate, weaken and otherwise undermine President Carter's chances for reelection. Aware that the hostage situation was contributing to Carter's rapidly declining popularity, there should have been no illusions in the White House over Khomeini's goals and the value of the hostage crisis to the revolution. However, I saw no evidence of any Iranian conspiracy to cooperate with any Americans to defeat President Carter despite the regular flow of information regarding Khomeini's desires.

Although Gary Sick, who was then a member of the staff of the NSC, has maintained that April 24 was the first available date for launching a rescue mission, there were operational indications in the Pentagon that one was in the works one week earlier, just prior to the New York presidential primary. It was postponed when the mother of one of the hostages, a U.S. Marine Corps guard, showed up unexpectedly in Tehran. Carter had needed to win the New York primary to slow down the momentum his Democratic challenger, Senator Ted Kennedy, was building. Instead, the hostages remained captive in Tehran and anti-American forces were able to score another victory.

The Next Pope Doesn't Need to Be a Catholic

Throughout the country, yellow ribbons were everywhere and time was marked on the 1980 calendar and by the media by the number of days Americans were held hostage in Tehran. In the Pentagon, Vince and I took turns updating the daily count on a large blackboard that hung in our office. As we grew ever more frustrated and angrier with our failed Middle East policy, we became increasingly irreverent, using "the board" to note scathing criticisms of the administration. Before too long, a tradition was established as others in NEASA began showing up in our office to add their perspective to the board with political cartoons and wicked one-liners. Even Murray wandered down occasionally to read the additions, laugh or scowl, but he never told us to knock it off. Everyone was consumed by the humiliation and with the frustrated rage which was a by-product of American impotence. Morale was terrible and the board provided a healthy means of venting frustration.

As the 1980 presidential campaign plodded on, friendly political rivalry within our small office grew increasingly intense. As far as one political appointee colleague was concerned, President Carter could do no wrong, and she constantly lobbied almost everyone to support him in the upcoming election.

Kern, a career civil servant, was disgusted with the results of Carter's foreign policy, and tended to favor Ted Kennedy. She was just aghast. In late 1979, Pope John Paul II had generated tremendous national fascination during his visit to the United States. One afternoon, at a time when Kennedy appeared to have momentum on his side, Kern asked whether anyone in the office had seen *The Tonight Show* the previous evening. Without looking up from her desk, our colleague said that she had missed it. "Why?" she asked. Without missing a beat, Kern recounted for us one of Johnny Carson's monologue lines in which Carson asked, "What do the pope and Jimmy Carter have in common? They are both going to be succeeded by Catholics." Kern and I laughed; it was a good joke. Our colleague, in all earnestness, looked up from her desk, shook her head and said, "I don't see what's so funny about that." "Come on," Vince said, trying to help her get the joke, "Kennedy, a Catholic, is going to unseat Carter as the Democrats' nominee at the convention." "I wasn't talking about politics," she replied, "but about religion. The next pope doesn't need to be a Catholic. He could be a Protestant." I laughed so hard that I actually fell out of my chair. But she really wasn't kidding.

A few weeks later, she dug herself into an even deeper hole when she came over to me one morning, leaned on my desk and asked me in a serious voice, "Howard, do the Jewish people have any holy books— you know, like the Koran?" Stunned by this question, I looked at her incredulously for a full five seconds before asking, "Perhaps you have heard of the Bible—you know, the Old Testament?" "Oh yes, yes," she said, drawing back stiffly, "of course, the Bible." As she walked back to her desk, I turned around to see Kern choking with laughter as he wiped tears from his eyes.

A Discreet and Cautious Dialogue

Throughout the summer of 1980, the core objective of our Middle East policy remained the buildup of a regional security network capable of supporting the RDF. The Defense Department estimated that over $10 billion would be required to purchase the capability necessary for turning the RDF into a real force. In addition to the agreement with Oman, an agreement with Kenya was also concluded in June 1980, while an access agreement with Somalia was signed in August. Unfortunately, no Gulf country other than Oman was ready to make available a rear staging area that would support the insertion of large, mechanized ground forces. Our Saudi pillar dismissed out of hand the notion of U.S. bases and a permanent troop presence on its soil.

Earlier in the year, Saddam Hussein had launched his own response to the Carter Doctrine and the Soviet invasion of Afghanistan. Anointing himself as the leader of the Arab world in February 1980, Saddam enunciated an eight-point "Pan-Arab Charter," which laid down Iraq's ground rules for the Gulf. Saddam's goal was to assert hegemony over the Gulf by pressuring the Bahrainis, Omanis and other Arabs to deny access to U.S. military forces and instead rely on Iraq for defense. The charter indirectly attacked the Soviet Union by chastising the Communist party of Iraq for alleged past misdeeds. Iraq's intentions were obvious for realists in the national security bureaucracy but eluded the many apologists for Iraqi ruthlessness. The Gulf states, though, had to take into account any number of threats: Soviet expansionism throughout the region, the spread of radical Islamic fundamentalism, traditional Iranian hegemonic ambitions and Iraq's revitalized vision for its enhanced role in the Gulf. In October 1979, Saudi Arabia, Kuwait, Bahrain, Qatar, the UAE and Oman had met in Taif, Saudi Arabia, without Iraq. The same group convened again in Taif in January 1981 and established the Gulf Cooperation Council (GCC), which began formally to operate in May 1981. Although Saddam Hussein attended the January 1981 meeting, Iraq was not made a member. Finally, in a February 1982 meeting of the GCC in Riyadh, representatives entered into a comprehensive joint security agreement.

Only Egypt, across the Red Sea from Saudi Arabia, was prepared to grant Washington access to a remote facility that could be turned into a rear staging area suitable to support an armored division. The Egyptian base, Ras Banas, was an old, run-down army base that had served as the jumping-off point for Nasser's troops en route to the Yemens in 1962. In early September 1980, a U.S. delegation, which included Vince Kern, traveled to Cairo in order to negotiate an understanding with Egyptians over U.S. use of the facility. Given its remote location—more than five hundred miles south of Cairo—and its being inhabited primarily by scorpions and snakes, we hoped that the Egyptians would permit permanent American troop presence and guaranteed access.

However, as with the rest of the Arab world, memories of British and French colonialism, coupled with the Soviet occupation of Afghanistan, left the Egyptians absolutely unyielding. In fact, upon his return, Kern described how difficult it was even to find the principal Egyptian interlocutors, particularly Presidential Advisor Osama el-Baz. They were visibly discomforted at the very idea of discussing American desires for a permanent presence. Osama el-Baz was known for his interesting excuses and pattern of behavior, which would emerge in other bilateral security matters through the years, particularly granting transit rights to American nuclear-powered warships through the Suez Canal. He wouldn't show up at scheduled meetings. His beeper didn't work. Other, unspecified issues suddenly developed of greater urgency than meetings with the American team. In the end, the team left Cairo having accomplished virtually nothing. It took the Iran-Iraq War to overcome the inertia of the Egyptian bureaucracy on this strategic matter.

The U.S. Army wanted Ras Banas (or some of the Sinai bases Egypt had gained from the withdrawing Israelis), and had prepared a program of improvements worth over $400 million. Egypt's posture proved too much for Congress, which was unwilling to make such large sums of construction money available for a facility that might never be used. President Sadat could not understand the Carter administration's insistence on a written agreement, nor could he understand the administration's apparent inability to comprehend the potential domestic problems that a foreign base in Egypt might encourage. Given the fate of the shah and the isolated position of Egypt following the peace treaty with Israel, it was difficult to argue with Sadat's logic, yet this would leave the RDF with no base structure to support operations in the event intervention in the Gulf became necessary.

Israel was the one country in the Middle East that was prepared to cooperate militarily with the United States. Early in President Carter's administration, Secretary of Defense Brown had initiated a discreet and cautious strategic dialogue with the government of Israel. Brown had assigned this responsibility to one of his most trusted strategic advisors, Dr. Andrew Marshall, director of the Office of Net Assessment. Marshall, a highly regarded professional, was known as the defense intellectual's intellectual, and no study came out of his office that had not been carefully analyzed and meticulously scrutinized for intellectual honesty. The mission of Net Assessment was to provide the secretary of defense with analyses of changing balances of power around the world, primarily involving the United States and the Soviet Union. Once completed, these forward-looking analyses contributed to various DOD documents, including the annual reports *Posture Statement, Defense Budget Request* and *Defense Guidance*. By assigning responsibility for a discreet dialogue to

Marshall, Brown had sought to avoid the injection of politics into the process, or having the "discussions" become subject to a bureaucratic tug-of-war within the DOD or between the DOD and State.

Marshall assigned the strategic dialogue to two men with whom I would develop long and significant relationships, commander James Roche of the U.S. Navy and Dennis Ross. Secretary Brown and Israeli defense minister Ezer Weizman had agreed to establish the dialogue during one of their many meetings in 1978. The dialogue began when Roche and Ross traveled to Israel in 1979 for a week of talks.

Proceeding under guidance from Secretary Brown, the limited purpose of the dialogue with Israel was to give both countries an opportunity to exchange views on evolving strategic trends in the Middle East and elsewhere. It was clearly understood, however, that there would be no discussion of military cooperation or coordination between U.S. and Israeli forces. The Carter administration wanted the dialogue limited to an intellectual exercise that, over time, could lead to enhanced mutual understanding of the strategic perspectives of both countries' national security bureaucracies, while providing a framework that might lead to some practical forms of strategic cooperation.

I first met Dennis Ross in December 1978 when we were assigned comanagement responsibilities for a RAND Corporation analysis, entitled *Alternative Security Arrangements for the West Bank in the Context of the Camp David Accords*, to be authored by Drs. Abraham Becker and Steven Rosen. The Departments of State and Defense had agreed to provide RAND with approximately $100,000 to perform this analysis, and Ross, Bill Kirby (an FSO in NEA at State), and I were to make sure that the money was spent appropriately. The U.S. government eventually received a first-rate study, the contents of which became even more germane in the wake of the 1987 Palestinian *intifada* and the direct negotiations, under way at the time of this writing, between Israelis and Palestinians for interim arrangements that might lead to a final peace settlement.

As Ross and I became more acquainted with each other's perspectives on the Middle East, America's declining position, the strategic realities engendered by the Iranian revolution and the Egyptian-Israeli peace treaty, it became apparent that we shared many similar ideas on what the United States might do to restore its influence and establish a balance of power more suited to the protection of American interests. One area we agreed on in particular was the need for strategic cooperation with Israel. The Arab-Israeli conflict had for too long been manipulated by Arabists in the national security bureaucracy to prevent military relations between the United States and Israel which would enhance strategic American interests in the Middle East.

As Ross briefed me on the nascent strategic dialogue with Israel, I began to assess the shallowness of U.S.-Israeli military cooperation. The Arab world had long assumed that the United States and Israel secretly conducted many different forms of military cooperation and coordination. In fact, aside from a regular exchange of military intelligence, typically involving comparisons of Arab order-of-battle information, regional assessments of the evolving balance of power and intermittent Israeli provision of intelligence (known as lessons learned) based on the collection and interpretation of how Soviet weapons systems performed in battle, there was no U.S.-Israeli strategic cooperation. If U.S. forces had to be deployed to the Middle East, the American and Israeli militaries had no experience cooperating with each other, and there were no plans for logistics, medical, air, ground or naval cooperation or joint operations.

A basic objective of most State Department Middle East experts and many others throughout the U.S. government was to maintain as much distance as possible between Israel and the United States, even if the result was to undermine the peace process that the Carter administration was trying to promote and to waste Israel's potential contribution to a more favorable balance of power. Arabists in and out of government consistently opined the "conventional wisdom" that U.S. ties to Israel were the primary factor leading Arab states to refuse to cooperate militarily with Washington. These experts argued that but for the power of American Jews and the Israel lobby to inject domestic political considerations into the struggle over foreign policy between the executive branch and the Congress, the United States would be able to devise and implement policies that would satisfy the political demands of Arab leaders, secure Arab military cooperation and guarantee American access to Middle Eastern oil.

Despite America's long-standing moral commitment to the security of Israel and the large and growing volume of American economic, military and technological assistance, Washington's relationship with Israel did not, in fact, have an operative strategic dimension. Not only was there no planning for combined operations, exercise activity or other forms of routine military cooperation, but most U.S. government officials, be they civilian or military, went out of their way to deny reports of U.S.-Israeli military ties and to resist all efforts to promote strategic cooperation.

For the most part, and with notable exceptions, most of these government Arabists based their Middle East expertise on their tours of service in Arab countries, rather than on academic, research-oriented study of Islam, the Ottoman Empire, Arab and Persian civilizations, or the history of Israel and the Jewish people. These experts claimed to understand the Arab people and the Middle East because they had lived in Arab countries and, therefore, knew "firsthand" what the Arab world would tolerate. But working or living abroad does not create foreign expertise. Nor does one become an expert on Israel (or any other country) merely by speaking the language while spending several years in the country. In my own case, I spent eight months working on a kibbutz in Israel following the October 1973 War and had become proficient in Hebrew. This did not make me a Middle East expert, however. Rather, my expertise resulted from years of studying the history, politics and culture of the peoples of the Middle East, together with the practical experience I gained working in the U.S. government.

Such "clientitis" is neither unique to government Arabists, nor is it inexplicable. The truth is that there are many more career opportunities in the Arab world than there are in Israel. A knowledge of Arabic, not Hebrew, Turkish or Persian, was more useful in career advancement, especially in NEA. Indeed, FSOs, no matter how distinguished, who developed clientitis toward Israel, as did their colleagues toward a particular Arab country, were regarded as suspect for challenging conventional wisdom.

The Arabists derisively labeled all those who disagreed with their expert views, or their unyielding stance that the Arab-Israeli conflict was the root cause of instability in the Middle East, as tools of the Israel lobby and powerful Jewish interests, which allegedly controlled the domestic political process as well as the media. A pro-Arab Middle East expert was deemed to be "objective." But a Middle East expert who supported strengthening U.S. ties with Israel, as well as with Arab states, was viewed suspiciously, especially if the expert was also Jewish and audacious enough to work on Middle East issues. In such a case, innuendos of "dual loyalty" were never far from the surface.

Unfortunately for U.S. interests, the Arabists were wrong insofar as the conventional wisdom goes. The Arab world, for various reasons, has been traditionally unstable and driven by intense rivalries. Arab leaders were convinced that Israel and the United States were "in each other's pockets." Given America's close relations with Israel, dating back to the Truman administration, they simply dismissed American protestations that the two countries did not cooperate militarily. Indeed, much frustration and misunderstanding between Arab leaders and U.S. officials was based on the bedrock belief of most Arabs that the United States could "deliver" Israel, if only U.S. leaders had the will to do so.

Notwithstanding this belief, and while it is indisputable that Arab nationalists and radicals could always inflame anti-Americanism among the Arab masses by linking Israel to the United States, most Arab leaders decided to cooperate with Washington, or not, based on realistic calculations of the value of American assistance in a given scenario. Arab leaders operated in a world of realpolitik, even if their American friends did not, and would accommodate themselves even to Israeli assistance when necessary.

The most well known example of U.S.-Israeli cooperation in support of an Arab state was the Israeli threat to intervene on behalf of Jordan in September 1970, a threat that helped forestall a Syrian invasion. Another example took place in 1962 when Egyptian intervention under Nasser in the Yemen civil war directly threatened Saudi Arabia. As the Egyptian role intensified and relations between Egypt and Saudi Arabia rapidly deteriorated, concern grew that open conflict might erupt between these two Arab countries. Although Washington was unable to assist the Saudis directly, Israeli warplanes flew south over the Red Sea to signal unambiguously to the Egyptians to keep their distance from Saudi Arabia. The realpolitik of the Middle East is: The enemy of my enemy is my friend.

Nor did the peace process, particularly the Egyptian-Israeli peace treaty, or even Iraq's menacing threats to the Kingdom of Saudi Arabia, prevent Saudi leaders from accepting American assistance when the situation so warranted. In February 1979, for example, while President Carter was shuttling between Egypt and Israel, it was reported that the Soviet-backed PDRY had invaded the Saudis' ally, the YAR. Fearful that the cross-border assault was the precursor of a PDRY attack against Saudi Arabia, the Saudis asked Washington to deploy AWACS aircraft, thereby enhancing the Saudi air-defense capability and presumably deterring a PDRY attack. AWACS aircraft were deployed because it served the interests of both Saudi Arabia and the United States. The Saudis accepted American AWACS planes because it served their interests, despite Saudi opposition to the Camp David peace process and the plight of the Palestinian people.

There were other fundamental reasons why Arab states were disinclined to cooperate militarily with the United States, reasons that were totally unrelated to America's relationship with Israel. First, in the wake of Vietnam and the Iranian revolution, the United States was, as previously noted, no longer viewed as a reliable security partner. Clumsy, slow to act and often provoking the very instability that U.S. policies were designed to prevent, Arab leaders realistically weighed the relative costs and often saw greater danger resulting from too close an American embrace. With Soviet regional power and presence growing and American power ebbing, confidence in American security assurances declined dramatically.

Second, the post–World War II history of the Arab world was characterized by the total rejection of residual colonialism and the permanent European military presence that had epitomized the emergence of the modern Middle East. Primarily British forces, but French as well, had come to symbolize Western oppression, imperialism and exploitation. In the wake of the British withdrawal, America had effectively replaced the United Kingdom as the foreign power in the Arab world. The most resonant theme of Arab nationalism, articulated by Egyptian president Nasser, was the thirst for independence from "foreign oppression." In these circumstances, Arab leaders found it difficult, if not impossible, to stand up to radical and nationalist pressures that were triggered by the presence of foreign forces, whether European or American. It was against this backdrop that the Arabists espoused the conventional wisdom and maintained that strategic cooperation with Israel was anathema: such cooperation would spark radicalism and instability in the Arab world.

Setting political considerations and deeply rooted prejudice aside, and analyzing the situation objectively, there was a broad range of potential benefits for the U.S. military posture in the Middle East if America and Israel could have undertaken genuine strategic cooperation. In the eastern Mediterranean Sea, for example, the Israeli Air Force and Navy could have conducted operations in coordination with U.S. forces. Such exercises would have acted to deter the Soviet Union and Syria from disrupting the long air and sea lines of communication through which the United States would deploy forces and their supplies. Owing to Israel's geographic location, Israeli air and naval facilities could have served as excellent staging areas, depots and distribution points for U.S. forces embarking on various operations throughout southwest Asia. To the south, the Red Sea represented another potential theater of operations where Israeli air and naval forces could have acted to support U.S. policies in deterring Soviet or proxy forces operating from Ethiopia. The southernmost entryway into the Indian Ocean from the Red Sea, the Bab al-Mandeb, was bordered by hostile Ethiopia and the PDRY. In a crisis, Israeli forces could have been employed to keep open this strategic waterway. Finally, well-equipped Israeli facilities could have been used for acclimatization exercises, bombing ranges, equipment maintenance and to support B-52 aircraft at Ben-Gurion International Airport.

Whatever the substantive or bureaucratic logic, the interagency review of U.S. southwest Asia strategy did not even *include* a discussion of Israel's potential contribution. It was not open to discussion, as if Israel did not exist. Nevertheless, many U.S. flag officers candidly acknowledged that "if the balloon goes up and we have to fight in the Gulf, the only country we can count on to help is Israel." Despite the comparative advantages of utilizing Israel, or at least considering the possibility, the conventional wisdom was that any form of U.S. cooperation with Israel would be a liability, not an asset.

When asked for the evidence to back up this line of argument, the Arabists would consistently say, "We know the Arabs, and the Arabs tell us not to cooperate militarily with Israel or the Arabs will not cooperate with the United States." Dissatisfied with these simpleminded arguments, I drafted a paper that analyzed the range of potential benefits and costs that could accrue from U.S.-Israeli strategic cooperation. At a minimum, I wanted to put strategic cooperation with Israel on the agenda, in order for the subject to receive full and fair debate despite the arrogant presumptuousness of careerists who insisted on ignoring the issue.

By this time, Bob Murray had moved on to become under secretary of the navy. My new boss, Ambassador Robert H. Pelletreau, was a Yale University–trained lawyer who had left the law to serve as a foreign service officer. Fluent in Arabic, Pelletreau had recently completed a tour as U.S. ambassador to Bahrain. Over the next several years, Pelletreau and I would work closely together on many issues, often traveling together throughout the Middle East. We were always friends. Although we often disagreed on particular issues, Bob Pelletreau was one of the most fair, intellectually honest and open-minded Arabists with whom I would ever work.

Having just returned from Bahrain, Pelletreau might have a more pragmatic attitude toward strategic cooperation with Israel than the typical Arabist. As the U.S. ambassador to Manama, Pelletreau was very familiar with the existing security environment in the Gulf and the tremendous difficulties the U.S. military was encountering there. Bahrain, an island nation strategically located in the Gulf, had been used by the British Navy until Britain's withdrawal. The ruler of Bahrain, Sheikh Khalifa, had agreed to grant the United States rights subject to a certain number of port call days per year, to include air delivery of spare parts and other consumables through the international airport. Unlike most of the other Gulf leaders, however, Sheikh Khalifa was outspoken in his support for the United States and his unequivocal opposition to the radical programs of the Rejectionist Front led by Saddam Hussein's Iraq. The government of Bahrain had granted limited access rights to a group of U.S. Navy ships known as MIDEASTFOR. The flagship of MIDEAST-FOR, the USS *La Salle*, was permanently deployed to the Gulf to establish an American presence and to perform various command, control and communications functions for the four or five destroyers and frigates that were rotated through the Gulf.

The government of Bahrain was extremely wary of Iran, which had on numerous occasions asserted historical Iranian claims to Bahrain. Iran had never unequivocally renounced its claim to the island nation, even after the fall of the shah. More than 50 percent of Bahrain's population is Shia. Following the revolution, Tehran helped establish a Bahrain Liberation Front, a small terrorist organization that sought to destabilize Bahrain, oust Khalifa, and create a Shia-dominated fundamentalist state. Aware of Bahrain's relative weakness, its declining oil resources, and the hegemonic intentions of its Persian and Arab neighbors, Khalifa was keen to establish a security strategy independent of the Saudis, a strategy that would be capable of keeping both the Iraqis and the Iranians at a distance. Through his relationship with the United States, Khalifa had managed to establish this balance, regardless of the many radical and conservative pressures he regularly endured.

I hoped that Pelletreau's relationship with Khalifa and his experience with the U.S. Navy and its local vulnerabilities might make him more open about trying to leverage Israeli power to serve U.S. interests. However, Pelletreau stood fast in his opposition to strategic cooperation with Israel, convinced that the political disadvantages far outweighed the potential military benefits. He was unwilling to send my paper forward or agree to even raise the proposal to consider Israel in the interagency review. It appeared that strategic cooperation with Israel would remain an intellectual exercise for the foreseeable future.

CHAPTER 4

WAR
IN THE GULF

———————◆·◆———————

A Policy of Contradictions

The situation along the Iraq-Iran border meanwhile continued to deteriorate. A brief history of Iraq's hegemonic aims toward its neighbors and
the Iran-Iraq War makes it clear that Saddam's invasion of Kuwait in
August 1990 was only his latest move in accomplishing his enduring goal
of becoming the predominant military power and arbiter of the supply
and price of oil in the Persian Gulf.

Iraq was in constant competition with Iran for Gulf leadership and
had long sought a deep-water port and offshore terminal to reduce its
dependency on pipelines running through other countries, especially
Syria. Its maritime access was extremely limited, and Iraq sought to claim
more of the Gulf's continental shelf.

While Great Britain had established its security relationships with
Aden and the various Gulf sheikhdoms in order to protect the sea-lanes
to its Indian empire, by the 1930s it was apparent that many of the Gulf
states possessed enormous oil resources. It was during this time frame that
many maritime and territorial boundaries throughout the region were
demarcated, including Iraq's. Nevertheless, boundary disputes, generally
involving oil rights, were commonplace and involved the Saudis, Iranians,
Iraqis, the Trucial States of the lower Gulf, Bahrain and Oman.

Kuwait had terminated its treaty relationship with the British in 1961
and became independent soon thereafter. Drawing on claims dating back
to the Ottoman Empire, Iraq immediately announced its annexation of
Kuwait. Iraq's "historical" claims to Kuwait focused mainly on the strategic Kuwaiti islands of Warbah and Bubiyan. Iraqi maritime access was
limited to the Shatt-al-Arab waterway and Iraq wanted to extend its
narrow coastline and increase its access to the Gulf. Iraq's three major
ports were Fao, Basra and Umm Qasr, located near Warbah and Bubiyan

islands. As the former protecting power, Britain dispatched troops to protect Kuwait against Iraq. British forces were later replaced by an inter-Arab force. In 1963, in exchange for a Kuwaiti "loan" of millions of dollars, Iraq acknowledged Kuwait's independence. In 1968, Kuwait declared that it would no longer accept any foreign presence in the region. Britain meanwhile had announced in January its intention to withdraw from the Gulf by the end of 1971.

In March 1973, two years after the British withdrawal from the Gulf and five years after the termination of Kuwait's defense agreement with London, Iraq again asserted its claims to parts of Kuwait and deployed Iraqi troops onto Warbah and Bubiyan islands. Kuwait protested this violation of its sovereignty, relying on agreements which purportedly settled Iraq's boundary claims dating back to the early 1930s. Iraq once more sought to compel Kuwait to grant Iraq rights that would enable it to assert sovereignty over the islands of Bubiyan, Warbah and the surrounding coastal area. Kuwait still lacked the ability to defend itself and Saudi Arabia moved troops to its border with Kuwait. Iraq agreed to drop its claims and withdrew, for the time being, having received another substantial "loan" from Kuwait in the process.

Notwithstanding its substantial relationship with Iraq, the Soviet Union did not support Iraq's 1973 aggression against Kuwait since Kuwait was one of the few Gulf states with which it maintained formal relations, due to Soviet support for radical antimonarchical movements throughout the Middle East. Strategically located and possessing enormous oil resources, Kuwait was an ideal regional alternative to Iraq and helped the Soviets compete for influence with the West in the warm waters of the Persian Gulf. More than any other conservative Gulf sheikhdom, the Kuwaitis adopted the rhetoric of Arab nationalism and opposed U.S. policy in the Middle East. Kuwait, with a substantial Palestinian population, was bitterly anti-Israel and vocally anti-Western and supported radical Palestinian movements. Through the years, Kuwait used large amounts of its enormous oil wealth to help ensure its safety and adroitly played Moscow off against the West. The Soviets supported Kuwait's nationalization of the Kuwait Oil Company in the early 1970s. Kuwait saw the Soviet Union as a means of countering historical Iraqi claims to Kuwait and preventing Iraq from exploiting its sponsorship of some radical Palestinian groups to destabilize the Kuwaiti monarchy. Newly conscious, however, of its military vulnerability, Kuwait began seeking to bolster its defensive capabilities. In the mid-1970s Kuwait began making substantial investments in the Soviet bloc and concluded a number of arms sales agreements with the Soviet Union to purchase Soviet weapons.

Notwithstanding the later Soviet invasion of Afghanistan in December 1979, Sheikh al-Sabah of Kuwait continued to oppose American policies and condemned the United States for establishing the RDF. With the Iranian revolution, however, and Tehran's efforts to destabilize the Arab states of the Gulf, Kuwait came to view Iraq as less of a threat than Iran. Kuwait, like all of the other Gulf states, was vulnerable to the export of militant Islam, and Kuwait feared internal instability among its Shia minority at the instigation of Iran. In the Middle Eastern world of realpolitik, Iraq was moderating its behavior and was willing and able to help deter Iranian-sponsored aggression against Kuwait and some of its other neighbors.

With respect to Iraq and Iran, Iraq had asserted traditional, historical claims to the oil-rich Iranian province of Khuzestan and its largely Arab population since the 1930s, when a treaty purportedly settled the boundary disputes. During the intervening years, each country had disputed various provisions of the treaty, and violent cross-border skirmishes characterized their relationship. One of the central issues in dispute between these two regional powers was control over maritime access to and jurisdiction and sovereignty over the strategic Shatt-al-Arab waterway.

Once the British announced that they would be withdrawing from the Persian Gulf and relinquishing their responsibility to protect the area, the regional powers maneuvered to position themselves to avoid a power vacuum. The smaller Gulf Arab states had to walk a delicate line between Iran and Iraq's regional ambitions regarding the assumption of responsibility for Gulf security. The British encouraged the sheikhdoms to form a cooperative security system. The shah of Iran, who had been surprised by Britain's announcement of withdrawal renewed Iran's "traditional" claims to Bahrain and opposed any confederation in which Bahrain might be included. He reasserted Iran's "long-standing" claims to the islands of Abu Musa and the Tunbs in the Strait of Hormuz and in November 1971 dispatched Iranian forces to occupy the islands. The military occupation of Abu Musa and the Tunbs by Iran continued through Khomeini and remains a source of regional tension even after Operation Desert Storm.

In the meantime, the British withdrawal also left the United States in the position of having continuing interests in the region without the presence of British forces to protect them. U.S. military strategy in the Middle East was based on rebuffing a strike by the Soviet Union across Iran to the warm waters of the Gulf in concert with our NATO allies.

The strategy was not geared toward protecting Western access to Middle Eastern oil. Under the emerging Twin Pillars policy, the United States began encouraging pro-Western Saudi Arabia and Iran to take Britain's place, urging the two countries to improve their bilateral relations in the process. The United States wanted its interests protected but did not want to do so itself, regardless of the strategic importance of oil.

Tensions between Iraq and Iran over the Shatt-al-Arab remained high. Final agreement on the Shatt-al-Arab question was not reached until March 1975, when the Algerians lent their "good offices" toward resolving the boundary dispute. The parties issued a communiqué known as the Algiers Accords, which was implemented by treaty in June. Iraq and Iran agreed on a demarcation of the waterway's boundary. As a condition of the agreement, the shah agreed to stop assisting the Kurdish nationalist movement in Iraq. Secret negotiations between Iraq and Kurdish rebels in Beirut had led to a peace agreement in March 1970 that had given the Kurds nominal regional autonomy. The Kurds had been used alternately by the Soviets, Iranians and Iraqis. The United States and Iran (with Israel) supported the Kurds in order to weaken Iraq and challenge the Soviets. Kurdish resistance collapsed after the conclusion of the Algiers Accords, and the Kurds were left to the mercy of the Iraqis.

Iraq used the lull created by its improved relations with Iran and its temporary renunciation of claims to Kuwait to enhance its role in Persian Gulf security by reducing its dependency on the Soviet Union and diversifying its suppliers. Iraq dramatically reduced imports from the Soviet bloc, increased its purchases of Western technology and established significant arms relationships with France and Brazil. After 1975, Baghdad adopted tactics which masked Saddam Hussein's intentions in order to improve relations with the West and its Gulf neighbors, particularly Saudi Arabia. Iraq began criticizing Soviet activities in the Horn of Africa and the PDRY and cracked down on the Iraqi Communist party. In May 1978, twenty-one Iraqi Communists were hanged. Iraq condemned the later Soviet invasion of Afghanistan.

After the shah fell, Iraq's relations with Islamic Iran quickly deteriorated as Khomeini sought to avenge his expulsion from Iraq in 1978 by trying to bring down the regime of Saddam Hussein. Competition between these two Gulf states intensified as Iran reasserted its "traditional" claims to Bahrain, and Baghdad correctly feared Khomeini was trying to destabilize Iraq through its large Kurd and Shia communities. Seeking to enhance its own relationship in the changing regional balance of power, Iraq demanded a revision of the Algiers Accords—to which Iraq had only agreed under "duress"—regarding the Shatt-al-Arab, the return to Arab sovereignty of Abu Musa and the Tunb Islands, and self-determination for Iran's national minorities, namely the Kurds, the Baluchis, the Azerbaijanis and the Khuzestani Arabs. Violent border skirmishing between Iraqi and Iranian forces resumed and increased in frequency and intensity.

Iraq sought to weaken Iran further and to project itself as the "moderate" defender of the Arab world. In early September 1980 Iraq formally abrogated the Algiers Accords and tried to seize the oil-rich Iranian province of Khuzestan in what Saddam Hussein expected would be a short war. On September 22, 1980, Iraq invaded Iran and began what became known as the Iran-Iraq War.

Despite the enunciation of the Carter Doctrine and our recent efforts to enhance the security structure in the Indian Ocean and Persian Gulf, the United States was unprepared to protect its vital interests in the region. Our former Iranian pillar continued to hold Americans hostage, and Saudi Arabia was militarily incapable of keeping the strategic sea-lanes open. Unable and unwilling to act on our own behalf and despite our evolving relationship with Iraq, the United States had not yet found another power on which to rely.

With the invasion of Iran on September 22, I renewed my campaign against the nascent tilt to Iraq. Having correctly anticipated that Saddam Hussein would invade Iran in order to seize Khuzestan Province, I vainly tried to rekindle debate within the Defense Department and among my colleagues in other agencies over the long-term danger that Iraq might pose to the United States. Unfortunately, the national security bureaucracy was too caught up in its attempt to manage this newly emerging crisis to think about the future. On the one hand, the Arabists in the U.S. government saw the Iraqi invasion as an opportunity to eliminate the growing threat of Iranian-sponsored Islamic fundamentalism, thereby reducing the danger to America's interests in the Arab world, while paving the way for improved U.S.-Iraqi relations. On the other hand, the war unambiguously demonstrated the pitiful ability of the United States to use its power to protect friends, such as the Saudis, and our vital oil interests in the Gulf, thereby creating potential opportunities for U.S. diplomacy to convince regional leaders of the value of granting more military access rights for U.S. forces.

Emergency efforts were undertaken to move American power from "over the horizon" into the region. With Iran threatening to lash out against the Saudis and Kuwaitis, the U.S. government immediately sought and received Saudi agreement for the temporary deployment of a squadron of AWACS aircraft to enhance the air-defense capabilities of Saudi Arabia, while hopefully deterring Iranian aggression. Suddenly faced with a tangible threat to its security interests, the Saudi leadership quickly agreed to the presence of American forces, despite the U.S.-Israel relationship and the unresolved Palestinian problem. The value of the facilities in Oman proved of considerable importance to the long-term support of the Indian Ocean fleet and the deterrence of attempts by Iran to stop the flow of oil through the Strait of Hormuz. The facilities in Kenya and Somalia were of limited value, however, in supporting a war being waged nearly two thousand miles away at the head of the Gulf.

In the months preceding his invasion of Iran, Saddam had received intelligence reports from King Hussein of Jordan and the Saudi leadership which summarized U.S. briefings on the steady decline in the military capabilities of the Iranians. Increasingly fearful that Iranian-inspired violence would intensify in the wake of the November 1979 riots in the Grand Mosque in Mecca and with a steady drumbeat of intelligence reports describing Iranian efforts to establish anti-Western revolutionary cells throughout the Muslim world, U.S. briefers had tried to allay the concerns of conservative Arab regimes over the combat capabilities of revolutionary Iran.

Much of Washington's information which was used to brief the Saudis and Jordanians on the Iranian military was derived from the DOD's expectations that Iran's advanced military systems were not being properly used or maintained. This conclusion led the American government to believe that the Iranian military, already racked by numerous purges of the senior officers, would not be capable of sustaining modern combat for more than several days. Although U.S. officials did not intentionally provide military intelligence on Iran to the Iraqis, U.S. officials were clearly aware that the American assessments would reach Baghdad. Given the significance the Arab leaders attached to these briefings, the United States had some responsibility for significantly contributing to Saddam's calculation that Iraqi power could overwhelm the remnants of the Iranian military.

American policy in the Middle East was constructed on contradictions. In order to strengthen the resolve of friendly Arab states, the United States began to enhance the ability of the principal Arab radical state, Iraq, to cast itself as the protector of the Gulf states and the West's vital interests, although Iraq was still bent on undermining the U.S.-brokered peace process. Historically feared because of its antimonarchical, radical behavior, Iraq suddenly became the shield of the Arabs and was becoming a de facto ally of the United States.

Other than acknowledging that my predictions of Iraqi intentions toward Iran had been borne out, none of my superiors or colleagues wanted to consider the range of consequences for American interests that might develop in the event that Iraq actually defeated Iran and became the undisputed arbiter of Persian Gulf oil supply and price. In fact, most of the bureaucracy was certain that Iraq would destroy the remnants of the Iranian Air Force in a matter of days, and the war would be over in little more than a month. Saddam had already succeeded in conditioning Washington to link Iraqi interests with American interests.

With the 1980 presidential elections little more than six weeks away, southwest Asia had become America's worst nightmare: the Soviets appeared to be consolidating their occupation of Afghanistan while America seemingly stood by; the United States remained incapable of securing the release of Americans held hostage for nearly a year; Iraq had invaded Iran, raising the specter of another oil cutoff, economic disruption and the spread of violence and instability throughout the Gulf; Ethiopia and Somalia continued to fight for dominance of the Horn of Africa as the Soviets increased their military presence in Ethiopian facilities on land and in the Red Sea; and the Arab-Israeli peace process had stalled while Israeli and proxy forces occupied southern Lebanon.

The most troubling strategic development for the United States, however, remained the Soviet invasion of Afghanistan and the potential for further moves against Iran or Pakistan. Coupled with the expansion of Soviet influence in and around the periphery of the Arabian peninsula over the preceding five years, by the middle of 1980, Soviet forces had established a network of air and ground bases in western Afghanistan near the southeastern Iranian province of Baluchestan va Sistan, providing Moscow with a forward staging area only five hundred miles from the strategic Strait of Hormuz. Although Soviet forces were engaged with Afghan rebels primarily in the north and east of the country, covert U.S. support for the rebels and overt military assistance for Pakistan raised the stakes and increased the potential for Soviet escalation. Having observed Soviet readiness to undertake naked aggression against Afghanistan, including "hot pursuit" into the North-West Frontier Province of Pakistan, U.S. planners could not ignore the possibility of a Soviet campaign designed to seize the Strait of Hormuz in order to pressure the West to cease its support for the Afghan resistance (Mujahadeen) as well as to provide Moscow with the ability to cut the West's oil lifeline.

With the war and the Iranian revolution draining the military and economic resources of Iran, Moscow might well have calculated that its forces would have met little opposition, despite the Carter Doctrine. With the United States immobilized by the hostage crisis, an election campaign, a post-Vietnam anti-interventionist legacy, and no permanent air, ground or naval presence in the region, there was little reason to believe that America or its Western allies possessed the military capabilities or the will to stop a rapid thrust by the Soviets toward their long-desired warm-water port in the Gulf.

The Eye of the Goat

Despite President Carter's election defeat in November, the bureaucracy proceeded with its plans to improve the Indian Ocean infrastructure necessary to support the RDF. Although military construction projects had already begun in Oman, U.S. engineers had not yet visited Kenyan or Somali facilities to conduct detailed site surveys. Both the Kenyan and Somali governments had come under considerable political pressure from NAM member countries for having entered into access agreements with the United States, but neither had yet received the benefits that they had anticipated. Responding to Kenyan and Somali requests and still interested in improving the facilities that the RDF might require, the DOD dispatched a Naval Facilities Engineering Command Team to the Horn of Africa in mid-December to move the process forward. I was assigned to this team in order to enhance my ability to support forthcoming legislative requests for the military construction funds that would be necessary to upgrade the facilities.

Neither Kenya nor Somalia matched the importance of Oman in U.S. strategy, owing primarily to their distance from the head of the Gulf, and, in the case of Somalia, its ongoing war with Soviet-backed Ethiopia over the Ogaden region. The most important facility in Kenya was the port of Mombasa. Located beneath the equator on the Indian Ocean, it sat astride a vital sea line of communication and provided significant logistics support for U.S. naval forces operating in the Indian Ocean. It had supported the British in a similar fashion. Moreover, as a large, relatively modern and Western-oriented city, Mombasa offered an excellent liberty port for the U.S. Navy. The principal facilities problem at Mombasa resulted from the port's shallowness, which prevented an aircraft carrier's turning around. As a result of this visit, the United States implemented a multi-million dollar dredging program, which along with several other modest improvements, enhanced Mombasa's port capabilities.

The Somali situation presented a more difficult political-military problem. The Horn of Africa was still caught up in the violent throes of the East-West conflict after Moscow replaced Washington as the superpower patron in Addis Ababa following the bloody ouster of Emperor Haile Selassie. Although the Somalis had made explicit their desire for Washington's embrace, the United States was wary of Somali efforts to draw America into playing an active role in countering the billions of dollars' worth of military equipment, the thousands of Cuban soldiers and the hundreds of Soviet and East German advisors that Moscow had committed to the conflict on behalf of the Ethiopians.

The airfield and port of Berbera, however, was one Soviet-built Somali facility which could be used either to provide naval logistics support for forces operating in the western Indian Ocean and Red Sea areas or for B-52 bombers operating anywhere in the region. Aden, the capital of the Soviet-backed PDRY, was about 150 miles away, while the Dahlak Archipelago in the Red Sea and Socotra Island in the Arabian Sea, both of which contained Soviet naval bases, were approximately 500 miles away from Berbera. Were any conflict to escalate to a U.S.-Soviet confrontation, Berbera could be an essential staging area for air and naval sorties against the Soviets and their allies operating in the Horn of Africa, the Red Sea, or the Arabian Sea. Berbera's strategic location and facilities, and particularly its long, strong runway, called for prompt U.S. attention.

The visit to Berbera was one of the most memorable experiences of my early career. The team flew out of Mogadishu early one morning in December aboard an Air Somalia prop plane with one small bathroom that had probably never been cleaned. There were more passengers than seats, and a number of chickens and goats ran up and down the aisle. One of our team members, an engineer, was violently ill, having drunk a glass of water at breakfast in spite of my having told him I had seen something black swimming in it. The U.S. ambassador to Somalia had strongly advised us against drinking Somali tap water, even though the U.S. Agency for International Development (AID) had constructed the system. When we finally reached Hargeisa in the early afternoon, our colleague was dehydrated and very weak, but doctors at a refugee camp were able to rehydrate him quickly and ensure a complete recovery.

Although we were already overdue for our visit to Berbera, the regional governor, hoping to encourage increased U.S. assistance, insisted on giving the team a tour of the Hargeisa refugee camps. We agreed in order to give the weakened engineer an opportunity to regain his strength for the two-hour ride through the desert to Berbera.

The tour was very depressing. Over a hundred thousand residents of the Ogaden region of Ethiopia had become political refugees in Somalia as a result of the continuing Ogaden war. Although their physical survival did not appear to be an issue at that time (these refugees seemed to be minimally fed, received international medical attention, and had some form of primitive shelter), the despair in their eyes spoke clearly to their helplessness and lack of hope, defenseless pawns in a postcolonial ethnic struggle that had taken on an East-West dimension.

Seeing a historic opportunity to conquer lands that had been awarded to Ethiopia during decolonialization, the Somalis had invaded the Ogaden region confident that revolutionary Ethiopia would lack the capability and will to fight back. Moreover, given the long-standing irredentist sentiments of the Ogadeni population, Mogadishu believed the war was politically justified. Although initially successful, once the Soviets turned from Somalia to support Ethiopia, the Somali invaders soon found themselves fighting heavily reinforced Ethiopian armor units that included several brigades of Cuban expeditionary forces. Hargeisa, capital of the northern province, was also the headquarters for the Somali forces still engaged in desultory combat with the Ethiopians less than fifty miles away.

Whatever the refugee situation in Somalia in 1980, however, by 1991, matters became horrific, as violence, senseless cruelty and mass starvation spiraled completely out of control, leaving Somalia and its people walking skeletons in a decaying graveyard.

The Somali desert is harsh and barren. For most of the two-hour drive in a Somali army jeep, we saw nothing more than an occasional shepherd with his camels and goats, a lizard scurrying across rocks baked by the blazing sun, and dry, dusty desert. We reached Berbera around two-thirty P.M. and were greeted by a group of Somali military officers. Very friendly, they escorted our team through the ramshackle facilities. They described how the Soviets, when they withdrew from the base, took everything with them, including furniture, toilets, windows, lighting fixtures, floorboards, and many other items that had actually been nailed down. The air base tower was little more than a broken-down, two-story wooden shack with no air traffic control instruments, electrical power or other implements necessary for managing air traffic. Nor were the storage facilities or the barracks (if you could call furnace-like bungalows barracks) in any better condition. While the runway appeared to be in good shape, it was going to require a major effort to install the minimum facilities necessary to enable U.S. Air Force or Navy aircraft to utilize this base. By contrast, the port of Berbera, located about one mile from the air base, required some upgrading but could immediately accommodate two U.S. Navy destroyers (or comparable-sized ships). The United States eventually spent $25 million to double the length of the pier and construct fuel storage and distribution facilities.

At the conclusion of our survey, the Somali commander invited us to a banquet in our honor at the Berbera Beach Club. Exhausted, hungry and dehydrated, we still had a two-hour drive back to Hargeisa, where we would spend the night before returning to Mogadishu the next morning. Although eager to depart immediately for Hargeisa, I convinced our team leader, a U.S. Navy captain, that protocol required us to accept the commander's hospitality.

The club was a two-room, thatched-roof bungalow at the water's edge. Inside, a long table was already set for the dinner. At each place was a bottle of red wine and a bottle of scotch, a residue of the influence of the Italian and British colonists who had occupied Somalia in the not-too-distant past. The commander displayed intense pride over the dinner, telling us that we were the first Americans whom he had the honor to host. Several excellent dishes had already been served, including pasta, fried meats, fried fish, and vegetable dishes when, with great relish, the chef brought in a whole roasted goat on a platter. He walked around the table demonstrating the Somali tradition of pulling handfuls of meat off the carcass with his hands. When he reached the commander, the chef gleefully yanked the eye out of the goat and ceremoniously placed it in the center of the plate. I watched the color drain from the Navy captain's face as he contemplated what might come next. Our Somali host respectfully bestowed upon the captain a great honor and offered him the eye. Shaking his head and looking down at his lap, protocol gave way. He turned to me and said, "Please, Mr. Teicher, as the political echelon of our team, I really believe this honor is yours." I swallowed hard, looked straight into the goat's eye (which seemed to be staring back at me), silently cursing myself for insisting that we stay for dinner, reached forward, picked up the slimy, discolored eye, and popped it quickly into my mouth. I swallowed without chewing, hoping that this approach would not offend the Somalis, who were clearly enjoying this traditional ceremony. I smiled and nodded at the commander, thanked him for bestowing such a great honor on our team, and then drained my glass of its remaining scotch. The Somalis cheered, pleased that the Americans had respected the Somali tradition, while several of my colleagues tried, barely successfully, to stifle their laughter. Following dessert and coffee, the Somali officers and our team walked along the beach through a thin, warm fog produced by the heat and dust of the desert and the chill of the sea. As we shook hands and said our good-byes, the commander gave me a strong slap on the back and a knowing wink.

The desert night turned chilly as we departed Berbera for Hargeisa. Accompanied by three young Somali soldiers, we tried to conduct a conversation. Unfortunately, neither their English nor my Arabic was up to the task and we rode silently but for the intermittent music and dialogue emanating from the jeep's radio. As I tried to comprehend what seemed to be a news report, I thought I heard a reference to John Lennon and the Beatles. My interest sparked by the English words in the broadcast, and hoping that they would start playing Beatles music, I asked the soldiers what was being reported. Although they had showed little interest in the news report before, one accommodated me by listening intently for a while. Eventually he turned back to me and said that although he did not understand what the Beatles meant, a man named Lennon had been shot and killed that day. "It can't be true," I said. "They are reporting that someone shot John Lennon?" The Somali soldiers had never heard of the Beatles, let alone John Lennon, and could not fathom why I was concerned about his death. They pressed me to explain why I cared, especially when I had answered that I did not know the man personally. Searching vainly for a way to communicate cross-culturally about Lennon and the influential role he and his music had played for so many people around the world, I recalled the Somali love for oral history and poetry. "Lennon has been the leading poet of my generation," I explained. "His poetry and the music of the Beatles is known to hundreds of millions of people around the world." The soldiers nodded solemnly. "The death of a poet is a loss for the whole world, whether we know his work or not," one of the soldiers said with sympathy.

Careening through the dusty Somali desert in a windowless jeep, I could not take my mind off Lennon and my memories of the Beatles. The irony overwhelmed me. Here I was, in the middle of nowhere, in a distant, hostile land, a goat's eye in my belly and working to help improve the ability of the United States to effectively wage war, yet I was so saddened by Lennon's death. His music had touched my generation and shaped our imagination. Perhaps it was the uncertain wisdom of what we were trying to accomplish in southwest Asia, my realism being tempered by the arduousness of the conflicts with which the United States was forced to deal. Still, I saw the world through a somewhat different prism because of John Lennon.

As we arrived at the U.S. Army headquarters in Hargeisa, I told the other members of the team about Lennon. They were bone-tired men who found it odd that I should really care. Falling asleep on a beat-up army cot, the sound of small-arms fire audible in the distance, I tried to convince myself that the contradictions did not need to be understood, only accommodated.

CHAPTER 5

A CHANGE IN DIRECTION

An Arabic Speaker

Despite the anti-Washington rhetoric of the 1980 presidential campaign, the election of Ronald Reagan lifted the spirits of many national security bureaucrats who had become enervated by the vacillation of the Carter administration and the feeling of impotence that pervaded the American security apparatus. While no one was quite sure where this right-wing, Republican conservative actor planned to take America, no one doubted his intention to swing the pendulum of world affairs back in America's favor. He promised the rapid development and implementation of a coherent strategy based primarily on the restoration of American military power and a "strategic consensus" among America's regional allies. Speaking of his plan for cabinet government, one had the impression that as president, Ronald Reagan would select Cabinet officers who shared a common worldview and would subordinate their egos to the genuine teamwork essential for fulfilling such a policy. Unfortunately, it did not take long for the contradictions between President Reagan's national security aspirations and those of his Cabinet to emerge.

The appointment of General Alexander Haig as President Reagan's first secretary of state introduced a strategic element into American foreign policy that had been absent throughout the Carter years. Whether or not he could speak eloquently, no one questioned that Secretary Haig understood the relationship between military power, political influence and the need for Washington to act vigorously to protect American interests to reverse our decline. Haig's realistic perspective and strategic priorities, unfettered by excessively moralistic notions of what to expect from allies and adversaries alike, boded well for the development of a policy to contain and perhaps roll back the steady expansion of Soviet influence throughout southwest Asia. CIA director William Casey,

111

whether or not he could be understood by someone with normal hearing, was intent on rejuvenating the operational side of the CIA in order to enable the United States to compete vigorously with the Soviet Union and again be taken seriously. By contrast, the appointment of Caspar W. Weinberger as secretary of defense initially caused considerable consternation within the Pentagon due to his reputation as a staunch budget-cutter during his earlier tenure as director of the Office of Management and Budget (OMB). Defense bureaucrats wondered how Reagan could reconcile his stated intention of rebuilding the U.S. military with "Cap the Knife" at the Pentagon's helm. Others questioned his substantive credentials to serve in this post, given his lack of national security experience during previous tours of government service. Of course, one learns in Washington that the only credential that counts is the confidence of the president. And Weinberger certainly had the president's confidence. It was a confidence that he (and others) would abuse over the next eight years.

U.S. vital interests in the Middle East did not change when Ronald Reagan defeated Jimmy Carter. They continued to be access to vital Middle Eastern oil and the halt of Soviet expansionism. Regardless of U.S. hopes under President Carter for regional security cooperation and a contribution to the defense of the Middle East by America's European allies, Secretary Haig understood the reluctance of friendly states to act on behalf of American interests. Under the rubric of "strategic consensus," the core goal of U.S. strategy for the Middle East was simple: strengthen conventional deterrence by preparing to act unilaterally in the event of a crisis.

Within ISA, we prepared for the transition from President Carter to President Reagan with trepidation and hopeful anticipation, notwithstanding his conservative domestic agenda. Despite Reagan's long-standing and firm pro-Israel convictions, Weinberger had a reputation for being pro-Arab. It did not require tremendous foresight to predict eventual tension on many issues between the secretaries of defense and state as Haig, unlike Weinberger, shared Reagan's views on the value of Israel to the United States. Haig had been quite outspoken in his criticism of the Carter administration's tendency to always blame Israel for the lack of progress in the Palestinian autonomy negotiations and constant repetition of the conventional wisdom that solving the Palestinian problem was the key to creating stability to the Middle East.

It was, therefore, a surprise when the transition team informed NEASA that Weinberger was going to nominate Noel Koch as the new deputy assistant secretary of defense for NEASA. Koch seemed an unlikely choice for Weinberger, unless the new defense secretary had decided to conform with the president's general stance on the Middle East and the Arab-Israeli conflict. I met twice with Koch to brief him on the situation in southwest Asia and our recent efforts to establish a security network that would allow the RDF to function in the region. When I arrived for our third session, however, I found Koch sitting dejectedly behind his desk, eyes staring upward with a glazed look about them. He turned his head and told me to sit down.

"Anti-Semitism, that's all it is," he stated tersely. "Excuse me," I replied. "What are you talking about?" Koch explained that he had just returned from a hastily scheduled meeting with Frank Carlucci, then Weinberger's deputy secretary of defense–designate. To Koch's surprise, Carlucci had summarily informed him that, despite what he had been told, he would not be the new DAS for NEASA. When Koch pressed for an explanation, Carlucci told Koch the job description now "requires that the DAS speak Arabic fluently." I confirmed that Bob Pelletreau spoke Arabic fluently but that neither his immediate predecessor, Bob Murray, nor the DAS before him, Les Janka, had spoken Arabic. Looking me straight in the eye, Koch said bitterly, "Weinberger does not want a Jew in this job. It's as simple as that."

Koch used all his political connections to try to regain the DAS job over the next month, to no avail. Although Weinberger and Carlucci tried to get Koch out of the Pentagon entirely, he showed remarkable persistence and endurance, eventually securing a job as the DAS for Africa and special operations.

Because the job offer to Koch was withdrawn on the basis that he didn't speak Arabic, it was somewhat surprising when Air Force major general Richard Secord was appointed as DAS, since he didn't speak Arabic either. While he had no formal Middle East training, Secord had served in the Middle East, working amiably with Israelis, Arabs and Persians at various times during his career. He came to ISA from the Air Staff, where he had been responsible for overseeing the Air Force's programs. Secord would later become somewhat notorious during the Iran-Contra affair.

It did not take long to discern that Secord's primary mission as DAS was to serve as the Pentagon's action officer for the sale of AWACS aircraft to Saudi Arabia. While he knew a great deal about AWACS technology and had good relations with the Saudis, Secord did not have good relations with the rest of the bureaucracy or with the Congress. In fact, several Air Force officers stated that Secord bore the principal responsibility for the Saudis' AWACS request. Immediately after the deployment of the AWACS aircraft to Saudi Arabia in September 1980, the Saudis had asked the Carter administration to update a survey of Saudi Arabia's air-defense requirements. Conducted by the U.S. Air Force, the survey concluded on technical grounds that AWACS aircraft offered the most cost-effective solution for the upgrading of Saudi Arabia's air-defense network. However, rather than waiting for the interagency policy review that is supposed to accompany the release of such a document to a foreign country, Air Force representatives informally briefed the government of Saudi Arabia on the study's findings.

Representatives at State, NSC and ISA were livid when news of this unauthorized disclosure became known, aware that the Saudis would never be willing to accept less than the full AWACS package recommended by the Air Force study. I was personally convinced that the Air Force had feared, whether correctly or not, that the Reagan administration might deny approval of the sale because of the stated intention of Haig to promote a regional strategy built on the presence of U.S. forces and systems, rather than rely primarily on proxies to defend U.S. interests. Whether or not the disclosures were designed to preempt these potential obstacles to the sale, it proved impossible to walk the cat back, leading the AWACS aircraft sale to become the first foreign policy crisis for President Reagan. From my vantage point as an ISA analyst, Secord's appointment as DAS could only be viewed as a promotion and reward for forcing the AWACS issue to the forefront of the national security agenda.

Wary of civilians who might be less respectful of the "chain of command," Secord preferred his subordinates to be military officers who would be less inclined to question his analysis or directives. Nevertheless, ISA was located in the OSD, a civilian organization, and I for one was not about to compromise my intellectual honesty to win the favor of Secord, even if he was my new boss. While always polite and respectful of his rank, I adopted a relatively combative attitude to what I believed was Secord's biased, Arab-centered view of the Middle East. To my pleasant surprise, Secord enjoyed a measure of debate and proved willing to listen, argue and occasionally change his mind.

For instance, in early 1981 we were still trying to find a staging area in the Middle East for the B-52s. Israel's Ben-Gurion International Airport was the only facility capable, with a minimum of improvements, of accommodating these aircraft. The airport at Berbera required too much upgrading to make it quickly usable and was in addition vulnerable to attack and interdiction. Reflecting the interventionist proclivity of the Reagan administration, I saw that there was a new receptivity to the notion of strategic cooperation with Israel throughout the national security and foreign policy bureaucracy, particularly at the State Department, despite the conventional wisdom which feared an Arab backlash. Advised that State supported the Ben-Gurion initiative, I worked with Under Secretary of Defense Fred Ikle and his special assistant, U.S. Navy commander Richard Barchi, to prepare a "justification" to request supplemental military construction funds for the necessary improvements. Although Secord was initially opposed on the timeworn basis that if the United States used Israeli facilities the Arabs won't cooperate, after reviewing our paper, which showed the lack of any alternative facilities in the eastern Mediterranean, Secord agreed that Ben-Gurion made the most sense.

With Secord's initials on the cover sheet, we convinced Ikle to send the memo forward and to seek a meeting with Carlucci to argue the case. Time was of the essence, as the supplemental budget request was essentially complete and would shortly be sent to OMB and on to Congress. Two days later, Barchi and I were given an appointment with Carlucci. Our memo was on the desk in front of him as we summarized the pros and cons of the Ben-Gurion arrangement and the purposes of the funding request.

Carlucci asked how we thought the Arab world would react to such an arrangement. "The B-52s would be deployed to Ben-Gurion only in scenarios involving Soviet aggression into the Gulf or other direct threats to Saudi Arabia or the oil flow through the Gulf," I replied. "We are not talking about Israeli aircraft flying missions on behalf of the United States against Arab countries. While I am sure elements in the Arab world will express their unhappiness with the arrangement, they will not permit this type of strategic cooperation between the U.S. and Israel to stand in the way of our coming to their defense."

"And General Secord agrees with this analysis?" Carlucci asked. Barchi pointed to Secord's initials signifying his concurrence. "Okay," Carlucci said. "Then I'll take this up with the secretary." We were elated, convinced that upgrading Ben-Gurion would significantly enhance the capability of the United States to project power into southwest Asia and send an unambiguous signal of America's determination to redress the U.S.-Soviet balance of power in the region.

As it turned out, our elation was short-lived. The next morning Barchi came by to inform me that Weinberger had rejected Carlucci's recommendation that he approve the supplemental request. According to Ikle's debrief, Weinberger disagreed with every element of the analysis, doubted that the United States would ever need to deploy B-52s into the Middle East, and strongly disagreed with our assessment of the reaction of the Arab world to such an arrangement with the State of Israel. For the time being, if B-52s were needed in southwest Asia, the only place they could operate safely from was from the middle of the Indian Ocean atoll of Diego Garcia, over 2,500 miles from the likely area of operations in the northern Gulf. Weinberger acted on the assumption that he alone of all President Reagan's advisors knew best what American policy should be in the Middle East. It was through this prism that Weinberger operated throughout his tenure as secretary of defense.

Don't Let Facts Get in the Way

As the fight over Saudi AWACS aircraft became a daily political struggle in Washington and the Reagan administration began promoting the concept of strategic consensus to the leaders of the Middle East, the groundwork for what would become the Reagan administration's 1984 debacle in Lebanon was being laid in and around Beirut. Since 1975, Lebanon had been torn apart by ever more violent combat among its many factions. Previously Lebanon had been viewed as a cosmopolitan symbol of hope for the Arab world. But the migration of many Palestinians from Jordan into Lebanon (with the strong encouragement of the United States) following the 1970 defeat of the PLO uprising known as "Black September" had disrupted the religious balance of power that had fostered a political equilibrium since the founding of the modern Lebanese state, which had been bolstered by President Eisenhower. However, with the incredible proliferation of powerful yet inexpensive and easy-to-operate small arms, such as AK-47 assault rifles and rocket-propelled-grenade launchers (RPGs), the carnage among Christian and Moslem Lebanese, Palestinians, Syrians and Israelis began to take on a life of its own.

Following six years of civil war, Lebanon, in 1981, had become the center of Middle East intrigue, terrorism and brutal violence. Damascus asserted traditional hegemony through the presence of the Arab Deterrent Force, a thirty-five-thousand-man Syrian force with long-standing political and financial ties with various Moslem and Christian ethnic groups and political parties. Israeli officials regularly traveled secretly to Beirut to meet with Christian allies, conducted violent covert operations against Palestinian terrorists, and attempted to influence the course of Lebanese politics so as to reduce Syria's historic domination of Lebanon. The Syrians competed vigorously for influence with the Israelis and with rival

Baathist Iraq as Baghdad worked to undermine the Syrians through Iraq's PLO and Christian allies. Palestinians, aligned primarily with leftist Sunni groups, brutally fought the Christians, nearly destroying the Christian militias until Syrian intervention on behalf of the Christians restored a shaky equilibrium to the balance of power in 1976. Effectively switching allegiances from their traditional ties with the Moslem community, the Syrians then turned on the Palestinians with a vengeance, redividing and weakening Lebanon's Moslem ethnic groups, enhancing Damascus's reputation among the Christians and strengthening Syria's overall power position in Lebanon and elsewhere.

These violent struggles were not limited to those between feuding ethnic groups: violence among members of the same ethnic group was common. The Maronite struggle grew particularly intense in 1978 and 1980, when Beshir Gemayel ruthlessly annihilated rival Christian leaders and many of the forces of his Maronite coethnics in order to become the dominant Maronite. Among the Druze, a mountain-dwelling ethnic group that had earlier lost its principal leader, Kamal Jumblatt, to Syrian assassins, the Jumblatt and the Arslan clans competed for preeminence. No ethnic group, except for the Shias of southern Lebanon, who were badly abused by the PLO throughout the late 1970s, was immune to intramural violence. That situation would deteriorate as well with the arrival of Iranian Revolutionary Guards (Pasdaran) following the 1982 Israeli invasion of Lebanon. The tragic patchwork of endless Lebanese conflict and violence was impossible for most Americans to comprehend, an incongruous and ever more violent blur on the evening news that flashed across television screens.

Having worked on U.S. policy toward Lebanon since my first day as an intern at the State Department in June 1977 (the United States was then trying to devise an FMS program to assist in the reconstitution of the Lebanese armed forces in the vain hope that the army might act as a force to end the civil war and restore the state), I had closely monitored Lebanese developments on a daily basis for nearly four years.

As the PLO and its affiliates launched terrorist attacks from the sea and across the Lebanese border into Israel, Israel's retaliatory and preemptive operations steadily escalated. Following the coastal road massacre in March 1978 in which thirty-four Israelis were killed, the IDF launched a major operation into Lebanon in order to destroy the PLO infrastructure in "Fatahland." Although Operation Litani, as the operation was known, had left Israel as an occupying power in southern Lebanon, the reinforcement of the pro-Israeli Lebanese militias under the command of Major

Saad Haddad had failed to secure Israel's northern borders by 1981. Indeed, terrorist operations against Israel had intensified while the Lebanese Forces, under the leadership of Beshir Gemayel, again triggered Syrian military pressure against the Christian communities.

Israel had conducted a dialogue with the leaders of two Maronite Christian clans during the years of civil war, Beshir Gemayel and Camille and Danny Chamoun. From the first encounter with Gemayel in 1976, the Israelis knew of his unabashed desire for Israel to intervene with decisive force to eliminate the Palestinian and leftist Moslem alliance. Removing Syrian forces from Lebanon would eventually become an even more important objective for Beshir Gemayel, Israel and the United States.

Under the Labor government in 1976 and 1977 and during the early years of Menachem Begin's premiership, Israel eschewed Gemayel's pressure, limiting its intervention to the supply of arms and equipment while improving its relations with both Camille and Danny Chamoun. However, with the violent consolidation of the Chamoun clan's Tigers with the Phalange militia of the Gemayel clan in mid-1980, the Israelis had little choice but to deal primarily with Beshir. Deftly manipulating Begin's deeply held Holocaust sentiments, Beshir eventually won from Begin vague promises to prevent the genocidal annihilation of Lebanon's Christian community.

By December 1980, Beshir finally managed to convince Begin to guarantee the safety of Christian towns, and agree that the Israeli Air Force (IAF) would interdict the Syrian Air Force should Syrian air strikes be launched against the Lebanese Forces. A Lebanese presidential election was to be held in 1982 and Beshir wanted to be elected. Unfortunately, the Syrians were backing Suleiman Franjieh, a bitter enemy of the Gemayel clan who was intent on avenging the Phalangist murder of his son Tony in 1978. If Beshir was to have a chance of winning the election, it was critical that the Syrians be pushed away from Beirut so that the Lebanese Forces could assert their hegemony and "ensure" a favorable electoral outcome. He had to find a way to convince the Israelis to intervene in order to tip the balance of power in his favor. The Israelis almost certainly did not know that they were being set up by Beshir Gemayel to do the Phalange's dirty work.

In early April 1981, Beshir instigated a violent confrontation with Syrian forces in the town of Zahle, a predominantly Greek Orthodox city in the Bekáa Valley. During the month of March, Phalangist forces had infiltrated the city and fortified their positions on the Sanin Ridge to gain a strategic advantage over the Syrian forces in the valley below. From a military perspective, it was essential for the Syrians to retake the Sanin Ridge and remove the Phalangists in order to secure their lines of communications. As the Syrians laid siege to Zahle, they prepared surface-to-air-missile (SAM) antiaircraft sites, but did not deploy any missiles. While the preparation of SAM sites was disturbing, Israeli experts took this limited escalation to mean that Syrian president Hafiz al-Assad did not want Israel to regard Syrian actions against the Phalangists to be in any way directed against Israeli interests.

Nevertheless, on the political level, Beshir Gemayel and Camille Chamoun traveled to Israel and succeeded in convincing Begin that if successful, the Syrian operation against Zahle would lead inevitably to a Syrian attack against the Christian "heartland," the possible destruction of the Lebanese Christian community and the total domination of Lebanon by Damascus. Several days later Begin won the approval of the Israeli Cabinet to conduct a limited air strike against the Syrians, presumably to convince the Syrians to lift the siege of Zahle. While the Cabinet was still in session, the IAF shot down two Syrian transport helicopters in the vicinity of Zahle.

Assad waited less than one day to answer the Israelis. To demonstrate his willingness to confront Israel, Assad deployed SAM-6 antiaircraft missiles to their prepared sites in the Bekáa Valley, together with additional SAM batteries and Soviet advisors along the Syrian-Lebanese border, and long-range surface-to-surface (SCUD) missiles near Damascus, where the SCUDs could reach targets in Israel. Beshir Gemayel had succeeded in escalating the situation from a Syrian-Christian battle into a Syrian-Israeli conflict, to include the possibility of direct Soviet involvement on behalf of the Syrians. Having gratuitously and unnecessarily injected Israel into this confrontation, Begin found that he had no choice but to declare Israel's intention to destroy the SAMs in Lebanon, if Syria did not withdraw them first.

Events in the eastern Mediterranean were being closely monitored by the national security bureaucracy in Washington throughout this period, although the situation in Lebanon was a low priority compared with the Iran-Iraq War and the Soviet occupation of Afghanistan. The world had grown almost weary of the Lebanese civil war and the grotesque violence that the Lebanese and their neighbors meted out to each other. No one in Washington or any other Western capital had calculated the high likelihood that Lebanon's strife could lead to a war between Syria and Israel. Although the Reagan administration was caught off guard by the developments of April, Washington reacted quickly, with a diplomatic initiative to try to prevent hostilities from erupting between the Syrians and Israelis.

Despite America's long-standing moral commitment to the preservation of Lebanon's territorial integrity and its unique form of consociational democracy, which dated back to the Eisenhower administration, America's vital interest in Lebanon was quite limited: the prevention of an Israeli-Syrian war on Lebanese soil that might escalate to a superpower confrontation. With SAMs stationed along Syria's border with Lebanon, however, it had to be assumed that these missiles could be fired against Israeli aircraft, should the IAF attempt to destroy the SAMs in the Bekáa Valley of Lebanon. In these circumstances it was doubtful that the conflict would remain geographically limited to Lebanon, and there was a great risk that Soviet advisors stationed at Syrian sites on the border could be killed. Although several members of the staff of the new National Security Council saw the crisis as an opportunity for Israeli military action to diminish Soviet influence in the Middle East, the extent of escalation and the outcome of hostilities were by no means certain.

President Reagan called on Ambassador-at-large Philip Habib to go to Syria to try to negotiate a political solution that would defuse the missile crisis. The situation was fast-moving. I participated in several internal ISA crisis discussions to try to anticipate what else might happen in this conflict, assess steps the United States could take to deter further escalation, and determine how to respond in the event that diplomacy or deterrence failed and a war between Syria and Israel actually erupted. In one of these meetings, the new assistant secretary of defense for ISA, Francis "Bing" West, was vigorously arguing that the confrontation was the result of Israel's desire to assert its hegemony in Lebanon and bring about the removal of the Syrian presence, a presence which had been mandated and legitimized by the Arab League. In these circumstances, he argued that the United States would need to "rethink" its relationship with Israel and not allow Israel to assume that U.S. assistance would be automatically forthcoming in the event of hostilities.

Having established a good working relationship with West several years earlier, I challenged his analysis, citing numerous intelligence reports and diplomatic cables from Israel, Lebanon and Syria that provided the basis for an accurate assessment of the nature of the escalation, particularly the manipulation of Israel by Gemayel and Chamoun. West was intrigued by this analysis, but concluded that my view was at odds with the DIA assessment and the position that Secretary Weinberger had instructed him to adopt in interagency discussions of the conflict.

According to West, Weinberger's posture was reinforced by the DIA analysis that argued that Begin and the chief of staff of the Israeli Defense Forces (IDF), General Rafael Eitan, were actually trying to provoke the Syrians in order to provide a pretext for another Israeli invasion of Lebanon. West noted that he had discussed this interpretation of events earlier in the morning with Carlucci, at which time he had received Weinberger's guidance. He said I was the first person he had heard to offer an explanation at odds with the DIA line.

The next morning Secord told me that West had discussed my analysis with Carlucci and that the deputy secretary wanted to meet with a DIA analyst and me to get a better understanding of the situation. After asking me several pointed questions about the chronology of events leading up to the early April Syrian assault on the Sanin Ridge, Carlucci asked the DIA analyst for his views.

To my surprise, the analyst agreed with me, adding several pieces of intelligence about Beshir's duplicity vis-á-vis the Syrians, Israelis and Americans. Carlucci expressed his confusion over why the DIA Lebanon analyst was presenting an interpretation of events so at odds with the official DIA position. Carlucci asked him about this contradiction, forcing the analyst to admit that he disagreed with the official line.

"But didn't you author the DIA report?" Carlucci asked, pointing to a document sitting on his desk. Taking a deep breath, the analyst replied, "I contributed to the report, but the product was considerably changed before the final version was released for distribution. I can only surmise that my superiors disagreed with my analysis and substituted their own. Perhaps they thought the conclusions were inconsistent with what they thought the secretary and chairman wanted to hear about Israel's role in Lebanon."

Visibly taken aback, Carlucci stiffened at the analyst's suggestion that conclusions were being modified to suit the policy objectives of Secretary Weinberger and General David Jones, then chairman of the JCS. Thanking us for our "interesting analyses," Carlucci abruptly ended the meeting without comment.

This recurring theme of "cooking intelligence" or slanting it to serve policy objectives would become a central and contentious issue during the Iran Affair and the subject of testimony during the later confirmation hearings of Robert Gates to become director of central intelligence. But these are issues that cut across administrations and political parties and go to the heart of national security decision-making.

As we left, I turned to the DIA analyst, stopping him before he went back downstairs to the National Military Intelligence Center (NMIC). "That was the most honest statement I have ever heard come out of anyone in DIA," I said, hoping he would take it the right way. Ruefully shaking his head, he acknowledged my backhanded compliment and replied, "There is just no interest in a comprehensive analysis of what's going on in Lebanon. Every time I suggest that the situation might involve Phalangist manipulation of the Israelis or that the Israelis are not simply looking for a pretext to fight the Syrians, I get an earful. No one will consider that anyone can manipulate Menachem Begin. Jones and the DIA director are convinced that everything Begin does is designed to manipulate us or embarrass Sadat."

Although the administration of Jimmy Carter had not been known for its friendly feelings toward Israel or for a willingness to use the U.S.-Israel relationship to help advance U.S. interests, the strongly anti-Israel environment at the Pentagon since Weinberger's arrival was unmistakable, notwithstanding the overtly pro-Israel sentiments expressed by President Reagan and Secretary Haig. The unstated message from Weinberger to the Pentagon bureaucracy was clear: regardless of the policy guidance that came from the White House or State, Weinberger was intent on putting his own imprimatur on Middle East issues. Given the potential for this Israeli-Syrian confrontation to degenerate quickly into a shooting war with the realistic possibility that the Soviets might intervene directly, escalating to a U.S.-Soviet crisis, Weinberger's cavalier attitude toward the critical need for a coherent policy and national security coordination was alarming.

Habib's diplomacy, coupled with the inclination of both Israel and Syria to step back from the brink of hostilities, prevented war from erupting in April. However, Weinberger's demonstrable pattern of antagonism toward Israel and the deteriorating situation in Lebanon did not abate.

You Can Be Certain the Job Will Never Be Boring

Having worked in ISA more than two years, I hoped that the election of Ronald Reagan would provide me with an opportunity to advance in my career, despite the fact that I was not a Republican. However, with the appointment of Secord over Noel Koch and the increasingly anti-Israel environment which pervaded the Pentagon in the spring of 1981, I decided to leave. Dennis Ross, who had moved from Defense to State, passed along my résumé to Jim Roche, who had become the deputy director for the State Department's Policy Planning (S/P) bureau. Robert C. "Bud" McFarlane, the new counselor of the State Department, had mentioned to Roche that he was looking for a new staff assistant with good bureaucratic skills and a working knowledge of current Middle East and political-military issues. While this position was essentially a lateral move, without any management responsibilities, Roche opined that, since McFarlane was a member of Haig's inner circle, my working for McFarlane would position me for other opportunities as they emerged. He arranged for McFarlane to interview me just before Memorial Day weekend.

The role of the counselor varies with every secretary of state. With a protocol rank equivalent to that of under secretary of state, the counselor, by definition, is one of the highest-ranking subordinates of the secretary. With three or four special assistants and a staff assistant, the counselor is able to participate in any issue of interest, typically receiving most sensitive diplomatic communications and intelligence reports seen by the secretary.

This was certainly the case for McFarlane, who had served with Haig on the NSC staff under Henry Kissinger during the Nixon and Ford administrations. A retired U.S. Marine Corps lieutenant colonel, McFarlane's career had included tours of duty in Vietnam, secret travel around the world with Kissinger, and a crisis management role as a member of the NSC staff during the *Mayaguez* Affair in May 1975. A realist who had worked for the late Senator John Tower on the Senate Armed Services Committee following his retirement from the Marine Corps, McFarlane was as experienced in the internecine world of Capitol Hill politics as he was with the high-level secrecy and bureaucratic maneuvers that typified the operations of Henry Kissinger. During Haig's tenure as secretary of state, McFarlane became one of his most trusted advisors, conducting public and secret diplomacy on behalf of Haig throughout the Middle East and Europe while overseeing the formulation and implementation of U.S. policies for the Middle East, Central America and European nuclear weapons matters.

McFarlane asked me to become his staff assistant just days prior to the June 7, 1981, Israeli bombing of the Iraqi nuclear reactor. When I told him that I was honored to accept the job, McFarlane replied, "I can't be sure of what lies ahead, but you can be certain the job will never be boring."

I arrived at my desk in the Pentagon on Monday morning, June 8, and was startled to find before and after photographs of Iraq's Osirak reactor. Neither the Israelis nor the Iraqis had yet publicly disclosed its destruction, and my first instinct was that the photo was a practical joke. A quick check with the NMIC confirmed that the reactor was, in fact, a pile of rubble, and that it was the Israelis, not the Iranians, who had conducted the strike. (Iran had unsuccessfully attacked the Iraqi reactor early in the Iran-Iraq War.) By midmorning, ISA was abuzz with concern over the Arab-world reaction and the impact on the U.S. posture in the Gulf. Particularly embarrassing was the failure of U.S. AWACS aircraft that were operating in Saudi Arabia to detect the Israeli aircraft on their way to or from the raid. I managed to get in to talk with Secord for a few minutes and got a sense of Weinberger's mood. A fighter pilot himself, Secord admired the skill and "chutzpah" of the IAF. After commenting that "the Israelis are the only people in the Middle East who solve their security problems unambiguously," Secord went on to say that "the only thing that will look worse than what's left of Osirak is U.S.-Israeli relations. Weinberger is really pissed off. He's convinced that Begin's real motive is to embarrass the U.S. and undermine our activities in the Arab world."

The fact that Saddam Hussein had actually been trying to develop a nuclear weapon capable of threatening Israelis, Persians or Arabs was irrelevant to Weinberger. He was not alone in regarding Iraq as Saudi Arabia's—and therefore America's—putative ally against Iranian-inspired Islamic fundamentalism in the Gulf. With the Israeli-Syrian missile standoff in the Bekáa Valley simmering just below the flash point, Weinberger had made clear to his deputies, who passed it on in no uncertain terms, that the United States had to punish Israel in order to mitigate the resultant damage to our position in the Arab world and send a clear message to Israel that the United States would impose a price for Israel's unilateral behavior.

In the ensuing days, Weinberger, together with other key advisors, successfully convinced the president to delay the scheduled delivery of six F-16 aircraft that had been purchased by Israel. While this action gave Weinberger something he could point to as a demonstration of U.S. unhappiness, it only reinforced Begin's worst instincts about the potential unreliability of the United States in the face of what Israel regarded as a fundamental and mortal threat to its very existence: an Iraqi nuclear bomb. Israel was widely denounced for bombing Osirak and paid a political price for its action. Nine years later, after Saddam Hussein invaded Kuwait and threatened a chemical holocaust in the Middle East, almost everyone looked back thankfully on Israel's "paranoia" and unilateral destruction of the Iraqi nuclear reactor.

Having given notice of my plans to leave ISA and move back to State in the midst of the post-strike policy crisis, I prepared for what I hoped would be a quick exit from the Pentagon. McFarlane had become the point man at State for managing U.S.-Israel diplomacy, as Washington worked with the Arab world in the U.N. Security Council to condemn the raid and suspend the F-16 deliveries.

Unexpectedly, the State Department Security Office advised that a new "background check" and "security clearance" would have to be undertaken, which would delay my going to State for several months. To my dismay, although I held TOP SECRET and Special Compartmented Intelligence (SCI) clearances (known as "CODEWORD" clearances), State refused to accept them. When I pointed out that my DOD TOP SECRET clearance had been passed to DOD by State Security, which had conducted my original background check, the security officer answered that "State does not accept third-party transfers, even when we are the originator of the first clearance, as in your case." During a chance encounter with West in the Pentagon gym the following day, he asked me how soon I would be going over to State. Although I had not yet had a chance to advise McFarlane's office of the delay, I told West that the move was hung up over the State Security Office's ludicrous refusal to accept back the clearances they had originally generated. Laughing with me over this ridiculous situation, West offered to "detail" me to State, thereby enabling me to start working for McFarlane while I remained on the DOD payroll. I gratefully accepted. Still drawing a DOD paycheck, I returned to the State Department in July 1981, staff assistant to the counselor.

CHAPTER 6

STRATEGIC CONSENSUS

Conventional Wisdom

By the time I went to work for McFarlane, a major shift had taken place in U.S. policy toward southwest Asian security issues. The conventional wisdom that the "unresolved Palestinian problem" was the root cause of instability in the Middle East was swept away. Despite the expertise of the proponents of this line of argument, it is indisputable that most conflicts in the Middle East have little, if anything, to do with Israel. While a resolution of the Arab-Israeli conflict, including the Palestinian problem, would certainly ease the suffering of Israelis and Arabs, improve the political and economic climate and increase stability in the region, resolving the Palestinian problem would not solve the myriad of problems plaguing the Middle East or threatening America's vital interests. The Soviet Union did not invade Afghanistan nor did Iraq invade Iran because of the unresolved Palestinian problem. Border disputes among the various countries of the Arabian Peninsula were not generated by the plight of the Palestinians. Libya did not invade Chad or try to destabilize Sudan, Egypt or other African countries because of its solidarity with the cause of the Palestinians. Wars in the Horn of Africa had nothing to do with the unresolved Palestinian problem, nor did Syria's claims on Lebanon and parts of Jordan.

In place of misguided conventional wisdom, the Reagan administration focused first, and foremost, on improving the ability of the United States to act unilaterally in protecting America's vital interests in Persian Gulf oil and to counter Soviet aggression in the region. With the worst-case scenario of a Soviet thrust toward the Gulf increasingly perceived as a realistic threat, it was important to act promptly to convince Moscow that the United States had the will and capability to use force to prevent a Soviet victory.

Reagan was convinced that U.S. interests could be protected only by enhancing America's capabilities for unilateral action in several potential

126

theaters of operations. Accordingly, Haig tried to forge a "strategic consensus" among America's key friends in the region, who were all, in one way or another, threatened by the Soviet Union. Although all shared this common interest and were willing to acknowledge some Soviet threat, in private if not in public, aside from Egypt and Israel, the countries of southwest Asia were reluctant to change their traditional threat perceptions.

Haig and his advisors acknowledged that numerous ethnic, religious, territorial and ideological factors contributed to the instability of the region; they recognized that the successful implementation of this new policy would require significant and sustained diplomatic efforts to overcome the local contradictions inherent in a new American strategy based on the Soviet threat. Although the conservative states of the Arabian Peninsula were frightened by the Soviets and the spreading waves of instability, radicalism and militant Islam, Arab leaders continued to hold fast to their bedrock belief that Israel was the principal enemy of the Arab and Islamic world. Despite inter-Arab rivalry, given the polarization of the Arab world which followed the Egypt-Israel peace treaty and the persistent escalation of hostilities between Israel and the PLO in Lebanon, Arab antipathy toward Israel was on the rise. Indeed, the conservative regimes virtually ignored the close ties between Moscow and the Arab radicals, which included Libya, Syria, Iraq, the PDRY and the PLO, because Moscow provided the military hardware which gave the Arabs the ability to threaten and confront Israel militarily.

Apart from Arab unwillingness to buy into the Reagan administration's notion of strategic consensus, Israel itself was also unwilling to agree, owing to the importance the United States placed on the Saudi role in the strategic consensus. Pointing to Riyadh's continuing hostility toward Israel and considerable financial support for the PLO and the confrontation states, Begin absolutely rejected the notion that Israel and Saudi Arabia had a common vital interest vis-à-vis the Soviet Union. Neither was Pakistan ready to declare the Soviet Union to be its principal threat, despite the brutal war being waged by the Soviet Union in adjacent Afghanistan. Islamabad's political attention, and the physical and intellectual orientation of the Pakistani military, remained focused on Pakistan's historic rival, India. For her part, Indian prime minister Indira Gandhi was convinced that Pakistan would never fight the Soviets, maintaining that Islamabad sought advanced fighter-bombers and other armaments only to attack India, eventually with nuclear weapons.

Despite the administration's best diplomatic efforts, and regardless of the military logic of a strategic consensus, these long-standing regional rivalries and threat perceptions were prone to die very hard indeed. Although a strategic consensus that supported unilateral U.S. military action seemingly offered a logical successor to the nearly defunct Twin Pillars policy, given the scope of violence sweeping southwest Asia in 1981, the vital interests and priorities of America's friends in the region would have to change in order to achieve a consensus. Regrettably, the widespread perception remained that America was in decline and weak. America needed to prove that it remained a genuine superpower which was capable of protecting its interests.

The Reagan administration used a variety of traditional instruments of influence to change the perceptions, interests and priorities of these states: arms sales, such as the AWACS aircraft for Saudi Arabia and F-16s for Pakistan; launching covert actions in Afghanistan and the African nation of Chad; economic assistance for pro-American but financially poor countries such as Egypt; and the measured use of military force to challenge the aggressiveness of Soviet-backed radicals, such as Libya.

Pakistan was located between Soviet-occupied Afghanistan and Soviet ally India and was regarded as a front-line state in the Cold War struggle with the Soviet Union. From Washington's perspective, it was essential to bolster Islamabad's capability and will to deter any Soviet advance southward toward the Gulf.

Deterring Soviet advances underlay the administration's rationale for the AWACs aircraft sale to Saudi Arabia, despite the vigorous opposition of Israel and its supporters in the Congress. The administration firmly believed that the AWACS planes would enhance Saudi security while deterring Soviet aggression in the Persian Gulf. Although regional conflicts, other than the Iran-Iraq War, assumed a lower priority for the Reagan administration, Haig was committed to preserving the gains of the Carter administration in the Arab-Israeli peace process, while framing U.S. policies for dealing with other regional conflicts through an East-West prism.

As Haig's principal advisor on security issues, McFarlane played a central role in the formulation and implementation of the emerging policies that provided the foundation for the strategic consensus. McFarlane was deeply involved in policy development, open and secret diplomacy, and creative thinking. Working closely with Secretary of State Haig on every sensitive policy issue, McFarlane was one of the few people in the State Department who received an advance copy of Haig's private calendar on a daily basis along with the restricted diplomatic cables and intelligence reports that went only to the secretary. Any assistant secretary of state who tried to "cut him out" or dared send a sensitive policy initiative up to Haig without first consulting with McFarlane risked serious consequences.

My first glimpse of the inner circle of State Department policy-making convinced me that this was a great job. My daily responsibilities were to vet the diplomatic and intelligence cables and media summaries before McFarlane arrived at the office early each morning, make sure McFarlane was fully briefed by the bureaucracy on key Middle East, Central American, arms control, international terrorism, and use of force issues, and ensure that his guidance was being implemented by the appropriate action officers. Bud's standard instruction was to think creatively and unconventionally about policy matters for which he was responsible. He continually emphasized that he did not want a sycophant for a staff assistant.

During my first week, Bud informed me that I would be accompanying him on a secret trip to India, Egypt and Israel designed to promote the southwest Asia strategic consensus. One month earlier he had met secretly with President Zia ul-Haq of Pakistan and then crown prince Fahd of Saudi Arabia in order to explain the emerging U.S. strategic framework and to solicit their perspectives on the new American approach.

He had also separately traveled to Israel to resolve the bilateral dispute that had ensued following Israel's destruction of Iraq's nuclear reactor. We were to fly with Haig to Marbella, Spain, for a meeting with Fahd, and then separate from the secretary's party in Belgrade, Yugoslavia, to travel on to New Delhi. From New Delhi, we would proceed to Cairo for meetings with Sadat, focused on Libya, and then conclude the trip in Israel, where McFarlane would initiate a strategic dialogue with Foreign and Defense Ministry officials. My job was to ensure that the logistical arrangements were made and that the working papers were being prepared consistent with the guidance McFarlane had given to Assistant Secretary of State for NEA, Nicholas Veliotes.

Despite the administration's hopes for an orderly, if difficult, implementation of the strategic consensus, attitudes and developments in the Middle East and Washington dramatically complicated Haig's design for change. Libyan leader Muammar Qadhafi's support for international terrorism and subversive activities throughout North Africa provided an opportunity for the United States to act forcefully against a hostile power closely allied with the Soviet Union, yet American relations with Saudi

Arabia and Israel became increasingly strained throughout 1981. It was McFarlane's responsibility to manage the AWACS aircraft sale while halting the slide in U.S.-Israeli relations.

In addition to reconciling the roles of Saudi Arabia and Israel in the emerging strategic consensus, it was essential for Washington to bolster Islamabad without further antagonizing New Delhi. U.S.-Indian relations had remained quite cool since the United States tilted in favor of Islamabad during the 1971 Indo-Pakistani War. New Delhi had adopted a consistently pro-Soviet line on every international issue, yet the Reagan administration hoped that a way could be found to improve U.S.-Indian relations without damaging its strategic relationship with Pakistan.

To this end, Reagan and Haig had held a brief discussion with India's Prime Minister Gandhi and Foreign Minister Narasimha Rao, earlier in the year at the Cancun Summit. Haig had tried to convince Gandhi to reconsider her lifelong antagonism and mistrust of the United States, emphasizing that the Soviet Union, despite its close ties with India, had emerged as an imperialist power with ambitions in southwest Asia that threatened the stability of the subcontinent. At that time, Gandhi acknowledged that the invasion of Afghanistan revealed the true nature and ambition of Brezhnev. However, she downplayed the likelihood that the Soviets would move beyond Afghanistan, into Iran or Pakistan, countering that the potential for increasing regional instability was related directly to Washington's decision to enhance the military capabilities of Pakistan.

Gandhi was convinced that President Zia of Pakistan was secretly developing a nuclear weapon that it would use against India and was providing military, financial and logistics support for Sikh subversives in India and Tamil rebels in Sri Lanka. She complained that America's confrontation with the Soviets in Afghanistan through covert support of the Afghan Mujahadeen had provided Zia with tremendous leverage over the United States. From India's perspective, the United States was to be faulted for responding unilaterally to the Soviet invasion of Afghanistan, rather than relying on the political and legal efforts of the United Nations or other international bodies to promote a settlement. Acknowledging the importance that President Reagan attached to the Soviet threat, she argued that Zia exploited this perception in order to get U.S. aid—most notably F-16 aircraft—to modernize the Pakistani military. Since U.S. F-16s were configured to deliver tactical nuclear weapons, Gandhi argued they were a particularly destabilizing menace and likely to lead to an escalation of tensions between India and Pakistan. Despite India's own nuclear weapons program, she warned that India would not sit idly by and permit Pakistan to test a nuclear weapon, intimating that forceful action might be taken to prevent such a development.

Perceiving an opening for a dialogue that might, over time, produce a change in the U.S.-Indian relationship, Haig and Gandhi agreed that the two countries would begin a strategic dialogue which would give them the opportunity to improve mutual understanding through candid and comprehensive presentations of respective interests, perceptions and policies. McFarlane was assigned responsibility for this dialogue on behalf of the United States, while Narasimha Rao appointed Director General of the Foreign Ministry Eric Gonsalves as head of the Indian delegation.

McFarlane and I accompanied Haig on his way to deliver a major speech in Germany. Haig made a one-night stop in Marbella to meet with Fahd at his summer villa. The discussion focused on the Arab-Israeli peace process and what became known as Fahd's Eight-Point Plan, the Israeli-PLO cease-fire in Lebanon, and the status of congressional consideration of the AWACS aircraft sale. We flew on with Haig to Belgrade, where we were to break away. The trip to India had so far remained secret, and it was our hope that it could remain so.

After we disembarked from Haig's airplane, McFarlane and I quietly wandered away from the rest of the secretary's entourage and the press corps, which were being shepherded into a motorcade for the drive into Belgrade. With over two hours to wait for our connecting flight to Athens, we casually reentered the airport and sat down at a cafe to have a beer. No sooner did we sit down than *Wall Street Journal* foreign correspondent Karen Elliott House abruptly sat down next to Bud. She had followed us off the plane and had become suspicious when McFarlane and I did not join the motorcade with the official party. Ever the gentleman, McFarlane ordered House a beer and asked her what was on her mind. "Why aren't you in the motorcade, Bud?" House asked. "Thinking about going somewhere else besides Belgrade?" Looking down pensively at his beer for a moment, McFarlane turned to House and replied, "You guessed right, Karen. Howard and I are not going to Belgrade. We are headed west from here and won't be traveling further with the secretary." House pressed for clarification, but McFarlane refused to be more specific. House finally finished her beer and walked away. After several more rounds of beer, we collected our luggage and left for Athens.

We arrived in New Delhi two days later, early on the morning of September 14, 1981. The fundamental goals were clear: foster an environment of understanding and trust between the United States and India that might eventually lead New Delhi to reassess its relations with Moscow, increase U.S.-Indian political cooperation, and reduce New Delhi's hostility toward Pakistan. McFarlane's schedule included a meeting with Rao preceded by several meetings and dinners with senior Foreign Ministry and Ministry of Defense officials. The substantive agenda for these talks covered a wide range of subjects, from strategic issues, such as the U.S.-Soviet competition in southwest Asia and the political-military implications for India, Pakistan and Afghanistan, to the prospects for improved U.S.-Indian relations.

From the outset, McFarlane emphasized that although the United States and India might often disagree on specific issues, particularly in the East-West context, and with regard to economic development policies in Third World countries, a sustained, high-level dialogue could help each country's leaders better understand the interests and perceptions of the other. The sessions were lengthy and intense. With friendly candor and precision, McFarlane summarized the U.S. perception of the dangerous trends of Soviet expansionism that formed the anvil against which Washington hoped to forge the strategic consensus.

In Afghanistan, Angola, the Horn of Africa and Central America, Moscow had demonstrated its increasing propensity to use force to achieve its goals. The Soviet Union was expanding its naval presence in the Indian Ocean, and upgrading the capabilities of Soviet Army forces adjacent to the Iranian and Chinese borders. Its policies combined intimidation and support for violence with an invitation to negotiate. This was also true in Pakistan, as the tempo of terrorist attacks in the North-West Frontier Province steadily increased. Although Soviet relations with Iraq had declined since the onset of the Iran-Iraq War, Moscow continued to sell arms to Baghdad and maintained its large advisory presence. At the same time, the United States knew that the Soviets were selling arms to Iran, positioning themselves to take advantage of opportunities for change in Iran. McFarlane emphasized that India and the United States had a common interest in peace, stability and stable economic growth. He assured them that the United States sought only to protect its vital interests in southwest Asia by helping foster stable economic development, expressing his respect for nonalignment and assuring the Indians that the United States was not seeking a permanent land presence in the region but only the capacity to project force in response to the Soviets' growing military capabilities. He sought their consensus on the need to resist Soviet expansionism, telling the Indians that this was the core meaning of strategic consensus. The second goal of the U.S. regional policy was to achieve a peaceful settlement of the Arab-Israeli dispute and reduce the tensions that create opportunities for Soviet troublemaking.

Turning to Pakistan, McFarlane attempted to convince the Indian interlocutors that their concerns about U.S. arms sales to Pakistan were misplaced. He made it clear that the United States agreed that while a full-scale Soviet invasion of Pakistan was presently unlikely, Soviet forces did conduct cross-border raids into Pakistan, and their capabilities were growing. Given the Soviet occupation of Afghanistan and without changing the regional balance of power, the United States was selling Pakistan the means with which to defend itself in order to act as a buffer against further Soviet inroads throughout the subcontinent. In each session, McFarlane reiterated this basic message, trying to convey to the senior leadership of the Indian Ministry of Foreign Affairs and the Army and Air Force chiefs of staff how the United States perceived the regional situation and what was being done to try to change it. Although most of the meetings were conducted in a formal atmosphere with delegations from both countries sitting across a table from each other in a Foreign Ministry conference room, McFarlane concluded the strategic dialogue in a more private meeting with Foreign Minister Rao on September 16. Rao welcomed the positive interest that President Reagan was displaying toward the subcontinent, and expressed the hope that the dialogue McFarlane had initiated would lead to a genuine and lasting improvement in U.S.-Indian relations and a reduction in tensions in southwest Asia. However, having been briefed by his subordinates on the substance of McFarlane's presentations regarding U.S. perceptions of East-West relations and intentions for strengthening America's ability to act to defend its interests in southwest Asia, Rao refused to reveal any change in India's attitudes toward southwest Asia matters or the Soviet Union and instead turned the discussion to philosophical issues.

Rao opined that it was vital for the two countries to discuss more than arms sales to Pakistan and that they shared common values, despite the temporary problems between the two countries. India wanted to remain, however, nonaligned and to work on improving itself. He warned McFarlane that Pakistan would get the arms it sought and also nuclear weapons but would not play the role the United States envisaged for it vis-à-vis the Soviet Union. Patience and the passage of time was essential to allow Pakistan and India to forge a new relationship with one another, notwithstanding America's desire for a strategic consensus. He expressed his country's pleasure that the United States was reaching out for a new relationship and for the opportunity to initiate a high-level dialogue on issues of mutual concern. At the conclusion of this meeting, Rao, who had conducted the dialogue while reclining on a long, aqua-colored pillow in his ornate office, rose to accompany McFarlane to the door. He asked McFarlane to understand that India saw their disagreements as temporary. If the dialogue continued, there might be real opportunities to reduce regional tensions and restore the natural relationship which should exist between two democracies, despite the East-West conflict.

Departing New Delhi early the next morning en route to Cairo, McFarlane and I reviewed the substance and scope of the talks. Concluding that the basic goals of the mission had been accomplished, we doubted whether any change would ensue in India's foreign policies toward the United States, the Soviet Union or Pakistan in the near term. While the Indian officials appeared to share Washington's desire to see bilateral relations improve, they remained convinced that U.S. perceptions of Soviet and Pakistani intentions were distorted and naive. Less than one year later, Prime Minister Indira Gandhi made an official state visit to the United States, where she met with President Reagan. In the course of her conversation with the president she pointed to the dialogue begun by McFarlane as the starting point in the process that convinced her to take a fresh look at improving U.S.-Indian relations.

Shoot-Down in the Gulf of Sidra

In addition to containing the spread of Soviet expansionism in southwest Asia, a fundamental objective of the Reagan administration was to change the radical, subversive behavior of Libyan leader Muammar Qadhafi.

During the last years of the Carter administration, considerable evidence of Libyan support for international terrorism had begun to surface publicly. Coupled with his outspoken pro-Soviet and anti-American attitudes, a perception of Qadhafi as a leading agent of Soviet subversion took hold in Washington. In pursuit of his long-standing goal of donning the mantle of radical, pan-Arab leadership, Qadhafi had for years been building up and modernizing his order of battle with the latest versions of Soviet tanks, artillery and aircraft, including long-range bombers. Qadhafi's avowed purpose for this military buildup was to participate in the Arab confrontation with Israel, an unlikely scenario given the long distances between Israel and Libya and the hostility that had developed between Libya and Egypt following Sadat's 1977 visit to Jerusalem. Nevertheless, with his impeccable radical credentials, preparation for war with Israel was ample justification for Moscow to sell him virtually whatever he would pay for, particularly since Qadhafi paid for his purchases with hard currency earned from oil sales to the Western world.

Despite the growing international concern over Qadhafi's alleged support of terrorism and his increasing tendency to try to subvert other Arab and African regimes, Western leaders were unwilling to take action against Qadhafi. Even when he unilaterally annexed portions of northern Chad in 1977, an area known as the Aozou Strip and believed to be rich in uranium deposits (a factor which could enhance Qadhafi's declared intention to develop a nuclear weapon), the international community hardly took notice.

By October 1980, however, Qadhafi had finally overreached, intervening in neighboring Chad with Libyan tanks, artillery, helicopters, strike aircraft and ground forces to support the regime of President Goukouni Weddei against the more capable forces of Hissein Habre, the former minister of defense of Chad, who controlled much of the country, including the capital city of N'Djamena. Similar in style to the Soviet invasion of Afghanistan at the "request" of the Afghan government, the Libyan intervention in Chad, supported by Cuban and East German technical advisors and logisticians, posed an ominous challenge to the Arab and African regimes of North Africa and the central Sahara. By early November, long-range Tu-22 aircraft were flying deep into Chad to conduct bombing raids against Habre's strongholds, while armor and mechanized infantry forces advanced on the ground, systematically destroying his forces. At the same time, Libyan forces conducted cross-border raids into Sudan, threatening to intensify their military pressure against the Sudanese unless they acquiesced to Qadhafi's fait accompli in Chad. By the middle of December, Libyan forces had captured N'Djamena, forcing Habre and the remnants of his command to flee from Chad, primarily to neighboring Cameroon. Less than three weeks later, Qadhafi and Goukouni announced their intention to merge Chad with Libya, arousing anger and great suspicion in European and African capitals over Qadhafi's long-range intentions toward other neighbors. Following such overt aggressive behavior, other African nations, including Niger, Mali, Ghana, Nigeria, Sierra Leone, Uganda, Liberia, Cameroon, Senegal, the Gambia and Gabon, began to produce evidence of Libyan support for subversive elements and terrorist acts in their countries. As Libyan-inspired subversion, tension and violence spread throughout the continent, diplomatic relations were broken, Libyan diplomats expelled, trade sanctions against Libya imposed and Libya's standing deteriorated rapidly.

As the evidence of Libya's subversive behavior became ever more public and incontestable, the incoming Reagan administration characterized Libya as a "cat's-paw" of Soviet expansionism and began to consider ways of challenging Qadhafi and stopping his aggressive behavior. The underlying strategy was that in challenging Qadhafi, the United States would demonstrate its capability to counter Soviet-inspired expansionism and would help restore the confidence of America's friends that the United States had the power and the will to act to defend its interests.

As early as March 1981, the U.S. Sixth Fleet began to conduct air and sea exercises in the Gulf of Sidra, an area of the Mediterranean Sea claimed by Qadhafi as part of Libyan territorial waters. (The internationally recognized limit to a nation's territorial waters is twelve miles. Nevertheless, Qadhafi claimed that Libya's territorial rights extended out to sea for two hundred miles.) Although this initial challenge did not result in hostilities between the United States and Libya, it was roundly denounced by Qadhafi and signified Washington's first test of Qadhafi's will to confront the U.S. military, as well as Moscow's readiness to back the claims of its Libyan ally.

By midsummer 1981 Qadhafi had as yet given no indication of any intent to back down on his territorial claims in the Gulf of Sidra or to stop his aggressive behavior throughout Africa. On August 19, the U.S. Navy conducted another naval challenge in the Gulf of Sidra. During the exercise, two Libyan aircraft were shot down when they took threatening action against two U.S. F-14s. Although the Libyans claimed that their aircraft had been illegally ambushed, the U.S. pilots insisted that they fired on the Libyans in self-defense only after the Libyan pilots had prepared to attack by activating their target-acquisition radars and the guidance systems of their air-to-air missiles.

The strategic goals of this naval challenge were clearly achieved. The United States used force effectively against Qadhafi's lawless behavior and the Soviet Union failed to take any action on behalf of its ally. The naval challenge came on the same day that a tripartite pact was formed which united the Soviet-backed states of Libya, the PDRY and Ethiopia in an anti-American alliance. The Sixth Fleet demonstrated that henceforth the world should expect the United States to use force to defend its interests and advance its policy goals at a time and place of its choosing.

The message was clear. The United States would no longer acquiesce to the continued pattern of Soviet and radical subversive behavior that had become commonplace. Should the Soviet Union decide to stand by radicals like Qadhafi, it was now on notice that it would be running an ever-increasing risk of a superpower confrontation. Although covert U.S.

support for the Afghan Mujahadeen had been under way for well over one year, the shoot-down of the Libyan jets represented the first overt manifestation of a resurgent American will to end the expansion of Soviet influence and the spread of radicalism throughout the Middle East.

Qadhafi, needless to say, viewed the shoot-down from a different perspective and attempted to exploit the incident and rally inter-Arab support for Libya and the tripartite pact. However, aside from rhetorical support, Libya received no help from any of its allies, Arab or otherwise. During his final meeting with Indian foreign minister Rao in New Delhi one month after the incident, Bud pointed to the Gulf of Sidra to illustrate that the Reagan administration, while not trying simply to pick a fight with Qadhafi, would take action when U.S. interests are threatened. Despite the administration's expectation that India would criticize the United States for the incident, Rao adopted a surprisingly neutral stand, saying that he didn't know enough about the Gulf of Sidra to make a clear judgment.

Enraged by the shoot-down and disappointed by the lack of international support, Qadhafi began to escalate his subversive behavior, keen to build on his successful intervention in Chad as well as to demonstrate that he would not be intimidated. Alarmed by Qadhafi's growing boldness, particularly his use of force and subversive activities against Sudan as well as threats against Egypt, President Anwar el-Sadat expressed his growing concern about Qadhafi and the need for greater bilateral cooperation between the United States and Egypt to neutralize Qadhafi's ability to carry out his threats. Sadat had earlier tried to convince the Carter administration to cooperate with Egypt against Qadhafi following a military clash between Libyan and Egyptian forces in Egypt's Western Desert. But Carter had been unwilling to use force and intervene militarily on behalf of Egypt, concerned that the United States would find itself caught in the middle of an Egyptian-Libyan war that might damage prospects for moving the Egyptian-Israeli peace process forward.

The Barrages

Throughout the summer of 1981, urban unrest in Egypt intensified in response to economic problems while militant Islamic fundamentalists fanned the flames of opposition. Sadat was especially concerned over the revival of militant Islamic fundamentalism in Egypt and Qadhafi's brazen expansionism in Chad and aggression against Sudan. Finally losing patience in September, Sadat ordered his security forces to crack down on the militants, as well as on outspoken secular opponents of his policies, such as the well-respected journalist Mohammed Haikal. Rioting ensued in several locations in Egypt, and hundreds of dissidents were arrested. In these increasingly tense domestic and regional circumstances, McFarlane and I arrived in Cairo in September 1981 to consult with Sadat about joint actions that Egypt and the United States could undertake to deter, and if necessary confront, Libyan expansionism.

One meeting was held with Sadat at his Nile River retreat, known as The Barrages. Presidents Reagan and Sadat had previously discussed the need for the United States and Egypt to plan measures that the two nations could take to counter Libyan and Soviet threats. Accompanied by Bing West and the U.S. ambassador to Egypt, Alfred Atherton, McFarlane was determined to lay the groundwork for concrete operational and exercise planning between the Egyptian Ministry of Defense and the U.S. military. McFarlane and Sadat discussed the regional situation for much of the afternoon, with Sadat focusing most of his attention on the Libyan threat to Sudan and the possibility that Ethiopia, in its capacity as tripartite power, might come to the defense of Libya by creating trouble on Sudan's southern border. He expressed Egypt's concern that, with Chad under Libyan domination, Sudan was the next strategic target for Qadhafi and the Soviet Union. Given Egypt's vital interest in Sudan, Sadat could not afford to see the country fall to Libya or Ethiopia. Such a development would leave Egypt flanked to the west and south by hostile powers able to put significant pressure on Cairo through their control of the Nile River, the lifeline of Egypt. Additionally, the radicals would gain a strategic advantage in the Red Sea, controlling nearly two thirds of the western littoral, from where the sea-lanes could be interdicted. With the Soviet Navy already exploiting naval facilities on Ethiopia's Dahlak Island, control over Port Sudan would further enhance Moscow's ability to dominate the Red Sea and disrupt the ability of the RDF to deploy to Saudi Arabia in the event of a crisis.

Libyan cross-border raids into western Sudan were especially troubling to Sadat. Although he acknowledged that the downing of the Libyan fighters was a positive act, it had not succeeded in deterring Qadhafi from his adventurous policies in Chad, Sudan or anywhere else. Indeed, Sadat noted that Qadhafi had actually been emboldened, certain that the United States would not engage Libya in a larger confrontation. Convinced that the Soviets were behind Qadhafi's efforts to encircle Egypt and unseat Sadat, the Egyptian president emphatically stated that he would not tolerate these developments. He wanted a commitment from the United States to help Egypt prevent the Libyans from making any further gains in Sudan. In the event of hostilities, Sadat wanted firm assurances that the U.S. Air Force would deploy AWACS planes and tactical fighters to fly combat air patrol missions in support of the air defense of Egypt. Should full-scale hostilities break out, ground combat would be the responsibility of the Egyptian Army. But the large Libyan arsenal of advanced fighter and ground-attack aircraft was cause for significant concern in planning any type of combat operations against Libya, and the Egyptian Air Force required more time to absorb the advanced fighters and associated U.S. equipment that were now flowing into Egypt as a result of the peace treaty with Israel.

Another matter of grave concern to Sadat was his conviction that Qadhafi intended to develop a nuclear weapon. Obviously impressed by Israel's destruction of Iraq's Osirak nuclear reactor, despite the embarrassment it caused Sadat, coming only four days after the Sinai Summit with Begin, Sadat made clear that Egypt must have a "long arm" capable of reaching Libya's nuclear reactor. Qadhafi had made no secret of his desire for a nuclear weapon, at one time offering to buy an atomic bomb from China. Of late, it had come to the attention of the United States and others that Qadhafi had proposed financing Pakistan's nuclear weapons program in consideration for gaining future access to nuclear technology and/or weapons. Although many U.S. intelligence and policy analysts dismissed or downplayed these reports, together with Qadhafi's pretensions to playing a leading role in Arab affairs, Sadat viewed the potential threat, with or without nuclear weapons, with deadly seriousness.

Although Sadat's crackdown on the domestic opposition had drawn considerable domestic and international criticism, the subject did not come up during the meeting. Aside from Sadat's passing references to some trouble with Islamic fundamentalists who had no vision except to try to make the past into the future, the discussion focused on strategic matters.

McFarlane assured Sadat that Reagan stood by his commitment to work with Egypt to prevent Qadhafi and the Soviets from making further gains in the Middle East. He said that the United States was ready to begin serious joint political-military planning to enhance the stability and security of friendly countries in the region. Pointing to the action in the Gulf of Sidra as an example of America's new resolve to counter Qadhafi and the Soviets effectively and to signal the joint determination of Egypt and the United States to confront Qadhafi's aggressiveness, McFarlane suggested that the upcoming Bright Star 82 exercise should be oriented toward Libya. If most of the exercise was conducted in the Western Military District, Qadhafi and the Soviet Union would be certain of Egyptian-American readiness to act against any threats to Sudan or Egypt.

Sadat expressed his satisfaction with U.S. readiness to begin joint planning for Bright Star 82, but stressed his belief that the two countries might need to act decisively in the near future, well in advance of the exercises being planned for early 1982. He pointed out that Qadhafi had not been deterred by the shoot-down, so why would exercises later in the year have a greater impact than what the United States had already done? He noted that Qadhafi believed that God and history were on his side. McFarlane opined that Sadat was probably right about Qadhafi, but that the Soviets would correctly interpret the serious message that Bright Star 82 would deliver and begin to rein him in. But if Qadhafi's aggression persisted in the interim, McFarlane assured Sadat, the United States would act with Egypt to stop him.

As we were leaving The Barrages for Cairo, Sadat proclaimed his great affection for the United States and President Reagan. Confident of the depth of U.S. support for Egypt and commitment to the peace strategy that Sadat had set in motion less than four years ago with President Carter, the Egyptian president appeared at peace with himself, as he prepared for what seemed to be Egypt's inevitable confrontation with Qadhafi. Sadat made no pretense about his ambition to attain a leadership role for himself and Egypt in Africa or the Arab world, nor of his strong belief that the Soviet Union was determined to eliminate him and regain its former position in Egypt. Eighteen days later, Sadat was assassinated by Islamic fundamentalists in the Egyptian Army.

Back at the U.S. embassy in Cairo, McFarlane and I huddled with Ambassador Atherton, Deputy Chief of Mission (DCM) Henry Precht, Bing West, and PM deputy director Rear Admiral Jonathan Howe in preparation for the next day's meetings with Egyptian minister of defense Mohammed Abu Ghazala. Precht had been assigned to Cairo regardless of the fact that many viewed him as one of several key individuals who bore a heavy responsibility for the policy that had undermined America's Iranian pillar. Three years earlier, the former Iran desk officer had truly fallen on his sword for NEA over my paper, insisting that there was no internal instability in Iran. Legitimate analysis was deleted so as not to challenge firmly held policy views. The myopic, institutional refusal to take a hard and honest look at the deteriorating situation in Iran had cost the United States dearly. Precht, more than any other individual, was most generally credited, perhaps unfairly, for being the one principally responsible for losing Iran.

Nevertheless, Precht had met the tests of a good FSO and received a plum NEA assignment as DCM in Cairo, one of the most important postings for American foreign service officers in the Arab world. Never let it be said that the foreign service does not take care of its own. The price paid by an FSO for substantive mistakes, no matter how great the consequences, was relatively modest as long as the game was played correctly, according to the unspoken rules of the foreign service.

I would come to learn this lesson the hard way some years later when I ended up on the losing side of a substantive foreign policy debate. When it appeared in late 1986 that I might finally be out of the foreign policy game and no longer able to fairly outmaneuver them in order to achieve substantive policy goals, my bureaucratic rivals in the foreign service and elsewhere in the bureaucracy brought out the long knives to make sure I never would get back in. I learned then the advantage of playing by their rules and having an institution behind me.

Strategic Cooperation with Israel

In seeking to consolidate the strategic consensus for the Middle East, a particularly difficult issue arose involving the nature of U.S.-Israeli strategic cooperation. The first exposure Haig and McFarlane had to the idea of strategic cooperation with Israel had come from S/P director Paul Wolfowitz and his principal deputy, Jim Roche, in early February 1981. At that time they explained the discreet strategic dialogue between the United States and Israel that had been quietly conducted by the Defense Department during the Carter administration. Although significant strategic issues had been discussed with key Israelis in the defense and foreign affairs ministries, nothing tangible had evolved, due largely to bureaucratic opposition within the NSC and the State Department.

Although Ronald Reagan and Menachem Begin often spoke in similar terms about the Soviet threat to the respective interests of the two countries, the attitudes of the two leaders toward genuine cooperation were based on contradictory assumptions. Begin firmly believed that Israel needed "freedom of maneuver" in both the strategic and tactical area in order to act against Arab threats. He was convinced that earlier Labor governments had placed excessive emphasis on prior consultation with the United States, to the detriment of Israel's security. Begin wanted to alter Israel's strategic relationship with the United States so as to enable Israel to act independently of it, while at the same time enabling the United States to tactically distance itself from Israeli actions that might damage U.S. interests in the Arab world.

Indeed, during the 1981 electoral campaign in Israel, Begin repeatedly emphasized that the Likud bloc's handling of the Americans afforded greater security because Israel was ready to act unilaterally, even if meant standing up to the Americans and provoking Washington's ire. In these circumstances, Begin hoped to forge a broad and somewhat ambiguous strategic consensus based on shared interests without formal structures for communication and cooperation. Some Israelis referred to this as the Begin Doctrine.

In early March 1981, David Kimche, the director general of the Israeli Foreign Ministry, visited Washington to begin a formal exchange of views with the Reagan administration. During this visit, Kimche and McFarlane established a dialogue that would evolve into an important channel of communications between the United States and Israel throughout much of the Reagan administration. McFarlane and Kimche acknowledged that U.S.-Israeli strategic cooperation would benefit the United States and Israel vis-á-vis the Soviet Union, while simultaneously triggering greater Arab suspicion of the intent of the policy. Both men agreed that the process would need to evolve carefully and deliberately in order to max- imize the benefits, while reducing the possibilities for misunderstandings and Soviet mischief-making. Other issues were also put on the agenda of the dialogue, including creative American diplomacy to enhance Israel's political and economic position in Central America, Africa and East Asia.

Based largely on the principles advanced by Wolfowitz and PM director Richard Burt, Haig introduced the basic tenets of strategic cooperation for southwest Asia during his visit to Israel in April 1981. Begin saw Haig's visit as an opportunity to implement his preferred relationship with the United States. From Begin's perspective, the United States and Israel agreed on the fundamentals: that neither the Soviet Union nor Soviet- backed Syria could be permitted to further expand their influence in Lebanon. Begin therefore thought it made perfect sense for Israel to act on its own against the Syrians without any need for advance consultations with Washington. Yet when Israel acted in Zahle, the situation only escalated, enhancing Syria's relative military position, while providing

Moscow with a pretext for expanding its involvement in the crisis, exactly the opposite of what Washington wanted to see happen.

The United States and Israel clearly had different objectives in mind. In contrast to Begin's desire for a strategic relationship based on greater Israeli freedom of action and independence from the constraints of subordinating Israel's interests to those of the United States, Haig wanted to build a structure that would afford the United States the orderly benefits of Israeli geography and military strength. The fundamental objectives were to enhance America's ability to project power to southwest Asia and deter Soviet expansionism, while reducing Israel's tendencies to act unilaterally in order to enhance Arab receptivity to the U.S. regional strategy.

Once strategic understandings were reached with key states, the United States hoped to be able to refocus its attention on the Arab-Israel peace process. By suggesting that Israel, Saudi Arabia and other conservative Arab states shared fundamental vital interests, the Reagan administration hoped to modify the threat perceptions of Israel toward its neighbors, who were weaker than Israel militarily, but of greater importance to the Reagan administration's plans for the defense of the Gulf. Based on a new sense of common interest, Haig and McFarlane sought to encourage greater risk-taking by Israelis and Arabs, which would, hopefully, lead to some measure of trust. While Haig and Begin discussed general principles, McFarlane met with Kimche and Abrasha Tamir of the Ministry of Defense (MOD) to organize a detailed agenda for political-military planning. A framework of ideas for cooperation, including joint military planning, pre-positioning of military equipment, a schedule of exercises and global political cooperation, was concluded.

In May 1981, McFarlane and Kimche met secretly in Geneva to develop a formal agenda for broad-based strategic cooperation and began an exchange of views on how to stimulate the peace process based on the preliminary understandings reached by Begin and Haig. McFarlane and Kimche agreed that the basis for strategic cooperation would be the mutual interest of the United States and Israel in deterring the advance of the Soviet Union into the Middle East.

The first phase of cooperation would be to develop military-to-military cooperation that would enhance the ability of the U.S. to project power into southwest Asia. Joint exercises, the pre-positioning of military hardware for the Rapid Deployment Force, access rights, increased intelligence exchange and joint planning were discussed. While such cooperation would also strengthen Israel's ability to deter Arab threats to the security of

Israel, McFarlane emphasized the U.S. position that strategic cooperation could never be directed against Arab states, even when such states were allies of the Soviet Union.

The question of Israeli "consultation" with Washington in advance of unilateral Israeli military operations never came up per se. McFarlane explained that strategic consensus from Washington's perspective meant that before Israel undertook military acts, it should calculate the probable effects of its actions on the interests of the United States, with a priority placed on not damaging Washington's interests. The United States, in turn, would hold up the same prism regarding Israeli interests. The talks concluded with both sides seemingly in agreement on the principles of cooperation and the political-military agenda for the next round of talks.

By the beginning of June, it appeared that the momentum of Haig's and McFarlane's talks with Israeli officials would shortly usher in an era of formal strategic cooperation. While in hindsight it is clear that neither side understood the fundamental goals of the other at the doctrinal level, and despite the growing fight over the AWACS aircraft sale to Saudi Arabia and the missile crisis in Lebanon, both the State Department and the White House were keen to accelerate the process. This was not true at the Department of Defense, however.

The bombing of the Iraqi nuclear reactor typified the Begin Doctrine. Having tried for several years to convince the United States, France and Italy that they viewed the reactor as a mortal threat to Israel's very existence, the Israelis had finally come to the conclusion that only decisive military action by Israel would prevent Saddam Hussein from completing a nuclear weapon. Believing they had sent strong enough signals to alert the United States of their intent without placing it in the position of having to either sanction Israel's move or act to deter it, the Israelis attacked.

The likelihood of Israel's unilateral action, however, was clearly signaled to Washington. Israel had repeatedly expressed grave concern over Saddam's intentions well in advance of taking unilateral military action. In January 1981, before Reagan took office, the U.S. ambassador to Israel, Samuel Lewis, had sent Washington a comprehensive cable which outlined, in exhaustive detail, Israel's repeated warnings. Ambassador Lewis's cable, however, did not receive high-level attention outside of NEA, which maintained that the Israelis were merely hysterical, exaggerating the Iraqi threat only to embellish their security assistance requirements. The conventional wisdom at State was that Saddam did not intend to build a nuclear weapon. Despite Sam Lewis's cable and other strong indications of Israel's concerns, the bombing of the Osirak reactor in June came virtually as a total surprise to the Reagan administration, although not to NEA.

Israel's "surprise" destruction of the Iraqi nuclear reactor provided the opponents of strategic cooperation with a simple pretext for stopping the process: Israel's actions were severely damaging America's ability to enhance its anti-Soviet position in the Gulf. Weinberger, in particular, was outraged by Israel's action. He went beyond calls for arms sales sanctions against Israel and said that the United States should reconsider its basic policies toward Israel; in particular the policy of not talking with the PLO and the role of the Camp David Accords as the touchstone of U.S. policy toward the peace process.

Weinberger was curiously oblivious to the potential negative consequences for Egypt were the United States to move away from the Camp David Accords. Weinberger was a vocal proponent of the line that the best way for the United States to advance its interests and help defend Israel was by strengthening America's ties with the Arab world. Weinberger repeatedly emphasized his strong conviction that Saudi Arabia, rather than Egypt or Pakistan, formed the front line of America's stand against Soviet expansionism. Throughout his tenure as secretary of defense, Weinberger demonstrated overt hostility toward Israel and tried to unilaterally change America's Middle East policy by distancing the United States from Israel, despite Reagan's stated desire for closer ties.

Despite their serious displeasure over Israel's military surprises in Zahle and Iraq, Reagan and Haig remained adamant that closer ties with Israel, not further distance and pressure, would help strengthen the anti-Soviet strategic consensus and increase Israel's willingness to take risks for peace in the negotiations for Palestinian autonomy. Reagan nevertheless acquiesced in the suspension of delivery of F-16 aircraft to Israel to signal U.S. displeasure with the raid on Iraq's nuclear reactor. In addition, he authorized the initiation of a formal dialogue with Iraqi diplomats. Yet Reagan essentially ignored Weinberger's attempts to change America's Middle East policy. Not until October 1981, when Begin overreached and intervened with the Congress to shrilly and openly criticize the AWACS aircraft sale, did Reagan finally lose his patience and demand that Israel stop meddling in America's domestic affairs.

At about the same time, the president announced what became known as the Reagan Corollary to the Carter Doctrine. This statement established that the United States would intervene militarily in southwest Asia not only to ensure the free flow of Persian Gulf oil but also to ensure that neither Saudi oil nor Saudi AWACS aircraft would fall into the wrong hands. With the enunciation of the Reagan Corollary, the policy groundwork was laid for Operation Desert Storm.

The F-16 suspension was to have been lifted on July 17. In late July, however, the IAF struck Beirut and the suspension was renewed. Just after the renewal, McFarlane convened a meeting in his office in the State Department to devise a policy that would move the United States and Israel toward a formal relationship of strategic cooperation based on the framework developed in the Jerusalem and Geneva talks. He reemphasized that the fundamental goals of strategic cooperation were to enhance the U.S. military posture in the eastern Mediterranean and to create a framework of bilateral military relationships for deterring Soviet threats in the Middle East. McFarlane charged the participants in the meeting to consider how this cooperation might evolve in a manner that would also diminish Arab threats to Israel and reduce Israel's tendencies to act unilaterally with apparent "disregard for American interests in the Arab world." Wolfowitz, Burt and Veliotes met with McFarlane to draw up the "terms of reference" for this initiative. Over the next six weeks, Dennis Ross (S/P), Richard Haass (PM), Edward "Ned" Walker (NEA), Dan Handel (McFarlane's special assistant for NEA matters) and I worked arduously to craft a policy paper and decision memorandum for the president that Haig could get Weinberger to support, no small task.

Reflecting traditional thinking and conventional wisdom, the NEA participants working on the analysis and draft decision memorandum were inclined to agree with Weinberger's firm opposition to strategic cooperation. Veliotes, however, understood the importance Reagan and Haig placed on strategic cooperation and was more open-minded. Despite their underlying misgivings, NEA gave considerable bureaucratic support to the policy paper in the face of strong opposition from DOD.

Under strict guidance from Weinberger, ISA refused to cooperate in drafting the analysis or in the preparation of the decision memorandum. Over the course of the next two months, Haig and Weinberger discussed the matter several times, but Weinberger refused to budge, insistent that he and not the secretary of state or president knew what was best for the United States in the Middle East. Communicating directly with McFarlane and Veliotes in an effort to prevent an actual showdown between Haig and Weinberger, Bing West, on several occasions, tried to convince McFarlane to reconsider the strategic cooperation initiative and to use his influence to turn it off.

Haig and McFarlane were convinced, however, that strategic cooperation would enhance America's regional military posture and dispel a measure of Israeli apprehension over the sale of AWACS planes to Saudi Arabia. McFarlane refused and gave Haig the paper and draft decision memorandum discussing the pros and cons of U.S.-Israeli strategic cooperation. The paper was jointly drafted by Wolfowitz, Burt and Veliotes. While explicitly acknowledging Weinberger's unequivocal opposition, McFarlane recommended that Haig sign the memorandum and request that Reagan approve guidance to the U.S. government bureaucracy directing that a strategic cooperation agreement be negotiated and implemented between the United States and Israel. Haig agreed and the memorandum went to the president in August.

Weinberger was still determined to prevent the United States and Israel from entering into such an agreement and sent a "personal dissent" to the president, arguing that strategic cooperation with Israel would irrevocably damage U.S. influence in the Arab world and would further discourage already tentative Arab leaders from participating in the strategic consensus. The secretary of defense strongly discouraged the president from agreeing with Haig's recommendation. To Weinberger's profound dismay, however, Reagan agreed with Haig and directed the national security bureaucracy to prepare the principles of a strategic cooperation agreement which Reagan could discuss with Prime Minister Begin during his forthcoming visit to Washington in early September.

Nevertheless, certain that he knew what was best for U.S. interests in the Middle East, Weinberger directed his deputies to avoid cooperating with the State Department, while he continued to work, unsuccessfully, to convince the president to reconsider his decision. The lack of DOD participation in the interagency preparation of the president's agenda for strategic cooperation talks with Begin permitted State and the NSC staff to monopolize the drafting and coordination process. Weinberger succeeded in cutting out the DOD bureaucrats from the process altogether, thereby undermining their ability to help shape the U.S. proposals more to Weinberger's liking.

Menachem Begin came to Washington during the second week of September in order to establish a personal relationship with Ronald Reagan. Just prior to the president's meeting with the Israeli prime minister, Haig met privately with Reagan in the Oval Office. Haig reiterated that Weinberger was opposed to strategic cooperation between the United States and Israel, but the president expressed his concurrence with Haig's recommendation that strategic cooperation would, on balance, provide the United States with more advantages than disadvantages. Haig then produced an index card for Reagan that McFarlane had personally prepared containing four key "talking points" on strategic cooperation which the president should propose to Begin during the course of the discussions.

The Americans and Israelis convened for their first official meeting in the Cabinet Room, which is adjacent to the Oval Office. After formally welcoming the Israeli prime minister, Reagan offered the opportunity to Begin to speak first. Keen to demonstrate how well he could manage the U.S.-Israeli relationship now that the tensions of the summer had abated somewhat (and fully briefed on the extent to which McFarlane and Kimche had agreed on the fundamental principles for cooperation along with a framework and agenda for detailed discussions), Begin took the initiative to propose that a formal strategic cooperation agreement be concluded between the two countries.

The president ran through the four talking points that Haig had given him and promptly agreed. He directed that Weinberger work with Israel's new minister of defense, Ariel Sharon, to work out the details of the agreement. Although it later became clear that both countries had premised strategic cooperation on conflicting principles, no effort was made during this formal discussion to lay out principles or agree to the goals that the parties hoped the agreement would help achieve. Reagan asked Weinberger for his comments as to how he saw the strategic cooperation process evolving. Weinberger held his counsel and carefully stated that he looked forward to working out the "details" in a manner that would enhance the mutual interests of both countries. For his part, Sharon enthusiastically shared his views as to where he saw the process headed. True to form, Sharon immediately overreached, delivering a high-handed lecture to the president and his advisors in the White House Cabinet Room about what Israel could do for the United States throughout the Middle East, as if the United States was absolutely incapable of conducting any type of military operation anywhere in southwest Asia.

Visibly shocked by the scope of Sharon's blunt talk and far-reaching goals, Weinberger did his best to dither and to slow the pace of the negotiations, eventually attempting to link the conclusion of the strategic cooperation agreement with an end to Israel's unwelcome and outspoken opposition to the sale of AWACS aircraft to Saudi Arabia. During the discussions, Begin assured Reagan that he would not actively lobby against the sale, yet he made clear that Israel remained staunchly opposed, fearful that the AWACS planes would dramatically undermine Israel's qualitative edge over its Arab adversaries and shift the Arab-Israeli balance of power against Israel. During subsequent meetings on Capitol Hill, Begin was cagey and refused to tell senators or House members that "he did not still oppose the sale." Reagan and his advisors viewed Begin's conversations on the Hill as a betrayal of Begin's Oval Office promise not to lobby against the sale.

On September 19, McFarlane and I traveled to Israel from Egypt for secret discussions with Kimche and Sharon. On our way from the airport to the ambassador's residence with Lewis, we listened as the five P.M. news on Israel Radio reported McFarlane's arrival in Israel for strategic cooperation talks. Shaking his head in frustration, Lewis said to Bud, "Welcome to the land of Arik Sharon. The only things that stay secret in Israel these days are what Arik wants to keep secret. He needs to point to your visit to demonstrate that the MOU [memorandum of understanding] is going to yield tangible results." McFarlane shrugged it off, commenting that "as long as the sensitive political subjects don't leak, it is irrelevant whether the fact of my visit is reported. I understand Sharon's stake in this process and his need to move forward promptly."

The following morning, McFarlane, Lewis and I drove to Jerusalem to begin two days of discussions with Dave Kimche and Hanon Bar-On, the deputy director general of the Ministry of Foreign Affairs (MFA). Separate meetings would be held with Sharon. McFarlane opened the meeting in Kimche's office at the MFA by acknowledging that considerable progress had been achieved to institutionalize military-to-military cooperation between the United States and Israel. Emphasizing that the DOD remained opposed, he reassured the Israelis that president Reagan was committed to cooperation and had made a decision that was being implemented. Reflecting the ongoing struggle over this subject between Weinberger and Haig, McFarlane emphasized that the impetus for what had been achieved had come from Haig, and that State would continue to reinforce the process. He told them that although the military-to-military talks would properly be shifting to other channels, Haig wanted the channel through McFarlane to continue in order to monitor the progress being made, while ensuring that each country's priorities received adequate attention. Kimche replied that he and Sharon were trying very hard to devise a means for the MOD and MFA to cooperate in order for there to be a smooth implementation of the MOU. Showing a healthy skepticism, Bar-On interjected there was no such word as "coordination" when it came to the Israeli bureaucracy.

Turning to the peace process, McFarlane expressed Washington's puzzlement over Israel's approach to the Palestinian autonomy negotiations. Acknowledging that the peace process was not the administration's top priority, progress remained an important objective of the United States. Haig wanted McFarlane to discuss peace process ideas on a preliminary basis to avoid misunderstandings when proposals were formally presented. The Israelis agreed that it would be a good idea to consider new ideas for the peace process quietly and outside normal channels, especially given the penchant for leaks in Jerusalem and Washington.

McFarlane went on to deliver a lengthy presentation on Washington's view of how the relationship had been sidetracked since the bombing of Osirak. After the bombing, the United States found itself compelled to cooperate politically with the Iraqis at the United Nations. The Israeli bombing of Beirut made it clear that Israel was not fully considering U.S. interests and the possible negative effects for Washington of Israeli unilateral action. McFarlane noted that he thought he had been understood during his meetings in mid-July, but it seemed that while the Israelis understood, they did not agree. McFarlane said that while the United States did not expect Israel necessarily to consult before operations were conducted, the administration certainly expected Israel to take into account American interests before decisions were implemented.

McFarlane pursued this theme by turning to the sensitive subject of the sale of AWACS aircraft to Saudi Arabia and the future of strategic cooperation. Describing the safeguards on the AWACS planes that would reduce the possibility of their being used to threaten Israel—including a proscription on the transfer of information to other countries in the region, geographic limitations that they not be deployed outside of Saudi Arabia and technical limitations related to the supply of critical components—McFarlane argued that other countries would sell more dangerous aircraft to Saudi Arabia, without any controls, if the sale didn't go through. Washington was growing quite weary of Jerusalem's failure to consider either the importance of Saudi Arabia to the United States or the extent to which Israeli interests were being taken into account by a sympathetic Reagan administration. He warned the Israelis of the potential negative and long-lasting effects on the bilateral relationship if the AWACS aircraft sale was defeated, since the administration was expending such extensive political capital to see it through.

The Israelis quietly listened to McFarlane's presentation and the not-too-subtle message regarding the future of strategic cooperation and the AWACS sale to Saudi Arabia. After a moment's reflection, Kimche asked the Americans to try to understand how Israel's security prism dominates the nation's politics and decision-making. Basing his explanation on the excessive legalism for which Israel is known, he emphasized the shared interest of blocking the Soviet advance in the region. Nevertheless, for Israel, regional threats sometimes outweigh global threats. Security overshadows all Israeli policies and the moment that AWACS planes were defined as a possible threat to Israel's security, Begin had no choice but to oppose the sale.

Begin understood that Reagan and his advisors felt betrayed and believed he had lobbied the Congress after promising not to, but Begin was convinced that he abided by his agreement to the letter. On Capitol Hill, he didn't say not to vote for the sale, but only that he could not say that the AWACS aircraft do not pose a security problem for Israel when it was obvious that they can pose a threat. Ambassador Bandar bin Sultan of Saudi Arabia (Prince Bandar) was actively lobbying on behalf of the sale, while the Israeli embassy in Washington was taking no role in the matter. The Israelis expressed their hope that, whatever the outcome of the debate, it would not damage strategic cooperation. Describing in further detail the domestic problems that this struggle was causing Begin, Kimche and Lewis described how opposition Labor leader Shimon Peres and others, such as former ambassador to the United States Simcha Dinitz, were accusing Begin of selling out the security of Israel by not waging an even more intense fight against the sale.

Turning to Lebanon, the Israelis believed that the IDF was on the verge of finishing off the PLO in Lebanon, but had stopped because of broader considerations. The United States wanted to establish and maintain a cease-fire in Lebanon, yet this would give the PLO the opportunity to strike at Israel on all other fronts aside from Lebanon. McFarlane acknowledged the dilemma of the evolving situation on the Lebanese border. He said that Washington's first priority was security for the northern border of Israel and stability in southern Lebanon. He emphasized Washington's belief that King Fahd of Saudi Arabia was working to minimize Palestinian violence against Israeli interests in order to sustain the cease-fire on the border. But neither the United States nor Saudi Arabia was sanguine about the prospects for an end to the violence. This contributed to Washington's ongoing efforts to devise a phased plan that would begin by stabilizing the situation on the Lebanese border before turning to the more complex problems in central Lebanon.

Sensing an opportunity to advance Israel's agenda for Lebanon, the Israelis suggested that the United States and Israel begin to cooperate to prevent a takeover of Lebanon by negative elements. They noted the close relationship between Beshir Gemayel and Israel. Israel wanted to work with him to improve the situation in Lebanon, pointing out that

Beshir was cultivating moderate Moslem leaders, including Druze leader Walid Jumblatt. Lewis interjected that Washington fundamentally disagreed with Israel's view that the Phalangists could become one with the central government, though he didn't doubt that Beshir or the government of Israel would like to see this come about. McFarlane ended the discussion by agreeing to ask Haig whether he wanted Lebanon to become a subject of the back-channel strategic dialogue or leave it to the efforts of Habib and Morris Draper.

The Israelis' purpose in raising the future of Lebanon was unambiguous. Israel was keen to work with the United States to ensure that its security interests along the Lebanese border were protected, and was ready to make compromises. But if the United States could not devise and implement a plan that would improve the long-term stability of Lebanon as well as the near-term security situation, Israel would act on its own, through its Lebanese friends and allies. Moreover, they made it perfectly clear that for reasons of domestic politics as well as daily security considerations, PLO operations against Israeli targets outside of the northern border of Israel would not be tolerated indefinitely.

Given the widely divergent attitudes in the national security bureaucracy in Washington over the relative importance of Lebanon and the role Saudi Arabia was playing, working with Habib and Draper in trying to maintain a PLO-Israel cease-fire, McFarlane did not need a crystal ball to recognize the political-military hornet's nest that Lebanon was fast becoming. Having delivered the core message, which was the fundamental importance the U.S. government attached to the consequences of unilateral Israeli actions on U.S. interests and the future of strategic cooperation, the rest of the discussions focused on Afghanistan, nuclear proliferation in Pakistan, Iraq and Libya, the spread of Soviet influence and threats to conservative states by the tripartite alliance, the growing boldness of Qadhafi and the prospects for change in Iran. The discussions of AWACS aircraft and Lebanon, however, illustrated the inherent contradictions between Israeli and U.S. regional interests.

Israel acknowledged that Pakistan had become a front-line state against the Soviet Union in the Gulf but reiterated their concern that Zia was determined to develop a nuclear weapon. Kimche stated that Pakistan was negotiating with China to conduct a secret test at a Chinese site in order to avoid detection by India or the West. Growing Libyan assertiveness throughout Africa, coupled with determined efforts to develop nuclear weapons capability, provided another cause for mutual concern between Israel and the United States. Niger, Gabon, Ivory Coast, Upper

Volta (now Burkina Faso), Mauritania, Morocco, Somalia and Togo were all targets of Qadhafi's subversive designs. But what most concerned Jerusalem was Qadhafi's determination to assume the leadership of the Organization of African Unity (OAU). He was willing to pay any price necessary to ensure that the OAU summit convened in Tripoli, Libya. In such circumstances, Qadhafi would not only assume personal leadership of the OAU, but would be able to appoint several key bureaucrats, extending Libyan influence throughout the OAU bureaucracy. Mentioning that Kenneth Adelman, deputy to ambassador to the U.N. Jeane Kirkpatrick, had raised Washington's interest in renewed African-Israeli ties during a recent African trip, McFarlane proposed to discuss the OAU matter with Assistant Secretary of State for African Affairs Chester Crocker upon his return to Washington. McFarlane suggested focusing systematically on the dangers posed by Qadhafi as well as the general subject of U.S. diplomatic support with African countries considering the renewal of relations with Israel. McFarlane saw numerous opportunities for Israel to dispatch doctors, agricultural development experts, educators, and other professionals to Africa and Central America who might be able to enhance the development of many Third World countries. He saw Israeli expertise, in some instances, competing favorably with Cuban expertise, thereby helping to roll back the spread of Soviet influence through Moscow's Cuban surrogates. The more difficult issue would be to arrange for U.S. financing of such Israeli activities.

McFarlane also briefed on the covert U.S. support for the Chadian resistance against the Libyan occupation of Chad. Washington was disappointed by the lack of French cooperation in Chad despite Paris's legacy as the colonial power. Paris simply refused to provide any support for opponents to Qadhafi. Despite Libya's alignment with Moscow, the shootdown in the Gulf of Sidra demonstrated that the Soviet Union would be very reticent about overt intervention on behalf of Libya. On the other hand, there was concern in the national security bureaucracy that Moscow would have to intervene if it appeared that Washington was acting openly to subvert Qadhafi.

Turning to Iran, McFarlane asked for Israel's assessment of the internal situation. The Israelis believed Iran was growing increasingly less stable as the war dragged on and the economic conditions deteriorated. It appeared that the Tudeh party (the Communist party of Iran) was trying to enhance its influence and position itself to play a more active role. Despite the Tudeh party's maneuvering, however, Moscow was trying to cultivate Tehran while distancing itself from Saddam Hussein.

In these circumstances, Israel perceived opportunities for helping re-store the U.S. position in Iran by working with elements in the Iranian military. The Israelis wanted to know why the United States refused Israeli requests to sell Iran military equipment. McFarlane explained that the United States essentially shared Israel's perspective on the internal situation in Iran as well as the deadlock in the war with Iraq and the significance of Soviet overtures. He refused to amplify, however, on the U.S. policy against the sale of military goods to Tehran but agreed that it was in the interest of both sides to restore Western influence in Iran and reduce hostility.

At the conclusion of six hours of talks, we left Jerusalem and drove to Beersheba, where Sharon was hosting a dinner at his Negev desert ranch in honor of the visiting commander in chief of the Sixth Fleet. The occasion represented the first official dinner for Sharon in his capacity as minister of defense, and it was clear that he relished the opportunity to indulge in a lecture on strategy to the American admiral and McFarlane, as well as the Israeli generals and admirals in attendance (IDF chief of staff General Rafael Eitan, Air Force chief Amos Lapidot and chief of naval operations Zeev Almog).

Although little of substance was discussed that night, the dinner pro-vided my first opportunity to meet Sharon and assess just how difficult it was going to be for the U.S. defense establishment to work with him. Sharon complimented the U.S. Navy for its shoot-down over the Gulf of Sidra and the determination of Washington to stand up to the Soviets in the Gulf. With barely a pause, however, he then launched into a lengthy attack on the AWACS aircraft sale, claiming that Saudi Arabia was fast becoming one of the most dangerous threats to Israel. He bombastically insisted that regardless of what the Saudis might say, Riyadh would never permit the United States to project power through Saudi Arabia into the Gulf. Describing Israel as the Western beachhead in a sea of radicals, reactionaries and Soviet-surrogates, Sharon warned that the only way to advance American interests was to rely on Israel. McFarlane, Lewis, William Brown (then DCM in Israel) and everyone else listened impas-sively to Sharon's tirade, convinced, I suspect, that little would be gained by challenging him. Sharon wanted to make sure that Haig's emissary would not be surprised by the next day's meeting at the MOD. He also wanted to make sure that no Israeli thought he would be any less willing to confront the Americans now that he was minister of defense than he had during the Israeli election campaign.

As the dinner ended and we bade Sharon farewell, I shook his hand firmly, looked him in the eye and told him, in the best Hebrew I could muster, that he would be well advised to listen to what McFarlane had to say and not just deliver his vision of strategic cooperation or Israel's place in the Middle East. Taken aback that I spoke Hebrew and had criticized his presumptuous attitude toward the United States, Sharon was momentarily speechless. Looking back at me, he grinned and replied, "I will listen if McFarlane has anything to say."

Early the next morning, McFarlane, Lewis and I met with Sharon, Kimche, Tamir, Eitan, Almog and several other MOD advisors to address next steps in the military-to-military cooperation process. Picking up on the prior evening's toast, Sharon wasted no time in returning to the theme that Israel was the only country that possessed the ability and will to counter further Soviet military advances toward the Gulf.

With a briefing map of the region posted on an easel behind his desk, Sharon resumed his lecture by explaining that U.S. strategy was inadequate for coping with the challenge. Pointing to a range of possible Soviet invasion routes into the Gulf through Iran, Iraq and Pakistan, he argued that the Soviets would advance along at least two main axes of attack directly into the Gulf or through Iraq into Syria and then south through Jordan to Saudi Arabia. Once the Soviets successfully intervened directly to ensure the survival of their proxies, as in Afghanistan, they were emboldened to do the same thing elsewhere in the Middle East. All Moscow needed was an invitation from its proxy and the United States would not be able to count on the support of any of the Arab regimes to halt further Soviet advances. Throughout this lecture, McFarlane sat stone still, his lips pursed tight as he stared at Sharon, patiently waiting for him to finish, while Lewis meditated over his ever present cigar.

Broadening the scope of his presentation and arrogantly indifferent to the sensibilities of his audience, Sharon argued that it was vital for the United States and Israel to tackle many problems together. But if political solutions could not be found, he warned, Israel would have to deal with problems, like the missiles in Lebanon, in a way that would embarrass the United States. Displaying another briefing board, which depicted the loss of IAF aerial reconnaissance coverage of Lebanon and Syria that resulted from the Syrian deployment of SAM-6 missiles in Lebanon, Sharon said Israel would alter this situation itself unless a way could be found to remove the missiles. If Habib was unable to convince Assad, Sharon suggested that perhaps the United States could provide Israel with satellite photography in real time, thereby eliminating aerial reconnaissance missions. He warned that Israel would answer any nuclear threat with preemption.

At the conclusion of Sharon's soliloquy, McFarlane replied by reviewing the principles upon which the U.S. strategy for the Gulf was based. McFarlane agreed that Arab states would not confront the Soviet Union without U.S. assistance, which is why the United States was trying to improve the military capabilities of regional states to defend themselves while enhancing America's ability to deploy its own forces quickly to deter further aggression. He acknowledged Israel's capabilities with regard to projecting power but disagreed that Israel could do so effectively in the Persian Gulf. He pointed out that were the United States to base its strategy on bilateral U.S.-Israeli operations, it would severely increase regional instability by exacerbating Arab and Soviet threats. He reiterated the security commitment to Israel but emphasized that the United States had Arab friends and vital interests which would not be ignored or subordinated to a strategy that, at least for the near term, was sure to be counterproductive. He noted the importance of Israeli geography and air power and stated it would be an important place to begin strategic cooperation. The United States hoped that over time, other forms of cooperation would evolve as the region became more stable and perceptions evolved.

Sharon could barely contain himself during McFarlane's presentation. With his barrel chest and huge gut almost bursting out of his shirt, Sharon leaned over his desk and loudly insisted that in order for Israel to cooperate militarily with the United States, the long reach of the IDF, including into the Persian Gulf, must be the cornerstone of cooperation.

To counter the negative impression Sharon was deliberately imparting and to emphasize that reach wasn't necessarily limited to the Gulf, Admiral Almog quickly interjected that the Israeli Navy was ready to help the United States in the Mediterranean. Sharon scowled at Almog, clearly displeased at his efforts to smooth the situation as the Israeli CNO went on to illustrate how the Israeli Navy could support the United States in the Mediterranean with a long reach, despite Sharon's more grandiose aspirations.

The meeting concluded after two hours, with both sides summing up by acknowledging the gap in goals and expectations. Sharon had put on a good show, blustering about Israeli power and U.S. timidity one moment, the next acting as the deferential politician. It was clear to our team that he would not stop pushing as hard as he possibly could to get the United States to agree with him. Sharon's goal of making Israel's long reach an integral part of the U.S. strategy for the Gulf typified his tendency to overreach in pursuit of his goals. McFarlane, however, had been polite but unambiguous: there was simply no way that the United States was buying into Sharon's strategic concepts.

But perhaps of even greater political significance for the brief time that Sharon would serve as Israel's minister of defense, he had demonstrated that he was not awed by America's potential power. On the contrary, he was convinced that he knew best how to confront the United States in a way that would maximize his domestic power base among the Israeli electorate while squeezing the United States for every diplomatic, military and intelligence advantage possible. No one spoke as we drove to the ambassador's residence in Herzliyya, this round of the strategic dialogue now complete.

Bud and I returned to Washington the following day. He was satisfied with the trip, despite Sharon. In less than a week, he had promoted the concept of strategic cooperation with the leadership of Saudi Arabia, India, Egypt and Israel. While considerable ground remained to be covered, the start of a new U.S. relationship with India seemed within reach, which would hopefully lead to a reduction in Indo-Pakistani tensions and a concomitant enhancement of Pakistan's front-line deterrent to Soviet aggression in Pakistan. In Egypt, Sadat appeared more confident than at any time in 1981, looking forward to Egypt's completion of the peaceful recovery of Sinai while steeling himself for a confrontation with Libya's Qadhafi. The Saudis, having adopted a public diplomatic role in facilitating a reduction of tensions between Israel and Syria and a cease-fire between Israel and the PLO in Lebanon, had now enunciated a peace plan that represented a major step toward Arab recognition of Israel. And while fundamental disagreements over the scope and pace of strategic cooperation still required considerable clarification, Washington and Jerusalem appeared closer than ever to implementing military cooperation, and at the same time a discreet channel for creative thinking and sensitive communications had been established.

Sadat Is Assassinated

Two weeks later, on October 6, President Sadat was assassinated in the suburbs of Cairo by Moslem fundamentalists during a military parade commemorating the anniversary of the October 1973 War. Uncertain over the nature and extent of the conspiracy, U.S. policymakers grappled with the prospects of major changes in the direction of Egyptian policy regarding the Soviet Union and Israel. In contrast to the circumstances surrounding the fall of the shah of Iran, the United States reacted to the death of Sadat with political and military vigor, in an effort to deter Libya and the Soviet Union from successfully exploiting the political situation in Egypt and the strategic setback to Washington's regional plans. U.S. naval forces were put on alert, as Sixth Fleet warships steamed into the eastern Mediterranean; AWACS aircraft were deployed to monitor the Egyptian-Libyan border; and additional military and economic assistance was immediately provided to Egypt and Sudan.

Barely hiding their glee over Sadat's assassination, the Soviets viewed his death as a potentially mortal blow to Reagan's notions of an anti-Soviet strategic consensus. Under Sadat, Egypt had become the most vocal Arab opponent of Moscow: publicly supporting the Afghan rebels; confronting the radical, pro-Soviet axis of Ethiopia, Libya and the PDRY; permitting U.S. troops to act as the centerpiece of the Sinai's MFO; providing the U.S. Army with access rights to the Red Sea port of Ras Banas (including Egypt's oral agreement to develop the facility into the much-needed rear staging area for forces that could be quickly deployed to Saudi Arabia); and agreeing, in principle, to permit U.S. nuclear-powered warships to transit the Suez Canal, thereby significantly enhancing the speed with which the United States could deploy carrier battle groups to the Indian Ocean. Egypt's peace with Israel and its commitment to support U.S. efforts to roll back the Soviet Union in the Middle East had made Egypt the cornerstone of Washington's regional strategy. With the Soviets on the march and militant Islamic fundamentalism spreading through the Middle East, the challenge to American policy represented by Sadat's assassination could not have been greater.

Leading a delegation comprised of former presidents Nixon, Ford and Carter, Haig departed for Cairo on the eighth of October. McFarlane was part of the U.S. delegation to the funeral. He had advised me that I would also travel to Cairo and then continue on with him for additional meetings in the Middle East or Europe. However, on the morning of the 7th, McFarlane found out that an important document for which he was responsible would require one more day to finish. Haig was very anxious to review the paper personally and was seriously displeased to learn that it was further delayed. In the circumstances, McFarlane instructed me to delay my departure in order to hand-carry the paper to him in Cairo.

The following day, carrying special papers designating me as a diplomatic courier, I flew to New York to catch a flight to Rome. There was a six-hour layover in Rome prior to my connection to Cairo. I had to pass through several rings of policemen, heavily armed soldiers, guard dogs, metal detectors and X-ray machines, finally arriving at the gate where a detail of special Italian police were inspecting every hand-carry item of baggage. Tensions were high in the gate area, and passengers and airport officials alike moved about nervously in the stifling airport heat, clearly worried about flying into Cairo on the day that Sadat was buried. When I put my briefcase up on the table, I showed the Italian inspector my diplomatic passport and courier papers. He ignored the documents and immediately tried to open my locked briefcase. I pointed to the diplomatic documents, but he brushed them away, obviously under explicit instructions to search everything. I refused to unlock the briefcase and he started to shout at me in Italian. A more senior inspector stepped over who also tried to open my briefcase. As I waved my diplomatic passport and the official courier papers in his face, he finally stopped for a moment to look at them. He set them down and indicated that he did not speak English. He then told me in Italian, according to the impatient Italian woman standing next to me, that if I wanted to get on the plane to Cairo I had thirty seconds to open the bag or he would have to take me to see his boss. Gambling that he would be satisfied by the diplomatic seals, I opened the bag and displayed the contents. He lifted up the gray fabric diplomatic pouch, pulled out scissors and clipped the seals before I could stop him. He reached in and pulled out the papers, a red, TOP SECRET cover page on top, quickly thumbed through them and returned them to the bag. "Why big deal?" he asked. With sweat pouring down my face, I leaned across the inspection table, took back the papers, the pouch and my briefcase and said emphatically, "No big deal, okay?" Shaking his head and mumbling something in Italian which made the woman next to me blush, he finally waved me through.

I arrived in Cairo around six in the evening; Haig and McFarlane were closeted with other foreign delegations in Haig's suite, taking advantage of an impromptu summit to discuss numerous issues. About an hour or so later, I handed over the document. Departing from Cairo on the morning of October 11, McFarlane, Bing West, NSC staff member Geoffrey Kemp, and I traveled to Sudan to meet with Vice President Ali Magid of Sudan. Vice Admiral Thomas Bigley of the JCS arrived separately in Khartoum. Jaafar Nimeiri, the Sudanese president, had met with Haig in Cairo and was staying in Egypt for an indefinite period, in part out of concern for his own security in the face of explicit Libyan threats, in addition to wanting a separate meeting to work out the details of the increased assistance that Haig had offered. A high-level visit to Khartoum headed by McFarlane would visibly demonstrate the U.S. interest in Sudan while providing an opportunity to turn rhetoric into action.

In recent weeks, Qadhafi's forces had grown increasingly bold, as the frequency of counterinsurgency air strikes had intensified. As a result of the covert support being supplied to the Chadian rebels by the United States and Egypt, several Libyan planes, primarily light, propeller-driven aircraft, had been shot down by Redeye missiles. The political and economic outlook for Sudan, apart from Libya, was grim.

Ali Magid wasted no time the following morning to convey a sense of dramatic urgency to McFarlane. Emphasizing the desire of Sudan to strengthen and enhance its relations with the United States, Magid focused his attention on what he described as the Libyan absorption of Chad. Describing the airfields, roads and military installations that the Libyan Army had under construction, with the assistance of East German advisors, Sudan believed an assault from Libya was imminent. While the Sudanese had expected Libyan support for subversion in Sudan and the infiltration of dissident Sudanese, the bombing of Sudanese villages, numerous cross-border raids in the past month and the buildup of facilities to support regular forces near the border had convinced the Sudanese government that the threat would be a conventional military attack.

Magid requested U.S. assistance. First and foremost, Sudan wanted air-defense systems to stop the Libyan air raids. Radars and fighter aircraft were at the top of the list, but they also wanted high-speed coastal patrol craft, the upgrading of forward facilities to support counterstrikes against Libyan forces in Chad, and new ground forces equipment for the army. It was imperative that the central government stop these attacks in order to protect its people while demonstrating the value of its relationship with the United States. Qadhafi's threat was obviously military, but his constant rhetorical attacks on the Sudanese as lackeys of the United States and traitors to the Arab cause was starting to succeed in fomenting unrest. Dissidents infiltrating from Chad were being trained in Libya to perpetrate terrorism through bombings and assassinations in order to destabilize the Sudan and create a loss of confidence in the government. The Sudanese told McFarlane that now that Sadat was dead, Qadhafi was ready to pay $1 billion to overthrow Nimeiri.

Secondly, Sudan desperately needed economic assistance. Although Sudan hoped to receive more aid directly from the United States and relief from the International Monetary Fund (IMF) for economic reforms, Magid made a special plea for the United States to convince Saudi Arabia to fulfill its aid commitments. The Saudi money was essential for the purchase of badly needed spare parts, British airplanes and the repair of older Russian equipment. He warned that if the central government ordered the price hikes the IMF was demanding, the people would riot and Qadhafi would offer them cash.

McFarlane answered the Sudanese requests by reiterating the U.S. determination to confront Qadhafi and the Soviet Union in order to ensure that Sudan did not succumb to their pressures. He, West and Bigley then proceeded to outline the increased aid levels, expedited deliveries of military hardware and regional exercise activity that the United States was prepared to undertake to bolster Sudan's security. Fiscal year 1982 military aid would increase from $30 million to $100 million, while economic assistance would total $115 million. Radars, tanks and tank transporters, howitzers, F-5 aircraft, and ammunition and ground-support equipment would start being delivered immediately. McFarlane also agreed to discuss the role of Saudi Arabia in supporting the economic and security needs of Sudan in order to try to convince Riyadh to fulfill its commitments. With regard to military exercises, the United States was ready to deploy Special Forces soldiers to Sudan to conduct exercises with Egyptian and Sudanese Special Forces units.

Magid displayed his satisfaction at the U.S. proposals, even though he repeated a request for higher levels of grant aid as opposed to the credits the United States had offered. McFarlane then brought up a potential problem. The United States had reason to suspect that Sudan might transfer U.S.-supplied tanks to Iraq. He noted that such an action would cause problems in the relationship. Disturbed by McFarlane's clear but informal demarche, Magid denied any possibility that such an action might occur. Following the conclusion of a long meeting and lunch, the delegation went directly to the airport to begin the return trip to the United States.

Immediately upon our return, McFarlane turned his attention to the sale of AWACS aircraft to Saudi Arabia. Coordinating the lobbying activities of the White House, State Department and Pentagon, McFarlane worked tirelessly to convince undecided senators that the sale of the aircraft was essential to the success of President Reagan's policy. Fearing a resurgence in Middle East turmoil in the wake of the Sadat assassination, fewer senators were prepared to challenge the president on an issue on which Reagan had personally staked so much. Making numerous calls himself, McFarlane lobbied for the sale in strategic, regional and political terms. Owing to his experience with the Senate Armed Services Committee, McFarlane was well respected on Capitol Hill. Although the outcome

was a cliffhanger until it was finally voted on on October 30, the administration prevailed by a vote of 52 to 48.

Despite Reagan's anger over Begin's continued vocal opposition to the
sale of the AWACS aircraft, once the Senate failed to block the sale,
Weinberger, prodded by Haig, moved forward to complete the negotiation
of a MOU on strategic cooperation between the United States and Israel.
In a fairly petty effort to reduce the significance of the MOU, however,
Weinberger had insisted that it be signed without ceremony and well
outside the formal confines of the Pentagon. The MOU was signed at
a bizarre reception for Sharon hosted by Weinberger at the National
Geographic Society headquarters building in Washington, D.C., on November 30, 1981. Clearly at pains to downplay the MOU's military
significance, and reiterating that it was oriented only toward the Soviet
threat to the Middle East, Weinberger refused to permit the media to
attend or photograph the event, and the Defense Department did not
issue the standard press release announcing it had been signed.

Although the MOU contained none of Sharon's grandiose designs, it
did provide a framework for the creation of military-to-military committees for planning joint exercises, the pre-positioning of military matériel
in Israel, access to Israeli ports for the U.S. Navy, U.S. support for the
manufacture of the Israeli-designed LAVI fighter aircraft, increased U.S.
military assistance and the agreement to negotiate a free-trade agreement
between the United States and Israel. While Sharon was disappointed
with the limited scope of the MOU, Begin viewed the document as a
major policy accomplishment, codifying shared strategic interests without
infringing on Israel's freedom to maneuver.

As important as the MOU was to the government of Israel, throughout
the month of November the attention of the U.S. government was focused
on the situation in Poland, where the Soviet Union was marshaling the
Red Army to intimidate the Polish government to crush the latest Solidarity uprising. President Assad of Syria, meanwhile, decried the MOU as
an aggressive Israeli act and publicly stated that Syria would never make
peace with Israel. Reinforced emotionally by the MOU, Begin, who was
recovering from a broken hip, used Assad's statement as a pretext to call
for the rapid extension of Israeli law to the occupied Golan Heights, an
act regarded by the rest of the world as an illegal annexation.

Herein lay the dilemma: From Washington's point of view, this was
exactly the type of unilateral act Israel was no longer supposed to undertake. For Begin, there was no obligation to consult with Washington
about political actions taken within Israel, regardless of the potential

political ramifications for the United States. The lack of prior consultation and the seeming disregard for the effect of such an action on U.S. interests in the Arab world, particularly coming immediately on the heels of the conclusion of the MOU, led Reagan, at the prodding of his advisors, to suspend its implementation. Weinberger, keen to distance himself from Sharon as much and as quickly as possible, stated that the Israeli action was a clear violation of U.N. Security Council resolutions as well as the Camp David Accords.

Begin, confounded by this unexpected U.S. response, summoned Lewis to Jerusalem, where he denounced the action of the United States. According to Lewis, Begin rhetorically asked whether Israel was a vassal state or a banana republic. Begin seemed genuinely unable to understand how his unilateral actions in Lebanon, Iraq or in the Golan Heights would undermine the doctrine upon which he based his concept of U.S.-Israeli strategic cooperation. Because the U.S. government could not convince the Arab world that Israeli actions were conducted independently, Washington found itself driven away from Israel and toward the Arabs as a direct result of Begin's policies.

Throughout October and into November, reports of spreading Libyan subversion in Africa, the Middle East and Europe grew in frequency and scope. These reports reflected the pattern of behavior that Qadhafi had pursued for some years, ranging from his murder of Libyan dissidents and his provision of military training facilities, equipment and money to international terrorists, to his buildup of advanced Soviet weaponry and his invasion of Chad. Following the August shoot-down in the Gulf of Sidra, Qadhafi had publicly intensified his overt confrontation with the United States, correctly noting that U.S. support for Egypt and Sudan was in large measure directed at Libya.

Indeed, he vowed to murder Reagan to retaliate for the humiliation suffered by his air force. Despite Qadhafi's conviction that U.S. policy aimed to bring about his downfall, the central goal of American policy toward Libya was to change his behavior, *not* get rid of him. While no one in Washington would have been unhappy were Qadhafi to be removed from power, to my knowledge the U.S. government did not engage in any type of activity, overt or covert, directly aimed at achieving that result. Libyan dissidents received some assistance from the CIA, but they lacked the strength to make a difference in the Libyan internal situation.

However, in mid-November, tensions in U.S.-Libyan relations dramatically escalated, as reports of varying degrees of reliability suggested that Qadhafi was not only plotting to assassinate President Reagan and

Cabinet officials, but that Libyan operatives had already penetrated the United States, Mexico and Canada. Viewing these reports as a direct threat to the United States as well as a personal threat to the president, Haig directed McFarlane to chair an interagency working group to devise a set of policy options that would convince Qadhafi to back down or risk ever-increasing international isolation, economic deprivation and potentially a direct military confrontation with the United States.

By the beginning of December, an interagency decision memorandum to the president had been completed and signed by Haig, Weinberger and Casey. Following a November National Security Council meeting in the White House, the president approved a package of near- and long-term measures to isolate Qadhafi; banned the export of U.S. goods to Libya and the importation of Libyan oil, the latter move dramatically reducing Qadhafi's principal source of hard currency; and ordered the preparation of a set of military options, ranging from more air and sea challenges in the Gulf of Sidra to large-scale strikes against Libyan military and economic targets. Turning up the heat on December 9, Deputy Secretary of State Judge William P. Clark urged all Americans to leave Libya as soon as possible. To begin a process that would start with economic sanctions but which might escalate to military action, Clark also announced that U.S. passports were invalidated for travel to Libya. The administration wanted to get the two thousand or so Americans out of Libya as fast as possible. The specter of the Iranian hostage crisis loomed large over every consideration of military action.

Against this backdrop, Qadhafi began a limited withdrawal of his army from Chad. He also stopped flying cross-border air strikes into Sudan. While no assassination attempts were conducted against U.S. officials in Washington, there were numerous reports that terrorist operations were in the works. Having earlier broken relations with Libya in June, declaring Libya's diplomats at its People's Bureau personae non gratae, another major threshold was crossed in mid-December 1981. These important steps paved the way for the military confrontation with Libya in 1986.

At the end of December 1981, I got away from Washington for a week of vacation in the Caribbean. I managed to avoid reading a newspaper the entire time I was away. I was, therefore, quite shocked upon my return to Washington to learn that McFarlane had been appointed as the new deputy national security advisor. Following the resignation of Richard Allen as Reagan's first NSC advisor, Judge Clark was called to the White House to assume that post. Clark had insisted that McFarlane join him as the deputy NSC advisor. I was not able to see McFarlane for several days after my return. When we finally met in early January, he offered me a job on the staff of the National Security Council. Whether the job would be as a special assistant to him or a member of the Middle East group remained to be determined. Stunned by my incredible good fortune at the age of twenty-six, I told him I would be more than pleased to take either job.

CHAPTER 7

THE NATIONAL SECURITY COUNCIL

———— ◆•◆ ————

More in Sorrow Than in Anger

McFarlane wanted me to be his special assistant, but Judge Clark decided that all the members of the NSC staff were essentially McFarlane's assistants and assigned me as a member of the Near East and South Asia Directorate. I had expected the three months of waiting at State to pass slowly, but events in Lebanon and a secret trip to London with Ambassador-at-Large Vernon Walters ensured that I had no time to cool my heels. McFarlane had received a call from Dave Kimche congratulating him on his appointment as Deputy NSC Advisor and inquiring about the future of the back-channel, strategic dialogue.

Since the suspension of the MOU, there had been no communication between the two men and Kimche was keen to find out whether the channel would remain open. McFarlane informed Kimche that responsibility for the channel would be turned over to Under Secretary of State–Designate Lawrence Eagleburger. However, inasmuch as Eagleburger would be unavailable for discussions for several months, McFarlane sent Walters and me to meet with Kimche to leave the dialogue in an orderly fashion.

Tensions in Lebanon seemed to rise on a daily basis, as Sharon and Eitan met semisecretly with Beshir Gemayel and the IDF mobilized armor forces and moved them back and forth from Israel's northern borders. Dennis Ross, Richard Haas and I met regularly to assess what would trigger the inevitable Israeli invasion of Lebanon and whether there might be some as-yet undiscovered means of preventing such a development. The upcoming dialogue with Kimche offered an opportunity to probe for a clear indication of Israeli intentions as well as to communicate our continuing interest in finding a way to prevent the cease-fire from collapsing as a broader diplomatic initiative for Lebanon was developed. Walters, who knew Kimche from his past life in the intelligence community, was more than willing to conduct the dialogue on behalf of McFarlane. At Walters's request, I arranged for the meeting to be held in mid-January 1982 at the U.S. embassy in London.

The State Department bureaucracy and the CIA prepared several position papers which Walters was to provide Kimche on such issues as the Libyan nuclear program; an assessment of the prospects for a change in Libyan behavior following the recent escalation in tensions; an evaluation of changes in the officer corps of the Iranian military; and an agenda for U.S. diplomatic initiatives in sub-Saharan Africa. I was also directed to communicate McFarlane's disappointment over the Israeli annexation of the Golan Heights by pointedly noting that Israel seemed unwilling to consider U.S. interests in the strategic actions it was taking.

Unlike the sessions in Israel the past September, this meeting lacked the energy or excitement that had pervaded the last round, and can best be characterized in diplomatese as cordial but correct. The meeting commenced at ten P.M. in the ambassador's conference room. The embassy was deserted, but for the Marine Guards who looked out from their perch into the misty, cold night onto Grosvenor Square. Walters delivered a lengthy but perfunctory review of the prearranged agenda items, essentially reading the position papers prepared by the bureaucracy.

Kimche waited until Walters had finished his briefing and then asked about the status of the MOU. I sat quietly for thirty seconds before delivering McFarlane's message, "in sorrow not in anger," about the Golan Heights and the apparent unwillingness of Israel to behave toward the United States like an ally that considers the consequences of its actions on the interests of its friends. Making known my personal disappointment over the manner in which Menachem Begin seemed intent on riding roughshod over U.S. interests to satisfy his own political vanity, I expressed my wonder at whether the United States was in for more of the same with Israel in Lebanon given the heavy IDF exercise activity, the recent meetings between Sharon and Beshir Gemayel, and Israel's escalating rhetoric. I pointedly made no mention of the MOU.

Kimche acknowledged my statement, and asked me to advise McFarlane that he, Kimche, clearly understood the message on the prospects for strategic cooperation. With regard to Lebanon and the PLO, he recalled that Sharon had been very explicit last September about the strategic needs of Israel and the desire to find political solutions to the threats posed by the PLO and Syria in Lebanon. Kimche noted that Israel was trying to find a solution to many problems in Lebanon, and it might have to resort to military options to achieve its goals. The United States should know that its interests would be given careful consideration but reiterated that the administration should not be surprised if Israel resorted to military means if political efforts prove fruitless.

Although Kimche did no more than repeat points that had been made to a number of American officials over the past year, the message that came through was that the time for political solutions was running out. The PLO was skating on thin ice. One or two provocations, whether against Israel proper or Israeli targets outside of Israel, would undoubtedly trigger a major Israeli action into Lebanon with the goal of destroying the PLO. In addition to the destruction of the PLO, he made clear that Israel had a political agenda in Lebanon designed to end the instability that the PLO had helped to create and had subsequently exploited. Lebanese elections would take place in 1982, and Sharon and Kimche's contacts with Beshir indicated that he was their candidate. For Israel to back Beshir meant war with Syria. Sharon undoubtedly believed he could quickly win such a confrontation regardless of the prospects for U.S.-Soviet escalation. Whether the Soviets would help Syria in Lebanon was highly problematic. It was unlikely that an Israeli-Syrian war could be limited to the ground and airspace of Lebanon. Even with the Soviets bogged down in Afghanistan, it was doubtful they would stand idly by if Syria suffered losses inside its recognized borders and called on Moscow for assistance.

Kimche's framework left me convinced that the calculation had already been made that the Israeli Army could solve Israel's strategic problems in Lebanon more quickly and more thoroughly than American diplomacy. Kimche was unwilling to be drawn out any further on Israeli intentions toward Lebanon, and I dropped the subject. The session concluded around one A.M. and we all left the embassy together. A sleek blue sedan with diplomatic license plates immediately drove up and stopped in front of us. As Kimche got in the car, he turned back and expressed the hope that we could meet again soon without the cloud of the Golan Heights hanging over us. As his car pulled away, Walters turned to me and said, "Sounds like war to me. Do you think we can prevent it?" Shaking my head I asked, "Have you met Sharon? He wants war with the PLO and the Syrians. He is convinced he has all the answers."

Back in Washington two days later, I drafted a summary of the discussions for Walters to send to Haig. After briefing Ross and Haas, we all agreed that Kimche's message was crystal clear. Although we wanted to believe that the upcoming, scheduled completion of Israel's withdrawal from the Sinai would prevent the war from starting before the end of April, little else stood in the way of a major IDF invasion of southern Lebanon and an Israeli strike against the Syrian SAM sites.

Finally arriving at the NSC in late March 1982, I was confronted with my first policy surprise. Two weeks earlier, a notice had been issued in the U.S. government publication the *Commerce Business Daily* advising that Iraq had been removed from the list of countries supporting international terrorism. On the surface, I found this to be a bizarre development, inasmuch as the CIA and other government intelligence agencies were continuing to report that Iraq harbored some of the world's most notorious international terrorists. Abu Nidal and Abu Ibrahim, to name just two of the most well known figures, were based in Iraq and continued to receive extensive support as well as financial and military assistance from the Iraqis for training their agents and managing terrorist operations. Given my ongoing interest in Iraqi developments and determination to reveal the true face of Saddam Hussein to U.S. officials, I asked my colleagues on the NSC how this decision had been made. Incredibly, none of them knew a decision had been made to remove Iraq from the list of countries supporting terrorism and had no idea who had made this decision. It was not until some years later that I learned that McFarlane himself had no prior knowledge of the decision. Engaging in some educated speculation, he said that he had assumed that Clark, Haig and Casey probably made the decision based on something Casey might have learned during one of his many secret trips to the Middle East. Beyond that, he had no explanation.

Think Creatively

Following Sadat's assassination in October 1981, Egyptian pressure on the Reagan administration steadily intensified over the prospect that the government of Israel would renege on its commitment to complete the withdrawal of Israeli forces from the Sinai Peninsula as called for in the treaty of peace. A number of factors contributed to this Egyptian perception. The most notable domestic political difficulty arose from the Israeli government's need to vacate Yamit, an Israeli settlement in the Sinai. Many Yamit settlers refused to leave, creating the possibility of a violent confrontation between Israeli pioneers and the Israeli Army. This led some Israeli government officials to express their hopes for some sort of compromise from Cairo that would help defuse the crisis. In the months leading up to the scheduled April 26 withdrawal, President Hosni Mubarak consistently made clear that Cairo was not going to help Jerusalem with this problem. There was no ambiguity over the location of Yamit inside occupied Sinai. Mubarak was not about to make any concessions to Begin that Sadat had not made.

The second issue involved allegations made by Sharon over violations by the Egyptian military in the limited force zones. The peace treaty included an elaborate set of annexes that divided the Sinai into four zones with very explicit limitations on the numbers of troops and types of equipment that Egypt could deploy in each zone. Sharon's shrill claims exacerbated the ever-present Israeli concerns over the fundamental intentions of the Egyptian government toward Israel and its intent to honor the peace treaty. Following Sadat's death, many Israelis had begun to question the wisdom of the treaty, given the strong possibility that the relatively unknown new Egyptian leader Mubarak might sacrifice it in order to burnish his Arab credentials and strengthen his domestic position in Egypt.

The third issue involved the exact demarcation of the international boundary at approximately thirty different locations along the length of the border. However, one boundary dispute, at a remote Red Sea location known as Taba, proved to be particularly onerous. Israel's claim to the approximately one-hundred-meter stretch of beach five kilometers south of Eilat was challenged by Egypt. Nonetheless, Israel had granted an international development group the rights to use the land and construction of a Sonesta hotel had already begun.

Coupled with the deteriorating security situation along the Israeli border with Lebanon and Sharon's bellicose and confrontational political style, the government of Egypt had convinced itself that the government of Israel might well renege on its treaty commitments. Whether the Israeli prime minister had made this decision or not, we recognized that Begin did not trust Mubarak and that Israel was going to test Egypt with brinkmanship over Sinai. Little if any of the mutual trust between the two countries, trust that Sadat and Begin had developed during the early years of Camp David, remained. Moreover, as U.S.-Israeli relations chilled over the Golan Heights, the suspended MOU, and the intensification of tensions in Lebanon, Washington became increasingly convinced that a unilateral Israeli act would soon take place somewhere on the Egyptian front.

About the same time I was moving over to the NSC, I met my future wife, Gayle Radley, a government lawyer from California. Our courtship was shaped in many ways by events in the Middle East. As I was settling into my job, a major crisis was coming to a head in Lebanon. For nearly a year, Israeli-PLO hostilities had assumed the proportions of a war of attrition, with both sides intermittently raising the stakes and trying to find new ways to goad the other into combat. At the same time, Syria was digging in with its surface-to-air-missile network in the Bekáa Valley, hoping to deter Israeli air strikes but ready to fight Israel if necessary. By the beginning of April 1982, few Middle East specialists doubted that a major confrontation in Lebanon between the IDF, PLO and Syrian Army was imminent.

In a memo to then deputy NSC advisor McFarlane I reiterated that an Israeli invasion of Lebanon was inevitable. My conclusion was drawn from the meetings Walters and I had in London; from a briefing given to Sam Lewis by Sharon on his concept for an incursion into Lebanon; and a separate briefing given to Haig by Israeli director for military intelligence, Yehoshua Saguy. U.S. diplomatic strategies simply would not yield results quickly enough to satisfy Sharon. Moreover, there was growing evidence to suggest that radical Palestinian factions were trying to undermine Arafat by conducting terrorist operations outside of Lebanon or Israel in order to goad Sharon into launching his military campaign. Additionally, Beshir Gemayel could not conceivably win the presidency of Lebanon without Israeli intervention to neutralize Syria and strengthen the political position of the Lebanese Forces.

When McFarlane and I discussed the situation further, I criticized what I saw as overly sanguine State Department assessments of the looming crisis in Lebanon and the option that the State Department was promoting: namely, to send Philip Habib out to the region to try to walk the Israelis, Palestinians and Syrians back down the escalation ladder. I did not believe this would succeed in averting war. Moreover, as if this situation was not dangerous enough, the Iranian Army and Pasdaran forces had completed their rollback of the Iraqis from Iranian territory and were making preparations for an invasion of southern Iraq.

McFarlane directed me to intensify the interagency crisis preplanning effort in the hope that some new ideas could be developed that would help head off escalation in Lebanon and deter Iran from taking military action against Saudi Arabia, Kuwait or other Gulf states. He pressed me to think creatively and not to succumb to the bureaucratic inertia that was confounding American diplomacy in the Middle East. As I would come to learn, however, it was dangerous to think creatively about U.S. Middle East policy.

The Taba Shuffle

Three days later, Geoff Kemp returned from a senior staff meeting and asked me whether my diplomatic passport was current. He informed me that the president had decided that morning to dispatch Deputy Secretary of State Walter Stoessel to the Middle East to shuttle between Cairo and Jerusalem in order to resolve the political crisis over the now uncertain Israeli withdrawal from Sinai and the dispute over the one-hundred-meter strip of beach known as Taba. Stoessel had invited Judge Clark to include a member of the NSC staff on his diplomatic team and it was to be me.

The international situation had become particularly tense in early April 1982. In addition to the multiple Middle East crises, Argentina and the United Kingdom were preparing for war over the Falkland Islands. (Haig was himself shuttling between both countries in what proved to be a vain effort to settle the conflict diplomatically.) The Stoessel team stopped in London in order for Stoessel to consult with Haig about his instructions for Israel and Egypt. Haig was quite calm about the situation and told Stoessel that he was confident that Israel could be convinced to complete the withdrawal without any delay. From the U.S. perspective, it was essential that the withdrawal be completed on time as any delay, regardless of the brevity of its duration, would significantly complicate U.S. diplomacy and further undermine the "cold peace" that had evolved between Israel and Egypt.

Dick Walters, a retired, highly decorated army lieutenant general fluent in at least eight languages, knew the Argentines extremely well and was supporting Haig's diplomacy. During our evening in London, Walters and I had dinner, comparing notes on our respective crises. "War in the Falklands," he said. "Neither side will back down. Looks the same in Lebanon. Just a matter of time." I had to agree, despite the optimistic prediction of Ambassador Habib that "diplomacy would yet work in solving the problems in Lebanon."

Immediately upon our arrival in Israel, Stoessel, accompanied by his wife and the rest of the team, were confronted by the Israeli media. We walked into a full-blown political circus with leaks, allegations, misinformation and high drama at every turn. There was no doubt that Begin and Sharon were suspicious about the intention of Hosni Mubarak to honor the peace treaty with Israel. Sharon in particular was exploiting the situation by whipping up nationalist sentiment with exaggerated claims of Egyptian "perfidy" and "unfair American pressure" on Israel. Every statement and action made by Mubarak or anyone else in the Egyptian government was given the absolute worst interpretation.

Stoessel, a career diplomat and Soviet expert, did his utmost to allay Begin's concerns for Israel. Fortunately, Begin was reassured by Stoessel's seriousness as well as by his grace and style. Stoessel demonstrated that he had come to listen to the Israelis, take careful notes, ask questions where there was uncertainty, and then carry these concerns back to the Egyptians. An astute negotiator who had spent most of his career dealing with the nuances of Soviet and East European affairs, Stoessel recognized that Begin needed to be treated with great courtliness and respect. Regardless of his lack of substantive Middle East experience, Stoessel was a statesman who knew exactly how to deal with a leader like Begin.

From their first meeting, Begin was visibly impressed with Stoessel. It was a large meeting, held in Begin's office, and included fourteen Israelis and twelve Americans. Begin and Sharon laid out their complaints, in meticulous detail, with Sharon typically raising his voice numerous times in order to demonstrate that he would not be bullied by Egyptians or Americans. Stoessel made few if any comments and took detailed notes on the Israeli presentation, asking several questions to seek detailed clarification of the Israeli concerns. Toward the conclusion of the meeting, Begin commented in Hebrew to Foreign Minister Yitzhak Shamir, "I like Stoessel. He's serious about what we have to say and he doesn't lecture us like Habib." Shamir merely shrugged, but Begin, from the outset of the shuttle, warmed to Stoessel and labored to work with him to resolve the mutual mistrust that had evolved between Begin and Mubarak.

In addition to Stoessel, our team included Morrie Draper, Michael Kozak from the State Department's Office of the Legal Advisor (L), NEA specialist Ned Walker, Army colonel Thomas Pianka and me. Following our initial round of exchanges with the Israelis, we traveled to Cairo in order to hear the Egyptian perspective. Unlike the "town meetings" in Jerusalem, the meetings in Egypt were limited to a smaller inner circle usually consisting of Mubarak and his key advisors: Foreign Minister Kamal Hassan Ali, Foreign Ministry Director General (now United Nations Secretary General) Boutros Boutros Ghali, Minister of Defense Abu Ghazala and Presidential Advisor Osama el-Baz.

As he had in Israel, Stoessel asked the Egyptians to present the issues as seen from Cairo's perspective. Listening to their presentation, I wondered how Haig could have been so confident during our meeting in London. It was as if we had passed through Alice's looking glass. Although the issues to be resolved were the same on both sides, it was obvious that both parties viewed the other from the most mistrustful possible perspective. What was black in Jerusalem was white in Cairo and vice versa.

Israel said it wanted to leave Yamit but needed more time to peacefully resolve the problems of the settlers. Egypt, on the other hand, was absolutely convinced that Israel was perpetrating a ruse to postpone the withdrawal and intended to hold on to parts of Sinai indefinitely. Contrary to Sharon's allegations about violations of the limited-force zones, Abu Ghazala read out the order of battle of his units in Sinai in excruciating detail, insisting that Egypt was in absolute full compliance with the limitations agreed to in the annexes to the treaty. From Abu Ghazala's point of view, Sharon was simply trying to stir up anti-Egyptian passions in Israel as a further pretext to hold on to Sinai, while enhancing his domestic popularity.

As for the demarcation of the Egyptian-Israeli border, the Egyptians insisted that there was no ambiguity about the disputed boundary markers. Israel was simply making claims on Egyptian land that it wanted to keep. Egypt did not see any border problems other than an attempted Israeli land grab. This was particularly true about Taba. "What is Taba?" Mubarak asked Stoessel rhetorically. "Taba, Taba, Taba! Until the Israelis claimed this beach belonged to them, neither I nor any Egyptian had ever heard of Taba. Now every schoolchild and peasant in Egypt knows about Taba and considers it as important as the pyramids. Suddenly my opponents, who also never heard of Taba or went to Taba, attach great political significance to it and its recovery. If Egypt does not regain Taba, there will be a political crisis here and I will be accused of giving away Egyptian land to Israel."

Stoessel replied unequivocally and consistently that the United States fully appreciated the importance of Egypt's regaining all of Sinai according to the treaty. The U.S. government was committed to use every effort to ensure that a political resolution of these three issues could be achieved and that all of Sinai would be in Egyptian hands by April 26. Having now heard both sides explain their versions of the impasse, Stoessel began to shuttle between Cairo and Jerusalem.

So began the fast-paced "Taba Shuffle." Returning to Jerusalem, Stoessel accurately reported on the talks in Cairo, leading Begin and his team to reject the Egyptian arguments out of hand. Begin, with great rhetorical flourish, insisted that Mubarak's explanations, coupled with what the Israelis viewed as a hostile speech in the United Nations by Egypt betrayed the true intentions of Cairo. In the Israeli view, Egypt had no intention of honoring its treaty commitments. It only wanted to recover Sinai, after which it would make its reentry into the Arab world its top priority at Israel's expense. Nonetheless, Begin said that he believed in the rule of law and would stand by Israel's commitments. He agreed to work with Stoessel to try to bridge the differences with Egypt and ensure that the withdrawal was completed on time. Stoessel listened quietly. He then commented that he thought he could obtain a letter from Mubarak to Begin reaffirming Egypt's commitment to adhere to the terms of the peace treaty.

Before commenting on the idea of a letter from Mubarak, Begin advised Stoessel to observe the confrontation that was escalating at Yamit. With great personal pain, Begin had ordered Sharon to send in the Israeli Army, unarmed, to physically remove the settlers who refused to depart peacefully. Nothing was more vital to Israel than reclaiming the land, Begin said. Yet here he was forcing Israeli pioneers to abandon their efforts in the desert. To fulfill Israel's commitments to Egypt, he was forced to violate the core of Israel's ideology.

Stoessel commended the prime minister for his actions to remove the settlers from Yamit, acknowledging that the United States recognized that the pain was undoubtedly genuine. However, it remained imperative that the process at Yamit be completed, despite the difficulties it was causing. As we worked carefully and deliberately through each of the other issues with Begin and Sharon, it quickly became clear that with the appropriate assurances from the United States, Begin would recommend to his Cabinet that the withdrawal be completed as scheduled. However, it became equally evident that one issue was not going to be completely resolved in time for the withdrawal on April 26: the issue of the infamous Taba.

Begin was adamant that Taba was historically a part of Israel, and he had no intention of abandoning Taba just because Egypt claimed it. Sharon argued that returning Taba to Egypt could pose a security threat to Eilat due to its proximity. Stoessel played down the dispute, suggesting that perhaps the withdrawal could go forward while both sides acknowledged that sovereignty over Taba and the border's demarcation remained to be resolved. Stoessel's suggestion was consistent with a provision of the peace treaty that allowed for disputes to be resolved through conciliation, and, failing conciliation, arbitration. Sharon and others quickly and loudly took issue with Stoessel's suggested compromise, albeit a temporary and essentially procedural one. Begin quieted his delegation and acknowledged that the dispute-resolution mechanisms contained in the treaty might provide a way of completing the withdrawal, leaving the final status of Taba open.

We returned to Cairo faced with the very difficult task that lay ahead. This was a very delicate situation. Without insulting the Egyptians in the process, Stoessel had to convince Mubarak to reassure the Israelis about Egyptian intentions. Moreover, since he had suggested the possibility of a letter from Mubarak to Begin, we had to try to find a way to get the president of Egypt to send a letter that Begin would find satisfactory. It seemed that it might be impossible for Israel to completely withdraw from Sinai by April 26. Israel was not willing to agree to anything more than to acknowledge that Taba was in dispute and agree to the procedures outlined in the treaty to try to resolve the dispute. It was not going to be easy to convince Mubarak to reassure Israel of Egypt's honorable intentions and give Begin a meaningful letter to that effect, knowing in advance that he would have a Taba problem on his hands.

The American ambassador to Egypt, Alfred Atherton, was especially dubious and questioned the political utility of Stoessel's suggested approach, especially the notion of Mubarak providing a letter that would satisfy Begin in these circumstances. Stoessel was unconvinced. Perhaps the United States could draft it for him, Stoessel commented during a team staff meeting. Atherton blanched at the idea and suggested that this would insult Mubarak. Since Atherton was unable to devise an alternative means of achieving this result, however, Stoessel decided to suggest the value of an instrument, such as a letter, and test Mubarak's reaction.

Working through the night in the U.S. embassy in Cairo, Kozak, Walker, Pianka and I worked up a draft letter that would satisfy Begin and might be acceptable to Mubarak. It was during this nocturnal episode that we discovered the lack of after-hours dining options in Cairo. Not even the embassy security personnel had a clue where we could find something to eat. Scrounging around shamelessly in the ambassador's office, we came across a package of Girl Scout cookies and half a bottle of scotch. The cookies were stale, but washed down by the scotch, they kept us going until we finished a draft letter at around four in the morning. In these circumstances, our traveling secretaries Susan Shea and Kate Milne were tireless, working at stretches of more than twenty hours without a break in order to keep up with the endless stream of papers and cables that flowed from the team.

Arriving at the presidential palace in Cairo to meet with Mubarak and his advisors, Stoessel deliberately opened the meeting by reporting the progress with Israel and some ideas we had developed that might move the process forward. Mubarak sat back in his chair and bluntly told Stoessel that he was listening.

After updating Mubarak on the status of our talks in Jerusalem, Stoessel gently broached the idea of a letter. Taken aback, Mubarak frowned and asked what would need to be in such a letter. Stoessel replied that we had prepared some ideas that Mubarak might wish to consider and handed him the draft. As he read through the paper, Mubarak visibly bristled. He expressed exasperation that the United States doubted whether he could write a letter to satisfy Begin. He reiterated that Egypt would honor all its international agreements, to the letter, including the treaty with Israel. Mubarak told Stoessel to please tell the Israeli prime minister that he would not send him a letter, but that Begin must rely on his word that Egypt would honor its commitments. He agreed, however, to consider the ideas Stoessel had proposed for Taba. Mubarak said all this while clearly straining to keep his temper under control. For several minutes, one could feel the tension in the air thicken as Mubarak and Osama el-Baz broke into a spirited argument in Arabic. Stoessel and the rest of us sat waiting for Mubarak to vent his anger.

After several minutes of back-and-forth with his advisors, Mubarak turned back to Stoessel and unexpectedly brought up the raging Iran-Iraq War. Mubarak asked Stoessel for his impressions of the situation in the Gulf. Stoessel paused, then turned to me to comment. I summarized the current information about the weakening Iraqi defenses in the face of sustained Iranian counterattacks, noting that I was sure the government of Egypt had more information on Iraq's situation than did the United States. I added that at the same time the United States was concerned about the implications of an Iraqi collapse for our interests in the Gulf, we were also troubled by the persistent efforts of the Soviet Union to gain some measure of influence in Tehran.

Mubarak replied that he and other Arab leaders were also growing very concerned over the downturn in Iraqi fortunes in the war. Despite its leadership of the Rejectionist Front against the Egypt-Israel peace and avowed hostility toward Egypt for its perfidy, Iraq still had a relationship with Egypt, as did Egypt with the rest of the Arab world. Other than Syria and Libya, which supported Iran, the Arabs of the Middle East feared an Iranian victory more than Saddam's well-known hegemonic aspirations. Mubarak warned that the implications of an Iraqi defeat were potentially catastrophic. Addressing his remarks to me and speaking in a voice charged with emotion, Mubarak stated that America must provide military assistance to Iraq in order to stop the Iranians. I replied that it was not possible for the United States to provide assistance to Iraq. Although it had been taken off the list of countries supporting international terrorism, Iraq was still not eligible to purchase American military hardware.

Mubarak paused before replying. Then, looking me squarely in the eyes, he told me not to act surprised, but that he knew that the United States was ready to trade thirty-six pieces of artillery to Baghdad in exchange for one Soviet-built Iraqi T-72 tank. He noted that Saddam himself had told him. Mubarak delivered a message from Saddam that Iraq could not supply even one T-72 because the Soviets continued to supply Iraq with the bulk of its military equipment and Saddam could not risk his supply line. He had asked Mubarak to deliver the message that he wanted the United States to help Iraq without imposing such conditions. I replied that Iraq did not need equipment but invigorated leadership in Baghdad, along with a new military strategy and tactical initiative on the battlefield. Moreover, regardless of any limited actions such as the artillery for T-72 trade, the United States would not establish a military supply relationship with Iraq.

At the conclusion of the meeting, we trooped outside and we all shook hands. I was the last in line to reach Mubarak. Without letting go of my hand, he stood with me for nearly five minutes of intense discussion. As Stoessel and the rest of our delegation started getting into the cars for the motorcade ride back to the U.S. embassy, Mubarak resumed his impassioned plea for U.S. help for Iraq. He said that the Omani minister of state for foreign affairs, Yusuf al-Alawi, had visited Cairo that morning and had met with Mubarak just prior to Stoessel's arrival. He had carried a message from Oman, the UAE and Bahrain asking Mubarak to convey to the Reagan administration the growing anxiety of the Gulf states over the deteriorating situation on the Iraqi border. He told me that he had also received a Saudi envoy in recent days who asked him to try to convince the United States to do something. Egyptian assistance, Mubarak argued, gave Iraq strategic depth by providing Iraq with millions of dollars' worth of weapons systems, ammunition and other supplies. He said that the relationship with Iraq could benefit the United States, but that Egypt needed the administration's help to do more for Iraq in order for Saddam to help the Americans in the Gulf. With a glint in his eyes,

Mubarak raised his eyebrows and noted that the arms supply relationship could be cut off at will, giving him substantial leverage over the situation.

He concluded by asking me what the U.S. position was in these circumstances. Mubarak had not let go of my extended hand throughout his remarks. Recognizing the seriousness of these statements, particularly at a time when the United States was also very concerned about the prospects for an Iranian breakthrough and an Iraqi collapse, I assured him that I would report what he had just told me to Washington and try to have an answer at our next meeting. Finally letting go of my hand, Mubarak grinned, wagged his finger at me and then slapped me hard on the back, telling me not to come back without a good answer.

When I caught up with the motorcade, Stoessel asked me what the exchange had been about. After I told him, he suggested that I report this to the White House directly and ask for instructions. Stoessel agreed to pass the information on to Haig himself when he next spoke to him and concurred that I should ask McFarlane for instructions over a secure telephone. Departing immediately for the airport from the presidential palace, we flew back to Israel to resume our negotiations over the withdrawal questions. On the flight to Jerusalem, Sue Shea christened our plane the *Taba Taxi*, since Taba was the one issue that seemed likely to preoccupy the team for the remainder of the trip. Before arriving in Tel Aviv, an exhausted Morrie Draper made up a jingle about the *Taba Taxi*, which soon became our team's theme song, known fondly as the "Taba Shuffle."

Upon our arrival in Tel Aviv that evening, Lewis informed us that Begin had decided to put the withdrawal decision to his Cabinet the following morning. After the Cabinet vote, he hoped to meet with Stoessel in order personally to inform him of the decision. Lewis opined that Begin would not put it to the Cabinet unless he was confident that he would have their support. Despite Sharon's bravado, it seemed very unlikely at this point that Sharon could stop the withdrawal.

The next morning we drove to the prime minister's office hoping that Lewis's surmise would be borne out. We walked up the stairs to the conference room and took our seats at the table. Begin walked in a more subdued state than we had previously seen him, his eyes squinting downward through his thick glasses. As a swarm of journalists, photographers and television cameramen was ushered out, I noticed that Sharon was absent and pondered why he would not be in attendance at such a historic moment. We sat in expectant silence, waiting for Begin to inform us of the Cabinet's decision. But the suspense continued for several more minutes as Begin opened the meeting by mournfully reporting that during the night, an Israeli patrol had driven over a land mine in the security zone of southern Lebanon. One Israeli officer, a young lieutenant, had been killed. Emotion choking his voice, Begin said that the dead officer was the nephew of one of Begin's close friends who had fought alongside him. He had attended the dead officer's circumcision ceremony (the bris) when he was just eight days old. Visibly distraught, Begin stated to the assembled group of Americans and Israelis that Israel viewed the terrorist attack as a PLO violation of the cessation of hostilities. He warned that Israel would not tolerate the murder of its children. After staring down silently at the conference table for nearly a minute, Begin seemed to regain his composure. Looking at Stoessel, he informed him that the Cabinet had voted to complete the withdrawal from Sinai as called for in the treaty, and asked that the United States convey this decision to the government of Egypt. He reaffirmed that this decision was contingent on the satisfactory conclusion of an agreement between Egypt and Israel which would define the procedures governing the resolution of the Taba dispute.

As we departed the prime minister's office, Stoessel refused to comment to the press, choosing to allow the Israelis to make whatever announcements they deemed appropriate in the circumstances. Getting into a limousine with Tom Pianka, I asked him what he made of Sharon's absence. "Based on what Begin told us about last night's terrorist attack and his especially sorrowful composure, I suspect that Sharon is back at the MOD issuing orders for some type of military action against Palestinian targets in Lebanon." Sure enough, within an hour of our return to the American consulate in Jerusalem, we received wire reports that the IAF had conducted air strikes against three Palestinian guerrilla bases in Lebanon. I had already telephoned McFarlane to inform him of the Cabinet decision when I heard the news of the strikes. I placed another call to update him on this latest development, adding that Begin was determined to demonstrate that Israel's completion of the withdrawal from Sinai should not be interpreted as an act of weakness or submission to American pressure. I gave him my opinion that the strikes were a limited response and would not be accompanied by an Israeli escalation on the ground. With Haig still shuttling between Buenos Aires and London, McFarlane thought there seemed little likelihood the United States could do more about the situation in Lebanon for the time being other than to wait and see who made the next move. Habib and NEA were at work on a new diplomatic initiative for Lebanon, but it would not be ready to implement for at least another month. "Stay focused on Sinai," McFarlane said. "An agreement on Taba must be worked out promptly."

With the Israeli Cabinet decision on withdrawal secure, Stoessel turned to Mike Kozak to draw up an agreement that could serve as the basis for a negotiated solution to the Taba impasse. Kozak is the quintessential international legal bureaucrat cum cowboy. A very creative lawyer, Kozak redefines the term workaholic. Whether working late in his office or at home tinkering on one of his five cars or electric guitar, Kozak never quit until he had accomplished his goal. Resolving the Taba question turned out to require not only his considerable creativity but also tremendous amounts of stamina. Working most of the night in the American consulate in Jerusalem, we came up with a four-page draft that acknowledged the disputed status of Taba and put forth a set of procedures that would move the dispute toward resolution, first through conciliation, and failing that, through binding arbitration.

Over the next few days, the *Taba Taxi* shuttled back and forth between Israel and Egypt as we tried to negotiate an acceptable agreement. It was not easy. The Israelis wanted to agree only to conciliation. The Egyptians wanted to skip conciliation and go immediately to arbitration. From the Egyptian perspective, the parties had made up their minds not to compromise one inch on Taba; therefore, what was the point of a conciliation process that would not resolve the dispute? In the meantime, Israel insisted that life had to proceed as before in Taba, permitting the construction of the Sonesta hotel to continue, something that might later strengthen Israel's position in any arbitration proceeding.

The negotiations proceeded slowly as the clock ticked toward April 26, 1982. Although the Cabinet had given its assent to the withdrawal, an agreement on Taba remained elusive. At one point, Kamal Hassan Ali, the foreign minister, came to Jerusalem in an effort to close the deal. His visit was potentially explosive for the Egyptians, as the international community had just condemned Israel for new settlement activities in the old city of Jerusalem and actions by fundamentalist Jews which had insulted the Islamic world. Yet Ali recognized that the risk was worthwhile if his visit could help convince the skeptical Israelis of the Egyptian commitment to the treaty with Israel.

Meeting in the American consulate in Jerusalem, Ali and his staff met with the Stoessel team to try to resolve various procedural details in the draft agreement. Later in the day David Kimche and Hanon Bar-On, the interlocutors of the U.S.-Israeli strategic dialogue, made the first visit ever of senior Israeli officials to the consulate, hoping to meet with Ali and find a way to conclude the agreement. To their surprise, Ali left just prior to their arrival, leading them to observe wryly that the Egyptians would come to Jerusalem to meet with Americans but not with Israelis.

We worked all night to refine the agreement, but one more day of shuttle diplomacy would be required to complete the process. With secretaries from Embassy Tel Aviv spelling the thoroughly exhausted Shea and Milne, a two-page agreement was finally produced. Meeting through the day, first in Israel and later in Egypt, then back again to Israel, final agreement was reached. It appeared that all that remained to be done was to type the final document and sign it. As we entered the consulate in Jerusalem to finish up this simple task at around ten P.M., we discovered that all of the secretaries, exhausted from four days and nights of endless work, had returned to their homes and hotels. Thus it fell to me, the best typist on the team, to type up the final Taba agreement, in duplicate.

We phoned over to Dave Kimche and advised him that we would conduct a signing ceremony at eleven-thirty P.M. in the Jerusalem Plaza Hotel, about 250 meters from the consulate. At the same time, we contacted Ambassador Mohammed Bassiouny of Egypt, who had been designated to sign the agreement on behalf of Egypt, to advise him of the time and place of the signing. To our surprise, he hesitated, then said that while the government of Egypt was ready to sign, it preferred to execute the agreement outside of Jerusalem.

The political cloud that had been created by the Israeli government's recent actions on the Temple Mount had thrown up a last-minute obstacle. To overcome this hurdle, Morrie Draper suggested that Bassiouny drive up to Jerusalem from Tel Aviv, where he lived and worked, in order to meet Draper outside the city limits of Jerusalem. Bassiouny agreed, drove to the rendezvous, signed the agreement by the side of the road and returned to Tel Aviv.

When Kimche arrived at the Plaza, he immediately asked where Bassiouny was. Without a moment's hesitation, Draper replied that Bassiouny had already signed the agreement and had returned to Tel Aviv. Kimche started to comment about the inappropriateness of the procedure but quickly relented to the fait accompli, signed the agreement and raised a glass of wine to toast Secretary Stoessel and his successful diplomacy.

Although the team expected to return immediately to Washington, the government of Egypt had graciously invited Stoessel to spend a day sight-seeing in Luxor in Upper Egypt. To show Egypt's appreciation for

The camels of Masirah Island, Masirah Island, Sultanate of Oman, December 1979

Negotiating the completion of Israel's withdrawal from Sinai, Jerusalem, Israel, April 1982. From upper left: Foreign Minister Yitzhak Shamir, Prime Minister Menachem Begin, Deputy Prime Minister Yehuda Ben Meir, Foreign Ministry director general David Kimche, Ministry of Defense advisor General Abrasha Tamir, cabinet secretary Dan Meridor. From upper right: American embassy political officer Paul Hare, Ambassador Morris Draper, Deputy Secretary of State Walter Stoessel, Ambassador Samuel Lewis, Deputy Chief of Mission William Brown, NSC staff member Howard Teicher.

*The "Taba Shuffle" team, following the conclusion of Sinai negotiations,
in the Valley of the Kings, Luxor, Egypt*

*Preparing to brief the president outside the Oval Office, October 22, 1984.
From left: Secretary of State George P. Shultz,
Assistant Secretary of State Nicholas A. Veliotes, and Howard Teicher*

White House state dinner in honor of President Zia Al-Huq of Pakistan,
December 7, 1982: President Ronald Reagan, Howard and Gayle Teicher

Vice-President George Bush, NSC staff member Richard Morris, Howard and Gayle Teicher
at a Christmas party hosted by the vice-president and Mrs. Bush, December 17, 1984

Oval Office discussion of the situation in Lebanon, January 27, 1983. Counterclockwise from right: President Reagan, Vice-President Bush, AID director Peter McPherson, NSC staff member Philip Dur (Commander USN), Ambassador Richard Fairbanks, Howard Teicher, NSC staff member Geoffrey Kemp, deputy NSC advisor Robert C. McFarlane, NSC advisor Judge William P. Clark, Ambassador Philip Habib.

Analyzing the situation in Lebanon, the cabinet room, September 6, 1983. From left: Philip Dur, Howard Teicher, and Chairman of the Joint Chiefs of Staff General John Vessey.

Briefing the president on the situation in Lebanon, the Oval Office, September 29, 1983. Counterclockwise from right: Philip Dur, Howard Teicher, Richard Fairbanks, Vice-President Bush, President Reagan, Judge Clark, and Michael Deaver.

Caspar Weinberger has forgotten more than you will ever know, U.S. delegation, U.S.-Tunisia Joint Military Commission, October 1984. From left: Pentagon spokesman Michael Burch, U.S. ambassador to Tunisia Peter Sebastian, Secretary of Defense Weinberger, Assistant Secretary of Defense Richard Armitage, Ambassador Robert Pelletreau, and Howard Teicher.

Restoring full diplomatic relations with Iraq, the Oval Office, November 26, 1984. Counterclockwise from right: President Reagan, Vice-President Bush, U.S. ambassador-designate to Iraq David Newton, Assistant Secretary of State Richard Murphy, Howard Teicher, NSC advisor Robert C. McFarlane, Iraqi ambassador-designate Nizar Hamdoon, Iraqi under secretary for foreign affairs Ismat Kittani, and Iraqi Foreign Minister Tariq Aziz.

Briefing the president, vice-president, and chief of staff on the outcome of the McFarlane mission to Tehran, the Oval Office, May 29, 1986. From left: White House chief of staff Donald T. Regan, President Reagan, Vice-President Bush, Robert C. McFarlane, and Howard Teicher.

For the record, the only cake in the shape of a key:
first birthday of Seth Benjamin Teicher, December 17, 1986

the Stoessel mission, special arrangements were made for a VIP tour of the Valley of the Kings and the Valley of the Queens. The latter stop was unusual, as the tomb of Queen Nephratari had been shut to the public for several years because of a deterioration of the hieroglyphics brought on by the outside air.

We had been up all night finishing the agreement and writing reporting cables to Washington; nevertheless, we flew directly to Luxor from Tel Aviv early in the morning. The heat was overpowering as we walked off the plane into the Egyptian desert, but the anticipation of the sights and of the long flight back to Washington later that night helped us overcome our fatigue.

Our last stop before lunch was the tomb of Nephratari. It was absolutely exquisite. Led by a prominent official from the Ministry of Antiquities, we descended to the bottom of the tomb, where our guide read the hieroglyphics to us. Fascinating as the tomb was, however, fatigue finally overcame Mike Kozak. As the rest of us listened to the guide, Mike found a comfortable slab against a back wall, lay down, and fell into a deep sleep. The guide finished his talk and started to lead us out of the tomb. Nearly fifty yards from the bottom, we realized that Kozak was missing. I went back, found him asleep and roused him. Pale and exhausted by this time, he would have felt right at home had we left him there with the spirit of Queen Nephratari.

CHAPTER 8

WAR
BY ANY OTHER NAME

---◆---

A Distinction with a Difference

Following the peaceful return of the Sinai to Egypt in April 1982, three issues began to emerge as the dominant threats to U.S. interests in southwest Asia: Israel's June invasion of Lebanon; the shifting balance of power between Iraq and Iran; and a resurgence of radical-inspired international terrorism. America's vital interests in the Persian Gulf were increasingly threatened by the spillover of these interlocking issues. The threat levels rose in direct proportion with each conflict's degree of violence. At the same time, opportunities emerged to establish a more powerful U.S. political and military position in southwest Asia in order directly to protect those vital interests.

Throughout this period, the president and his principal advisors were increasingly forced to grapple with crucial issues of life and death for Americans, Europeans and the peoples of the Middle East. The members of Reagan's National Security Council held strong and often conflicting views on the proper role for military power in the pursuit of American interests in the Middle East. Policy papers and decision memoranda were tools to influence the outcome of debates and were carefully prepared to reflect a balanced articulation of opposing points of view; the pros and cons of specific policy options; and the recommendations of each NSC member to enable President Reagan to weigh the arguments and decide which view was more persuasive. If a consensus among the NSC members was achieved in advance of a presidential decision, a National Security Decision Directive (NSDD) was drafted and staffed by the relevant agencies to enable the directive to be executed by the president when decisions were reached. When policy disagreements could not be resolved without presidential intervention, the NSDD would be drafted after a decision was made. These were standard operating procedures.

The process was designed to allow decisions to be made and subsequently implemented.

Unfortunately, despite the apparent clarity of national security decisions, their implementation was often stymied, as Reagan's Cabinet officers waged unconventional warfare against each other to achieve their objectives after finding themselves on the losing side of a policy debate. Regrettably, it was standard practice for Cabinet officers who were dissatisfied to choose to interpret presidential decisions, however unambiguously they were drafted, to suit their own preferences. Weinberger, in particular, acted with disdain toward a number of President Reagan's key decisions simply because he maintained, quite openly, that he knew what was best for the United States in the Middle East. To my amazement, there was no discipline imposed by the president on wayward Cabinet officers, especially not on Weinberger, for deliberately refusing to implement numerous presidential decisions bearing on the use of force in the Middle East. Ronald Reagan's failure to exert decisive leadership would lead to America's humiliating defeat in Lebanon in 1984, the 1986 Iran Affair and the blind tilt toward Baghdad, the latter contributing directly to the 1990 Iraqi invasion of Kuwait and the resulting Operation Desert Storm.

The palpable sigh of relief in Washington that accompanied Israel's withdrawal from Sinai quickly turned into a gasp for air as Israel intensified its preparations for invading Lebanon. By the middle of May 1982, only wishful thinking and prayer stood in the way of an Israeli onslaught against the PLO. No one in the administration was unaware of Israel's preparations for war, despite the administration's continuing hope that diplomatic solutions could be found to overcome the tangled web of political-military problems involving Israel, Lebanon, the PLO and Syria.

As important as prayer can be for the human spirit—particularly in the Middle East—neither prayer nor diplomacy offered comprehensive or realistic solutions to the violence that typified the whole of southwest Asia. Despite his best efforts, Phil Habib's creative diplomacy could not achieve miracles when it came to the competing interests of the numerous Lebanese factions, Arafat and his Palestinian opponents, Sharon, and President Hafiz al-Assad of Syria.

Sharon outlined the thrust of his operational plan for Lebanon during a December 1981 meeting with Habib and Draper in Jerusalem. Habib had reacted vigorously, insisting that the United States would never support an Israeli military initiative either to eliminate the PLO or to redraw the political map of Lebanon. Inasmuch as Sharon was telling numerous U.S. officials about Israel's strategic interests in Lebanon, and despite his disclaimer that he was only expressing his "personal ideas" and not the official Israeli position, Washington reacted and strongly voiced its opposition to an Israeli war of choice in Lebanon. To ensure that American opposition to a military solution was accurately and unambiguously conveyed to the government of Israel, Reagan wrote a letter to Begin in early 1982, urging the prime minister not to go to war while making plain the commitment of the United States to continue to pursue diplomatic solutions.

With the resumption of Palestinian attacks on Israeli targets and Israeli reprisals in late April 1982, however, the prospects for a diplomatic solution to the Lebanon crisis seemed increasingly remote, if not outright illusory. Habib, NEA and Geoffrey Kemp persisted in their best efforts to devise a new initiative that would promote European as well as American diplomacy in order to avert a war and achieve the desired political results. In part a reflection of America's conviction that because diplomacy had worked before, a way could be found to make it work again, a diplomatic initiative was the essential leverage necessary if the United States was to have any credibility in its consistent pleas to Israel to show maximum restraint.

The national security bureaucracy was divided as an increasingly strident debate developed between Haig, on one side, and Vice President George Bush, Weinberger and Clark on the other. While he recognized, but did not emphasize, the East-West dimension of the conflict between Israel, the PLO and the Syrians in Lebanon, Haig insisted that Israel's right to self-defense could not be denied simply out of deference to U.S. interests in the Arab world, or the potential negative ramifications for the U.S. position in the Gulf. In support of his position, Haig opined that the Saudis would not ask for a refund on their AWACS aircraft just because Israel was at war with the PLO or Syrians. Nor did he believe that the ability of the United States to project power into the Gulf would be advanced or hindered by a war in Lebanon, despite the negative, anti-American rhetoric that was sure to ensue. On the other side of the debate, Weinberger became increasingly shrill in his anti-Israel rhetoric, arguing that Israel was exaggerating the PLO threat and that many of the military acts that Israel undertook were part of a deliberate Israeli strategy designed to split the United States from the Arab world.

In May 1982, Sharon and a large contingent of Israelis came to the State Department to meet with Haig, Habib and others, including myself, in order to restate Israel's position that the escalation of violence and the failure to find a diplomatic solution left Israel in a position where it would soon have no choice but to act with force. I found it ironic that both Sharon and Weinberger, the ranking military advisors to their respective governments, were men of such extremes and passion on Middle East issues and the nature of the U.S.-Israeli and U.S.-Arab relationships. In an odd way, I believed that they deserved each other.

Sharon lectured at length about the essential requirement for Lebanon to be rid of PLO terrorists, not only for Israel's sake, but also for the sake of the United States and other Western countries that suffered from Syrian and Soviet-sponsored terrorism emanating from Lebanon. Sharon's extensive presentation left no doubt that he was itching for war. Aware that Sharon was looking for any signal that he might arguably interpret as a U.S. "green light" for an invasion, Habib firmly, loudly and unambiguously opposed Sharon's agenda. Haig also expressed his firm opposition to an invasion but pointedly noted that Israel must, in the end, make its own decisions on how best to act in self-defense, and if military action proved necessary, he expected Israel to act with a response proportionate to the provocation.

According to many, Sharon viewed Haig's final comment as the green light he had been seeking. But the entire meeting must be analyzed to evaluate whether Haig gave Sharon Washington's blessing for military action. Throughout the meeting, Haig repeatedly emphasized that the United States did not believe military solutions could cure the problems of Lebanon. But as a matter of international law, moral principle and realism, Haig reiterated that Israel enjoyed the same rights as any other country to act in its own self-defense. Whether it was reasonable for Sharon and Israel to interpret Haig's remarks as an okay to invade Lebanon is not for me to judge. But considering the glint in Sharon's eye and the forceful, overbearing way he clutched his briefing papers and pounded the conference table that day, I believe that Sharon would have found a way to interpret Haig's comments about the nice weather in Washington as encouragement for an Israeli invasion of Lebanon.

I was eating lunch in my office in the Old Executive Office Building (OEOB) on June 3 when the White House Situation Room, the twenty-four-hour, seven-day-a-week intelligence and communications hub of the president and NSC staff, telephoned to inform me of the assassination attempt in London against Shlomo Argov, Israel's ambassador to the United Kingdom. Argov had been shot in the head at point-blank range by Arab assailants. As news wire and intelligence reports describing the incident and its likely perpetrators poured in throughout the day, a sense of dread anticipation settled in among national security bureaucrats working Middle East issues. We were all certain that Israel would retaliate with air strikes against PLO targets in Lebanon and that the PLO would respond with artillery and rocket attacks against northern Israel.

However, early reports led some to believe that Israel's response might be restrained because the attackers appeared to belong to the Abu Nidal organization operating out of Baghdad, and not the PLO. Long outcast from the PLO mainstream, Abu Nidal was in the midst of waging a vicious war against Yasir Arafat and his supporters. Arafat had sentenced Abu Nidal to death, in absentia, for his wanton perpetration of international terrorism directed against civilian targets. Abu Nidal had replied by trying to assassinate Arafat and by killing Palestinian leaders who supported him. Despite the U.S. conclusion earlier in the year that Iraq had ceased its support for international terrorism, Abu Nidal continued to reside in and launch terror operations from Baghdad. Indeed, the next day we learned that the terrorists' orders had been delivered by an Iraqi courier and that the weapons used in the attack against Argov were provided by the Iraqi military attaché to the United Kingdom. The close relationship was undeniable.

In these circumstances, the United States had to speculate whether Abu Nidal had connived with Saddam Hussein to try to assassinate Argov, in order to provoke an Israeli attack on the PLO and the Syrians, Iraq's bitter Baath rival in the Arab world, which had firmly allied itself with Iran in the Iran-Iraq War. Baghdad's support of the Argov attack represented the standard modus operandi of Saddam Hussein when it came to dealing with his Arab opponents. It would also be sweet revenge for Israel's June 1981 destruction of the Iraqi nuclear reactor. Given the indications, from Saddam's point of view, a Middle East war involving Israel might even facilitate U.S. interest in helping bring about an end to Iraq's war with Iran.

While my colleagues scoffed at my "instant analysis" of Iraqi motives, they did not dispute Abu Nidal's role and the potential value it might have in convincing Israel not to strike the PLO in Lebanon. Convinced that an Abu Nidal provocation was different from a PLO provocation, "a distinction with a difference" for those who followed international terrorism, Kemp, Veliotes and Robert Ames (a highly regarded national intelligence officer for the Middle East at the CIA), argued that the very rapid implementation of a new U.S. diplomatic initiative could prevent a total breakdown in the cease-fire and the inevitable Israeli invasion. Perhaps Israel could be restrained. I did not agree, but we spent the balance of the day cobbling together a letter for Reagan to send to Begin urging restraint and promising diplomatic action.

As we passed drafts of a letter back and forth and the day passed into night without Israeli military action, a faint hope emerged that Israel might indeed choose restraint, rather than the prompt retaliation that would undoubtedly escalate into a major military confrontation. Such hopes proved false, and the die of war was cast the following day when Israel launched its retaliatory air strikes against PLO targets in Lebanon. Two hours later the PLO unleashed artillery and rockets against northern Israel. The cease-fire between Israel and the PLO, a condition that Israel did not even wish to acknowledge out of concern that it might be perceived as de facto recognition of the PLO, broke down. The final threshold to war had been crossed.

The PLO, which had during the previous year strengthened the military capabilities of its fighters in southern Lebanon with heavy weapons, including rockets, artillery and surface-to-air missiles, responded to the IAF strikes by attacking twenty-nine towns and cities throughout northern Israel with over five hundred artillery and rocket rounds. Israeli civilians were forced into bomb shelters as the PLO gave Begin and Sharon what they needed to invade Lebanon. The government of Israel made no secret of its intentions. Within a matter of hours, the Israeli Defense Forces moved quickly to organize its ground forces for maneuver operations in Lebanon, while the artillery, Air Force and Navy pounded PLO targets to soften them up for the ground forces' advance. No attempt was made to preserve secrecy. Sharon had made every effort over the preceding months to be as public as possible about his intentions. Judge Clark, who was with the president at the economic summit in France, urged Reagan to act. On Saturday night, June 5, President Reagan finally approved the dispatch of a letter to Begin urging restraint and calling for a cease-fire to take effect at nine A.M. Sunday morning. Although Ambassador Lewis managed to deliver the message to Begin at six-thirty in the morning, we quickly learned that Begin had brushed him off, refusing to even consider a cease-fire. Lead elements of the IDF began to cross the border at eleven A.M., June 6.

I spent Saturday night in my office in order to monitor the escalation and work on a statement for the president. With reports of IDF movements flooding into the Situation Room all night, it was obvious that the Israeli juggernaut would soon begin to roll forward. Anticipating a rapid advance and the systematic destruction of the PLO forces in the south, the fundamental questions facing the United States were the prospects of Israeli-

Syrian combat, Soviet intervention and an Arab response that might include an oil embargo. Sitting in the Situation Room's secure conference room with Oliver North and other NSC staff members, maps of Israel, Lebanon, Syria and the Middle East propped against the wall and intelligence reports, diplomatic cables and wire stories piled up around us, we analyzed a range of scenarios and possible initiatives the United States could undertake in order to contain the conflict, reduce the prospects for a wider war and end the fighting as quickly as possible.

State was already engaged in diplomatic consultations with Saudis, Syrians and indirectly with the PLO, in order to try to restore the cease-fire. While this diplomacy was certainly well-intentioned, there seemed to me no sense of realism about Israel's agenda, which was to destroy the PLO as a military and political force, or the level of Israel's frustration with the growing PLO military infrastructure in south Lebanon. It was clear that American diplomacy had failed, due in part to Iraqi intrigue, but primarily due to the irreconcilable interests of the Lebanese ethnic groups, the Palestinians, the Israelis and the Syrians.

The natural state of politics in Lebanon had become one of violence and coercion. America's good offices were incapable of altering the basic goals of the parties. Shortly after dawn, the invasion well under way, I went over to the State Department to receive Prime Minister Begin's letter to President Reagan, which outlined the goals and scope of "Operation Peace for Galilee." Begin informed Reagan that the goal of the operation was to destroy the ability of the PLO to shell and rocket northern Israel. To accomplish this goal, the IDF would advance only forty kilometers into Lebanon and would do its best to avoid confronting the Syrians. Well aware of Washington's many reasons for opposing an Israeli invasion, Begin clearly sought to calm U.S. leaders, at least to the point where the IDF could accomplish its minimal goals without U.S. intervention. No one in the White House, from the president on down, accepted Begin's letter at face value.

In an analysis of the letter we sent forward, Kemp and I jointly expressed the opinion that while the IDF would crush the PLO, it was difficult to believe that the Syrians, for a variety of political and military reasons, could afford to sit idly by and permit the IDF to gain a position which threatened the Syrian Army's lines of communication back to Syria. Moreover, it was inconceivable that Syria's SAM batteries in the Bekáa Valley would not be destroyed by Israel. Having listened to Sharon brief anyone who would listen about his solutions to Israel's multiple problems in Lebanon, it would have been naive to actually believe what Begin wrote the president. Sharon unambiguously promoted a vision of Eretz Israel that called for an expansion of Israel's border and wanted to force the United States to accommodate itself to his vision through a fait accompli. Indeed, it quickly became apparent that Sharon and Begin had not been candid about the extent of Israeli intentions, flagrantly abusing the American commitment to Israel's security to engage the United States in a policy with which Washington did not agree.

Reagan, Bush, Clark, Chief of Staff James Baker and Michael Deaver were outraged, and their reaction led to the Reagan and Bush administrations' mistrust of Israel's Likud-led government through 1992. The president, having arrived in Versailles, France, over the weekend for an economic summit, appeared to have been caught off guard by Israel's action. Clark in particular perceived the timing of the action to be directly related to the president's travel. He believed Begin had deliberately sought to embarrass the United States by creating a crisis that would put the president on the spot with the other summit leaders. When I politely challenged Clark's analysis upon the president's return, he fiercely glared at me and then said it was obvious to him that the Israelis wanted to make us look weak and were taking advantage of the president's strong friendship toward Israel. "Israel takes America for granted and wants to be treated like an ally while acting contemptuously towards us. We cannot let the Israelis have it both ways," Clark said with considerable anger in his voice.

Reagan immediately dispatched Habib to Israel and Syria in order to try to restore the cease-fire as well as to promote a more ambitious diplomatic initiative that would complete the task of removing the PLO from southern Lebanon. The Syrian military, however, had begun to engage the IDF at various points along the eastern axes of advance. While Assad was pleased to have the IDF weaken the PLO's military capabilities, Syria needed to protect its own position in Lebanon. With IDF-Syrian ground combat starting to intensify, the Israelis wiped out the Syrian SAM network in Lebanon and shot down twenty-nine Soviet-supplied Syrian fighter aircraft on June 9. Over the next two days, the Israelis and Syrians fought a number of bitter tank, infantry and air battles before Habib succeeded in convincing both sides to agree to and implement a cease-fire on June 11.

Yet no sooner did the cease-fire begin than Israeli units began to creep forward in order to consolidate their lines and attempt to cut the Beirut–Damascus highway. In what could only be described as a new level of Israeli chutzpah, Sharon responded to Habib's furious demarche that

Israeli movement violated the cease-fire by stating that Israel had never agreed to a cease-fire in place. When the dust settled at the end of the first week of the war, Israeli artillery was virtually in range of Damascus, Beirut was surrounded from the south and west, and the Syrian Army in eastern Lebanon, although fighting fiercely, appeared to be poised for destruction.

The roots of America's vital interests in Lebanon were found in the legacy of the Eisenhower Doctrine and the long-standing American commitment guaranteeing the independence of Lebanon against Syrian encroachment. But in the current circumstances it was essential that the United States prevent Lebanon from becoming an Arab-Israeli battleground that could escalate into a U.S.-Soviet confrontation. Since the April 1981 missile crisis had erupted, the Soviet Union had demonstrated that it intended to stand by its Syrian ally, even placing Soviet advisors in harm's way on the Syria-Lebanon border in order to deter Israel from acting against the missiles in the Bekáa Valley. As soon as the war began, the Soviets began to prepare a resupply effort, a move which we had anticipated and which did not appear threatening to U.S. interests. However, following the destruction of the missiles and the post-cease-fire maneuvers of the Israeli Army, the situation quickly grew more ominous.

Putting Teeth into the Message

Early in the second week of the war, the watch officer in the Situation Room called me at home at four A.M. to instruct me to come in immediately and read a letter that had just arrived. When I asked whether it was another Begin letter, he would say only that it wasn't from Begin, but that Dick Pipes just arrived to start translating it. The reference to Richard Pipes (the principal NSC staff member responsible for Soviet affairs) could only mean one thing: a "hot line" message from Brezhnev. This was the first time the hot line had been used since the start of the Reagan administration. I had gotten only two hours of sleep, but I leaped out of bed and raced back to the White House.

Dick Pipes is a Harvard scholar, well known for his hard-line, anti-Soviet views. He interpreted the letter as ominous in tone, with Leonid Brezhnev effectively threatening to intervene if the United States was unable to restrain Israel. A threshold had been crossed and the situation in Lebanon could no longer be viewed as a regional problem. We immediately convened the interagency Crisis Pre-Planning Group (CPPG) in order to prepare for a seven A.M. Special Situation Group (SSG) meeting, which Vice President Bush would chair. As the CPPG reviewed the latest intelligence, we debated how to interpret Brezhnev's letter and tried to assess what, if anything, the Soviets might do to back up their threat.

I asked the representative of the JCS, Lieutenant General Paul Gorman, whether we had picked up indications of any change in the status of Soviet forces. He emphatically replied that the United States had not observed any change. This led the CPPG to conclude that for the present, at least, Brezhnev was simply posturing rhetorically. The United States would, therefore, not need to do more than reply with a firm letter from Reagan to Brezhnev. Robert Gates, the deputy director for Intelligence (DDI) at the CIA, concurred, noting that there were no signs of unusual activity in Moscow or among Soviet leaders.

As the CPPG meeting concluded at six-thirty A.M., I felt unsettled and decided to call the National Military Intelligence Center (NMIC) in the Pentagon to ask the officer responsible for real-time monitoring of Soviet forces whether our assets had detected unusual Soviet activities. Calling on a secure phone from inside the Situation Room's conference room, I queried the watch officer, a lieutenant colonel, who was unaware of the hot-line message. He immediately replied that it was funny I should ask. He proceeded to brief me on a dispute that was then under way within the intelligence community over some information that had been received several hours earlier which included orders from Moscow to a Guards (Soviet airborne forces) regiment in Odessa and their associated strategic airlift to go on an alert status. I knew that this was the same unit Moscow had put on alert during the October 1973 War.

He went on to recount the ongoing debate. Although some analysts believed the orders were for a genuine alert, other intelligence analysts argued that it simply reflected an exercise about which the United States was unaware. He said the argument was going on at the "colonel level," and, as far as he knew, the unevaluated information had not even reached the director of the DIA, let alone the chairman of the JCS or Secretary Weinberger. When I asked him what time the information had come in, he read me the date/time/group (DTG) from the report. With a copy of the hot-line message in my hand, I compared its DTG with the one read to me by the watch officer. The DTGs were identical.

Momentarily stunned by the enormity of the implication that the Soviets had placed airborne forces on alert in order to "put teeth" into the hot-line message, I asked him to hold on while I called General Gorman to the phone. Taking a deep breath, I saw Gorman at the end of the table pointing to a map of Lebanon which showed the extent of the Israeli advances as he talked with Lieutenant Colonel Oliver North, the NSC staff's political-military affairs officer who handled Middle East and Central American issues. "General," I called out, "you better come over here and talk to this guy at the NMIC. It appears that Moscow has placed airborne forces on alert in Odessa."

A pall of silence descended over the room as everyone watched Gorman slowly turn away from North and walk over to where I stood, the secure phone in my hand. After speaking with the NMIC himself, he turned back to the group and nodded his head in confirmation. Although the information was still being evaluated, it certainly appeared that Moscow was signaling that it was preparing to send troops to Syria. He went on to say that we didn't have any indication that they had begun to deploy yet, only that they had given orders to prepare to move. The room virtually exploded with a barrage of verbal expletives about the Israelis in general and Sharon in particular. A few minutes later Gorman restored a semblance of calm and we began to analyze the implications of this new information.

The hot-line letter had suddenly taken on a much more ominous meaning. The Soviets were clearly preparing to do more than simply resupply their ally in Damascus or bluster rhetorically in an effort to convince the United States to put significant pressure on Israel. Following the incredible humiliation to Syria's Soviet-supplied air-defense network in Lebanon and the "threat in being" that the IDF now posed to Damascus as a result of Israel's continued advance, Moscow was compelled to act in order to demonstrate that it was prepared to confront the United States and stand by its allies in the face of "American-backed" Israeli aggression.

The dilemmas for the United States were profound: Was Moscow bluffing? Would it help the Syrians in Lebanon, or was its commitment to Damascus limited to the territorial integrity of Syria? Would Moscow, already deeply involved in Afghanistan, be willing to deploy forces to Damascus in response to a request for assistance? Should Washington increase the alert status of selected U.S. forces in order to match the escalation of Moscow, thereby demonstrating that the United States would not be intimidated, but also possibly forcing Moscow to climb further up the escalation ladder? How far up the ladder might both super-powers have to go before Moscow or Washington would start to back down? The United States absolutely did not want to go to war with Moscow in the Middle East. Were there steps that could be taken to convince Israel to observe a cease-fire in place and desist from further action against Syria, without appearing that the United States was caving in to Soviet threats? There were no clear answers to these questions; only speculation, more questions and analyses of options.

When Bush arrived along with the other principals of the SSG to review the letter, we advised that the situation had suddenly grown muddy and threatening because of the apparent alert orders that had been given to the Soviet forces. Bush instantly absorbed the gravity of the new information (he had received a copy of the letter as soon as it was translated around five-thirty A.M.) and fired off a list of questions that he wanted considered while he went upstairs to the White House residence in order to brief the president on the latest developments.

The vice president returned about thirty minutes later and directed the CPPG to prepare a draft response for the president to send to Moscow. Reagan was taking a very firm line. He did not want Moscow to perceive any lack of will on the part of the United States to stand by Israel or that the United States could be intimidated by Soviet threats. As for the alert of Soviet forces, the United States would not adjust the posture of the U.S. military, for the time being, in order to assess the seriousness of Soviet intentions. The United States already had significant naval and marine forces in the Mediterranean and on balance it seemed unnecessary to shift them in a manner that might appear even more threatening to Moscow. On the diplomatic level, the president directed that Habib somehow intensify his efforts and "pull out all the stops" to convince Israel to observe the cease-fire.

In addition to Moscow, only two other countries tried to help the Syrians cope with the Israeli invasion: Libya and Iran, allies in the Iran-Iraq war. Libya sent cash and some mobile surface-to-air-missile equipment with accompanying troops. Iran's assistance, on the other hand, proved to be much more important, although the significance was not immediately apparent. Several days after the invasion, we learned that Tehran wanted to dispatch several thousand Pasdaran fighters (Revolutionary Guards) to fight alongside the Syrians. Ostensibly due to Syrian support for Iran in its war with Iraq, the Iranians wanted to return the favor, while demonstrating that even the bloody struggle with Iraq would not prevent Iran from contributing to the fight against Israel. At first Assad was opposed to the deployment of Pasdaran, clearly troubled about how to keep them under effective Syrian control. But Iran persevered and induced Damascus with financial assistance. Suddenly IranAir flights were flying over Turkey en route to Damascus. Assad tried to keep the Pasdaran out of Lebanon, but neither the Pasdaran nor Iran's ambassador to Syria Mohammed Mohtashami-Pur would agree, and the Pasdaran quickly drove into Lebanon, taking up residence at the Sheikh Abdullah Barracks in the Bekáa Valley.

From this lodgment, Iran finally had secured a forward staging area, a training center and management headquarters for the export of the Islamic revolution to the Shia community of Lebanon. While we were clearly distressed by Iran's successful penetration of Pasdaran units into Lebanon, we had no idea that this action would inevitably lead to the radicalization of large elements of the Lebanese Shia community, the widespread taking of hostages, a dramatic upsurge in international terrorism and what would eventually become known as the Iran Affair.

Begin came to Washington one week later to meet with Reagan on June 21. Bush, Clark, Michael Deaver and Weinberger all advocated imposing military supply sanctions against Israel on the basis that Israel's use of U.S.-supplied weapons violated its agreements to limit their use to self-defense. They urged the president to cancel Begin's visit and thereby distance the United States from Israel's actions in Lebanon. Weinberger also argued that the United States should consider departing from its traditional stand of opposing a dialogue with the PLO. Haig, U.N. ambassador Jeane Kirkpatrick and Casey disagreed, arguing that the invasion was a justifiable act of self-defense. They believed the invasion created opportunities for the United States to expand its regional influence at Soviet expense, while significantly damaging the infrastructure of international terrorism.

During one meeting, Weinberger opined that since Begin had once himself been a terrorist, Arafat could also change and become a statesman. Weinberger continued in this vein for several minutes, urging the president to seize the initiative in the peace process by reconsidering the U.S. policy toward the PLO. Kirkpatrick was visibly shocked by Weinberger's attitude, and finally interrupted him. "Cap, you talk about Yasir Arafat as if he's some kind of agrarian reformer. Arafat is a Soviet-backed international terrorist. You have lost your sense of perspective." At this point, his National Security Council sharply divided, Reagan spoke up to "agree with Jeane." Reagan said he believed that the best chance the United States had to influence Begin to end the fighting and revert to diplomacy would result from a personal meeting between the two men. In this context, Reagan resisted the pressure to cancel Begin's trip.

The ensuing struggle between what became two distinct camps on Middle East issues illustrated the lack of presidential leadership in this area and it reflected Reagan's consistent failure to control the members of his Cabinet. With the Begin meeting confirmed, Haig immediately prepared a briefing memo and accompanying talking points, which contained no criticism of Israeli policy, emphasized America's desire to see the fighting stop as quickly as possible and noted, with some satisfaction, the blow that Israel had dealt to international terrorism. Clark reacted angrily to Haig's proposed messages. He was livid with what he characterized as a "kowtow" to Begin and instructed Kemp and me to draft an alternative paper that clearly informed Begin of the president's great unhappiness with Israel's invasion of Lebanon and the absolute requirement for the violence to end immediately. Clark decided to have the president meet privately with Begin in the Oval office, where this harsh message could be delivered without the need for either leader to posture before his subordinates.

To Begin's dismay, after a brief pleasantry Reagan picked up the stack of index cards that contained the demarche and read the harsher NSC statement. Begin was visibly shaken when he, Reagan and Lewis entered the Cabinet Room after Reagan had finished delivering this tough message. Although Begin proceeded to deliver a lengthy statement about the hordes of arms captured from the PLO in southern Lebanon, his voice cracked several times; he was apparently distracted and perturbed by the schizophrenic reception he was receiving. On one side of the president, Haig was smiling warmly and nodding enthusiastically as Begin presented the results of the operation. On the other side of the president, Bush, Weinberger and Clark tried to reinforce the tough private message that Reagan had delivered, hardly masking their anger over what they perceived to be Israeli exploitation of American generosity and goodwill. Haig had been arguing that no pressure should be applied to force Israel to lift the siege of Beirut before the PLO was ejected. Veliotes and Habib sought to use the opportunity to force a weakened, but not destroyed, PLO to support peace talks between Jordan and Israel. They discounted Israel's goal of destroying the PLO militarily and politically. The Reagan administration was not speaking with one voice.

On the diplomatic level, the divided Cabinet also contributed to the communication of mixed signals to the Saudis, the Syrians and the PLO. One matter that Arab leaders kept raising with U.S. diplomats was their concern that the IDF would physically enter Beirut in pursuit of the PLO. Never before had Israeli ground forces invaded an Arab capital city, and great stock was placed in convincing the United States to prevent Israel from invading Beirut. At the mid-June funeral for King Khalid of Saudi Arabia, Bush and Weinberger informed the Saudis that the United States agreed with this perspective and would not permit the IDF to enter Beirut.

Understandably, the Saudis immediately communicated this news to the Lebanese leadership and the PLO, thereby severely undermining Habib's indirect negotiations with the PLO, negotiations that seemed close to reaching an agreement on a political solution. Arafat interpreted Bush and Weinberger's assurances to mean that he should hold out, despite the fact that the Lebanese Moslem leaders were putting tremendous pressure on him to agree to leave Lebanon.

Filling the Gap

Against the backdrop of Israel's invasion of Lebanon and the gnashing of teeth it was causing throughout much of Washington, the Iran-Iraq War continued to go in Iran's favor. By the middle of June 1982, an Iranian offensive seemed imminent. Armor, infantry and artillery units were massing in several locations astride the border, while Iranian hospitals were emptied of all but the most serious cases. The strategic Baghdad–Basra road appeared to be the target. If the Iranians could cut the road, many analysts concluded, Iraqi forces along the front could be routed, bringing about the collapse of Iraq and the victory of Iran. In such circumstances, Iranian forces would march on Baghdad, intent on eliminating Saddam Hussein and imposing a fundamentalist regime answerable to Tehran. With the region in flames, the prospects of an Iranian victory against Iraq were extremely ominous.

The United States had identified a gap in the lines of the Iraqi forces just north of Basra. Tehran also appeared to be aware of this vulnerability, since Iranian forces were poised to launch a major assault upon the Iraqi forces at the gap. Were the Iranians to succeed in breaking through this point, they might indeed be able to outflank the forward-deployed elements of the Iraqi Army, destroy them from the rear and then turn toward Basra and Baghdad.

As Israeli escalation in Lebanon continued, and as Arab pressure on Washington grew more intense daily, the attention of the Middle East bureaucracy was almost as focused on the situation in the Persian Gulf as on the war in Lebanon. Despite the fact that Iraq might well have deliberately provoked Israel's invasion by instigating the Abu Nidal assassination attempt in London, the United States found itself grasping for some way of preventing Iraq's collapse. All of us involved in the ongoing policy review agreed that there was little, if any, short-term assistance that the United States could provide that would make a difference on the ground. Nevertheless, as had Mubarak in April, Arab leaders continued to press U.S. officials at every opportunity to sell Iraq arms, or at least permit them to transfer U.S.-supplied arms and equipment to Baghdad. All these overt entreaties were refused, as the United States held firm. We told the Arab and European interlocutors that the Iraqis did not need more weapons but needed intelligent battlefield leadership. They needed to make better use of the equipment they already owned.

Faced with the grisly prospect of an outright Iranian victory, however, one option was debated that might help the Iraqis fend off the Iranian attack without requiring the United States to allow Iraq to gain access to U.S.-supplied matériel. The United States could inform Saddam of the weaknesses in Iraq's own lines and the apparent plans of Iran to attack those positions. This proposal was hotly debated by the same CPPG that was simultaneously coping with the situation in Lebanon. Toward the end of June, a decision was finally made that this was the only option the United States could pursue that might make a difference in preventing an Iranian victory. Communicating through the Saudis and the Jordanians, the U.S. government sent a message to Saddam Hussein that it wanted to offer Iraq some assistance in the war with Iran. Both Saudi Arabia and Jordan were provided with the information about the vulnerabilities in the Iraqi lines so that they could pass it along. However, the offer went further. It suggested the possibility of dispatching a U.S. intelligence officer to Iraq to illustrate the deployments with satellite photography and maps. The Iraqis quickly accepted the entire package. They received the briefing and took immediate action to adjust their defensive positions. When the Iranian assault came some weeks later, Iraqi defenses had been significantly fortified and the Iranians were repulsed with very heavy casualties.

After this, Baghdad's relationship with the United States began to improve rapidly. To get a better idea of what might be possible in U.S.-Iraqi relations, President Saddam Hussein dispatched Nizar Hamdoon to Washington, both to try to ferret out the truth behind the growing "tilt" toward Iraq and to propagandize on behalf of Baghdad. Hamdoon, a trusted Baathist deputy, had been responsible for the activities of the Iraqi Baath party in Syria. It was ironic that for the second time during the Reagan administration, an action taken by Israel, first against the Iraqi nuclear reactor and now Israel's invasion of Lebanon, dramatically affected the environment in Washington and helped to reinforce the nascent American tilt toward Iraq.

A Multinational Force

In early July, Habib reported that the PLO was close to making a decision to withdraw, if a way could be found to provide for the security of the Palestinians left behind. Certain that Israel would refuse to agree to a U.N. peacekeeping force, Habib argued that the United States should organize an alternative multinational force (MNF). The commitment of U.S. forces would provide him with the necessary leverage to convince Arafat that the safety of Palestinians would be ensured during and after the withdrawal of PLO forces.

Despite strongly stated objections by Baker, Weinberger and the JCS to Habib's recommendation that U.S. forces be committed, Kemp, North and I were directed to draft a lengthy decision memorandum for the president which analyzed Habib's request as an opportunity for the United States to deploy forces and bolster America's strategy for southwest Asia. By demonstrating American readiness to use force to help end the bloodshed in Lebanon while enhancing our political leverage there, the United States could try to make the most of a bad situation and convince other Middle East states that the option of U.S. military intervention had been reinvigorated.

The situation was very complex. Reagan needed to get the Congress to support him in committing U.S. forces to back up U.S. policies, and countries had to be found which would accept more Palestinians. In addition, European partners had to be found to act as peacekeepers with U.S. forces. The president approved the recommendation that the U.S. participate in an MNF for "temporary peacekeeping" in Beirut on July 3. Owing in part to the July 4 holiday, consultations with the Congress had not been scheduled to take place until the following week. However, State immediately cabled the decision to Habib, who passed it along to Begin. News of the decision leaked out of Jerusalem the following day, setting off another mini-crisis in Washington between the executive branch and Congress. In this situation, a foreign government knew about the administration's intentions to send U.S. forces to Lebanon before the Congress was consulted. Although the congressional leadership was eventually mollified, and pressures to invoke the War Powers Act successfully resisted, it would still take Habib another six weeks, which included dramatic Israeli military escalation, before he could negotiate the final arrangements for the PLO's withdrawal. The Reagan administration's failure genuinely to consult with Congress in advance represented a pattern, cutting across administrations, which typified the struggle between the executive branch and Congress in the field of foreign affairs.

In the midst of the war in Lebanon and the latest developments in the Iran-Iraq War, larger southwest Asian strategy took center stage when India's prime minister Indira Gandhi made a state visit to Washington. The result of nearly a year's effort beginning with the strategic dialogue, the prime minister's visit marked a watershed in U.S.-Indian relations. Still convinced that advanced arms sales of U.S. weapons to Pakistan posed a threat to India, Gandhi remained skeptical of Zia's long-term intentions. The United States continued to receive reports suggesting that Pakistan was working on a nuclear weapon, but had not confirmed them. Gandhi proved surprisingly receptive to the president's arguments about the growing Soviet threat to southwest Asia posed by the invasion of Afghanistan. She agreed that the shared political cultures should enable the United States and India to restore the promise to bilateral relations that had preceded the Indo-Pakistan war and the polarization of the relations along East-West lines.

Because this was formally designated as a state visit, a black-tie White House dinner was hosted by the president and Mrs. Reagan in honor of Prime Minister Gandhi. By coincidence, my parents were visiting Washington and I invited my mother, Charlotte, to accompany me to the event. Following the Rose Garden dinner, we mingled with the Indian guests and U.S. government officials while Zubin Mehta prepared to give a concert on the White House lawn. Vice President Bush, with whom I was meeting almost daily on the fluid situation in the Middle East, stopped by to chat and asked me whether anything new had come in on Lebanon that day.

After a brief substantive exchange about the day's fighting I introduced my mother to the vice president. Visibly touched, Bush commented that it was really wonderful that I had brought my mother to a state dinner. He said it made him think of his own mother, whom he had not seen lately, and whom he would now give a call. He looked at my mother and said with perfect grace, "Everyone should be able to take their mother to a state dinner, at least once." Needless to say, Bush made her day.

While Habib would be forced to negotiate numerous technical details in order to conclude the withdrawal deal, one of the most revealing and distressing aspects of this phase of the war was the refusal of the Arab states to accept PLO fighters despite the Arab states' rhetoric for the Palestinian cause. Although Syria finally agreed to take most of the fighters, weeks of negotiations were required with Egypt, Tunisia, Jordan, Algeria, Iraq, the YAR and Sudan to get these countries to agree to take any at all. Each state was unambiguous in its opposition and every effort was made by the leaders of these countries to try to extract concessions from the United States on the matter of American recognition of the PLO as the sole, legitimate representative of the Palestinians. Through all of this, Beirut remained the PLO's hostage. As the bombs rained down, the city's power and water was cut by the Israelis to increase the pressure on the Lebanese leaders and the PLO. Yet no Arab leader was willing to accept responsibility for taking in the latest wave of PLO fighters or Palestinian refugees and so help to end Beirut's suffering. The problem was finally overcome by U.S. diplomatic persistence and a final plea from Arafat and his colleagues to key Arab leaders that there really was no alternative but to cut a deal through the United States.

Earlier in the summer, Haig had resigned as secretary of state when he concluded that Judge Clark, Edwin Meese and Jim Baker were undermining his role as the president's principal advisor on foreign affairs. Despite a suggestion from Weinberger that he was well suited to assume the leadership of the State Department, Reagan appointed George P. Shultz as the new secretary of state. As Shultz prepared for his upcoming confirmation hearings, he asked to meet with the NSC staff responsible for the Middle East in order to listen to our perspectives on the problems and prospects of the region. Meeting with us in Clark's office, Shultz listened intently as Kemp and Veliotes briefed him on settlement activity in Israel's occupied territories, the military situation in Lebanon, Habib's negotiating efforts and the difficulties the United States was experiencing in its regular dealings with Begin and Sharon.

After an hour of this, I finally interjected that there were other problems in the Middle East, not involving Israel, worthy of Shultz's attention. Agreeing that he had already heard a great deal about Lebanon and the West Bank, he asked me to proceed with my brief. I presented him with a *tour d'horizon*, painting a grim picture of a region beset by tension, conflict, subversion, terrorism and war. I told him that while today he was focused on the eastern Mediterranean, there were other dangers to the long-term interests of the United States than the war in Lebanon or the future of the PLO. Solving the Palestinian problem would not protect vital U.S. interests in Gulf oil, nor would it cause the Soviet Union to withdraw from Afghanistan.

In response to these comments, Shultz acknowledged that he had not considered Lebanon in the broader regional context, but repeated what had become his trademark criticism of the Israelis and the apparent lack of interest of the United States or Israel in offering the Palestinians a realistic approach to find a peaceful solution. After he finished, I looked at him and politely noted that in listening to his criticism of U.S. policy toward the Arab-Israel peace process, I was forced to conclude either that he had not read the Camp David Accords or else he was somehow not satisfied with the substantive leverage that the accords provided the United States over Israel, if the Palestinians would agree to negotiate within the Camp David framework.

Shultz nodded his head and said quite candidly, "In fact I have not read the Camp David Accords. I don't even have a copy of them." I pulled out my annotated copy of the accords and offered it to Shultz. "Camp David is not perfect, Mr. Secretary," I said, "but I think you will find it can provide a much better basis for progress, especially because the government of Israel has already agreed to it, than if the U.S. tries to craft a completely new process." During his confirmation hearings shortly thereafter, I was pleased to hear that Shultz had explicitly stated how he had recently read the Camp David Accords carefully and had come away convinced that they contained considerable value for the Arab-Israeli peace process.

Last In, First Out

Over the next two months, Habib negotiated with the PLO through intermediaries, and the national security bureaucracy labored day and night to complete an agreement that would enable the peaceful evacuation of the PLO from Beirut and permit the deployment of an MNF to prevent Israeli interference during the withdrawal and to protect the Palestinian inhabitants of the refugee camps.

At the same time, Secretary Shultz convened a small group of advisors, headed by Paul Wolfowitz, to devise a Middle East peace initiative that would offer the Israelis, Palestinians and other Arabs, notably the Jordanians and the Syrians, a reinvigorated peace process. Based squarely on the Camp David Accords, it was premised on a secret understanding concluded between Assistant Secretary Veliotes and King Hussein of Jordan. Unlike the Camp David Accords, which were silent on the final status of the West Bank and Gaza Strip (it was a subject to be negotiated but one on which the United States had not taken a position), the United States now proposed to promote a final status arrangement that returned sovereignty over the occupied territories to Jordan. Veliotes and U.S. ambassador to Jordan, Richard Viets, were led to understand by King Hussein that within forty-eight hours of President Reagan's public enunciation of this new U.S. position, the king would issue a public statement expressing his willingness to participate in a negotiating process based on these new principles. As a result of the assurances King Hussein had provided to Veliotes and Viets, President Reagan delivered a major speech on September 1, 1982, just as the last Palestinian fighter left Beirut on a ferry to Cyprus.

The speech became known as the September 1 Reagan initiative and drew considerable praise in the United States and abroad. In Israel, however, Begin correctly perceived that the U.S. goal was to create a political opportunity for the Palestinians that would deny Israel the victory it sought through the destruction of the PLO. He rejected the Reagan initiative outright. Bewildered by the U.S. conduct of secret diplomacy with the Arab world which had led to a fundamental shift in the U.S. position over the final status of the occupied territories, Begin did not comprehend how his behavior and that of Sharon over the past year had generated deep mistrust.

Within the Middle East bureaucracy, the first days of September were filled with heady visions of a new dawn for the peace process as we waited for King Hussein to make the historic announcement that he would accept the Reagan initiative as the basis for Jordan's participation in the peace process. Meeting in Morocco, the Arab League issued the "Rabat Declaration," which neither supported nor opposed the Reagan initiative. Unfortunately, however, the Arab leaders did not grant King Hussein the clear authority he needed to enable him to join a process as the representative of the Palestinians.

Several days later, the NSC staff received word that Weinberger, without any interagency discussion, had on his own initiative ordered the Marines to depart Beirut and return to their ships on September 10. West Beirut dignitaries called on the American embassy to express their fears of potential violence and instability, but it was too late. As part of the withdrawal agreement, the MNF was authorized to stay in Beirut for up to thirty days in order to allow the Lebanese Armed Forces (LAF) to move in to provide for the security of the Palestinians who were left behind.

Weinberger, however, chose not to wait for these arrangements to be made and instead acted on his own authority, ordering the Marines out. "LAST IN, FIRST OUT," read the Beirut newspaper headlines the next day, as the Lebanese grimly watched the Marines depart. Without the multinational framework, the French and Italians quickly followed suit, leaving Beirut denuded of the international guarantees that had been provided to the PLO as well as to the government of Lebanon. Immediately upon receiving word of this development, I called Secord at ISA to ask what had happened. He said he did not know, other than that "Weinberger told Vessey [now chairman of the JCS] to get the Marines out of Beirut. Their job was finished."

Although the Rabat Declaration had not broken any new ground vis-à-vis recognition of Israel, and King Hussein still had not made any announcement of his willingness to participate in the process, other events had occurred in the region. Beshir Gemayel was elected president of Lebanon, Israel had pulled back slightly from lines near Beirut and President Reagan's peace initiative continued to receive good press, holding out hope for progress in the Arab-Israeli peace process. As usual, however, just when the situation in the Middle East appeared to be calming down and perhaps even turning in the direction of American interests, the world turned upside down on Tuesday, September 14, when reports started to come in that Beshir Gemayel had been assassinated. With his death confirmed later in the day, and the MNF already removed from Beirut, there was little the United States could do to prevent Israel from acting unilaterally to take control of the situation in the Lebanese capital. In direct contravention of agreements Habib had negotiated, Israeli forces immediately entered Beirut and began to search for Palestinian holdouts and exercise their authority through force.

Once again, the U.S. and Israeli governments were accusing one another of bad faith as tensions soared regarding the IDF's presence in Beirut. Despite U.S. assurances to the Arab world, an Arab capital had been violated by Israeli armor. Diplomatic hell was breaking loose as Washington tried to cope with a political-military situation that was spreading out of control. Kemp had already gone off for a much-needed break in the Caribbean. I had planned to sleep late on Saturday morning, September 18, before going to my synagogue to celebrate the Jewish New Year. I woke with a start when the phone rang early in the morning, but whoever it was hung up before I could answer. Within minutes, though, I heard my beeper go off in the other room while a voice called out to me by name from the beeper's miniature loudspeaker, directing me to telephone the Situation Room immediately. What now? I thought to myself, wondering what else could have gone wrong in the six or seven hours that had passed since I left my office. Still half-asleep, I sat and listened in horror as the watch officer read to me from the cable the American embassy in Beirut had just sent, reporting political officer Ryan Crocker's firsthand account of a massacre of men, women and children in the Sabra and Shatila refugee camps. "The Judge wants you in here right away," the watch officer said after finishing the executive summary of the telegram. "Right away."

Dressing quickly, I arrived at the Situation Room within the hour. I got my stack of cables and press clippings and sat outside Clark's office, reading the latest updates as I waited for him to call me in. I was struck by how ragged Clark looked when I walked into his office. He had obviously been in since the early morning, and the fatigue showed in his face. He looked up at me, slowly shook his head, and said, "They cried out for vengeance and vengeance they have wrought. Do you think these people can ever make peace? How could this happen?" Clark spoke with what seemed to be genuine disbelief. "This massacre is truly appalling and sickening, Judge Clark," I said. "But the greatest tragedy is that the people of Lebanon have been slaughtering each other for hundreds of years. Change will come when they decide to stop using violence to advance their interests. But in this circumstance, we bear a heavy responsibility for this tragedy." Clark looked at me with a question in his eye. "What do you mean?" he asked. "The Israelis went back into Beirut and let the Phalangists have their vengeance. What does it have to do with us?"

I swallowed hard and said, "A key part of the deal with Arafat was for the MNF to protect the Palestinians who stayed behind from Phalangist vengeance. When the U.S. Marines left, and the French and Italians followed suit, who was there to protect those Palestinians? No one. On the contrary, once the Phalange saw the MNF depart, it was only a matter of time before something like this happened. Personally, I blame the secretary of defense for unilaterally withdrawing the Marines and creating the environment where the Syrians could assassinate Beshir Gemayel, who Damascus saw as an American agent, and then be confident that the Phalange would take it out on the Palestinians." This was clearly something Clark had not considered. We spoke a while longer before he was called up to see the president. He directed me to draft a statement condemning the massacre and said he wanted to discuss the draft upon his return. Clark came back to the Situation Room about thirty minutes later and placed a secure conference call to Shultz, Meese, Weinberger, Vessey and Casey in order to discuss the massacre and what to do about it.

The call was laden with emotion, and a sense of guilt. Shultz suggested that we should consult with the government of Lebanon and offer to reorganize a multinational force to provide a presence that could help bring about the prompt withdrawal of the IDF from Beirut while contributing to a sense of calm throughout the city. Weinberger disagreed, countering that there was no role for the U.S. military to play, although he "was angry as hell at Sharon for his role in this tragedy." In the end, Shultz, Meese, Casey and Clark favored the return of the MNF with a U.S. component, while Weinberger and Vessey remained adamantly opposed to any U.S. participation. Clark hung up and called Reagan to brief him on the discussion. As he put down the phone again, Clark looked at me and said, "The president believes we have a moral responsibility to help the Lebanese. If the government of Lebanon wants an MNF, we will help put it back together and contribute."

There was nothing more for me to do. As I walked out, Clark was phoning Shultz with the president's guidance. Later that evening I went back to the Situation Room. A cable of instructions had already gone out to Ambassador Robert Dillon in Beirut to consult with the Lebanese government. The instructions implied that the decision to offer a U.S. component to a new MNF had already been made. The Lebanese wasted no time in accepting the U.S. offer, and the diplomatic process to form a new MNF began.

CHAPTER 9

A PEACEFUL
PRESENCE

Assad Gave Me His Word

On September 29, a new MNF was reconstituted and the U.S. Marines returned to Beirut. Unlike the earlier deployment, there was no time limit imposed on their tour of duty, nor were the forces given a clear, unambiguous mission. American, French, Italian and now British forces were sent to Beirut to serve as a "peaceful presence" symbolizing the determination of the West to support Lebanese efforts to rid itself of foreign forces, rebuild its economy and reform itself politically. The United States was not sending in the Marines to secure Beirut. Chief of Staff James Baker, in particular, was concerned about triggering a confrontation with Congress over the War Powers Act. Indeed, to avoid possible invocation of the act, Reagan explicitly stated that there was no intention that U.S. armed forces would become involved in hostilities.

The deployment of the second MNF prompted the Reagan administration to try to articulate a clear set of policy goals toward Lebanon. In the end, President Reagan did little more than reiterate the declaratory goals Habib had enunciated during the summer which called for the removal of all foreign forces, political reconciliation and economic reconstruction of Lebanon and security for Israel's northern borders. This became the stated U.S. policy toward Lebanon.

To accomplish these goals, Habib and Draper labored for nearly nine months to broker an agreement between Israel and Lebanon that would have secured the withdrawal of the Israeli Army from Lebanese territory, created arrangements in southern Lebanon to guarantee the security of northern Israel and laid the groundwork for political and economic relations between Israel and Lebanon. The flaw, however, was obvious and proved to be fatal.

Habib resolutely insisted that in exchange for Israel's agreement to withdraw from Lebanon, he could "guarantee" that Syrian and PLO forces would also withdraw. He based his conviction on assurances provided to him by Assad during the summer. Moreover, despite America's declaratory goal of Lebanese reconciliation, Habib never made political reform a priority of his diplomacy. During many of the conversations we had, he repeatedly told me that it was unrealistic to expect the central authorities to deal with political reform as long as Lebanon was occupied by foreign powers.

The U.S. government and the Lebanese government wanted to conclude a withdrawal and security-arrangements agreement as quickly as possible. The government of Israel also wanted a prompt withdrawal, although initially it was in much less of a hurry than the other parties. The Syrians stated their agreement with this general goal, but in practice Assad did all he could to hinder any agreement that was not on his terms. As precious time passed, the Soviet Union resupplied the weakened Syrians with increasingly sophisticated weapons. Divergent interests, particularly the administration's emphasis on the Reagan initiative and Syria's requirement to restore its military strength, provided both the Israelis and the Syrians with ample justification to stall the process.

Israel remained resentful of Washington for what it considered a betrayal of trust over the Reagan peace initiative. Recognizing that Jordan and the PLO were linking their willingness to support the initiative to Israel's withdrawal from Lebanon, Begin's team worked as slowly as possible, negotiating with the Lebanese on several tracks at the same time. During negotiations over the future of trade relations, the two sides were literally arguing over the price of pickles.

Syria was concerned that it would be left out of the peace process due to Reagan's emphasis on the Palestinians and Jordan. Damascus used the months immediately following the withdrawal of the PLO to recover from the war with $2 billion worth of supplies from the Soviet Union. The Soviet Union had been humiliated when U.S.-made weaponry destroyed Soviet-supplied military hardware in Lebanon. In particular, the Syrians used the end of 1982 to install a strategic air-defense network that would ensure that the IAF would never again be able to act with impunity over Lebanon or Syria. Time was on Syria's side.

The Lebanese government, under the leadership of Beshir's brother Amin Gemayel, was primarily interested in getting rid of the Israelis, the Syrians and the Palestinians, while preserving the primacy of the Maronite Christian community within the Lebanese political structure. Against this backdrop and as months passed, Judge Clark grew increasingly impatient with the pace and scope of Habib's efforts, eventually demanding that Habib set a target date for concluding an agreement. Within the NSC staff, we were concerned that the longer the Israel-Lebanon negotiations dragged on, the more difficult it would be to assure the cooperation of the fast-recuperating Syria. I agreed with Kemp and U.S. Navy commander Philip A. Dur, a new member of the NSC staff responsible for political-military issues in the Middle East (I had worked with Dur previously, at the DOD). We argued that the Syrians would soon be able to use their power against the Lebanese factions, the Israelis and the United States if Habib continued to ignore Assad and failed to make significant political progress before the end of 1982. Nor did we have any illusions that the Reagan initiative could endure indefinitely without some movement toward the start of negotiations.

Habib, however, did not want to hear any criticism of his approach from the NSC staff, and on the margins of King Hussein's December 1982 visit to Washington told me bluntly to "butt out, I don't need the NSC staff telling me when and how to get things done in Lebanon. We will get an agreement and the Syrians will withdraw." Habib, to be fair, gave the same assurances to President Reagan. He sincerely believed that the Syrians would eventually agree to withdraw. During the "prebrief" for a visit to the White House by President Mubarak in February 1983, the president pointedly asked Habib whether and why he believed that the Syrians would withdraw from Lebanon. "Assad gave me his word," Habib replied. "The Syrians will withdraw when Israel withdraws. There is no doubt in my mind."

As we walked from the Oval Office to the Cabinet Room for the plenary session with Mubarak and his advisors, Habib pulled me aside and angrily said, "Did you write those talking points for the president? Goddamn it, Teicher! You guys are trying to ruin me. You're supposed to be a Middle East expert. I can't negotiate a deal between the Israelis and the Syrians that gives Israel special rights in Lebanon just like that. The White House has got to let me do it my way." Pausing momentarily, I replied, "Look Phil, I don't have any illusions about the Syrians, Lebanese or the Israelis. Nor do I expect you to produce a miracle. But we simply don't share your confidence that the Syrians will agree to withdraw once Israel and Lebanon reach an agreement. I understand that you don't want to engage Assad now because it will enhance his leverage over the negotiations that are under way. But don't expect Clark to let up." Habib scowled as he stomped off, shaking his head and swearing under his breath about young jerks at the NSC.

The administration's preoccupation with Lebanon and the Reagan initiative prevented the national security bureaucracy from looking farther east to try to do anything about the situation in the Gulf, other than the minimum necessary. The JCS had spent several years resisting the president's instructions to establish new command arrangements for southwest Asia, arguing that existing arrangements were sufficient. It seemed that the JCS would never voluntarily agree to restructure the command arrangements due to interservice rivalries and competition for resources. President Reagan eventually forced the issue by demanding that the Central Command (CENTCOM) be established. Although the headquarters remained at MacDill Air Force Base in Tampa, Florida, CENTCOM assumed operational responsibility for the RDF, and an orderly, if long-distance, planning, coordination and exercise process was set in motion.

Yet U.S. security policy in the Gulf remained unstable. Saudi Arabia was neither strong enough nor willing to adequately protect U.S. vital interests in the Persian Gulf. Our tilt toward Iraq remained still nascent. And the strategic consensus that was to assist the United States in advancing and protecting its own interests based on the common threat posed by the Soviet Union had virtually evaporated with Haig's departure. Nonetheless the strategic framework remained intact and the national security bureaucracy continued to deliberately press ahead to strengthen America's ability to act unilaterally to defend Gulf interests.

Do Not Lock or Load

Shultz viewed the participation of United States Marines in the MNF as a demonstration of U.S. resolve to use force in the Middle East to protect vital interests and to provide an element of leverage to our regional diplomacy. Clark and the NSC staff shared this view. The Marines' return to Lebanon for the first time since the Eisenhower administration was a clear signal that the United States meant business; at least it was supposed to be a clear signal. Weinberger, however, remained adamantly opposed to the participation of U.S. forces in the MNF and argued strenuously for their withdrawal at every opportunity.

At Weinberger's direction, the DOD went out of its way to put further distance between the United States and Israel. The Defense Department publicly highlighted the growing number of confrontations between Israeli soldiers and U.S. Marines, as the visceral acrimony between Sharon and Weinberger continued to intensify. The DOD emphasized these differences in part to reassure the Saudis and others that the United States would not cooperate with the Israelis in the defense of the Gulf. Weinberger did his best to cast Israel as a strategic liability, despite the president's public contention that Israel represented a strategic asset for the United States in the Middle East.

Even as the command arrangements provided by CENTCOM were being put into place to defend against Soviet or other threats to our oil interests in the Gulf, Tehran was intensifying the export of the Islamic revolution and attacking the soft underbelly of Western interests in Lebanon. Having established its beachhead in the Bekáa Valley in June 1982, Tehran's proponents of militant fundamentalism were actively strengthening their influence among the large déclassé Shia population of Lebanon. The number of Iranian Pasdaran that Iran had deployed during the early days of the war had remained fairly constant at around two thousand, but the numbers of Lebanese Shias who gravitated toward a more militant, anti-Western orientation had grown dramatically. Particularly in the Bekáa Valley, where Syrian forces remained in control opposite the IDF, the Shia militias grew in numbers, strength and determination to usurp power from the traditional Shia leadership and to drive the Israelis and the MNF out of Lebanon. Through the office of Iranian ambassador Mohtashami-Pur in Damascus, money, guns and guidance flowed from Tehran to the Bekáa.

The defense of U.S. interests in Beirut fell to the Marines of the MNF. This was not the purpose, however, for which the Marines had been deployed. The Marines were neither prepared nor enabled to contend with the emerging terror threat. The bizarre rules of engagement (ROE) that governed their ability to fire in self-defense severely hobbled them. Despite the extreme violence of Beirut, the Marines were prohibited from locking ammunition clips into their personal weapons. However much Weinberger might have opposed the presence of U.S. Marines in Beirut, however correct he believed himself to be, it was simply outrageous to severely restrict the Marines' ability to defend themselves.

On January 9, 1983, I asked Gayle to marry me. Fifteen minutes later, my beeper went off and I was summoned to the Situation Room, where the watch officer informed me that we had received confirmation that long-range, high-altitude SAM-5 air-defense missiles had been delivered to Syria and were expected to become operational in the very near future. Supported by Soviet advisors and technicians, the SAM-5s and the very sophisticated electronics that supported the missile systems gave Syria the ability to cover all of Lebanon, northern Israel and northern Jordan. This new capability, coming in the wake of the Israeli destruction of the Syrian air-defense network during the war, was sure to strengthen Assad's resolve to stand up to U.S. efforts to negotiate a political arrangement between Israel and Lebanon. The prospects for Habib's efforts to succeed looked worse than ever.

Improving Relations with Israel

In February 1983, Israel's Kahan Commission of Inquiry issued its findings regarding the Sabra and Shatila massacres. Sharon was forced to resign from his Cabinet post as defense minister, and several other Israeli officials were severely reprimanded. In this context, and with U.S.-Israeli defense relations at a historic low, McFarlane instructed me to propose a strategy for improving U.S.-Israeli relations predicated on the need for moving the peace process forward and enhancing the overall U.S. military position in southwest Asia. Aware that several of my colleagues on the NSC staff favored increasing the pressure on Israel, McFarlane explicitly directed that I compose the paper secretly and not coordinate my ideas with anyone else on the staff.

The strategy paper was completed in early April. It argued that the mutual mistrust that had evolved since the first days of the Reagan administration and the Israelis' failing confidence in U.S. commitments to the security of Israel had reached a point where, unless reversed, the U.S. government would find it very difficult if not impossible to achieve its diverse regional political objectives. Israel's control of occupied territories and its military strength and preoccupation with security, in the absence of Arab conciliation, made Israeli cooperation essential if progress was to be made toward the withdrawal of Israeli forces from Lebanon, a resumption of the broader peace process, and increased political-military cooperation from key states in the Gulf. The United States could not expect any of these goals to be accomplished while Washington and Jerusalem remained at loggerheads over so many fundamental issues.

Given this deteriorating state of affairs, a strategy designed to improve U.S.-Israeli relations and restore Israeli confidence in American reliability in order for the United States to exert effective influence in Israel was proposed. This influence would enhance U.S. diplomatic leverage and increase the likelihood that three core American goals could be accomplished by the end of June: a Lebanon withdrawal agreement, a Jordanian movement toward direct negotiations with Israel over transitional arrange-

ments for the West Bank and Gaza, and a restoration of strategic cooperation between the United States and Israel directed against the Soviet
Union in the eastern Mediterranean.

Against the backdrop of the Kahan Commission, it was apparent that
Begin had become increasingly detached from Israeli politics. (In addition
to his deep sorrow over the massacres at Sabra and Shatila, Begin had
also recently lost his beloved wife.) Moshe Arens, Yitzhak Shamir and
David Levy were all maneuvering to assume the leadership of the Likud
bloc in the expectation that Begin would soon step down. It appeared to
me that the emergence of Arens as a friend of the United States could
prove essential to any effort to improve our relations. Unlike Shamir,
who was prone to approach U.S.-Israeli relations from a confrontational
stance, the tough-minded Arens was a realist who understood the importance of the U.S.-Israeli security relationship. I did not believe that Arens
would gratuitously jeopardize the relationship in order to enhance his
domestic political position or to gain a tactical advantage over an enemy
of Israel. Sharon, by contrast, regularly sought to exploit the U.S. relationship for his own political gain. He played on chauvinistic impulses in
Israel to bolster his position as the one Israeli leader on whom Begin could
count to stand up to an America he characterized as driven solely by oil
interests in the Gulf and Arab pressures. The challenge for Washington
was to find a way to take advantage of the opportunity created by Begin's
passivity, the probable leadership vacuum, Sharon's demise and Arens's
potential ascendancy in order to influence Israeli leaders and policy in a
direction that would advance and support American interests.

I argued that our key goal should be to help strengthen Arens and
others who understood the need to minimize friction between the two
countries. The best way to achieve this goal would be to refocus on
security issues in a manner that would improve Arens's influence and
prestige in the Cabinet and with the Israeli public. Owing to Arens's
background as an aerospace engineer and his interest in the development
of Israel's high-technology defense industries, U.S. assistance to this sector would strengthen Arens's influence in addition to contributing directly
to the well-being of the Israeli economy. I pointed out that Weinberger
had grown especially tough in his opposition to several defense-coopera-
tion initiatives, including the provision of defense manufacturing technology that would support Israel's LAVI program (an advanced tactical fighter
aircraft Israel wanted to produce for internal use and export), joint U.S.-
Israeli development of military technology resulting from lessons learned

in Lebanon, conversion of FMS credits for defense purchases in Israel, and the like.

Israeli confidence in the U.S. commitment to Israel's security had weakened over the past two years, despite the genuine friendship that Ronald Reagan felt toward Israel. In the eyes of many Israelis, the United States had unfairly penalized Israel for its destruction of the Iraqi nuclear reactor. We had promised to maintain Israel's qualitative edge over its Arab adversaries but suspended shipments of F-15s and F-16s even while continuing to sell advanced arms to Arab states. The United States had sought Israeli restraint, promising to get the Syrian SAMs out of the Bekáa Valley, but succeeded only in talking about the problem. We promised to treat Israel like a strategic partner but suspended the very limited MOU. The United States had promised to consult with the leadership of Israel before promoting any major initiatives in the peace process but consulted with King Hussein of Jordan, not Israel, in advance of the September 1 Reagan initiative. It made little difference to the Israeli polity that immoderate Israeli behavior had triggered U.S. actions. Looking at things through an Israeli prism, the United States seemed driven by Arab sensibilities at the expense of Israeli security needs.

Reduced Israeli confidence in America decreased Israel's willingness to take risks. Focusing on the stalemate in the Lebanon negotiations over security arrangements, it was essential that Washington recognize its responsibility for Israel's lack of confidence in our assurances. Deserved or not, Jerusalem believed that the arrangements negotiated by Habib in 1981 actually had contributed to the PLO buildup in southern Lebanon. The administration's subsequent failure to take seriously Israeli intelligence on the PLO and the ensuing discovery of vast quantities of PLO arms and equipment in the south hardened Israel's growing conviction that confidence in U.S. security assurances had been misplaced. Given the volatile nature of Israeli electoral politics and the fundamental role of the security issue in the consciousness of every Israeli, the United States had to understand that American performance was essential to the ability of Washington to convince Israel to take risks for peace. In domestic Israeli politics, politicians who urged Israelis to run risks in the peace process based on unfulfilled American security promises would simply not be reelected.

Equally important to the successful development and implementation of this strategy was a clear understanding of the Arab dimension of U.S.-Israeli relations. A large measure of U.S. influence within the Arab world derived from Arab perceptions of U.S. influence over Israel, particularly Washington's ability to "extract" concessions on a range of issues. Even in private discussions, where many Arab leaders acknowledged Israel's right to exist, most Arab officials recognized neither the moral and strategic interests that the United States had in a strong Israel nor the relationship between healthy U.S.-Israeli relations and Israeli risk-taking in the peace process. It was difficult for the Arab world to believe that our ability to extract concessions from Israel derived as much from Arab as U.S. actions. Arab leaders recalled Eisenhower's policy dictates to Israel in 1956 and regularly called for the United States to impose its will and cut off aid to Israel. While such actions might have yielded short-term praise in the Arab press, it would have guaranteed stiffened Israeli resolve, reduced prospects for Israeli concessions and would have led quickly to even shriller Arab rhetoric and exaggerated expectations.

In attempting to advance our goals, the United States was confronted by the following dilemma: take actions which might anger the Arab world but bolster Israeli confidence, and so induce a greater Israeli propensity to take risks; or try to encourage the Arabs to be forthcoming by pressuring Israel, thereby reducing the likelihood of Israeli concessions. On balance the United States needed a strategy that would be as tough or as forthcoming with the Arab world as we chose to be with Israel. While this approach could be counted upon in the short term to provoke the Arabs, it would increase U.S. influence within Israel. If that influence led ultimately to Israeli concessions, Arab confidence in the United States would grow, thereby eventually increasing our influence in the Arab world as well.

McFarlane gave my strategy paper to Eagleburger, who in turn passed it on to Shultz. During the second week of April, McFarlane called me to his office, where he informed me that Shultz was so impressed with the paper that he had decided to make it his strategy. Several days later, Shultz asked to see Reagan. With McFarlane, Eagleburger and me present, Shultz presented the strategy, having first graciously acknowledged me as the author, recommending that the president immediately instruct Weinberger to release the licenses necessary for the export of manufacturing technology that would enable Israel to proceed with the development of the LAVI aircraft. Reagan agreed to the general outlines of the strategy as well as to Shultz's specific request for the release of the LAVI licenses. He directed that the strategy be implemented and the licenses released. McFarlane passed the president's guidance along to Weinberger. However, Weinberger strongly objected, and protested the decision to Reagan.

Despite Weinberger's opposition, Reagan refused to change his mind and directed Weinberger to support Shultz's approach. Recognizing the importance of the licenses in building Arens's stake in the U.S. relationship, Ambassador Lewis promptly communicated the news of the president's decision to Arens, thus initiating a turnaround in U.S.-Israeli relations.

It was too late, however, for the Reagan initiative. On April 10, to the intense disappointment of many, King Hussein of Jordan announced that he would not enter into negotiations with Israel on behalf of the Palestinians or for Jordan. The Arab world had not mustered the resolve necessary to convince Arafat to agree to such a role for the king. Fed up with the PLO, Israel and the United States, King Hussein threw up his hands in despair, effectively ending the Reagan initiative. Hussein's rejection of the Reagan peace plan initiative helped intensify the thaw in U.S.-Israeli relations and increased George Shultz's frustration with Arab leaders.

But We Must Have Revenge

Even as the administration was trying to recover from the collapse of the Reagan initiative, a blow was struck directly against American interests in Lebanon. On April 18 the U.S. embassy in Beirut was destroyed by a terrorist car bomb. Sixty-three people were killed, including seventeen Americans. Although the murder of Americans is always sobering for national security bureaucrats, I was especially saddened by the death of Bob Ames, the NIO for the Middle East. Ames and I had engaged in frequent and heated debate over the pros and cons of various policy alternatives for the United States in the Middle East over the past year. We had met earlier in April to discuss some of the questions he might explore before he left for the Middle East. Although he and I disagreed fundamentally about issues involving the Arab-Israeli conflict, he was a genuine expert and I respected him very much. With a tremendous depth of knowledge and experience in the Middle East, his loss was a deep blow to the United States government.

Later that afternoon, the White House announced that Eagleburger would lead a U.S. delegation to Beirut in order to demonstrate America's resolve not to be intimidated by terrorists and to bring home the bodies of the slain Americans for burial in the United States. McFarlane had already called to inform me that I would be the White House representative on this delegation, which would include Veliotes, Deputy Director of Central Intelligence (DDCI) John McMahon, Noel Koch and Marine Corps lieutenant general Bernard Trainor, representing the JCS.

We arrived at Beirut International Airport early on the morning of April 20, protected by squads of heavily armed Marines and Lebanese security forces. We careened through the crazy-quilt streets of Beirut to the hulk of the bombed-out embassy, where Eagleburger delivered a statement to the media. Squinting into the bright, hazy glare of the sun rising up over Mount Lebanon, the ruins of the embassy smoldering as rescue workers continued to search for bodies, I stood behind Eagleburger as he spoke firmly about the determination of the United States to press ahead and help liberate Lebanon from the violent madness that was starting to engulf Americans along with Lebanese. Following his statement, Eagleburger and I went to the American University of Beirut hospital, where many of the victims were being treated.

We walked through the wards. I came across one embassy employee, a Lebanese national, who had been my driver for three days in October 1982 when I had come to Lebanon to consult with Lebanese leaders about the prospects for national reconciliation and reconstruction. The man smiled when I walked into his room and immediately called out my name. He had lost both his feet, one hand and one eye in the explosion. Tears started to well up in my eyes and I found it impossible to find words. Holding out his one remaining hand, he took my hand and said simply, "Do not worry about me. I am glad you have come. But we must have revenge." Such was the reality of Lebanon.

That evening, I received a call from Kemp that President Reagan had decided to send Shultz to the Middle East to try to finally conclude an agreement between Israel and Lebanon, and that I would represent the NSC on Shultz's team. Veliotes and I stayed on in Beirut for the next two days, conferring with Lebanese officials who were clearly concerned that the destruction of the U.S. embassy was the prelude to America's withdrawal from Lebanon. Seeking reassurance about U.S. resolve, Lebanon's U.N. ambassador Ghassan Tueni was particularly concerned over Shultz's intentions: Would Shultz squeeze concessions out of Israel or the Lebanese? Did the United States remain confident in its ability to produce a Syrian withdrawal along with an Israeli withdrawal? Did Shultz understand the terrible pressure that the negotiations with Israel had brought to bear on Lebanon from the rest of the Arab world? Expressing the view that concessions would need to be made by all parties, Veliotes, Habib and I emphasized that Shultz would not be invoking his own prestige unless he was confident that he could conclude an agreement.

The Sour Commentary

Shultz began his shuttle in Cairo with a chiefs of mission meeting. Shultz wanted to give his Near East ambassadors an opportunity to express their perspectives directly to him, while also trying to give them a sense that they had a stake in his shuttle. However, one issue immediately surfaced that would confound Shultz for the balance of his term as secretary of state: Syrian opposition to U.S. policy. U.S. ambassador to Syria Robert Paganelli was outspoken in his criticism of U.S. Middle East policy in general and in particular with Habib's assumption that Syrian cooperation with the Israel-Lebanon arrangements would be delivered by other Arab leaders. Shultz listened patiently to Paganelli but eventually grew tired of his criticism. After the meeting Shultz took me aside and asked me what I thought "of Paganelli's sour commentary." Not wanting to be caught in the middle of what was sure to become a bitter feud between the secretary of state and several of the senior Arabists in the foreign service, I reiterated my own serious doubt that the Syrians would withdraw simply because Assad had said so to Habib. Despite Habib's repeated assurances to Shultz and everyone else, I believed that Syria had regained sufficient strength to advance its own agenda in Lebanon, which was very different from ours. I also downplayed the potential value of any role the Saudis might play. Saudi Arabia was highly vulnerable in light of the Iran-Iraq War, and despite its warm friendship with America, Riyadh needed to avoid putting itself in a position where Assad could exert pressure on Saudi Arabia through Syria's relationship with Iran.

By the beginning of May, Shultz resolved the key issues that had separated the Israelis and Lebanese, and a final agreement appeared within reach. Knowing full well of Assad's opposition to the agreement, Gemayel dispatched his foreign minister, Eli Salem, to Damascus on May 2 in order to brief Assad and seek his concurrence. Visibly shaken, Salem briefed us the following day on his talks with the president of Syria. Assad had asked Salem why Amin Gemayel believed he needed to sign an agreement with Israel. He went on to compare Lebanon to Egypt, noting that both countries had a strong national consensus, but that when Sadat deviated from that consensus and signed an agreement with Israel, the people of Egypt had killed him. According to Salem, Assad told him that Lebanon was capable of enduring much more war than the eight years of conflict it had already suffered. He pointedly and unmistakably warned Salem that the losses Lebanon would suffer if it signed an agreement with Israel would pain Syria. There would be no Syrian withdrawal in the context of Israeli withdrawal. Salem said that Assad had explicitly warned him that Syria would terrorize the government of Lebanon and all the Christian communities, except for those who swore allegiance to Syria, if the agreement was signed.

There was only one way to interpret Assad's presentation: Syria would forcefully oppose any agreement concluded between Israel and Lebanon. While Assad was ready to discuss withdrawals and security arrangements, he had not as yet been consulted about the terms on the table and he would not agree to the terms as presented to him by Salem. It was clear that Assad was throwing down a gauntlet, not only to the Lebanese but to Washington. Knowing full well what Assad's intentions were, the United States encouraged the Lebanese to sign the agreement, but then, over the course of the ensuing year, it failed to step up to its responsibility to prevent the Syrians from destroying the Lebanese government and abrogating the agreement with Israel. This failure was a direct result of the Cabinet divisions which President Reagan was unwilling to reconcile.

I had been directed to use a privacy channel that enabled direct, secure communications with the White House, thereby bypassing the State Department Operations Center. I sent my own message back to Clark reporting on Salem's briefing and offering my opinion that Syria was prepared to go to war to spoil the agreement. Backed up by the Soviet Union and intent on flexing his muscles, the Syrian president was keen to demonstrate that Syria's strength and resolve were fully restored.

By this time the U.S. government had gathered considerable information linking the embassy bombing directly to Iran and Syria. No military action was taken, however, to hold either country responsible for this heinous act of terrorism. The administration's failure to respond to this blatant act of direct aggression against the United States emboldened Syria and Iran. Assad quickly perceived the large gap between America's tough rhetoric and its willingness to take action in response to terrorist acts. With the Iranians operating in the shadows and militant Lebanese Shias performing most of the dirty work, Assad constructed a facade of "plausible deniability" and was able to slowly turn the screws on American diplomacy with a long-term campaign of escalating terror, subversion, and rocket and artillery attacks.

Shultz traveled to Damascus on May 8 to try to convince Assad and Foreign Minister Abdel Halim Khaddam that the agreement made sense for Syrian interests in Lebanon. Meeting first with Khaddam, Shultz outlined the various components of the agreement, and urged Syria to consider how it would benefit from its implementation. Khaddam listened politely but made clear that Syria was totally opposed, considering Lebanon's agreement a betrayal of the Arab cause. Over lunch at the Foreign Ministry, Shultz grew weary of Khaddam's endless debating and not-so-veiled threats, and had steered the discussion to other topics. All of a sudden, Shultz noticed that Khaddam was being served a different meal from everyone else and asked him why. Khaddam told Shultz that he had become a vegetarian, emphasizing with outstretched arms that when "you stop eating meat, you are supposed to become more peaceful inside." Shultz took in this remark with a deadpan expression, then started to laugh as he cocked his head and replied, "Oh really? How's it coming?" Even several members of the normally grim-faced Syrian team started to laugh when they understood how Shultz had made fun of their boss. Khaddam turned beet red with embarrassment and remained quiet for the balance of the meal.

The subsequent meeting with Assad was fairly bizarre. Entering Assad's office, I was immediately struck by the famous oversized picture of Saladin defeating the crusaders at the Horns of Hittin, which hangs prominently in Assad's office directly opposite the visiting delegation. After pointing out the picture to Shultz, Assad embarked on an hour-long monologue, talking about tactical nuclear weapons in Europe and other subjects before finally asking Shultz about the agreement between Lebanon and Israel. Shultz was an experienced negotiator who understood Assad's tactics. He briefed him in detail on the agreement itself and then described the side letters that would ensure that Israel's withdrawal would precipitate Syria's withdrawal.

Unfortunately, Assad correctly understood that if he refused to withdraw from Lebanon, Israel would be under no obligation to withdraw its forces, thus ensuring that the agreement would never be implemented. Instead, working through proxies to the maximum extent possible, the Syrians could slowly bleed Israel, which was already experiencing significant and growing domestic opposition to Israel's extended and debilitating presence in Lebanon. Thanking Shultz for visiting Syria, Assad advised him that Syria would not be withdrawing its army from Lebanon.

On the way back to the airport, my Syrian escort, the Foreign Ministry's director for North American affairs, asked me how I enjoyed my brief visit to Damascus. "Things appear fine in Damascus," I replied coldly, "but tell me, how are things in Hama these days?" (In February 1982, the

Syrians had destroyed much of the city of Hama in order to crush a Moslem Brotherhood rebellion. At least twenty thousand Syrians were murdered at Assad's direction.) Turning around to face me head on from the front seat, his eyes narrowed to slits as he replied with steel in his voice, "We've built a lot of parks in Hama." As I shook my head in disgust and mock disbelief, he continued, "There are no problems in Hama for you to worry about." Listening to his callous commentary, and knowing how many thousands of his own people Assad had killed in order to maintain his grip on power, I contemplated what Assad might have in store for Lebanon. It was more essential than ever that we get the Israelis out and find a way of honorably withdrawing our forces before we found ourselves in the middle of a Hama-like situation.

Despite Assad's rejection, Israel and Lebanon finally signed the agreement on May 17. Over the next six weeks, little if any progress was made toward implementation of what became known as the May 17 agreement. Secretary Shultz lobbied hard to convince the Saudis and other Arab leaders to pressure Assad to cooperate. But, as accurately predicted by Paganelli, neither the Arabs on whom Shultz had counted nor Assad were prepared to play ball. Indeed, claiming that Habib had guaranteed that Israeli forces would not advance toward the Syrian lines during the June fighting if Syria agreed to a cease-fire, Assad chose to signal his outright rejection of the May 17 agreement by informing Washington that he had lost confidence in Habib's role as mediator. Habib was no longer welcome in Damascus, and he resigned as special envoy to the Middle East in July.

CHAPTER 10

HELP THEM MAKE PEACE

The Bermuda Triangle

Gayle and I were married in California on July 2, 1983, and enjoyed a three-week honeymoon oblivious of the politics of Washington or the Middle East. However, on the day we returned to Washington, McFarlane replaced Habib as the president's envoy for the Middle East. I immediately called the White House. Wilma Hall, McFarlane's secretary, told me not to unpack, and within the week I left for the Middle East.

I later learned that in the months preceding the appointment, McFarlane had decided he would resign from the NSC owing to a growing sense of frustration with the national security bureaucracy. Following Assad's decision to make Phil Habib persona non grata in Damascus, Clark and McFarlane had asked Prince Bandar, the Saudi ambassador to Washington, whether Assad would refuse to engage with any American mediator, or whether it was limited to Habib. Bandar said that Syria was trying to play the United States off against the Soviets and that Assad wanted the United States involved. Riyadh also wanted the United States to stay involved, and Bandar offered to find out whether Assad would agree to resume a dialogue over the May 17 agreement with a different American interlocutor.

With the failure to implement the May 17 agreement, Israeli wariness of what had become their Lebanon quagmire grew steadily. On the political level Amin Gemayel refused to communicate with the Israelis, leading to growing mistrust about Gemayel's intentions to live up to the May 17 agreement. Nor was Gemayel prepared formally to ask Syria to leave Lebanon, rightly fearful that Assad would say no and start the war that he had threatened during his meeting with Salem. On the military level, the readiness and morale of the Israeli Army was being worn down by trying to maintain order between the warring Maronite and Druze forces in the Shouf Mountains, a strategic region where Maronites and Druze had lived for centuries. In these circumstances, the government of Israel indicated that it was preparing to initiate a partial withdrawal to the southern bank of the Awali River. The Israelis knew that this would weaken the putative "threat in being" that they maintained against the Syrian Army. Nevertheless, they hoped it would coerce Amin Gemayel to exchange the instruments of ratification of the May 17 agreement. Israel wanted Gemayel to ask the Syrians to withdraw in order to reduce the danger the Shouf-dwelling Maronite Christians faced from the Druze.

The Syrians did their best to unsettle the Gemayel government further by claiming that the partial withdrawal was no more than an Israeli cover story for the partition of Lebanon. In a move remarkably similar to Syria's earlier activities in Lebanon in 1958, Damascus brought together the Druze warlord Walid Jumblatt; Nabih Berri, leader of Amal, the Shia militia; and Rashid Karami, a Sunni leader, to form the National Salvation Front (NSF). The NSF pursued two objectives: the rejection of the May 17 agreement and the creation of a new Lebanese government dominated by Lebanon's Moslem majority.

This was the emerging situation in Lebanon when, in mid-July, Bandar informed Clark that Assad was always open to a dialogue with the U.S. government on any subject. Clark asked McFarlane to travel secretly to Damascus to determine whether Assad would engage with him and if so on what terms. Having been told by Clark that Shultz agreed with the proposed probe of Assad, McFarlane and Bandar flew to London in Bandar's executive jet to meet with Dr. Wadi Haddad, Gemayel's national security advisor. Haddad supported the initiative, and McFarlane and Bandar flew on to Riyadh. McFarlane and Bandar spent the day alone in the home of Bandar's brother, ensuring that no one would observe the ambassador or his guest. At two A.M., McFarlane boarded Bandar's jet and flew alone to Damascus. Upon arrival, he was taken directly to the Presidential Palace for a six-hour meeting with Assad.

As is Assad's style, for the first several hours he and McFarlane discussed a range of subjects that had nothing to do with the Middle East. In meetings with U.S. officials, Assad typically sought to cloak himself in mystery to disorient his guest and maintain a negotiating upper hand. Characterizing Assad as a sort of "brutal mystic," McFarlane recalled that he asked about such issues as beings from outer space and the Bermuda Triangle. Assad wanted McFarlane to be impressed and to sense an element of danger when dealing with him. He mentioned several times that Dr. Henry Kissinger had respected him. McFarlane had learned from

Kissinger's experiences in the 1970s that Assad's style was to try to keep negotiators off balance and alarmed, unsure of what his next move might be. After four hours of discussion, McFarlane finally asked Assad point-blank whether he acknowledged the existence of the State of Israel. He replied that the Jews were a people, not a state. When he was pressed on the issue of Syrian withdrawal from Lebanon, Assad spoke elliptically of Phoenicia being one people forever, hinting that Syria would withdraw from Lebanon after the Israelis withdrew. Once they reached the fifth hour of discussions, McFarlane asked whether he was ready to engage in a process to withdraw all foreign elements from Lebanon. Assad replied that he was ready to begin that process. Having secured what appeared to be the basis for discussion, McFarlane departed the Presidential Palace and returned to Saudi Arabia, where he briefed King Fahd on the Damascus meeting. Based on the apparent willingness of Assad to resume the dialogue, with the direct involvement of Fahd and Bandar, Clark and Shultz agreed that McFarlane would become the new Middle East envoy.

At the office the day after Gayle and I returned to Washington, Kemp and Dur told me about McFarlane's secret trip, adding that no one at the American embassy in Damascus was aware of the visit. It was essential, they said, that no word of this visit leak out. I had clearly missed a great deal of activity during my month-long absence. Later that morning McFarlane summoned me to his office. "I promised I would not let anything disrupt your wedding," he said with a grin on his face, "and I didn't. But now I need you to help get me organized for this trip we're taking at the end of the week." McFarlane instructed me to develop a strategy paper that he wanted to give to the president for his approval. The first half of the paper was to deal with the various measures the United States could undertake to manage the partial withdrawal that Israel seemed intent on pursuing in the near future. The challenge was to find a way to facilitate Israel's partial withdrawal in the context of the U.S. goal of a total withdrawal of foreign forces.

One idea that Shultz proposed was to term Israel's partial withdrawal to the Awali River line a "redeployment" that would lead to total withdrawal, thereby minimizing the partition perception being fomented by the Syrians. But whether we called it a redeployment or a partial withdrawal, the southward movement of the IDF would reduce whatever leverage remained against Syria. McFarlane directed that I assess whether other countries might be able to help induce Syria to cooperate with blandishments or threats, such as Turkey, Iraq, France or Saudi Arabia.

As difficult as this first problem was, the second half of the assignment was even more ambitious: devise a strategy to promote "national reconciliation" among the disparate Lebanese factions, particularly the Maronites and the Druze, and thereby help bring an end to the civil war. Shultz and McFarlane believed that the central issue was to redraw the political map of Lebanon to avoid Maronite domination of the country and establish a renewed sense of Lebanese nationhood. But to the extent that there ever was a "nation" in Lebanon, it was Mount Lebanon, the core and the heart of the people from which the French built the country of Lebanon in 1943.

While it seemed a straightforward matter to identify the types of structural changes that might contribute to minimizing the Maronite domination of a new Lebanon, such as the reallocation of cabinet portfolios, national elections for the president, and the reorganization of the LAF along nonethnic lines, devising a realistic process that would change the attitudes of the factional leaders and their followers was a totally different matter.

While I agreed that U.S. success would be much more likely in the context of genuine national reconciliation, I doubted that it could be achieved for at least another generation. (For example, the Jumblatt clan had fought the Gemayels for control of the Matn region as far back as the mid–nineteenth century.) Given Lebanon's long history of blood feuds, hatred and mistrust and its seemingly natural tendency to exploit foreign interests to advance ethnic interests, I feared that U.S. attempts to reenergize Lebanese democracy, however worthy and enlightened, would be problematic at best. Nonetheless, it was decided that McFarlane would try to reach out to the leaders of every community in an effort to convince them that the U.S. could do more for all of them, and that they could do more for themselves, through a process of national reconciliation.

The administration's top priority was to prevent the Israelis from withdrawing from the Shouf until the LAF could move in to replace them. After the government of Israel made clear its determination to withdraw, regardless of the deteriorating relations between the Druze and Maronites, it became essential for McFarlane to convince the Druze to agree to permit the LAF to deploy into the Shouf as the IDF withdrew. With the LAF providing security, and at least the veneer of a national institution, perhaps the forces could serve as a bridge between the two communities and lay the groundwork for a process of reconciliation. It was a tall order, but one that had to be achieved to avert more Lebanese bloodshed and the collapse of U.S. policy.

Neither Gayle nor I was prepared for another separation so soon after our marriage. Nevertheless, I headed back to the Middle East on July 29 with Bud and his wife Jonda (Jonnie), Ambassador Richard Fairbanks, Phil Dur, Christopher Ross, Wilma Hall and Fairbanks's secretary Pat Schaubel.

We arrived in Lebanon intent on finding a way of moving the various factions toward a process of national reconciliation by taking immediate advantage of the imminent redeployment of the IDF to the Awali River line. There had never been much communal harmony between the Druze and Maronites of the Matn and the Shouf. Yet throughout most of the eight-year civil war, the inhabitants of this region had managed to avoid outright communal warfare. When Sharon arrived with the Lebanese Forces in the summer of 1982, Druze-Maronite violence erupted with a vengeance, however, as the militias began to settle scores. Having carelessly stirred the simmering embers of hatred by upsetting the delicate balance of power in the Shouf, the IDF found itself caught in the middle of a blood feud that could best be understood by Americans as "the Hatfields versus the McCoys." National reconciliation would become that much more difficult to pursue if war broke out in the Shouf. It was essential that an agreement between the Druze and the Maronites be reached to permit the peaceful entry of the LAF into the Shouf or widespread fighting would break out when the IDF withdrew.

While there was no love lost between Druze and Christian leaders, neither was there any love for the Baathist leadership in Damascus. Syria demanded its due in Lebanon, and what it could not achieve by persuasion it secured through force. Syrian agents murdered Walid Jumblatt's father, Kamal Jumblatt, after he had tried to assert his independence from Assad in 1977. Despite what he might otherwise have wanted and regardless of ties to Israel through the vibrant Druze community of Israel, Walid was very susceptible to Assad's threats and blandishments. He was also the leader of the Druze and he was committed to improving their political influence and economic conditions in Lebanon.

With the creation of the NSF and the issuance of demands identical to those espoused by Assad, there was no ambiguity over the nature of the diplomatic struggle. Syria would not allow Walid Jumblatt to reach any agreements with the central authorities in Beirut unless and until the May 17 agreement was abrogated. Assad was well aware that Israel's staying power in Lebanon was waning, but he had no incentive to cooperate with the United States. To this end, Assad bluntly told McFarlane during a six-hour meeting in early August that there would be no reconciliation among the Lebanese until the May 17 agreement was dead. The easiest way for Assad to prevent the United States from using the MNF as leverage to ensure an orderly withdrawal of the IDF from the Shouf and its replacement by the LAF was to ensure that Jumblatt refused to cooperate. In many respects, however, the Maronite president of Lebanon proved even more difficult to move than Jumblatt. Proclaiming his readiness to work toward national reconciliation one minute, the next minute Amin Gemayel would refuse even to place a telephone call to Jumblatt as we used our best efforts to bring the two leaders together.

On the technical level, considerable progress was made under McFarlane's direction to coordinate an operational plan between the IDF, the LAF and the MNF to ensure that the IDF redeployment went as smoothly as possible. The lessons of Sabra and Shatila and the dwindling value of U.S. security assurances had not been lost on the Druze community. The premature withdrawal of the MNF had given the Phalangists the freedom to enter the camps and commit their atrocities. The Druze feared that this could happen to them this time. From the Druze perspective the LAF, commanded by General Ibrahim Tannous, a Christian, was just another Christian militia, though it included thousands of Moslems and several hundred Druze. In contrast, McFarlane believed that the deployment of the MNF, with a new mission, along with the LAF would contribute to greater security in the Druze villages. McFarlane saw this as a way for the "peaceful presence" of the MNF to contribute to the reconciliation process and stimulate a diplomatic momentum to end the factional bloodshed in Lebanon despite the ruthless opposition of Damascus.

Following an initial round of consultations with the Lebanese and Israelis, we met with Assad, King Fahd, King Hussein and President Mubarak to explore how to reconcile Gemayel and Jumblatt to the point where the Israeli redeployment could take place peacefully. Assad spent considerable time discussing the spiritual forces at play in the Middle East and pointedly asked McFarlane whether he had any new information on the Bermuda Triangle. With respect to national reconciliation in Lebanon, he would say only that the NSF represented the will of the Lebanese people. The other Arab leaders offered their best wishes for McFarlane's success, but none would agree even to attempt to persuade Assad to permit Jumblatt to participate in the reconciliation process.

Upon our arrival in Damascus for McFarlane's second meeting with Assad, the team drove to the embassy to first meet with Ambassador Paganelli, DCM Robert Rugh and political officer April Glaspie before commencing the formal meetings with Assad and Khaddam. Paganelli and his staff had prepared a briefing for us on Syria's perspective toward Lebanon and the United States. McFarlane and Fairbanks took Paganelli aside and told him they needed to speak with him privately prior to the country team meeting. Paganelli ushered the two envoys into the embassy's secure conference room while the rest of us mingled outside. Aware that Paganelli was about to learn of McFarlane's earlier secret visit to Damascus, Dur and I hoped the embassy staff would still support our mission. Paganelli emerged from the conference room thirty minutes later pale and almost speechless from the disclosure that an envoy from President Reagan had come secretly to Syria and had met with Assad, yet he had not been informed. Suddenly aware of the extent to which Shultz had lost confidence in him, despite his thoroughly accurate assessment of Assad's adamant opposition to the May 17 agreement and the flaws in American policy, Paganelli sat in remote silence during the discussions while Rugh and Glaspie presented the case that we could expect to hear from the Syrians.

Glaspie presented what by this time had become Embassy Damascus's "I told you so" analysis of the Syrian position toward the May 17 agreement and the impossible task McFarlane faced in trying to convince Assad to compromise. She was considered to be one of the most prominent Arabists in the State Department. An extremely hardworking and ambitious FSO, she possessed a thorough knowledge of Arabic and much experience in the Arab world, yet this background may have contributed to her tendency, shared by nearly every Arabist at State, to adopt an attitude of almost reverential deference toward Arab positions on the Arab-Israeli conflict and other Middle East issues. During the subsequent meeting with Khaddam, I noticed that Glaspie took very detailed notes, apparently not missing a word. After the meeting we chatted about writing up reporting cables and similar issues. She had noted that I also took detailed notes. She shared with me a "trick of the trade" and suggested I use a felt-tip pen rather than a ballpoint, in order to avoid hand and finger fatigue. "Joe Sisco taught me that," she said proudly.

I recalled her note-taking tip years later during Operation Desert Shield when Ambassador Glaspie, who had gone on to win State Department awards for her reporting skills, was apparently unable to report accurately on her demarche to Saddam Hussein just prior to Iraq's invasion of Kuwait. Yet then, Glaspie was unfairly made a scapegoat by senior members of the Bush administration who hid behind her skirt as they shirked their own responsibility for the failed policies which had led inevitably to Desert Storm.

We spent the evening at the Damascus Sheraton, where Deputy Foreign Minister Farouk Shara hosted a dinner in our honor. When we went to Dur's room to change for the dinner, Dur found a hidden microphone. Often irreverent, he began to describe graphically his impressions of our Syrian hosts and their manners in colloquial Russian. If the Soviets were listening, they would have had to wonder who Phil really was.

The next morning, the team was led to a large room adjacent to Assad's office. Our group had grown quite large and included McFarlane, Fairbanks, Paganelli, Rugh, Glaspie, Chris Ross, Dur and myself. An equal number of Syrian security agents, each armed with pearl-handled revolvers stuck into their belts, waited with us. Ten minutes passed before a protocol officer emerged from Assad's office to summon McFarlane. Stating that Assad wished to begin with a private meeting before enlarging the session to include the full delegation and his staff. McFarlane obliged, taking Ross in with him to serve as his interpreter. No sooner had the door closed behind him when several more Syrians came into the waiting room. One of them carried a Nikon camera with a very long telephoto lens. He immediately began trying to take head-on photographs of each of us, presumably for dossiers they were compiling as well as to try to intimidate us. Fairbanks reacted angrily, ducking behind a column to avoid the photographer. When the photographer refused to relent, Fairbanks grinned mischievously and raised his middle finger at the camera.

Four hours later, with McFarlane still engrossed in private discussion with Assad, two Syrians sidled over to Phil and me to strike up a conversation. The Syrians politely asked if I spoke Arabic. I replied that I did and we conversed in Arabic for a few minutes. Then they began to speak with Phil in French and Russian, two of his languages, before turning abruptly back to me to ask in Hebrew whether I spoke Hebrew. Initially taken aback by their flawless command of the language, I replied in Hebrew and asked them how they had come to speak so well the national language of a country they claimed did not exist. "Do you plan to go shopping in Tel Aviv?" I asked. Laughing, one of the agents replied that whatever else might happen between Syria and Israel, there would never come a time when Syrians would go shopping in Tel Aviv. Two hours later, McFarlane and Assad finally joined the rest of us in the holding room where Assad greeted us and bade farewell to McFarlane.

Returning to Paganelli's residence before departing for Riyadh, McFarlane reported that the session, like his previous encounter with Assad, had wandered all over the globe before settling down to a restatement of general principles. Assad's clear goal was to convince the United States to stop supporting the May 17 agreement, emphasizing that failure to do so would only lead to more violence and hardship for everyone in Beirut. He warned that the Lebanese communities could not resolve their political differences as long as the sovereignty of Lebanon was violated by Israel.

For his part, McFarlane noted to Assad that the U.S. Marines had been coming under mortar fire from Druze batteries located in the hills above the airport since late July. The ROE prohibited the Marines from firing at any targets except those that fired at them. It was virtually impossible for the Marines to pinpoint the source of fire owing to the terrain and the lack of specialized artillery-targeting radar. McFarlane pointedly told Assad that the Marines had recently acquired advanced radars that could pinpoint the source of artillery fire and accurately direct return fire onto the attacking gun batteries. He told Assad that the U.S. forces would defend themselves. While Assad took careful note of McFarlane's statement, he questioned the will of Washington to endure in Lebanon any longer than Israel. As we left Damascus for Riyadh, it was evident that Assad held a strong hand and was playing a mean game of poker.

Arriving in Riyadh late that evening, we took up residence in one of King Fahd's luxurious guest palaces. A sumptuous feast awaited us. Halfway through the meal, however, I began to feel ill and broke into a cold sweat. As waves of nausea began to overwhelm me, I stood up from the table and walked to the nearby elevator. Dur saw me wobbling and quickly came to my side to see if I needed help. He told me that he had been looking for an opportunity to leave, since he also was beginning to feel ill. Riding up the elevator to our floor, I assured him I would be just fine. However, as the elevator stopped and the doors opened, I took one step, then fainted to the floor. When I came to several moments later, Dur was literally lifting three Bedouins off me, who seemed to materialize from nowhere. Obviously the security wardens of our floor (we were the only guests in the entire palace of some 450 rooms), they were shouting and accusing me of being drunk. Phil fended them off and helped me to my room. It had clearly been a big mistake to eat the parsley in the tabbouleh in Damascus.

Over the next few days, we had several meetings with Bandar and Fahd in order to coordinate our strategy and tactics. The king emphasized his willingness to make every effort to convince Assad to be reasonable and to find a solution to the impasse on the May 17 agreement, as well as to continue to work with the Lebanese leaders to counsel reconciliation. However, the Saudis were convinced that the Syrians, stronger than ever with renewed Soviet backing, would prove very difficult and uncompromising.

From Riyadh we flew on to Cairo to exchange views with the Egyptians. Our meetings with Mubarak and other Egyptian officials covered many issues, and were less focused on the problems of Lebanon and trying to convince Assad to cooperate. Mubarak's primary concern remained the situation in the Gulf and Iran's use of human waves to attack Iraqi positions. The fanaticism of the Iranians was frightening, even if their tactics had yet to break through the Iraqi lines. Mubarak continued to lobby for increased U.S. support for Iraq and Jordan, arguing that strengthening these countries would provide the best bulwark against the radical threat to the Gulf.

We were in our airplane getting ready to leave Egypt. The plane had just taxied over a mile to the end of a runway and we were waiting for our takeoff clearance. I was sitting across from Dur. A RDF exercise, Bright Star 83, was under way, and a stream of U.S. Air Force C-141 transports were in the process of landing on our runway. I was looking out at the barren Egyptian desert and watching the C-141s land when I suddenly saw smoke appearing to come out of our starboard engines. I told Phil to look. "Nah," Phil said casting a quick glance out the window, "it's only dust." But the crew chief must have heard me: he unbuckled his seat belt, cracked open the door, looked out at the engines and landing gear and immediately yelled "Fire!" Grabbing a fire extinguisher, the chief emptied the bottle on the landing gear, but to no avail. McFarlane, Dur and I jumped out of the plane and started to run into the desert as rivets popped off of the engines' casing. Wilma Hall was still standing inside the cabin of the plane, struggling to gather up her notebooks, camera bag and God knows what else. Turning around, I ran back onto the plane and got her. While Egyptian soldiers standing guard at the end of the runway shouted at us in Arabic to stand still, Wilma and I ran to the others, who had moved fifty or so meters away from the plane. The U.S. Air Force crew worked furiously for several more minutes to try to extinguish the fire but had to deplane when their fire extinguishers were depleted. The landing gear and one of the engines burned for nearly ten more minutes before the Cairo Airport fire trucks arrived to smother the fire and all our belongings with foam. It turned out that a magnesium brake had been dragging during the long taxi from the terminal to the runway, eventually overheating and setting the landing gear, wheel well, and engine on fire.

Short of Breath

Pressure within Israel to withdraw the IDF continued to mount as Lebanon's communal struggles intensified and Assad made plain his intention to do whatever was necessary to restore Syria's position of preeminence in Beirut. In this environment, Israeli defense minister Arens decided to proceed with the redeployment of the IDF regardless of whether the Lebanese could agree on how to secure the Shouf from bloodshed. Back in Beirut, Phil Dur and I watched the IDF prepare to leave. We would cross the Green Line, which separated East from West Beirut, every morning and evening on our way from our West Beirut hotel to the ambassador's residence in Yarze overlooking Beirut, where McFarlane and Fairbanks were living. Roadblocks with earthen barricades were set up as Israeli tanks and APCs would unexpectedly appear at an urban crossroads. The IDF had begun to move its armor from north of Beirut, around the city's eastern suburbs, and south toward the Awali River near Sidon. Manned by Phalangists, the roadblocks were supposed to secure these checkpoints from forces hostile to the Israelis.

Late one night, Chris Ross and I were driving back to the hotel when we were stopped at the "Galerie Simaan" crossing by a filthy, scarred Phalangist, armed with an AK-47 assault rifle, which he shoved into Ross's face as he demanded to see our papers. We could see his backup partially hidden behind an earthen wall, armed with an RPG-7, as a Lebanese Army sentry looked on passively, less than fifty meters ahead. Dur was in another car behind us. His driver was a Moslem who became terrified when he realized that a confrontation was brewing between Ross and the Phalangist. Ross was incensed by the Phalangist's demand that we show him our papers. In flawless Arabic, Ross told him that we were American diplomats, and he could "stuff" his request. The Phalangist was outraged by Ross's insult and became even more threatening, but Ross refused to budge and just looked ahead calmly, the muzzle of the AK-47 pointed at the side of his head. After what seemed an eternity, but was probably no more than thirty seconds, the Phalangist swore and waved us on. Dur's car came roaring by as the embassy's bulletproof Impala instantly overtook Ross's VW Rabbit. Reaching the LAF checkpoint, Ross indignantly chastised the sentry who had watched the Phalangist while sitting atop his APC. "What do you want me to do?" the soldier asked. "The Israelis are leaving Beirut. Why do you argue with the Phalangists? He'll kill you just as soon as he won't. You don't have any problem with me. No problem." Disgusted with the apathy of the sentry, Ross told him that he was why things weren't going to get any better in Lebanon. The soldier shrugged and we drove off to the Riviera Hotel on the Corniche Mazra, our home away from home.

There was no doubt that the IDF was leaving Beirut. Although Israel claimed to want to coordinate the redeployment, it was well under way by the middle of August. By then we had been in the region several weeks. Having been stymied by the Syrians in his efforts to promote reconciliation and an orderly redeployment in the Shouf, McFarlane asked Israel to agree to postpone the withdrawal of the IDF. As August came to a close, however, Syrian-backed forces recognized that a unilateral withdrawal of the IDF appeared imminent and that the MNF would not be replacing them. At the direction of the Syrians, the NSF moved to fill the vacuum and began to attack the Lebanese Forces and the LAF from the mountains overlooking Beirut. The Marines also became targets of the NSF and came under mortar fire at the end of August. Two Marines were killed.

In an effort to convince Syria to stop undermining U.S. policy in Lebanon and the attacks against the MNF and to permit the Lebanese to begin to work out their political differences peacefully, McFarlane directed Dur and me to devise additional options, within the existing ROE, that would strengthen the ability of the United States to achieve its political objectives in Lebanon and deter Syrian and NSF fire. Dur suggested that the only way to counter Syria's artillery threat to the Marines and Beirut was with the long-range guns of the USS *New Jersey*. Although relatively inaccurate without an airborne spotter to correct the fire of the guns, the firepower of the *New Jersey* would be more capable of deterring, and if necessary destroying, the guns from the Matn that were raining death down onto the MNF and Beirut.

As the political-military situation continued to deteriorate and communal war in the Shouf appeared increasingly certain, McFarlane intensified his pressure on Gemayel to reach out to Jumblatt and the other leaders. The Lebanese president reluctantly agreed to authorize his national security advisor, Wadi Haddad, to meet with Jumblatt, if McFarlane could arrange the meeting. In Paris, after completing a round of consultations with the leaders of Italy and France, we received word from Uri Lubrani, Israel's former ambassador to Iran and now the MOD's Coordinator for Southern Lebanon, that Jumblatt would be in Paris from August 26 to 28. Lubrani believed that he could convince Jumblatt to meet Haddad, although Paganelli had independently informed Jumblatt that only McFarlane wanted to meet with him. Apparently convinced that the Syrians were prepared to sacrifice the Druze of the Shouf in order to kill the May 17 agreement, Lubrani met with Jumblatt late into the night of August 26 to urge him to meet with Haddad.

The following morning, Lubrani and his associate, Brigadier General Meir Dagan, came to the residence of the American ambassador to France, where we were staying while in Paris for a breakfast meeting. Lubrani briefed us on his discussions with Jumblatt, stressing that Jumblatt was under tremendous pressure from the Syrians. I telephoned Jumblatt to invite him to the residence for a meeting with McFarlane later that afternoon. I added that Dr. Haddad would join us, having been advised by Lubrani that Jumblatt was ready to acquiesce to this development. Speaking on the telephone, Jumblatt said he would be pleased to see McFarlane but he did not want to see Haddad. I tried to convince him to at least talk with Haddad, but Jumblatt continued to resist. We agreed to talk again later. I told McFarlane that we needed to offer Jumblatt something else, but I was not sure what.

After a moment's reflection, McFarlane telephoned François de Grossouvre, a trusted advisor of French president François Mitterrand, who told McFarlane that he was surprised to hear that Jumblatt was backing away from a meeting with Wadi Haddad, as he and Jumblatt had met the previous night and Jumblatt had agreed to the meeting. He offered to speak with him again and then get back to us. Just then, Haddad arrived. Lubrani and Dagan quickly moved to another room of the residence. While Haddad was very interested in learning of Israel's ideas, he was not authorized to meet with them. We hastily arranged "proximity talks" between the parties. Lubrani and Dagan sat together in one room while McFarlane and Haddad kept an open phone line in another room about fifty feet away. The Lebanese and Israelis exchanged questions and ideas. As Dur and I shuttled between the two rooms, participating in both conversations, de Grossouvre called back to report that Jumblatt was ready to meet at a neutral site, namely de Grossouvre's Left Bank apartment. I phoned Marwan Hammadeh, Jumblatt's deputy, to propose a three P.M. meeting. Although he balked at first when I suggested that Haddad would join at 3:05, we quickly compromised on "some time later."

If the morning's proximity talks appeared bizarre, the rendezvous with Jumblatt resembled a Keystone Cops movie. We arrived at de Grossouvre's apartment at two-thirty, just as a stunningly attractive "housekeeper" left, bidding us adieu. McFarlane wanted to create a nonthreatening atmosphere for Jumblatt, so he decided that Dur and I would listen from the adjoining kitchen, rather than participate in the salon. For half an hour, McFarlane and Jumblatt grappled with the fundamental issues of reconciliation, Syrian threats to Jumblatt, the suffering of the Druze and America's interest in helping the disparate communities find a mechanism for overcoming the hatred and mistrust which had plagued Lebanon for centuries. Dur and I listened intently, through the old-fashioned keyhole, straining to pick up everything that Jumblatt was saying. At 3:35, Dr. Haddad and Lebanon's ambassador to France, Farouk Abilama (a Druze who had converted to Christianity), arrived.

The discussion immediately deteriorated as the two sides leveled numerous accusations and counteraccusations of crimes, betrayals, greed and avarice at each other. Suddenly the door to the kitchen burst open, as Jumblatt got up to help himself to a drink. Momentarily startled by Dur's and my presence, he leaped back, then steadied himself when he realized that we did not pose a physical threat to him. Recognizing me from our previous meetings, Jumblatt started to laugh as he took a bottle of cognac off a shelf and poured three fingers into a large glass. The growing tension was unexpectedly broken, and Haddad and Jumblatt began to discuss whether indeed a mechanism could be devised that would lead to the peaceful departure of the Israelis from the Shouf.

As the meeting concluded about five-thirty, McFarlane pressed Jumblatt to agree to another meeting the following day. Jumblatt said he would consider it, along with the ideas that had been raised. As he stood up to leave, Jumblatt extended his hand to McFarlane and said, "I am sorry that I shelled the airport. My shells were not meant for your Marines. Please come and visit me at my home in Mukhtara. I shall be at your disposal." Driving away from the "secret" meeting as hordes of journalists and photographers (who had been tipped off by de Grossouvre) descended upon us, it seemed that we might be on the verge of making real headway on the problem of Lebanese reconciliation. The stakes were very high. If we were unable to make progress between the Druze and Maronites now, it would not be long before the war for the mountain would erupt.

Later that evening, we debriefed Lubrani and Dagan on the meeting with Jumblatt. Lubrani had already spoken briefly with Jumblatt, who had expressed considerable anxiety about Syria's threats to him and his family. Could Jumblatt be invited to visit the United States? wondered Lubrani, suggesting that it might alleviate Jumblatt's concerns, while signaling to the Druze people that he essentially supported the American approach. McFarlane agreed with the suggestion and I telephoned Marwan Hammadeh the following morning to extend an invitation to Walid Jumblatt to visit the United States, telling him that we would be pleased to receive Jumblatt and his family and make all the necessary arrangements for their comfort and security. Hammadeh thanked me for the offer and suggested that Jumblatt might wish to meet with McFarlane later in the day. Several hours later we heard from Lubrani that Jumblatt's Syrian "keepers" had showed up unexpectedly. He found that Jumblatt and his party had departed for Geneva. I immediately called Hammadeh, but a housekeeper who spoke no English answered the phone.

Meanwhile in Beirut a firefight had broken out during the day between the Amal militia (Shia Moslems) and the Lebanese Forces (Maronite Christians). The LAF intervened, and a cease-fire was brokered during the night of August 28. Keen to demonstrate his "control" of the situation, President Gemayel ordered three LAF brigades to conduct a sweep to disarm the Amal units, triggering more fighting and Druze shelling from the Shouf onto Lebanese Army units. By late morning on the 29th, with negotiations under way between Gemayel's representatives and Amal leader Nabih Berri, Syrian and NSF artillery from the upper Matn began to rain down on Beirut.

We departed Paris immediately to return to Lebanon. Coming directly from the airport where we arrived by helicopter from Tel Aviv, McFarlane and I met with CIA station chief William Buckley to get his assessment of the fighting. (Buckley was abducted seven months later by Islamic Jihad and died in captivity.) Buckley had worked through the night and was as agitated as I had ever seen him, seething with anger as he pounded his fist on the table throughout the briefing. Systematically pointing out the coordinates from where Syrian and Druze artillery and rockets had fired during the past twenty-four hours, Buckley said that he had incontrovertible information from a variety of sources that the previous day's firefight had been instigated by Syrian intelligence agents in Beirut.

This was Assad's answer to Jumblatt's meeting with Haddad in Paris, Buckley said. He went on at length. The Syrians knew that the NSF would collapse if Jumblatt cut a deal with Gemayel, and Syria wanted a war for the Shouf. They were doing everything they could to start the war immediately, while ensuring that the Lebanese Army either sided with the Lebanese Forces or fell apart under the ethnic pressures the civil war would undoubtedly produce. A war in the Shouf would create an impossible situation for the United States. Gemayel would have no choice but to back the Lebanese Forces, making national reconciliation even more difficult, if not outright impossible. The United States would be forced to sit by passively while a bloody tribal war raged or choose sides. In either case, Assad was convinced that only he could win.

Buckley then returned to the map of Lebanon, which highlighted the Syrian and Druze gun positions. He urged McFarlane to recommend to Washington that the time had come for U.S. intervention in order to save Lebanon from Syria. The United States must destroy the Syrian positions immediately, he said. Spare the Druze sites, and Jumblatt and his people would understand that the United States was not against them. He concluded that Assad believed Lebanon would always remain a part of Syria and that Assad would fight to the last drop of Druze, Shia, Sunni and Maronite blood if that's what it took. We concurred with Buckley.

McFarlane met with Foreign Minister Salem and National Security Advisor Wadi Haddad that afternoon to try to devise a way of convincing Jumblatt to resume the dialogue of the 27th, stopping the fighting, regaining the momentum to form a new government with a commitment to national reconciliation and coordinating the peaceful entry of the LAF into the Shouf. Salem and Haddad were ready to resume talking with Jumblatt but requested that the United States issue a statement that it would use all means to prevent the partition of Lebanon, the fall of the central government and the return to hostilities. McFarlane demurred, arguing that such a statement would be seen as U.S. intervention in a civil war. Frustrated, Salem said the Lebanese people needed more from the United States. McFarlane said that there was no consensus on political compromise among the factional leaders, pointedly noting that the only consensus was that the United States should solve Lebanon's problems and not expect factional leaders to make meaningful compromises.

In the circumstances, McFarlane, Fairbanks, U.S. ambassador to Lebanon Robert Dillon, Ross and I concluded that the moment had come to pull out all the stops to work with Gemayel to form a new government that would include the NSF leaders, Rashid Karami, Nabih Berri and Walid Jumblatt. To achieve this ambitious result would require the United States to act with firmness, forcefulness and finesse with the Lebanese, the Syrians and the Israelis. McFarlane reported this analysis back to Shultz and Clark and was authorized to proceed. The first stop would be Israel, where McFarlane was to convince Begin to delay further the withdrawal of the IDF which was due to commence that evening. This was to give us some time to organize the European and Arab pressure we needed to bring to bear in Beirut and Damascus in order to work out an agreement between Gemayel and Jumblatt. A letter from President Reagan in hand, we flew by helicopter directly from Beirut to Jerusalem.

To save time, we had requested a landing clearance at the Knesset helipad. Before departing Beirut our Marine pilots were informed that clearance had been granted. As we approached Jerusalem, however, with fuel supplies running dangerously low, our pilots were instructed to land at the Israeli airport in Atarot, outside of Jerusalem in the occupied West Bank, as only Israeli pilots were permitted to land on the Knesset pad. Atarot was deserted, as Ambassador Lewis was waiting at the Knesset. He arrived fifteen minutes later. Lewis was as angry as I had ever seen him. Finding me before McFarlane, Lewis expressed his outrage that we had landed at Atarot, loudly complaining that we had violated the policy prohibiting official United States use of this airport. The premise of this policy was that the use of an airfield in the occupied territories might be interpreted by Israelis or Arabs as de facto U.S. recognition of the permanence of the occupation. I said it was my mistake and told him I would take responsibility for the matter if it came up with any Israeli officials. Sure enough, the moment we arrived in the prime minister's office, Arens asked how our landing at Atarot had been. McFarlane did not reply, so when Arens repeated his query, I said that I had made a mistake with the clearances and that the matter of our landing was irrelevant to the business at hand.

McFarlane briefed Begin and his advisors on our plan and requested for the last time a two-to-three-week delay in the withdrawal of the IDF. Begin was skeptical that an agreement could be reached between Jumblatt and Gemayel, arguing that between Assad's pressure and the communal hatreds, it was hard to see how an agreement could be negotiated. After confirming that McFarlane would not again ask for more delays, Begin agreed to delay the withdrawal through Saturday, September 3. We had gotten a little breathing room but did not know whether it would be enough.

Around three P.M., we tried to fly back to Beirut (from Ben-Gurion Airport in Tel Aviv), but the hydraulics system on one of the helicopters had failed and we had to wait until nearly six o'clock before another helicopter could arrive to fly us back to Beirut. By the time we reached the Beirut coast, the city was being heavily rocketed and shelled from the Shouf and the upper Matn, while firefights between factional militias raged throughout the city. Fairbanks, who had remained behind to work with Gemayel on a national reconciliation speech, was trapped in the bomb shelter of the Presidential Palace, which was sustaining multiple direct hits. All of our landing zones were under heavy fire, as was the airport, and we were forced to land and spend the night on board the USS *Iwo Jima*. The fighting continued well into the early hours of the morning, tapering off finally around four-thirty A.M.

When we awoke Beirut was quiet, save for occasional bursts of machine-gun fire. A heavy pall of acrid smoke hung over the city. The Marines at the airport informed the embassy that we would fly to the landing zone at the Ministry of Defense and proceed directly to a meeting with Gemayel. Our helicopter, a lightly armed Huey transport, was escorted by two menacing Cobra gunships. Lifting off from the *Iwo Jima*, we flew low and fast over the sea, flying directly over the Shia suburbs of Hay es-Salloum toward the Baabda Heights overlooking the city. Small-arms fire crackled below us as Shia militiamen took potshots at the helicopters. Wearing a flak jacket over my dark blue suit, I sat on my helmet for added protection. Once the shooting began, the pilots took evasive action, veering sharply away from the suburbs as they flew as low as possible to reach a steep ravine on the east side of Beirut. Almost able to reach out and grab the trees below us, we flew up through the ravine to the top of the ridge line overlooking Beirut. Seemingly out of harm's way, the pilots circled back to the south to find the Baabda landing zone (LZ), and we touched down in the smoke-filled Defense Ministry LZ several minutes later. As we stepped out of the helicopter, our security officers rushed to us shouting that we needed "to get the hell out of here," as thirty mortar rounds had hit the LZ within the last two minutes and more incoming fire was expected. From the LZ we drove to the Presidential Palace to meet with Gemayel.

McFarlane immediately impressed upon Gemayel that the success of the LAF in stopping the previous nights' attacks needed to be exploited politically. It was imperative that he immediately reach out to the other communal leaders, notably Jumblatt, to try to reach an accord. Through meetings and telephone calls, efforts were made throughout the day to try to end the killing and begin a process of reconciliation. These efforts proved futile. Between the pent-up mutual hostility of the militias and the manipulations of the Syrians, the fighting intensified and hope for a political solution waned.

On the afternoon of September 3 at the ambassador's residence, we were meeting with McFarlane when we received an urgent message from the Marines. They had just intercepted communications from Jumblatt's headquarters to Druze gunners ordering them to open fire on the Ministry of Defense and the U.S. ambassador's residence with their artillery. McFarlane, a retired Marine artillery officer, immediately started giving orders to shutter the windows, turn off the gas and electricity and take cover in the makeshift shelter, the silver closet inside the kitchen. Meanwhile McFarlane telephoned Jumblatt personally and told him we were aware of the orders to his people and advised the Druze leader not to take any irreversible actions. Less than a minute later, incoming artillery started to land near the residence. Artillery shells were falling outside on the grounds when suddenly two rounds crashed into a corner of the building. With a vicious crack, the vibration of the exploding shells knocked us down to the floor of the silver closet. A third round landed in the alley alongside our communications center, destroying our satellite dish and cutting off our communications. For several minutes we waited in darkness, unsure whether the shelling had stopped. McFarlane and Fairbanks went to the palace to speak with Gemayel while I set to work helping to clean up the mess. The residence was filling with smoke, as many of the trees on the grounds had caught fire during the attack. Our water pressure had dwindled to a trickle, and there was little to do but wait until the fire department could arrive.

That night, Gemayel finally addressed the Lebanese people, but his speech lacked the specific offers of compromise or suggestions of how to try to begin to overcome the hatred and mistrust that were engulfing Lebanon. The Druze and Syrians answered Gemayel's speech by immediately resuming their shelling. From beyond the ridge at Suq al-Gharb, heavy fighting went on all night, with artillery and rocket shells intermittently landing near the residence. Since the fighting had erupted several days earlier, I had been unable to return to my hotel in West Beirut, as the crossing points between West and East Beirut were closed. McFarlane had generously offered me the spare bed in his room. The rocket and artillery barrages were earsplitting. Nevertheless, to my amazement, McFarlane went right to sleep and snored through the night's heavy fighting, even as our windows seemed to shake out of their frames from the pressure of the exploding artillery shells. I, on the other hand, lay awake all night, certain that the next shell would land on top of us. Finally, I fell asleep. Not fifteen minutes later, Bud bounded out of bed and told me it was time to get moving.

As fighting spread through the mountains and the city, Gemayel and his advisors intensified the pressure on us to get the MNF to intervene on behalf of the government. Sitting in Beirut, reading the intelligence traffic and talking with the leaders of the various factions, there was no question that Syria was prodding its NSF allies to intensify the conflict. Damascus made no effort to conceal its objectives: bring down the government of Lebanon and annul the May 17 agreement.

In this cauldron, our diplomatic leverage diminished significantly as the IDF completed its preparations for withdrawal. The NSF had little reason to accommodate U.S. diplomacy. Drawing a parallel to the U.S. defeat in Vietnam and the failure to stand with the shah of Iran, Foreign Minister Khaddam of Syria told the Saudi and Lebanese foreign ministers that "the U.S. is short of breath." Syria astutely perceived that by intensifying the level and scope of violence, the MNF would be forced to leave Lebanon, the government of Lebanon would fall, and the May 17 agreement would be abrogated.

Aggressive Self-defense

Frustrated by the growing conflict between Shultz and Weinberger, who was still unwilling to consider an expanded role for the MNF, Clark scheduled a National Security Planning Group (NSPG) meeting for Saturday, September 3, 1983. McFarlane was directed to return to Washington to brief the president in order for the administration to come to some decisions on how to proceed in Lebanon.

Clark had convened the NSPG to find a way to further delay Israel's withdrawal to prevent the mountain war and the threat it would pose Beirut and the MNF. The meeting proved to be an exercise in tough rhetoric but divided results. McFarlane briefed on the limited progress the United States had made in pushing Amin Gemayel to try to organize a government of national unity that might start the process of reconciliation. Whether more time would have made a difference was problematic, but Reagan decided on the spot to call Begin to request yet another delay of the IDF withdrawal. As the meeting drew to a close, Arens called back on behalf of Begin to advise that it was too late.

Reagan's advisors were divided along familiar lines. Throughout the preceding month, the national security bureaucracy had fiercely debated whether and how the MNF role and mission could be expanded in coordination with the Israeli withdrawal. Such an expansion would provide more time for U.S. diplomacy to promote political reconciliation among the Lebanese factions while reducing the possibility of communal violence in the Shouf. State (primarily PM and S/P, Shultz and Eagleburger), Clark, McFarlane and the NSC staff argued in favor of an active-presence mission for the MNF. An active presence would have permitted the MNF to be interposed between the Lebanese factions in order to reduce the direct pressure that Syria could bring to bear on the Lebanese government. Bush, Baker, Weinberger and the JCS strongly opposed any change in the role and mission of the MNF, other than its withdrawal from Lebanon. But all the members of the NSPG were in agreement that the limited mission of the Marines gave the Syrians a means of undermining the confidence and interest of the various Lebanese factions in working with the United States. The Syrians were probing the limits of the U.S. ability to use force in response to their aggression directed against American interests. We did not have the power in place or the will to win, and the Syrians knew it.

With occasional reference to the recent Soviet shoot-down of KAL 007, President Reagan made it clear that it was imperative that the Marines ashore receive defensive fire support if they were attacked. But Chairman Vessey emphasized that it would be hard to answer the Syrian shelling unless the U.S. Navy were to conduct carrier-based air strikes against the Syrian guns. Shultz argued that a Syrian victory in Lebanon would be perceived as a Soviet victory, and would undermine the U.S. position throughout the Middle East. U.S. credibility would suffer to the benefit of our radical adversaries.

At the end of the NSPG, no new decisions were made. The rules of engagement were not changed. The United States would continue to act only in self-defense, if fired upon directly. The only thing that was agreed upon was that McFarlane should return immediately to Lebanon to rejoin Fairbanks, who had stayed behind to continue U.S. efforts to negotiate a cease-fire, while trying to convince the confessional leaders to agree to join a government of national unity. McFarlane asked Kemp to accompany him, and I stayed in Washington to work the issues at the NSC.

The military situation deteriorated dramatically after the IDF pulled back to the Awali River. By September 7, Syrian and Druze forces had filled the power vacuum, and reports of civilian massacres and atrocities in the Shouf and Matn became increasingly common. Brigadier General Carl Stiner of the U.S. Army, the representative of JCS chairman Vessey at the Lebanese Ministry of Defense and the American embassy in Lebanon, reported that the LAF was surrounded and running low on ammunition. In this context, the LAF commander, General Ibrahim Tannous, decided that the LAF would make its last stand at Suq al-Gharb, a village on the most prominent ridge overlooking Beirut. If Suq al-Gharb fell, little would stand in the way of the advancing radical forces, which now included Iranian Pasdaran, PLO fighters, Druze and leftist Lebanese militias.

At an NSC meeting on Friday, September 9, President Reagan decided to send the battleship *New Jersey*, with its sixteen-inch guns, to Lebanon to enhance the United States' ability to answer long-range Syrian artillery. This decision reflected an inherently contradictory compromise within the National Security Council. (The statutory members of the NSC are the president, the vice-president, the secretaries of state and defense, the NSC advisor, the director of central intelligence and the chairman of the JCS.) On the one hand, some of the members of NSC wanted to strengthen U.S. diplomacy and saw the *New Jersey* as serving that end. President Reagan wanted to ensure that Americans in Lebanon were not reluctant to defend themselves against attacks and directed the Marines to conduct more "aggressive self-defense." But the threat to Americans and American policy came from Syria, which had effectively declared war on U.S. policy back in May 1983 during Shultz's shuttle, and the United States did not want to engage in war with Syria. Herein lay the dilemma and the contradiction. Weinberger and Vessey argued strongly against the dispatch of the *New Jersey*, but the president agreed with the opposing view of Marine Corps commandant General P. X. Kelley and directed that the battleship sail immediately to the eastern Mediterranean. The NSDD signed by Reagan forbade the Marines to move outside the Beirut area and directed that they avoid a confrontation with the Syrians. But it simultaneously authorized the Marines to conduct "aggressive self-defense."

Despite brave talk of reconciliation, neither the central government nor the NSF showed any genuine inclination to stop fighting and settle differences politically. The Syrians brushed off Saudi and other Arab entreaties as they directed their allies to turn up the heat. On September 11, Stiner and McFarlane reached the conclusion that the fall of Suq al-Gharb was imminent, threatening the entire city of Beirut as well as what was left of the tattered U.S. effort to promote a political settlement and implement the May 17 agreement. McFarlane sent back a lengthy message, which became known as the "sky is falling" cable, that analyzed the situation in terms of Syrian control of the attacking forces and requested that U.S. forces be authorized to provide direct fire support, including carrier-based air strikes if necessary, to bolster the Lebanese Army.

Washington received McFarlane's message later that day, and Judge

Clark conducted several secure conference calls with his counterparts before convening an NSPG at six P.M. to evaluate McFarlane's request and U.S. options. At seven-fifteen, the president, having been briefed by Clark, approved McFarlane's request. Although Clark directed Weinberger and the JCS to implement the president's decision immediately, the military "chain of command" advised Colonel Timothy Geraghty, the commander of the Marine amphibious unit on the ground at the airport, that the discretion to fire would be his as the on-scene commander.

The Lebanese Army managed to hold on at Suq al-Gharb without immediate U.S. fire support, though the combat grew fiercer as the week passed and supplies were exhausted. During the predawn hours of the 19th, Stiner concluded that the LAF would not be able to continue their resistance without U.S. intervention. Geraghty had no illusions about the Lebanese or his tightly constrained mission. Convinced that U.S. fire support would dramatically increase the danger to the Marines at the airport, however, Geraghty had exercised the authority by refusing to issue the orders to fire. Hamstrung by the Pentagon since the Marines were initially deployed, the "presence" mission that the MNF was pursuing was unrealistic in an environment in which the Syrian regular army and their Lebanese allies were waging a real war against a less capable foe, the Lebanese Army and the Christian militias. In the face of General Stiner's conclusions and McFarlane's pressure, Geraghty finally relented and the USS *Virginia* began to fire in support of the LAF at Suq al-Gharb. The naval gunfire support had the desired effect, bolstering the spine of the LAF and causing the Syrians and their allies to pause. Five days later, with the *New Jersey* one day away from arriving off the coast of Beirut, McFarlane and Fairbanks succeeded in negotiating a cease-fire and returned to discussions of a political settlement. The U.S. fire support had achieved what had become the primary American objective, which was to prevent the fall of Suq al-Gharb, a development that would have significantly increased the threat to all Americans in the Beirut area. It had also injected a measure of uncertainty into the Syrian calculus regarding how far the United States was prepared to go to achieve its political objectives.

But the U.S. escalation created the impression that America had chosen sides in Lebanon's civil war on behalf of Gemayel and the Christian militias, inciting hostile, anti-American feelings among many Lebanese, particularly among the Druze and the Shias. In this changed environment, it became more important than ever to broker a political solution that would reconcile the opposing factions, bring about the removal of foreign forces and help restore Lebanese independence.

Unfinished Business

The cease-fire held into October, and U.S. diplomacy, bolstered by this measured use of force, resumed the pursuit of a political dialogue among the disparate Lebanese factions. Pressed by McFarlane and Fairbanks, Gemayel finally agreed in principle to participate in a reconciliation conference, assuming the other confessional leaders also agreed to participate. On October 7, Fairbanks's associate, Charles Patrizia, called me in Washington at four A.M. to advise me that Fairbanks wanted me to return immediately to Beirut to assist in the effort to convene the reconciliation conference. I argued that the mission might be better served by a representative from the State Department, perhaps David Mack, who was responsible for Lebanon matters. Fairbanks, however, rejected my suggestion, based on my relations with the confessional leaders and the continuing need to work with them on a daily basis.

By the time I arrived in Beirut on October 10, most of the Lebanese leaders had agreed to travel to Geneva for a reconciliation conference at the end of the month. There was one notable holdout: Walid Jumblatt. As a result of the mountain war, the Druze had significantly strengthened their hold over the Shouf, and Jumblatt was in no mood to make any political concessions to Amin Gemayel. Elusive as ever, Jumblatt had left Lebanon to break free from Syria's grasp momentarily and to consider his options in the more peaceful environment of Amman, Jordan. With the cease-fire starting to come apart, however, it was essential that we get Jumblatt to agree to come to Geneva. His failure to attend would guarantee a worthless reconciliation conference and signal the likely resumption of full-scale war.

Working through various diplomatic channels, I asked whether Jumblatt would agree to receive me in Amman to discuss the plight of the Druze people and our "unfinished business" from the Paris meetings. After several days of silence, Jumblatt signaled that he would be pleased to meet with me on Saturday evening, October 22.

Patrizia and I were on a Marine helicopter at five-thirty P.M. and flying toward Beirut Airport. En route, the pilot received a message that our airplane, which was kept at Ben-Gurion for security reasons, had not yet arrived. Because of the delay, the pilot was instructed to fly to the *Iwo*

Jima to pick up some equipment, before flying us to the airport to wait for our plane. Lieutenant Colonel Harry Slacum, Geraghty's executive officer, met our helicopter and took us over to Geraghty's office to ensure that the communications with the plane and Embassy Amman were properly coordinated.

It turned out that no one in Embassy Tel Aviv had alerted the air crew to our travel and it would take about two hours before they could be located and fly up to Beirut. In the interim, Geraghty had come by and asked us to join him for a beer in the barracks. After about thirty minutes he was called away, and we went back to his office with Slacum. I used the opportunity to tell Slacum what I thought about the tactics the Marines were employing to counter the growing number of sniper attacks coming from the deserted buildings on the airport perimeter. In my view, the Amal was testing the Marines, probing to determine how far they could push before getting a response. Everyone in Beirut knew the Marines walked around with unloaded weapons, despite the fact that they had tanks. I suggested that using the tanks to take down the buildings where the snipers were positioned would send a clear message that there was a price to pay for shooting at Americans. I argued that countersniper tactics may work in conventional combat, but that this was an unconventional situation. Slacum did not take kindly to my gratuitous advice. His response reflected a deep-seated disdain for civilians giving advice to the military and, in my opinion, a complete lack of understanding about the symbiotic relationship between violence and power in Lebanon. "Don't lecture me about how to deal with snipers," Slacum replied. "Our response is just right. We don't get them all, but we get some of them." I tried to make the point that in Lebanon sniping at the Marines was a political act. In this Middle Eastern context, it was imperative for the Marines' response to reflect greater, not equivalent, power, if force was to have any deterrent effect. Slacum dismissed my arguments with a wave of his hand and walked out, leaving Patrizia and me to wait alone in Geraghty's office until our plane arrived to take us on to Amman.

We met with Jumblatt in the ambassador's residence in Amman from eleven P.M. until two A.M. The discussion followed familiar lines, as Jumblatt vented about Gemayel's untrustworthiness, the vulnerability of the Druze and the extremity of Syrian pressures. Although I expected harsh criticism from him for the U.S. military intervention at Suq al-Gharb, there was none. Instead, Jumblatt asked whether the United States would really help with the economic reconstruction of Lebanon, particularly in the Shouf and in southern Lebanon, where humanitarian and economic assistance was badly needed. I told him that a successful reconciliation conference in Geneva would help lay the groundwork for such assistance, but it was important for Jumblatt and the other leaders of the NSF to understand that the United States would not implement major assistance programs without peace. Emphasizing the essential need for reconciliation, I said that the best chance for establishing trust among the leaders of Lebanon was for them to sit and talk without the threat of violence hanging over their heads. "Maybe not your head," Jumblatt replied bitterly, "but it will hang over mine. I can assure you of that." Aware of his justifiable paranoia, I repeated that the United States was ready to receive him and his family, should he wish to go there. Jumblatt agreed to consider attending the conference.

Toward the end of the meeting, seeking to draw him out, I told him I was interested in learning more about the Druze religious beliefs, how they differed from Sunni and Shia Islam, and the role played by mysticism in the Druze faith. I knew that he had lived in India for some years and was a leader who inspired his followers through spiritual charisma as well as bravery. Jumblatt smiled, rolled his eyes but demurred, saying that I should not ask him about such things that night. He told me he was glad I was interested in the Druze and their faith and offered to discuss the meaning of the Druze existence all night when I came to Mukhtara. He put it off, however, for another time. As we parted, Jumblatt repeated his skepticism about Gemayel and the prospects for peaceful reconciliation, but agreed to try to see his way to Geneva.

I had asked for a wake-up call for eight A.M., but my phone rang at six forty-five. It was the communications officer at the embassy. Word had just come in reporting a large explosion at Beirut Airport. He said that the airport was closed and there was no word on when it would reopen. Initial reports indicated there had been an attack on the Marines' barracks, but no casualty reports had come in as yet. I quickly got dressed and ran across the street to the embassy. By the time I arrived, the embassy was starting to receive casualty reports, as well as word that the French barracks had been hit simultaneously.

Only When They Die

At 6:20 A.M. a suicide truck bomb had crashed through the perimeter of the Marines' barracks, destroying the building and killing 241 Marines. The French barracks, located in downtown Beirut, was also destroyed, and 58 French soldiers had died. The terrorists used the same *modus*

operandi as with the destruction of the American embassy in April and
the bombing of the Iraqi embassy—by Syrian agents—several years earlier. With Iran and Syria allied against Iraq in the Gulf, it was becoming
clear that a radical alliance was opening up a new terrorist front of
the Iran-Iraq War inside Lebanon. The successful export of the Iranian
revolution required foreign foils, the same way Iran needed the "Great
Satan" to mobilize the mass martyrdom that gave Khomeini and the other
mullahs so much power.

Although such suicide bombings were in the style of fundamentalist
Shias prepared to martyr themselves like their brethren in Iran, such
terror operations in Beirut, particularly against targets that might hold
Syria responsible, could not have been undertaken without the tacit
acquiescence, or perhaps even the outright instigation, of Damascus.
Assad, however, read the United States correctly. He calculated that the
United States would use force only in retaliation for discrete conventional
attacks. If U.S. forces could not ascertain the precise source of an attack,
then there would probably be no reaction. Against a country that played
by Hama rules we imposed an American standard of justice, where one is
innocent until proven guilty. Here, we imposed a burden of proof beyond
a reasonable doubt on ourselves, rather than on the states sponsoring
terrorism against American interests.

In an effort by the administration to avoid a War Powers challenge,
and to reduce the likelihood of casualties, the ROE forbade the Marines
to behave like Marines. It seemed as if Weinberger and Vessey believed
that because they would not accede to a more forceful role for the MNF,
or an expanded ROE, the Marines were not actually in a war and they
would not be badly harmed. The situation was tragic. U.S. Marines were
forced to occupy the worst possible terrain in Beirut and to carry unloaded
weapons in what was undoubtedly one of the most dangerous cities in the
world. Over time, their peaceful presence, defenseless posture and limited
ability to defend themselves brought upon them contempt from the population of Beirut. This was, after all, the Middle East, not Montana. The
Syrians read the newspapers and knew full well that Washington was
deeply divided over the presence mission of the Marines in Lebanon.
They also knew that the United States was grappling with how best to
cope with terrorism. There had been no retaliation following the hostage-
taking in Tehran, nor was there one after the destruction of the American
embassy in Beirut. Ronald Reagan's tough talk had not been matched by
tough action. Beirut had indeed become America's Bermuda Triangle.

Flying directly from Amman to Beirut, Geraghty met our plane on the runway and immediately drove Patrizia and me over to the smoking ruins of the barracks. Geraghty and I had developed a good working relationship during his tour as the Marine amphibious unit (MAU) commander. During the preceding months, he had commented several times to me how strange it was that both he and I could hail originally from St. Louis, Missouri, yet somehow end up representing the United States in Beirut. We had talked politics, Cardinals baseball and the realities of the Middle East on several occasions, but we had never spoken about death and the risks that come with soldiering.

Nothing in my life prepared me for the appalling disaster that confronted me that morning at Beirut Airport. The barracks where I had sat and sipped beer less than eighteen hours before had been flattened. Voices racked with pain were calling out from the rubble as search parties dug for survivors and ambulances careened around the tarmac. Walking through the ruins of the barracks to the makeshift morgue that had been set up next to a hangar, I saw Marines look up at Geraghty from their grim work, prying slabs of concrete from dead comrades, collecting body parts, filling body bags, their emotions and anger somehow calmed by the steadiness of their leader. Standing in the doorway of the morgue, Geraghty took off his helmet, put his hand on my shoulder and grimaced as he shook his head. Before we could talk, we heard the whistle of bullets flying by outside the doorway where we stood. "Snipers," Geraghty said. "Motherfucking snipers shooting at us while we're trying to deal with all this." Rage mixed with nausea; I wanted to stay at the airport, to talk with Geraghty, to offer whatever comfort or assistance I could. But out of nowhere an embassy driver appeared, calling out that Fairbanks was waiting for me to go and meet with President Gemayel. "Help them make peace," Geraghty implored, as we said good-bye in what proved to be our last encounter.

My Lebanese driver was frightened by the situation at the barracks, and was anxious to leave the airport area immediately. He said the whole city was on edge, fearful of another act of terrorism and waiting for American and French retaliation. As we left the airport, he pressed the accelerator to the floor and careened toward the city, trying to get away as quickly as possible. When we reached the Shatila circle, he made a sharp right in order to take a shortcut across the northern end of the Shia suburbs.

He had made a grave mistake, we found, as we turned a corner and found ourselves confronted by four Amal militiamen, armed with rocket-propelled grenades and AK-47 machine guns, who had placed a roadblock with tall spikes in our path. Although our van was allegedly bulletproof, it was not RPG-7–proof. Nor was the single Uzi submachine gun that the driver had tucked away under the seat likely to do us any good against the overwhelming firepower of the militiamen. The driver was a Christian and he turned to me with a terror in his eyes unlike anything I had seen in a man before. "I am sorry," he said, as he grabbed his rosary and started to pray.

From one nightmare to the next, I thought, as one of the militiamen banged on the door of the van and signaled to me to get out. "I'm not getting out," I said in English. Holding up my black diplomatic passport, I stated that "I am a diplomat. I am not getting out of the car." He tried to open the doors, but thankfully, they were locked, causing him to bang the door again with the butt of his rifle. Two others came up to the front of the van and pointed their RPG-7 directly at the windshield, but neither the driver nor I budged. The militiamen walked back to their roadblock and caucused for a few minutes, then one of them returned and started screaming at me again to get out of the van. Shouting through the closed windows, I told him to call my friend, Nabih Berri, and ask him if he wanted his men to bother me anymore. At the mention of Berri's name, the militiaman backed off, then picked up a radio and began to talk into it. Several minutes passed before he picked up the radio again. When he put it down, he came over to the van, hit it with the butt of his rifle, and signaled to his associates to move the roadblock. Rivers of sweat pouring down his head, the driver laid a patch of rubber fifty yards long as we sped away. Fearful that we would be shot from behind, the driver told me to keep down until we were safely across the Green Line, which separated Moslem West Beirut from Christian East Beirut. With the faces of maimed and dead Marines carved vividly into my brain and with my heart racing and my mouth dry from this close encounter, I could not help but think that Beirut had become the gate to hell.

Still in shock and unable to sleep, I returned to Washington on Tuesday, October 25, certain that our mission to Lebanon was over. During the week before the attack, McFarlane had been named NSC advisor, following Judge Clark's sudden reassignment as secretary of the interior. I was thrilled for McFarlane and assumed that the responsibility for the U.S. peace initiative would return to State. I was, therefore, taken aback when McFarlane called me down to his office to inform me that I would accompany Fairbanks to Geneva on Friday to support the Lebanese reconciliation talks. Enervated by the harrowing events of the past weekend and fed up with the constant maneuvering of the Lebanese leaders, I told

McFarlane that "I am not volunteering to go to Geneva." McFarlane paused momentarily and then said, "The success of this initiative is very important to the president. I am sure you will make the correct decision." I could not refuse, regardless of how I felt about the prospects for success or the importance of the issue. I had only to think of so many dead Marines to know that I could not turn my back on their sacrifice.

In Geneva, Fairbanks and I met with Amin Gemayel and every communal leader in attendance in an effort to squeeze political reconciliation out of the Lebanese. But we were not the only interlocutors attending the reconciliation conference, as Syrian Foreign Minister Khaddam was also in Geneva. We spoke to the leaders about the essential need to reformulate the French-sponsored 1943 National Pact, which had created modern Lebanon, and the fundamental need to create a new political system based on the demographic realities of 1983. We talked about reconstruction of their country. Khaddam, on the other hand, gave them the Syrian perspective, insisting that anything that resulted from the Israeli invasion must be canceled and the Israeli occupation resisted. The price for liberating the land of Lebanon from the Israelis, he lectured them, could not be the independence of the Lebanese people. "People cannot change their nature or the color of their skin just because they want to," he warned, "Only when they die can people change."

Khaddam did not pull any punches in Geneva as he hammered away at the U.S. position and Amin Gemayel day in and day out. In his own words, he said that continued Lebanese support for the May 17 agreement would be answered by death. Syria would not permit the agreement to stand. Coming less than a week after the destruction of the French and American barracks, without any retaliation, and pressure intensifying on Washington to cut its losses and leave Lebanon, the communal leaders lost whatever confidence remained in America. Washington's willingness to take action to back up its diplomacy could not be relied upon. Nevertheless, we kept on slugging away at each leader until the conference ended.

On the final day, November 4, Fairbanks and I met with Shia leader Adil Usayran, Foreign Minister Eli Salem and Maronite leader Suleiman Franjieh. As we concluded our discussions with Franjieh, the Swiss security officers came in and advised Fairbanks and me that they had intercepted what they believed was an Iranian communication indicating that a bomb attack would be launched against us when we left the Intercontinental Hotel. Riding down the freight elevator to the loading dock, where the security forces had moved our cars, Fairbanks turned to me and said,

"You ride in my car." I looked him in squarely in the eye and thanked him for that vote of confidence. I don't know why I got in his car, but I did. Driving to the U.S. mission, I grimaced in anticipation of an explosion as we drove past several parked cars.

A secret meeting and dinner between Wadi Haddad, Dave Kimche, Fairbanks and me had been arranged. Regardless of the final outcome of the reconciliation conference and the fate of the May 17 agreement, the U.S. wanted to continue to facilitate communications between the governments of Israel and Lebanon, communications that might contribute to an atmosphere of confidence-building and mutual trust. The meeting provided a cordial starting point for a face-to-face dialogue between Haddad and Kimche, as both parties tried to put the past behind them and devise a way of coping with mutual security and political interests, particularly involving the Syrians and the Palestinians. No agreements were reached, nor did anything tangible emerge from the meeting. But it demonstrated that Israeli and Lebanese officials, despite their mutual bitterness, possessed some will that might eventually lead to peaceful solutions of problems that plagued both countries. Unfortunately, our diplomacy fared less well trying to get the Lebanese to achieve comparable results amongst themselves.

CHAPTER 11

A FAILURE OF PRESIDENTIAL LEADERSHIP

A New Presidential Envoy

The reconciliation conference over, I returned to my office in Washington on Thursday, November 10, and learned that the newly appointed presidential envoy for the Middle East, Donald Rumsfeld, wanted to see me as soon as possible. Rumsfeld assumed this high-profile position in November 1983 after Reagan appointed McFarlane as his third national security advisor. A former congressman, secretary of defense, White House chief of staff and ambassador to NATO, Rumsfeld had taken a six-month leave of absence from his post as chief executive officer of G. D. Searle and Company, the pharmaceutical company best known for its development of the sugar substitute NutraSweet, to become the Middle East envoy.

Undoubtedly one of America's most qualified national security executives, Rumsfeld moved vigorously to place his imprint on U.S. policy on the Middle East in general and on Lebanon in particular. A realist who recognized the role military power played in the pursuit of diplomatic objectives, Rumsfeld had only limited familiarity with the politics and people of the Middle East. He used his "innocence" to best advantage as he began to educate himself about the regional situation, the personalities of key leaders and American policy options. Rumsfeld was especially interested in forging personal relationships with the key leaders of the Middle East. Indeed, by the time he relinquished the title of Middle East envoy, Rumsfeld had met the head of state of every country in the Middle East with which the United States maintained diplomatic relations.

One of the most forthright, serious and articulate politicians I have ever met, Rumsfeld wasted no time in coming right to the point. He wanted me to be a member of his negotiating team, which would be leaving for the Middle East the following week, and he would not take no for an answer. He said that he knew that I had recently been married but had spent most of the time in the Middle East, rather than in Washington. McFarlane, Fairbanks and Shultz had all told him that I knew the players in Lebanon, Israel, Syria and the rest of the Middle East better than anyone else and that I had a measure of institutional memory that cut across several different Middle East missions over the past two years. I thanked Rumsfeld for the compliment. (I recalled Ambassador Vernon Walters's sage advice: "Anyone who tells you that flattery gets you nowhere has never been flattered.") Try as I might to convince Rumsfeld that he needed me more in Washington backing up the mission than in the region, he stubbornly refused to take no for an answer. After an hour of discussion without any progress, we agreed to meet again on Monday to try to work out a mutually acceptable arrangement.

As exciting and potentially rewarding as it would be to participate in Rumsfeld's team, my reticence was in part because I wanted to stay in Washington but also directly related to the failure of President Reagan to impose discipline on his feuding advisors. I also believed we needed to devote more attention to U.S. policy in the Gulf. Reagan's tough rhetoric about "swift and effective retribution" against terrorists and their backers was proving to be hollow, as the weeks wore on without any military response to the terrorist attack against the Marines. Not knowing whether or when a decision to retaliate would actually be made, Rumsfeld believed it was essential that some way be found to bolster American diplomacy. U.S. credibility was at stake.

The relative progress the United States had made from the days of the Carter administration in "putting our money where our mouth was" in advancing U.S. policy interests was really fairly minimal. During the Carter years, there was neither the capability nor the will to use force to defend and advance American interests. In contrast, the Reagan administration had significantly built up conventional military capabilities and strengthened America's ability to project force. Yet the razor-sharp divisions within the National Security Council and the Vietnam legacy hampered our will to act. In some respects, the United States was in an even more vulnerable position than it had been under Carter. While we finally had our ammunition together with our tanks, we were very reluctant to actually use either. Our words were brave, forceful and tough. Ronald Reagan had put the world on notice that "America was back in the saddle again," yet the administration kept issuing swaggering warnings without backing up words with deeds. Thus, those who opposed U.S. policies, especially state sponsors of terrorism, were able to manipulate America's weakness and outmaneuver Washington. They knew an Achilles' heel when they saw one.

Perfidy

Notwithstanding the president's unequivocal declaratory posture on Lebanon, Reagan's National Security Council members were still badly divided over the proper role for the United States in Lebanon and how to respond to terrorist attacks. As I returned to my office in the second week of November, Phil Dur advised me that as a result of his initiative, Deputy NSC Advisor Admiral John Poindexter had communicated with General Jacques Saulnier, French president Mitterrand's military advisor, and agreed that a joint strike against the Sheikh Abdullah Barracks should be prepared in the event a decision was made to retaliate. President Reagan and Secretary Shultz believed it was essential for the United States to act with force. The barracks had become the headquarters of the Pasdaran in Lebanon. We had received information from numerous sources confirming that Islamic Amal and the Hizbollah were training terrorists and launching operations from this former LAF barracks. The Sheikh Abdullah Barracks represented the nerve center of Tehran's western front in its war with Iraq. The barracks was a target worthy of destruction not only for the central role it was playing in the terrorism afflicting Lebanon but as an important adjunct in the war for the Gulf. But Weinberger and Vessey opposed striking back at terrorists.

Despite Reagan's decision that planning for a joint U.S.-French strike proceed, Weinberger resisted. He did not believe that the battle for the Gulf was now fully joined in the suburbs of Beirut. Yet the evidence of the Hizbollah's perpetration of the attack against the MNF, in the name of Islamic Jihad, mounted. We received reports that the operations had been approved and coordinated by Colonel Ghazi Caanan, the Syrian officer in charge of military operations in Lebanon. Weinberger repeatedly argued with Shultz against retaliation unless the evidence was absolute. It seemed he would agree only if culpability could be proved in an American court of law.

Weinberger was convinced that retaliation and/or an expanded role for the MNF in support of American diplomacy would lead to ever-increasing casualties and U.S. responsibility. He exploited the Soviet role in Syria and Lebanon to bolster his constantly growing defense-budget requests, in spite of the fact that he and members of his staff regularly criticized the State Department and the NSC staff for "not having a policy in Lebanon." Yet Chairman Vessey's personal representative in Lebanon, Brigadier General Carl Stiner, was fully involved in McFarlane's and later Rumsfeld's diplomacy. Stiner understood the goals of President Reagan's policy, and, to the dismay of the JCS, concurred in the need for the United States to escalate its military activities in order for diplomacy to succeed. But Stiner's perspective had virtually no influence on Weinberger's abhorrence of the role of force in support of a policy with which he did not agree, despite the fact that it was Ronald Reagan's policy.

In spite of the logjam in the JCS, a plan to strike the Sheikh Abdullah Barracks was prepared by the Navy staff under the supervision of Vice Admiral Ace Lyons, the Navy's deputy chief of naval operations for plans, and the Sixth Fleet Task Force 60 commander off the coast of Beirut, Rear Admiral Jerry Tuttle. Following up on Dur's communications with Saulnier, the French on-scene commander approached Tuttle to say that he had been empowered by Paris to collaborate in a joint U.S.-French strike against the Sheikh Abdullah Barracks. Working from the U.S. plan, U.S. and French military planners devised an operational plan for a combined U.S.-French naval-aviation strike force to destroy the Sheikh Abdullah Barracks in Baalbek. The French and American officers were united in their determination to avenge the deaths of their comrades some three weeks earlier.

On November 14, NSC Advisor McFarlane convened a National Security Planning Group (NSPG) meeting to address the matter of the joint U.S.-French strike. Reagan unambiguously decided that the strikes were to be executed on November 16. The president's order was to proceed. Admiral Tuttle, however, never received word of the approval or the order to execute the plan.

With the plan expected to be completed and approved during the night of the 15th and the weather forecasted to be clear, Dur and I stayed late in the Situation Room monitoring the final preparations for the attack. As the night wore on, Dur volunteered to stay and call me the moment we received word that the attack force had launched. I awoke with a start at six A.M., suddenly aware that I had not heard from Dur. When I reached him he was beside himself and quite morose. "Weinberger disapproved the strike this morning. He came over to the West Wing of the White House and advised McFarlane that the French minister of defense, Charles Hernu, had called him about the joint plan but Weinberger claimed that he did not know anything about it. Hernu informed Weinberger that the French would attack at 9:00 A.M. Washington time, a condition which Weinberger claimed made it impossible for the U.S. to comply with." It was clear that Weinberger scuttled the joint operation because he did not agree with the president's decision.

During the afternoon of November 15, Tuttle had sent a request for approval of the plan to the Pentagon, but it was held up at the U.S. Command in Europe (EUCOM). EUCOM had direct responsibility for Sixth Fleet operations and controlled the flow of communications between the Fleet and the Pentagon. Tuttle's request arrived at the Pentagon between three A.M. and four A.M. on the sixteenth, at which time Weinberger and Vessey decided not to authorize its execution. "Weinberger refuses to carry out the president's decision," Dur said with total incredulity in his voice. "An order has gone out from Weinberger to the Fleet ordering them not to execute and to stand down." The French aircraft had launched first from the carrier *Foch* and were prepared to link up with the American bombers. With the French already airborne and holding, Tuttle had no choice but to inform his French counterpart that America would not, in fact, be joining the French in the attack on the terrorist base.

Weinberger had blatantly disregarded the instructions of the commander in chief, behaving with total insubordination because, once again, he arrogantly believed that he knew what was best for the United States in the Middle East as well as how best to use (or not use, as was the case) American military power. Perhaps of even greater significance was Weinberger's confidence that the president would not impose any discipline on him for disobeying orders. Although Weinberger argued afterward that the president never made the decision to conduct the strike, a clear and unequivocal record exists with regard to the decision as well as Weinberger's stand down order. (Perhaps the personal detailed notes which we now know Weinberger kept will shed some light on exactly what Weinberger thought the president had directed in the November 14 NSPG.)

One theme was continually addressed during these NSPG debates: Should the United States rely on regional powers or must it act itself to achieve American goals and protect its vital interests? Under Weinberger, DOD was consumed in seeking every possible means to withdraw U.S. forces from Lebanon and instead rely on Arab powers to resolve the crisis and protect American interests in the Middle East. With respect to responding to acts of terror directed at American interests, Chairman Vessey argued—out loud—that it was "beneath the dignity of the United States to retaliate against the terrorists responsible."

He insisted that a U.S. military solution in Lebanon would require the deployment of six U.S. Army divisions. Vice President Bush went to Lebanon the day after the Marine headquarters was bombed and surveyed the carnage himself. He argued forcefully in favor of retaliation, as did McFarlane and Shultz. James Baker and Edwin P. Meese, then Ronald Reagan's principal political advisors, however, saw the 1984 election approaching and urged caution.

The November 16 failure to carry out the joint U.S.-French strikes typified how Reagan's cabinet government had run amok in the national security arena. The struggles within the National Security Council were fierce, and internal guerrilla warfare contributed as much to undermine U.S. interests in the Middle East as did the terrorist attacks. On several occasions NSPG meetings with the president degenerated into all-out shouting matches between Shultz and Weinberger. Furious with Weinberger's constant efforts to move the Marines out of harm's way in early 1983, Shultz had angrily told one NSPG, "If anyone in this room hears me suggest that the United States should send in the Marines to protect U.S. interests, just choke me on the spot."

While one could respect Weinberger's determination to argue his point and his courage to forcefully disagree with the president, once Reagan had made a decision, it was Weinberger's duty to implement it, not prevaricate and obfuscate. The time to debate should have been over. Yet the endgame never seemed to end. As I sat in meeting after meeting, with neither President Reagan nor Vice President Bush ever intervening to resolve the disabling disputes or assert discipline, I grew increasingly doubtful about the ability of the United States to succeed in its conduct of foreign policy, particularly in the Middle East. Policy could not be successfully implemented as long as the administration remained polarized. In addition, the administration's willingness to communicate meaningfully with the Congress and citizenry to form a consensus in the field of foreign affairs, and to exert genuine leadership, was almost nonexistent. President Reagan and his advisors and the congressional leadership engaged in a rhetorical power play in a divisive attempt to control the foreign policy of the United States. This critical failure to communicate, as well as the tendency to posture with "macho bravado," also directly contributed to the U.S. failure in Lebanon.

Time after time, Reagan would make decisions authorizing the use of force to invigorate American diplomacy. Yet Weinberger and Vessey consistently reinterpreted the president's decisions to argue that the circumstances on the ground did not warrant naval or marine gunfire unless and until Americans died again. They did not comprehend the role played by American power in the perceptions of the Lebanese and Syrians and the relationship of that perception to the success or failure of American diplomacy. Moreover, following the destruction of the Marine barracks, it should have been obvious even to the members of the "New Never Again Club" that Syria and Iran had declared war, albeit unconventional war, on the United States and the other members of the MNF. (The Never Again Club was a term used by General Matthew B. Ridgway and other senior Army officers, stung by the stalemated ground war in Korea, to argue that the United States should never again engage in a land war in Asia. The New Never Again Club was a term coined by the Army's post-Vietnam leadership. It expressed the view that U.S. military force would be used only during "genuine" national emergencies.)

I bluntly explained to Rumsfeld that the fissures within the NSC argued for me to remain in Washington, where I could support his efforts working with the bureaucracy while helping to ensure that the hard decisions that would need to be made in support of his diplomacy would be put before the president and actually implemented. Acknowledging the value of an ally in the NSC staff, he still refused, assuring me that McFarlane and he worked well together and he was confident that he would receive the necessary decision support. As a compromise, I proposed that I travel with his delegation fifty percent of the time, spending the balance of my time in Washington. Rumsfeld agreed and scrupulously honored his word, limiting my travel to three of the six months that he served as Middle East envoy.

As a new participant in the process, Rumsfeld realized that clear-cut decisions were unlikely to emerge from this paralyzing ongoing debate, leading him to conclude that other "pressure points" needed to be developed. Israel and France, the two key powers that still lent some strength to American diplomacy, were under political assault from mounting domestic opposition to their presence in Lebanon. Rumsfeld fully appreciated the spectrum of domestic and international forces, including the power of the media, that needed to be brought to bear to strengthen American diplomacy. Intensely aware of the opposition of the Pentagon to an increased military role for the United States, he immediately undertook to identify other measures that might strengthen our diplomacy, while increasing the pressure on Syria. I suggested he consider trying to engage the support of two other countries which had severe problems with Syria but which had not yet been included in the group of nations supporting U.S. diplomacy: Turkey and Iraq. I asked Rumsfeld whether any of the briefing materials he had received from NEA included a discussion of

Turkey. "Turkey?" Rumsfeld replied. "Why no, there has been no discussion of a role for Turkey."

Despite the history of the Ottoman Empire and its fundamental relevance to the political geography of the modern Middle East, Turkey and its affairs are considered a European matter by the national security bureaucracy, owing to Ankara's membership in NATO and Turkey's tendency to look north toward the Soviet Union and west toward Greece when analyzing conventional threats to its security. The realities of Turkey's geography and demography nonetheless combine to make it a Middle Eastern state, with the potential for effective influence in the eastern Mediterranean as well as the Persian Gulf. This would finally became apparent with Operation Desert Storm.

With regard to Lebanon and Rumsfeld's interest in finding new ways of bringing additional influence to bear on Syria's strategic calculus, I explained that a number of border disputes between Turkey and Syria, as well as Syrian support for the Armenian terrorist organization ASALA, had contributed to a deep chill in Turkish-Syrian relations, a chill that he could exploit. A visit by him to Ankara would signal a clear determination by the United States to strengthen the balance of power in Washington's favor and force Assad to consider the possibility that Turkey might intensify its pressure on Syria.

NEA and EUR were appalled when Rumsfeld informed them that he wanted Ankara added to the list of countries he planned to visit during his first trip to the Middle East. Because of his former positions of secretary of defense and ambassador to NATO, Rumsfeld had maintained excellent relations with the Turkish president as well as with many senior Turkish military officers. Convinced that the Turkish angle would at a minimum introduce an element of uncertainty into Assad's calculus about Rumsfeld and the direction of U.S. policy, he overruled the opposition and made Ankara one of the first stops on his trip to the region in mid-November 1983 where he was warmly welcomed by Turkish political and military leaders. Turkish officials were quite hostile to Syria, particularly because of the sanctuary for ASALA that Assad was providing. They were very willing to consider means for enhancing the pressures on the Syrians. Rumsfeld did not need to make direct requests for Turkish action, as the Turks had their own reasons to keep Assad off balance. Rumsfeld agreed to work to intensify the assistance that the United States was providing Turkey in its war with ASALA. Less than one month later, Ankara conducted "previously unscheduled military exercises" in a disputed border region, sending an unambiguous signal to Assad at the same time as the United States, France and Israel conducted air strikes over Syrian and Hizbollah positions in Lebanon.

Through various means, we learned that the Syrians were surprised and concerned that a new player, one that Damascus had reason to fear, was being brought into the Lebanon equation. Although we could not detect an immediate change in the Syrian posture toward U.S. policy, we worked hard to stanch the erosion in American credibility brought on by our weakness following the barracks bombing. Indeed, by choosing to travel to Turkey and not Syria on his first trip, Rumsfeld made clear to all parties that he intended to adopt a hard-nosed posture toward America's chief antagonist in the region.

While Turkey offered significant potential leverage against Syria, Iraq appeared to offer greater immediate impact on Syrian behavior. Baathist rivals, Syria had no greater adversary in the world than Iraq. Saddam and Assad had become bitter enemies, occasionally trying to assassinate each other. At the national level, this rivalry was best illustrated by the military and political support Syria was providing Iran in the Iran-Iraq War, as well as the long-running, violent struggle for domination of the Arab radicals being waged by proxy forces of Damascus and Baghdad throughout the Middle East.

Strategic Cooperation with Israel, Part II

As Rumsfeld departed for the Middle East, I focused the bureaucracy's attention on ways to bolster our position vis-à-vis Syria and the Soviet Union in the eastern Mediterranean and against the Soviet Union and Iran in the Persian Gulf. Two subjects of immediate interest were the restoration of strategic cooperation between Israel and the United States and the hotly debated question of improving U.S. relations with Iraq. If managed properly, these relationships might contribute to our short-term goals in Lebanon as well as to the overall position of the United States in the region.

Restoration of strategic cooperation with Israel would help convince Syria that the political ruptures in U.S.-Israeli relations had been overcome and that some military cooperation was once again taking place. With regard to Iraq, improved U.S.-Iraqi relations would presumably enhance Baghdad's ability to cope with the Iranian threat in the short term while complicating Assad's calculus regarding an intensified Iraqi threat to Syria. With respect to Iraq, I continued to argue that Saddam Hussein's long-range intentions and goals had not changed and that neither Saddam's ruthlessness nor his anti-Americanism had waned. However, given the alternatives, neither the United States nor its Arab allies wanted to see Saddam swept away by Islamic fundamentalists answering Tehran's call. I kept an open mind as to the possibility of improved relations with Iraq, if Iraq demonstrated a genuine and lasting change in its behavior. The challenge was to define and agree on the tests that could be applied to determine the extent and meaning of any such change.

Following the withdrawal of the PLO from Beirut in August 1982, McFarlane directed that the bureaucracy resume its formal interagency review of southwest Asia security strategy as provided for in an earlier National Security Study Directive (NSSD). Largely stimulated by the deteriorating position of Iraq in its war with Iran and indicators that Moscow was trying to improve its position in Tehran, the broad-based interagency NSSD effort gave every part of the bureaucracy an opportunity to participate in the formulation of a new policy toward this critical part of the world. In addition to the usual national security participants, the departments of Agriculture, Commerce, Energy, Justice and Treasury and the Office of Management and Budget were asked to participate. The NSSD study had originally been initiated in early 1982 to provide an interagency framework that would fill in the details of the strategic consensus policy. Geoff Kemp was the chairman of the resulting organization. Due to a combination of constantly changing circumstances and serious differences of opinion among the participating agencies, this NSSD process on U.S. policy in southwest Asia continued through the spring of 1985 without reaching a consensus on U.S. security strategy in the region.

Strategic cooperation between the United States and Israel had been suspended in December 1981 following the extension of Israeli law to the occupied Golan Heights, an act perceived by the rest of the world as annexation. Fifteen months later, in March 1983, the president decided to improve relations with Israel. The decision was made to help restore Israeli confidence in the United States and thereby improve the prospects for Israeli risk-taking in the Lebanon negotiations as well as in the Palestinian autonomy negotiations, should King Hussein finally agree to join the peace process. At the time of the decision, Reagan directed that the bureaucracy reexamine whether and how to restore the moribund MOU with Israel on strategic cooperation. Weinberger proposed taking some time to work on a different approach. A consensus emerged within the bureaucracy to support Weinberger's variation on the president's theme, so that the Defense Department would have a stake in the final outcome.

On the earlier assumption that the May 17 agreement would be ratified and that Israeli withdrawal from Lebanon would be under way sometime during the summer of 1983, the United States felt no pressure to begin formal strategic cooperation discussions before the IDF withdrawal was completed. However, with the inability of the Lebanese government to rectify its deteriorating domestic political situation or cope with the related Syrian pressure, and with the American escalation and the unilateral Israeli withdrawal, the bureaucracy was unable to complete a proposed structure for strategic cooperation until the fall of 1983.

Following the bombing of the Marine barracks and the failure of the United States to retaliate, the perception of American lack of resolve and enhanced Soviet regional strength once again began to prevail throughout the region. The DOD came under particularly harsh criticism for turning aside Israeli offers of emergency assistance in the immediate wake of the bombing of the Marine barracks. Severe and life-threatening American casualties were flown to U.S. military hospitals in Germany, nearly four hours away, rather than being taken to Israel's Rambam Hospital in Haifa, which is especially well prepared to treat victims of bombings. Yet Weinberger was unable to reconcile his inherent opposition to U.S.-Israeli strategic cooperation with the obvious need to act in a manner that would strengthen the U.S. ability to confront Soviet threats in the eastern Mediterranean, whether or not they involved the Syrians.

In late November, Prime Minister Shamir and Defense Minister Arens visited Washington in order to review a wide range of bilateral issues, including military and economic matters. In the month leading up to the visit, the national security bureaucracy worked feverishly to resolve minor disputes over such matters as who would chair and manage subgroups, where meetings would be held, and how many and which agencies would be invited to participate in specific groups. On the substantive level, more important questions needed to be resolved, particularly the command arrangements, when and where U.S.-Israeli military exercises would be conducted, and what the nature and extent of joint military planning would be.

President Reagan had accepted the recommendation of Weinberger and the JCS and excluded Israel from CENTCOM when it became operational in 1981. Fearful that the Arabs would not cooperate with the United States if Israel were part of the same command structure, Israel was effectively pulled out of the Middle East and designated a EUCOM area of responsibility. In order to ensure the maximum amount of coherence in the emerging southwest Asia strategy, however, the NSC staff put the command arrangements issue back on the agenda. The Defense

Department, with the support of NEA at State, argued passionately that it was essential to limit any Israeli military interaction to EUCOM, due to the eastern Mediterranean role the JCS envisaged for Israeli forces. Moreover, the DOD added that integrating Israel into CENTCOM would detract from the Soviet dimension of strategic cooperation which the United States wanted to emphasize. The NSC staff, along with PM, contended that Israel's inclusion in CENTCOM would reinforce the putative strength of CENTCOM, whose primary mission was to stop a Soviet invasion of Iran coming through the Zagros Mountains. Joint planning would hardly be meaningful for southwest Asian contingencies if Israeli planners were not allowed to meet and plan with the CENTCOM planners. By excluding Israel from CENTCOM, it was clear that the Defense Department wanted to say yes to the president without taking concrete measures to implement and institutionalize his decisions. As the visit drew near and final preparations were made, the proponents of integrating Israel into CENTCOM, led by Donald Fortier, then senior director for Political-Military affairs on the NSC staff, decided to compromise on command structure and focus instead on the substance of the working groups.

The United States and Israel announced the formation of the Joint Political-Military Group (JPMG) following Reagan's November 29, 1983, meeting with Shamir and Arens. An umbrella organization composed of senior national security officials from both countries, the JPMG established working groups to conduct joint operational planning and improve military-to-military communications; plan combined exercises; and work together to determine how best to pre-position U.S. equipment and ammunition in Israel. Related to strategic cooperation, but outside of the context of the JPMG, Weinberger offered to send a high-level DOD procurement and research-and-development delegation to Israel to evaluate areas of potential collaboration. Taking careful note of the Beirut medical debacle, he sent his assistant secretary for health affairs to negotiate a special MOU on medical cooperation.

On the political level, it was agreed that the principal issue to be addressed by the JPMG would be the Soviet threat. Despite the long history of Soviet support for its more formidable Arab adversaries, many Israelis were troubled by the formal designation of the Soviet Union as an enemy and continued to lobby to soften the designation or to broaden the category to include regional threats. Throughout the national security bureaucracy, there was no dissent on this question and the United States did not budge. Although many observers of U.S.-Israeli relations questioned the extent to which strategic cooperation would produce tangible enhancements to the U.S. position in the Middle East, once formed, the structure developed a life of its own. The United States–Israel relationship became institutionalized for the first time. The people who participated in the JPMG began to meet with increasing regularity and soon developed bureaucratic stakes in the results of the process. To the surprise of many, sensitive activities, such as joint planning, remained secret and depoliticized, reflecting the seriousness with which both countries' military planners took their obligations.

While Arab leaders, as anticipated, publicly and privately complained about the renewal of strategic cooperation, arguing that Israel was a liability for America rather than an asset, none of Washington's Arab military allies decreased the level of their ongoing joint planning or cooperation with the United States. The sky did not fall down when the United States began working with Israel on issues of mutual concern, despite the dire warnings of the proponents of the knee-jerk "Israel is a strategic liability" school of conventional wisdom.

To Tilt or Not to Tilt

The question of improving U.S relations with Iraq was much more complex. The relationship had been inadvertently assisted by Israel's bombing of the Iraqi nuclear reactor in 1981 and its invasion of Lebanon in 1982. The idea gained a momentum that enabled Iraq and the United States to gingerly dance toward diplomatic relations. For nearly eighteen months, the U.S. government had been providing valuable intelligence information to the Iraqis to help the Iraqi Army repulse the Iranians. In addition, the United States had been giving Iraq considerable political support at the United Nations. Political pressures to go further with Baghdad steadily built from both domestic and foreign interests, and the Commerce and State departments joined the chorus of entities anxious for the United States to loosen its restrictions on trade with Iraq. With the success of the intelligence-sharing program and the reduction, but not elimination, of Iraqi support for international terrorism, the farm lobbies, farm-state senators and congressmen, and the Department of Agriculture succeeded in offering $400 million in Commodity Credit Corporation (CCC) guarantees to Baghdad to help finance Iraqi purchases of American wheat. The decision was made quietly by the Department of Agriculture with the consent of State and Commerce. The NSC staff was informed of this action only after it was announced in late 1983.

Although food aid would almost assuredly have been approved had the issue been brought to an interagency forum, the sale of Hughes helicopters, ostensibly civilian models for agricultural purposes, was another matter. Initially disapproved in the spring of 1983, the sale of Hughes helicopters resurfaced later when Commerce took an active lead in promoting the civilian functions of the craft. Proponents of the sale insisted that the frames of the helicopters were too light for any weapons system to be mounted on them and that the helicopters did not have the range or payload capacity necessary for transporting troops and equipment into combat. NSC advisor Clark acquiesced and the sale went through.

The tempo of commercial sales accelerated rapidly following the Hughes sale. Based on Hughes's quiet success, Bell Helicopters wanted to sell Iraq ten UH-1s, Vietnam-vintage transport helicopters, still in use in the U.S. military. The NSC was asked to participate in the interagency dispute. I strongly opposed the sale of the UH-1s and argued that the civilian model could easily be modified by the Iraqis to carry machine guns and transport troops. But I was in Lebanon for the entire month of August 1983 and others on the staff disagreed with me and the issue was elevated "above our pay grade." I was told that Secretary of Commerce Malcolm Baldrige and Secretary of State Shultz lobbied NSC advisor Clark hard over a period of weeks, leading him to acquiesce in August 1983 to authorize the issuance of the licenses. In an environment increasingly dominated by commercial and political considerations, license requests for the sale of dual-use technologies to Iraq, and the accompanying interagency disputes became frequent and contentious.

Observing this "commercial" activity, I took strong issue with my colleagues in the State Department, primarily James Placke, the deputy assistant secretary for the Arabian Peninsula responsible for Iraqi affairs. I argued that the United States was doing much more than simply helping Iraq withstand the Iranian onslaught. Baghdad remained irreconcilably opposed to a political settlement with Israel, had not renounced its long-standing claims to Kuwait and continued to harbor international terrorists, despite its having been removed from the terrorism list. Placke did not dispute my portrait of Saddam and the dangers he posed. But he countered my arguments with the perspective that the United States had to do everything possible to prevent Iraq's fall, and, in the process, perhaps we could reinforce the positive trends in Iraqi behavior that had begun to emerge. Most notably, Placke viewed Baghdad's statements on the Arab-Israeli conflict, that it would support agreements reached between the PLO and Israel and a toning-down of its virulent anti-Zionist rhetoric, as indications of change. Judge Clark, then NSC military assistant John Poindexter and Kemp tended to agree with Placke's view.

Still skeptical of these rhetorical indications of Iraqi moderation, I suggested we devise more substantive tests for determining the extent of changes in Iraq's behavior. One such test was the proposed Iraqi pipeline to the Jordanian port of Aqaba, the Aqaba pipeline. In January 1984, I met with a Bechtel Corporation vice president at McFarlane's request in order to explore how the NSC might assist in securing the necessary political guarantees that would enable the one-million-barrel-per-day pipeline to be built. (I later learned that McFarlane's involvement had been instigated by Attorney General Edwin Meese, acting at the behest of his former associate E. Robert Wallach.) The pipeline offered many advantages, including economic benefits for Jordan, less vulnerability to Iran-Iraq War interdiction and more oil on the international market. However, of particular significance in my calculus about Iraqi intentions toward Israel was Saddam's willingness to place a strategic Iraqi asset, an oil pipeline that would export at least $20 million worth of oil per day, adjacent to Jordan's border with Israel. Baghdad understood that the proximity of the pipeline to Israel's Red Sea port of Eilat would make it an easy target during any Arab-Israeli hostilities. Were Baghdad to move forward to construct a pipeline with an outlet less than five miles from the Israeli border, this would indeed be a convincing demonstration that Baghdad's behavior, as well as its long-term intentions, were moving in a positive direction. Not surprisingly, however, the Iraqis did not trust Israel. Bechtel, the Jordanians and Iraqi diplomats lobbied U.S. government officials to provide political guarantees that Israel would not attack the pipeline and, if it did, Iraq wanted financial guarantees to cover losses and reconstruction.

As the bureaucracy continued to debate how far and at what pace to move with Iraq, Arab leaders, notably King Hussein of Jordan, President Mubarak of Egypt and King Fahd of Saudi Arabia, continued to encourage Washington to reach out to Baghdad at a political level. These and other leaders argued out of fear and hope—fear that Iraq would fall to the Iranians if the United States did not provide Baghdad with political, economic and matériel assistance, and hope that once the war ended, a stable Iraq with strong economic ties with the West could serve as the bulwark against radicalism in the Gulf. Use an Arab computer to understand Iraq, Hosni Mubarak told me, not an American computer. I was missing Baghdad's signals.

From inside Baghdad, U.S. Interests Section chief William Eagleton also lobbied hard for greater U.S. involvement in Iraq. Reporting on subtle shifts in Iraqi attitudes toward the United States, Eagleton urged the bureaucracy to look for an opportunity to help Iraq "save face" by taking the first initiative toward the restoration of full diplomatic relations. But since Iraq had broken diplomatic relations following the June 1967 War, claiming that Israeli occupation of Arab lands seized during that war was tantamount to American occupation, protocol required that Baghdad formally propose the restoration of relations. Both Baghdad and Washington wanted to elevate the relationship, but a way had to be found that would not create a perception of Iraqi or American weakness by either party's acting first.

In November 1983, a message was passed through the Iraqi Interests Section in Washington to the State Department that should an American emissary visit Baghdad, President Saddam Hussein would welcome the opportunity for an exchange of views that might lead to a renewal of full diplomatic relations. Although Saddam had recently conducted extensive discussions with Senator Bill Bradley of New Jersey and Congressman Stephen Solarz of New York, these were unilateral in nature and not at the behest of the president of the United States. Within one month of receiving Saddam's message, the first U.S. Air Force plane to land in Iraq since the June 1967 war would arrive in Baghdad with a presidential emissary bearing a letter from Ronald Reagan to Saddam Hussein. Rumsfeld's second trip to the Middle East provided the opening for this high-level dialogue to commence.

November 1983 represented a watershed in U.S. Middle East policy. In the wake of the most blatant and murderous terrorist operation ever conducted against American interests, the United States chose not to retaliate. Nor did we waver in our continuing efforts to convene a conference of Lebanese leaders in Geneva to promote political reconciliation while preserving the May 17 agreement. Within a matter of weeks, a practical arrangement for U.S.-Israeli strategic cooperation was concluded even as a decision was made to send a presidential envoy to Baghdad to accelerate the dialogue that would lead to the restoration of full diplomatic relations. At the same time, Syria and Iran, the principal adversaries of Iraq, Israel and the United States, were intensifying their struggle to destroy U.S. policy in Lebanon and the Arab-Israeli peace process. Against this backdrop, Iraq publicly embraced Egypt, a country it had several years earlier condemned for its peace with Israel, thereby helping to usher Egypt back into the Arab mainstream. Dramatic changes were afoot in the Middle East, but the only certainty was the uncertainty over what would happen next.

Rules of Engagement

The situation in Lebanon continued to deteriorate as Syria and its allies infiltrated men and matériel through the Shuwayfat Gap throughout November and December of 1983. To bolster Lebanese confidence in America's staying power and commitment to a peaceful resolution of Lebanon's problems, Reagan hosted President Gemayel in Washington immediately following the departure of Shamir and Arens.

In the face of clear questioning from Reagan regarding the prospects for national reconciliation in Lebanon and being told of the fundamental importance attached to such a process by the United States, Gemayel eloquently assured the president that reconciliation, as demonstrated by the Geneva conference, along with the withdrawal of all foreign forces remained his top priority. He also reaffirmed Lebanon's commitment to the May 17 agreement but asked President Reagan what more he was prepared to do to help Lebanon cope with growing Syrian pressure to abrogate the agreement. Reagan asked NSC advisor McFarlane to update Gemayel on additional steps the United States was prepared to take to demonstrate its commitment to the Lebanese government, steps that would clearly signal U.S. determination and resolve to the Syrians.

As part of his earlier decision to strike the Sheikh Abdullah Barracks, President Reagan had ordered the rules of engagement to be broadened. The ROE governed, among other things, when and how U.S. forces could fire in self-defense. Despite the failure of the United States to conduct the joint strike, this had been completed and documented in an NSDD that authorized U.S. forces to return fire against targets "associated" with the source of the fire. No longer would Americans be restrained to fire only at a person or position that had fired first. Perceiving American timidity, the Syrians and Druze had begun to fire surface-to-air missiles (SAMs) at the F-14 Tactical Aerial Reconnaissance Pod System (TARPS) missions the U.S. Navy was flying over Lebanon. However, by the time the source of fire was detected and reported to the carrier, the direct target had vanished, making it impossible to conduct air strikes within the previous narrowly defined ROE. The new rules permitted U.S. forces to attack any target in Lebanon associated with those firing the SAMs, thus creating numerous opportunities for preplanned U.S. strikes.

The political objective of the expanded ROE was clear: to demonstrate that the United States would use force to defend itself and its diplomacy.

The Syrians obliged two days later on December 3, when Syrian forces fired SA-7 missiles at a TARPS flight. I had arrived at the office early in the morning to finish preparing for my Monday departure for the Middle East with Rumsfeld. Suddenly the door to my office burst open as Phil Dur came in with copies of the reports of the attempted shoot-down of the F-14. "The JCS wants to go after them," Dur said, true amazement in his voice. "They have unanimously recommended to Weinberger that the Navy carry out air strikes on the Syrian SAM batteries as soon as possible." By midday we had the Weinberger-JCS position. Dur had prepared a memo for McFarlane recommending that the president approve the strike, and a decision to strike was quickly made. Dur informed me that the operational plan called for an afternoon strike in order to take advantage of sunlight in the eyes of the defenders on the ground. Expecting the strike to be launched at 1:00 P.M. Beirut time the following day, we agreed to meet at the Situation Room the following morning to monitor the operation.

The Situation Room called me during the night at two-thirty A.M. to advise me that the strike had already been conducted and that two aircraft had been shot down. One plane had crashed in the sea, the pilot apparently safe and on his way back to the carrier. The other plane, however, had gone down over land, and although two parachutes had been spotted, there was no word on whether the men were dead or alive.

I tried to grasp how U.S. forces, with an arsenal of sophisticated weapons and highly skilled personnel, could have been shot down by the Syrians. The Israelis conducted air strikes in Lebanon every day and never lost a single airplane. Yet when the United States had finally summoned the resolve to try to destroy those who shot at our reconnaissance planes, we lost two aircraft right away. Such a demonstration of American political and military prowess would hardly inspire fear, caution or respect in our adversaries, in the Middle East or elsewhere. As dawn broke in Washington we learned that one of the pilots, Lieutenant Mark Lange, had died, while the other crew member, Lieutenant Robert Goodman, was injured but alive in Syrian captivity.

After consultations in London and Paris, I arrived with Rumsfeld in Lebanon on December 8. The team immediately set up quarters in the penthouse of the otherwise abandoned "Comfort Hotel" in Yarze, about one mile from the American ambassador's residence. The composition of the Rumsfeld team had changed from the group that had supported

McFarlane and Fairbanks. Lawrence Silberman had been added. Tom Miller, a hard-charging FSO, had been assigned responsibility for managing the team's day-to-day affairs. Bob Pelletreau, my former boss in ISA and shortly to become the NEA DAS for Israel, Syria, Lebanon, Jordan and Egypt, was also appointed to the mission. In the hope that discussions might move beyond mere exchanges to negotiations, the team also included a representative of the State Department's Office of the Legal Advisor (L), Alan Kreczko, the principal attorney for NEA affairs. Personal security was provided by Robert Booth, a State Department security officer with considerable experience in protecting dignitaries and coping with unstable political-military situations. To my pleasant surprise, Sue Shea and Kate Milne, the very talented secretaries that had supported the Stoessel mission nearly two years before, had been plucked out of their regular NEA assignments to provide secretarial and administrative support for the team. Chris Ross, who had relocated his family to Tel Aviv in order for them to be relatively close together, and Carl Stiner continued to support the presidential envoy.

The Comfort Hotel was one of the more bizarre accommodations in which I stayed during the course of my Middle East wanderings. With the fighting escalating throughout Beirut, the embassy did not want us to stay in any West Beirut hotels because it was impossible to provide security and difficult to move daily back and forth across the Green Line. I had spent a night in the Comfort Hotel in May 1983 when I accompanied Shultz to Lebanon. Recalling that trip, I remembered that when I had checked in, the first thing the clerk did was to apologize that the hotel was not very comfortable. It had been hit by artillery some months earlier and most of the rooms were still being renovated. Throughout the night, rockets were fired in the direction of the ambassador's residence, perhaps sending a message to Shultz. The rockets flew over the residence and down into the valley where the Comfort Hotel was situated, landing about a hundred meters away. Since that last visit, the renovation had been completed but the hotel had not reopened. To accommodate the embassy, the owner generously rented us the penthouse in order for the team to be located together in one place in East Beirut near the residence. While it seemed like a good idea at the time, the day after we arrived the LAF deployed a battery of 105-millimeter howitzers in the rubble of a vacant lot a hundred feet away. In addition to making the neighborhood a high-value target for Syrian and Druze artillery, the constant thump and vibration of outgoing rounds made the Comfort Hotel particularly uncomfortable. We were in addition required to wear our flak jackets and helmets even to walk around the hotel.

The fundamental purposes of this trip to the region were for Rumsfeld to determine whether there was any room to maneuver on the May 17 agreement and to reinforce America's strong commitment to finding a way for the Lebanese to reconcile their bitter political differences.

Working closely with the new ambassador to Lebanon, Reginald Bartholomew (leader of the interagency delegation for establishing U.S. access to Omani military bases in the Carter administration who had the misfortune of arriving in Beirut the weekend the barracks were bombed), Rumsfeld set out to meet with all the leaders who had participated in the Geneva conference in November. Following meetings with Nabih Berri, Adil Usayran and Saeb Salaam, the team departed for Muscat, Oman, on December 11, where Rumsfeld would begin to familiarize himself with the perspectives of Gulf leaders and to encourage them to apply pressure on Syria. Rumsfeld had immediately grasped the direct relationship between U.S. policy in Lebanon and the implications for American interests in the Gulf. Meanwhile, Bartholomew was directed to focus his efforts on the domestic political situation in Lebanon. Bartholomew carried out the responsibilities of his new mission with energy, wisdom and courage, and was tremendously helpful in supporting Rumsfeld's mission.

During the two days of wide-ranging discussions with Sultan Qaboos bin Said and the minister of state for foreign affairs, Yusuf al-Alawi, in Muscat, a series of terrorist attacks occurred in Kuwait, which led to an intensification of the struggle between militant Islam and the West in Lebanon and elsewhere. On December 12, 1983, Shia terrorists had attacked four major targets, including the American and French embassies in Kuwait City. The *modus operandi* was identical to the earlier attacks in Beirut: fast-moving suicide trucks with dynamite strapped to compressed-gas bottles.

The Kuwaiti authorities quickly captured seventeen individuals who were members of al-Dawa, a Tehran-backed, militant Shia organization dedicated to the export of the Iranian revolution. Three of the seventeen were Lebanese, including the brother-in-law of Imad Mugniyah, one of Hizbollah's most notorious operators. With trials of the Dawa Seventeen about to commence, Mugniyah began kidnapping Americans in Beirut in order to pressure the Kuwaitis through the Americans. Intent upon preventing the execution of his brother-in-law by the Kuwaiti authorities, Mugniyah used the Western hostages in Lebanon to serve as bargaining chips in an effort to bring about the release of the terrorists. In just over one month, three Americans, including CIA station chief William Buckley, were kidnapped by Mugniyah. Buckley was kidnapped the same morning that Libyan Tu-22 aircraft conducted a surprise attack on Sudan, dropping bombs on the city of Omdurman, adjacent to the capital, Khartoum. Many other people, including Germans, Italians and Britons, would be kidnapped for the same purpose in the coming few years. Although death sentences were imposed by Kuwaiti courts on several of the Dawa prisoners, these sentences were commuted to life imprisonment. All of the Dawa Seventeen were freed when Iraq later invaded Kuwait in August 1990.

The attacks in Kuwait on December 12, 1983, and the capture of the Dawa Seventeen represent the beginning of what became known as the Iran Affair. Although I was hundreds of miles away in Oman on the morning of the blast, on hearing the news I immediately broke into a cold sweat, recalling the horrifying images of the barracks bombing and the American embassy in Beirut. I urged Rumsfeld to deviate from our itinerary and travel to Kuwait. He chose not to go, concerned that it would produce an image of excessive concern and that our unscheduled presence would be seen to be rewarding the terrorists with even greater media play, perhaps thereby exaggerating their sense of accomplishment.

We continued on our scheduled itinerary to Amman, Jordan, to meet with Walid Jumblatt on December 15. At a lunch in Jumblatt's honor hosted by Edward Djerejian, the American DCM, we spoke for over two and a half hours about U.S. and Druze ideas regarding the prospects for reconciliation; Syrian, Iranian and Libyan sponsorship of international terrorism; humanitarian needs of the residents of the Shouf; new ideas that General Stiner had developed for security arrangements in the Shouf and Iqlim al-Qarrub; and the Iran-Iraq War. Jumblatt kept pressing us to stop cooperating with the LAF, asserting that Druze gunners wanted to attack only the Lebanese Army, not the Marines. He didn't want to kill Marines or have the Sixth Fleet on his back, Jumblatt protested. Turning to the Iran-Iraq War, Jumblatt was especially candid, asserting that Iraq would lose to Iran and be divided up between Turkey, Iran and Syria. He warned us that we didn't realize just how fragile the regime in Baghdad was. Khomeini didn't care what it cost him to win. He emphasized that America did not begin to comprehend the extent of Shia extremism.

As soon as the meeting ended we boarded our airplane and took off for Damascus, where the situation had suddenly become unstable in recent days. Assad suffered a heart attack and his brother Rifaat had tried to seize power. Although violence was temporarily averted, we had received reports that several of Rifaat's praetorian-guard tank brigades were massing to strike at the regular army. Unfounded rumors contributed to wild speculation about Assad's supposedly grave medical prospects, the implications for civil strife in Syria, and the consequences for the situation in Lebanon. In addition to his illness and the frantic and potentially violent internal maneuvering that was swirling around him, international pressures were intensifying on Assad.

The Guns of the *New Jersey*

In the previous two weeks, U.S., French and Israeli air strikes had been conducted against Syrian targets in Lebanon. The Turkish Army was exercising along the Syrian border. Soviet and Arab political pressure had increased in response to Assad's undisguised effort to foment a rebellion against Yasir Arafat within the PLO. Coupled with widespread death and destruction in Tripoli, Lebanon, where the PLO was holed up as the Syrians and the forces of Abu Musa relentlessly attacked the PLO's dwindling strongholds, Moscow was angry at Damascus over its campaign to undermine Arafat. The Soviets had also issued a clear warning to Damascus to be cautious in its confrontation with the United States. Moscow was taken aback by the U.S. air strikes and expected them to continue and perhaps escalate in response to the continuing Syrian provocation. During an exchange of toasts with the Syrians in Moscow at the beginning of December, the Soviets had unambiguously stated that their commitments to Syria did not extend beyond Syria's borders. On the East-West level, the Soviet Union was not going to confront America over Syrian policy in Lebanon. And the Syrians had Lieutenant Goodman in captivity, a card that we knew the Syrians very much wanted to play.

As Rumsfeld, Silberman, Pelletreau, Miller and I sat around a conference table on the airplane discussing whether and how to discuss the status of Lieutenant Goodman, Carl Stiner walked back to us from the cockpit, where he had just been summoned to the radio. "Mr. Ambassador," Stiner said in his "good old boy" Tennessee drawl, "I have just received a message from the fleet. A TARPS mission was flown over Lebanon earlier today. Syrian SAMs fired on the plane and missed. But in response, the *New Jersey*, about fifteen minutes ago, opened up on the Syrian SAM sites with her sixteen-inch guns." In other words, at the exact time that our airplane was entering Syrian airspace, the battleship *New Jersey* had fired her Volkswagen-sized shells at Syrian positions. "The

Syrians will believe that the *New Jersey*'s firepower is being coordinated with your arrival," I said. "They would think you are lying if you told them that the timing was pure coincidence." "Do you think they will shoot us down?" Rumsfeld asked, only half jokingly. "I doubt they will fire at us, but they will want to demonstrate how they can withstand U.S. pressure by keeping us waiting or refusing to see you. In either case, coupled with all the other activities going on in and around Syria, this visit will give us an excellent opportunity to test how well Assad is coping with the pressure." Arriving an hour later at the Damascus Airport, we were greeted by a barely civil Foreign Ministry representative who refused to shake hands with the members of the team.

Arriving at the American embassy, where we were to wait to be summoned to our eight-thirty meeting with Khaddam, Rumsfeld convened a meeting with Paganelli and his people in order to get every possible perspective on what was going on in Damascus. Paganelli assumed that Rumsfeld's top priority would be to try to secure the release of Lieutenant Goodman. Rumsfeld quickly disabused him of that idea, informing him that he had no intention of getting caught up in negotiations with Syria over Goodman's fate. "Goodman's captivity is a symptom of the problem in Lebanon," Rumsfeld said. "He is not the problem I am trying to resolve. Nor do I want to give the impression to the Syrians that an individual is what this is all about. We all care about Lieutenant Goodman, but he does not define our interests in Lebanon or Syria."

The call from the Foreign Ministry came at eight P.M. confirming that Khaddam would receive us at eight-thirty. At about the same time, the Syrian media reported the arrival of Rumsfeld in Damascus, "riding in on the guns of the *New Jersey*." Khaddam usually kept his guests waiting, a technique he hoped would keep visitors off balance. But he didn't keep us waiting that night, obviously keen to gauge the political dimension of the U.S. military escalation. Greeting us politely and without rancor in his conference room, Khaddam was pale and sweaty, displaying uncharacteristic nervousness. Following an exchange of pleasantries, including our offer of U.S. medical assistance for President Assad, Khaddam noted that the complicated problems confronting the United States and Syria needed to be solved without the involvement of Marine generals. Listening carefully to Rumsfeld's presentation, Khaddam said that he was disappointed to hear nothing new from Rumsfeld, as he had expected Gemayel to convince Reagan that the time had come to change the U.S. position on the May 17 agreement.

Choosing his words with utmost care, Rumsfeld asked Khaddam

whether Syria would be ready to begin talking about the range of issues in Lebanon on the basis that neither Israel nor Syria would achieve their first choice in Lebanon. Asking numerous questions for clarification, Khaddam would not agree to a process based on anything less than Syria's first choice. He did agree that if all parties put all the elements of the problem, including the May 17 agreement, on the table, he would be willing to meet the next morning to try to work out a new framework, although he repeatedly qualified his comments, stating that he had not yet agreed to anything.

True to form, Khaddam tried to throw Rumsfeld off balance during this three-hour meeting. Abruptly changing the subject, he asked Rumsfeld whether he planned to be a candidate for president of the United States in 1988. Rumsfeld smiled as he slowly cleaned his pipe, packed it with fresh tobacco and relit it before answering this very undiplomatic question. Telling Khaddam that he sounded like his wife, Rumsfeld deliberately proceeded to summarize his essentially political résumé, noting that he had considered running for the presidency in 1980 but backed out in the face of Reagan's popularity. The one gap in his career had been the private sector, which he had now accomplished through his work at G. D. Searle. Leaning forward as he tried to gauge the purpose behind Khaddam's query, Rumsfeld simply said, "What's your next question, Mr. Foreign Minister?" Without missing a beat, Khaddam laughed and returned once again to the American attitude toward the May 17 agreement.

We returned to the embassy following the meeting and worked all night to prepare an agenda that Rumsfeld could present when he met with Khaddam the following morning. Accompanied only by Pelletreau and Paganelli, Rumsfeld informed the rest of us after the morning meeting that he believed Khaddam had accepted the basic principle of no first choice and that Khaddam's careful word choice suggested that we might be close to working out a formula for moving the dialogue along. Pelletreau, by contrast, argued that Khaddam had placed many issues on the table, leading him to believe that Khaddam was mainly trying to "buy time" while the dust settled in Damascus. The matter of Lieutenant Goodman had not even been mentioned, although Khaddam had clearly wanted to hear from the U.S. side toward the end of the meeting when he had asked whether there wasn't anything else the United States wanted to raise.

As we departed Damascus for the airport that afternoon, soldiers belonging to Rifaat's Defense Companies were particularly evident throughout the city. Tension was in the air and we could see battle-ready concentrations of tanks and APCs moving in the outskirts of Damascus. Perhaps as a result of the international and domestic pressure, Khaddam's reception suggested that there might yet be a compromise political solution that would enable us to achieve our objectives in Lebanon.

A Pearl-Handled Revolver

Following stops in Israel and Egypt, we flew on to Baghdad on December 17 in order to lay the groundwork for the resumption of full diplomatic relations between the United States and Iraq. Our arrival in Baghdad at dusk was a staged media event. The Iraqis wanted to make sure that Iran and Syria were fully aware of this high-level American visit. Rumsfeld, who usually avoided talking to the media, used the photo opportunity to emphasize that the United States would not be intimidated by the terrorist attacks in Kuwait, and that he particularly looked forward to his meetings with the Iraqi leader.

The long drive into Baghdad was uneventful, and we were put up as guests of the government of Iraq at the al-Rasheed Hotel. Built originally to accommodate the 1982 Non-Aligned Movement Summit Conference, which because of the Iran-Iraq War was never held, the hotel offered the most modern conveniences to Iraq's foreign guests. A nightclub, replete with belly dancers, dancing girls and rock and roll in a deafening Western-style disco, beckoned guests, as the team returned to the hotel late that night from a dinner at the home of William Eagleton. Before leaving the residence, we were warned to be extra careful in the hotel as it was known to be staffed by Iraqi intelligence officers who would be looking for opportunities to entrap unsuspecting Americans looking for a good time.

The next morning we met with Iraq's foreign minister, Tariq Aziz. A Christian Arab of medium height, dressed in olive green fatigues with a pearl-handled revolver holstered at his waist, Aziz met us at the entrance to the Foreign Ministry, a somewhat tawdry, brown cement building. Tariq Aziz conveyed the image of the reasonable, Western-oriented modern man, able to represent his government at the intellectual and social level of his Western counterparts, while maintaining the Iraqi Baath party's well-deserved reputation for ruthlessness.

As we walked in the door, the foreign minister drew Rumsfeld away from the rest of the team, including from his State Department bodyguard, Bob Booth, and led him into a small elevator. Rumsfeld motioned Booth to get into the elevator with them, but Aziz's two bodyguards stood in Booth's way, forcing him to run up the four flights of stairs to catch up with Rumsfeld and Aziz as they emerged from the elevator. Chiding Booth good-naturedly, Rumsfeld asked him, "What kind of bodyguard lets his boss get into an elevator alone with a host who has a revolver sticking out of his pants?"

The ensuing discussions were cordial, even friendly, as if the bitter, sixteen-year hiatus in relations had already been forgotten. Following Rumsfeld's introductory remarks, where he expressed the U.S. desire to restore a balance in America's relations with Iraq, Aziz delivered a long speech that covered many regional and global topics. Emphasizing how Iraq had politically matured through its bitter experiences with Iran, Aziz suggested that improving relations with the United States might help Iraq achieve a better balance in its relations with Iran. Noting Iraq's ambition to assume its rightful role as a leader of the Arab world, Aziz admitted that Baghdad required a stable, long-term relationship with the United States in order to promote economic development and rebuild after the end of the war. On the Arab-Israeli conflict, Aziz argued that Iraq's struggle with Israel was "logical," while conflicts with Syria and Iran were not. Rumsfeld showed Aziz a copy of President Reagan's letter to President Saddam Hussein to ensure that there would be no surprises. Aziz expressed great satisfaction with the letter, particularly its reference to U.S. opposition to the continuation of the Iran-Iraq War.

After reading Reagan's letter, Aziz asked Rumsfeld if the United States would consider taking steps to help promote an early end to the war in addition to political cooperation in the United Nations. In reply, Rumsfeld informed Aziz that the United States would work harder to stop the flow of arms to Iran, and that he would take a personal interest to ensure that such a policy was implemented. Following lunch, the call came from the Presidential Palace that Saddam was ready to receive Rumsfeld. However, he could be accompanied only by Mr. Eagleton and by Pelletreau, the senior State Department representative on his team.

Rumsfeld briefed me after the meeting, describing Saddam as polite but tough. He was visibly pleased to receive Reagan's letter and had expressed the hope that bilateral relations would continue to improve and move toward full restoration on the basis of mutual respect and dignity. The balance of the discussion was dominated by Saddam Hussein, who described in considerable detail the heroic struggle being waged by the Iraqi people against the Iranian onslaught. Portraying Iraq as the last defense against Iranian barbarism, Saddam made no requests for further U.S. assistance, as if to suggest that Iraq did not need America's help. Nor did he agree to work with the United States against Syria. The fact of the meeting with an envoy from the president of the United States appeared to have been Saddam's principal objective. No date for the resumption of relations was set or even proposed, but the die was cast and the bureaucracy moved inexorably forward to increase America's stake in ever-expanding political and commercial relationships with Iraq.

Stay the Course

Immediately upon my return to Washington I met with Dennis Ross to review a new strategy for Lebanon he had devised. Ross had returned to the Pentagon as the deputy director of net assessment and we regularly collaborated closely off-line. Ross had to be discreet, because Weinberger did not want anyone in the OSD deviating from his views or assisting anyone else in the bureaucracy in thinking creatively about the Middle East. The essence of Ross's strategy for Lebanon was to intensify the pressure on the Syrians by augmenting and redeploying the Marine presence and capabilities. This would enhance America's ability to negotiate a Syrian withdrawal simultaneously with the withdrawal of the Marines. Nevertheless, Assistant Secretary of Defense Richard L. Armitage, who had discussed the idea with McFarlane, later told me that Weinberger was unwilling to consider any movement of the Marines except to ships offshore. In this context, Armitage encouraged me "to spend less time thinking about what to do with the Marines, and more time thinking about a Lebanon policy without Marines."

Shortly after Christmas, the Long Commission, which had been established immediately following the destruction of the Marine barracks, issued its report assessing responsibility and analyzing how such a debacle could have taken place. Geraghty and Lieutenant Colonel Howard Gerlach, the commander of the battalion landing team, were assigned most of the blame for the Marines' inadequate security. This was very unfair. The Long Commission had inculpated the entire chain of command. Since Weinberger wanted to exculpate General Bernard Rogers, the Supreme Allied Commander, Europe, the president was persuaded by McFarlane and Fortier that neither Geraghty nor Gerlach should be disciplined. While the Long Commission could easily find technical fault with perimeter security measures, the military responsibility for this debacle lay squarely on the shoulders of Weinberger and Vessey. They had consistently obstructed presidential decisions and had convinced themselves that because they did not want to commit U.S. forces to combat in Lebanon, U.S. forces would not find themselves in danger. Weinberger was unwilling to accept responsibility for a policy environment in and around the Pentagon which placed field officers in untenable positions.

In the Middle East in general and in Lebanon in particular, it is more important to be feared and respected than to be loved. Neither Weinberger nor Vessey accepted any responsibility for the deaths of the Marines of the MNF, although they undoubtedly shared the pain and sense of loss experienced by all Americans. Instead, they argued that it was the escalation encouraged by McFarlane at the battle of Suq al-Gharb, and that the ensuing naval gunfire against Druze positions had inspired the attack.

This charge typified their bias and demonstrated a lack of in-depth knowledge. Proponents of this argument fail to distinguish between the Druze, who were on the receiving end of U.S. naval gunfire, and the Iranian-backed Hizbollah, who perpetrated the terrorist attack. The attacks against the French and U.S. barracks were part of a continuing pattern of Syrian and Iranian warfare. We were building up militarily to wage large-scale conventional warfare against a conventional enemy when we should have been preparing to counter the terrorist tactics that were working so well at undermining U.S. policy and at taking American lives. Because of the lack of discipline of U.S. decision-making authorities, America's adversaries understood exactly how best to undermine U.S. policy.

The ultimate responsibility for the political environment that led to this debacle and its aftermath, however, rested squarely on the commander in chief, Ronald Reagan, for failing to discipline and manage the members of his National Security Council. Reagan took formal responsibility for the bombing in order to avoid lengthy and politically unsavory tribunals. But Reagan admitted to no error, nor was anyone held responsible or chastised. No, the administration of Ronald Reagan would consistently do everything necessary to "circle the wagons" and protect itself, deflecting blame onto others, who were to be sacrificed on the altar of expediency.

No Reverse Gears

The *Long Commission Report* triggered an earthquake in Congress. Coupled with the diplomacy of the Reverend Jesse Jackson, who traveled to Damascus to recover Lieutenant Goodman from captivity, the little remaining domestic consensus supporting U.S. policy in Lebanon totally unraveled. Congress immediately began to call for the withdrawal of the

Marines and the renegotiation of a bipartisan resolution, concluded just prior to the October 23 bombing, authorizing the Marines to remain in Lebanon through April 1985. With public support dwindling rapidly, the Syrians, suddenly aware of the flimsiness of the pressure that America had so recently applied, generated a full-court press, infiltrating antiregime forces through the Shuwayfat Gap into southern and western Beirut to exploit the situation.

Faced with a clearly untenable political situation, in early January I began to draft a strategy paper that was predicated on the withdrawal of the Marines to their ships offshore. Having sat through another NSPG just prior to my departure for the Middle East with Rumsfeld in mid-January—where Shultz and Weinberger were practically yelling at each other across the conference table—there was no longer any justification for further risks to Marines or other members of the MNF. Decision-makers were not doing their job. Weinberger had dug in his heels long enough and now had the majority of the Congress and public opinion on his side. The strategy proposed that the United States might still be able to convince the Syrians to back off by doing more with less following the redeployment of the Marines offshore. Unfinished when I left for Beirut on January 15, the essence of the policy would be implemented shortly after my return in early February. On the morning of January 17, Rumsfeld convened his staff to work together to draft a proposed "input" for President Reagan's forthcoming State of the Union Address. The most difficult challenge was how to deal with the degenerating political problems in Beirut while still calling for the implementation of the May 17 agreement and the withdrawal of all foreign forces.

The fighting had tapered off in recent days and Bartholomew had arranged for several of us to have lunch with Dr. Malcolm Kerr, the highly respected Arabist scholar who had succeeded David Dodge as the president of the American University of Beirut (AUB). But late that morning, Bartholomew received a call that Kerr had been murdered outside of his office by Hizbollah. Although I had never been a student of Kerr's, I had heard him lecture several times and had read many of his books and articles. He had come by to visit at the NSC prior to his departure for Beirut, filled with hope and optimism that he could help maintain the AUB's standing as an institutional friend of all the people of Lebanon free of the conflict that was being waged outside its walls. If any one event clearly signaled to me that the end had come for American policy in Lebanon, it was the shocking and tragic murder that morning of Malcolm Kerr. Our opponents were perfectly willing to kill all of us if necessary and they understood that while U.S. forces might eventually retaliate or act in self-defense, the United States would not initiate an attack against them.

By the end of February, U.S. policy in Lebanon had collapsed. Nabih Berri, leader of the Shia Amal militia, successfully implored most of the Shia members of the LAF to desert, pulling the final prop of support out from under the central government. The predominantly Shia Sixth Brigade effectively removed itself from the Army and joined the Amal forces, bringing with them tanks, APCs, artillery and other stores of ammunition and consumables. Convinced that President Reagan would not simply cut and run in Lebanon, Rumsfeld returned once more to Beirut in an effort to bolster Gemayel by personally conveying the president's determination "to stay the course."

Phil Dur had gone back to Beirut with Rumsfeld as the NSC representative. A man of considerable intellect, courage and a sense of history, Dur was intimately familiar with Lebanon's tortured legacy and the responsibility of Western powers in its creation. As the end drew near, Dur and Rumsfeld called the Situation Room over our portable, secure tactical satellite communications (TACSATCOM) system on the afternoon of February 6 to implore the president to issue a strong statement of support for Lebanon and to direct the U.S. forces to fire in support of the collapsing central authority and fulfill U.S. commitments to the Lebanese.

Speaking over the sound of heavy artillery shelling landing nearby, Dur gave one of the most impassioned speeches I have ever heard delivered. He called for a statement that would say, among other things, that the United States and like-minded democratic governments could not stand idly by while external forces opposed to the legitimate government of Lebanon intervened forcibly to dictate the terms of Lebanese internal affairs, supplied instruments for terrorist attacks and subverted the legitimate authorities. The government of Syria, which occupied the territory of Lebanon from where the bulk of the shelling and subversion originated, should cease this activity immediately. McFarlane related that the authority to fire on Syrian-controlled areas had already been released to the fleet as per a previous NSDD. He could only assume that the failure to fire reflected Weinberger and the JCS's continuing tendency to tell the White House it would act but then refuse to do so.

With Shultz out of town on a long-scheduled trip to Latin America, and Reagan on his way to California, Weinberger convinced McFarlane to convene another NSPG to come to grips with the death of America's policy in Lebanon. Some months earlier, Reagan had assured Foreign

Minister Eli Salem that he had "no reverse gears" when it came to America's commitment to Lebanon. Since the first days of Israel's invasion of Lebanon in June 1982, Vice President Bush had maintained a low profile of cautious opposition to U.S. involvement in Lebanon. Egged on by congressional Republicans who suddenly feared that Lebanon might become a devastating campaign issue in November 1984, however, Bush, sensitive to the winds on the Hill, moved quickly to reinforce Weinberger's request to redeploy the Marines offshore. Fed up with the deadlock between Weinberger and Shultz and with the president's willingness to talk tough without taking action, McFarlane concurred with Weinberger's request. Acting for Shultz, Eagleburger articulately and courageously, but in the end vainly, argued that the precipitous withdrawal being contemplated would dramatically erode U.S. capability in the Middle East and beyond.

Since his first day as secretary of state, Shultz had committed significant amounts of his time and personal prestige to help end Lebanon's agony and to restore momentum to the Arab-Israeli peace process. He worked very hard to achieve concrete results. In the end, however, he was bitterly disappointed by the Arab leaders on whom he had relied to prevent Syria from exercising its veto over direct negotiations between Israel and its Arab neighbors and by his colleagues in the National Security Council, most notably Weinberger.

Having finally gotten his wish to withdraw the Marines, Weinberger immediately authorized the Navy to cover their retreat with constant fire from the *New Jersey*—as if it would somehow look better if the United States shot its way out of Lebanon, more like a John Wayne movie. I sat in the Situation Room as reports arrived from the fleet describing the *New Jersey*'s fire. By the time the guns had finished, nearly three hundred 16-inch shells and an additional five hundred 5-inch shells had been hurled into the mountains of Beirut. I was appalled. According to the reports I had seen, there had been no fire at the Marines that would justify any shelling, let alone the orgy of firepower the fleet had unexpectedly unleashed up on the Druze and Syrians in the Matn. There was no logic to what Weinberger and the JCS were doing, unless they were somehow convinced that this macho display of firepower would restore credibility to the policy that their consistent behavior had undermined. Indeed, Weinberger could hardly wait to go out to the fleet to try to "boost the morale" of the Marines who were now back on board their ships. He told the Marines that their mission had been "one of the toughest and most miserable tasks that was ever assigned. You couldn't move out or take high ground or improve your position." But who did Weinberger believe was responsible for keeping them in that untenable position with ROEs which made it impossible for them to fulfill their mission?

Notwithstanding the failure of presidential leadership, the U.S. failure in Lebanon significantly colored Reagan's confidence in the State Department's ability to formulate and implement policy in the Middle East. Philip Habib's herculean efforts should not be dismissed. But Shultz's decision to rely on Habib and upon Saudi assurances that Syria would withdraw, instead of a decision to make the removal of the Syrian Army from Lebanon America's top diplomatic priority, doomed U.S. policy. American influence was wasted on the laborious negotiation of a flawed agreement between Israel and Lebanon, an agreement which Gemayel could never implement and which gave Syria ample time to restore its military strength and political position in Lebanon.

CHAPTER 12

TAKING THE BARK
OFF THE TREE

———— ◆ ————

The Enemy of My Enemy Is My Friend

In early March 1984, his six months as Middle East envoy nearly finished, Rumsfeld gamely returned to the region in order to shift the flag of U.S. interest from the eastern Mediterranean to the Persian Gulf. Understanding the direct relationship between America's defeat in Lebanon at the hands of Syrian and Iranian-sponsored terrorism and the likely erosion in America's already limited ability to defend vital interests in the Gulf, Rumsfeld sought to invigorate the confidence of Gulf leaders in the United States. His goal was to encourage Saudi Arabia, Kuwait, Bahrain, Qatar and the UAE to expand the scope of military-to-military planning to prepare for contingencies involving an Iranian victory against Iraq or a Soviet breakout from Afghanistan into Pakistan or Iran.

This last trip also gave him an opportunity to visit those Middle Eastern countries he had not yet visited. By the time he resigned as presidential envoy, Don Rumsfeld had met with the leaders of every country in the Middle East except those of Iran, the PDRY and Libya. At every stop a consistent theme emerged: intensifying Iranian human-wave suicide attacks against dug-in Iraqi defenses might yet lead Iran to win the war, threatening the stability of all of America's friends in the Gulf and continued Western access to vital Gulf oil supplies. There was no lack of consensus with regard to the need for the United States to do whatever was necessary to prevent such an outcome, just as long as U.S. forces stayed over the horizon.

The U.S. military recognized the shortfalls in its ability to rapidly deploy forces, particularly heavy armor, to the Persian Gulf region. CENTCOM forces did not exercise much in the Gulf. This was in part due to local political concerns, as well as the expense and logistics difficulties involved in large-scale exercises. Rumsfeld, therefore, made it his mission to encourage key leaders, notably the Saudis, to begin joint contingency planning and to agree to the pre-positioning of supplies and equipment at their military facilities, much the same as Bartholomew had negotiated with the Omanis in 1980. While this approach would still fall short of a permanent U.S. presence, such efforts would significantly reduce the amount of time it would take for U.S. Army and Air Force units to deploy to the region and assume combat-ready status.

Following the discovery of an Iranian-inspired coup plot in Bahrain, and the unilateral dispatch of crack Jordanian troops to strengthen the regime's security there, Washington and Amman initiated a secret military cooperation program known as Joint Logistics Planning (JLP). One alternative to the RDF pursued by Washington was to encourage Jordan to perform a comparable role. The United States proposed providing Jordan with modern transport aircraft, 1,600 man-portable Stinger antiaircraft missiles, sophisticated communications equipment and other tactical equipment that would enable Jordan to dispatch rapidly two brigades (eight thousand troops) of elite forces to trouble spots in the Gulf. The Reagan administration hoped that a Jordanian RDF would be readily accepted by Arab leaders. Such a force could help defend U.S. interests without the potentially negative effects of a U.S. military presence. While a Jordanian RDF would not be enough to counter Soviet or Iranian aggression across the Gulf, the JLP would have contributed to the quick defense of the smaller Gulf states, particularly in crises that escalated faster than the United States could respond.

The JLP was strongly opposed by Israel and its supporters in the Congress. Israel argued that until peace, or at least an end to the state of war, was negotiated between Jordan and Israel, the JLP would significantly contribute to the Jordanian threat to Israel. The national security bureaucracy was united in its belief that the JLP was a sensible program that did not threaten Israeli security. Indeed, we argued that the JLP would enhance confidence in U.S. security commitments to Jordan as well as to other conservative Arab states, thereby increasing the potential for Jordan to take risks for peace in the face of Syrian threats. While it was difficult to argue with the same logic that applied to motivating Israel to take risks for peace, opponents of the program delayed its funding and implementation, pending King Hussein's acceptance of the Reagan initiative. When Hussein formally rejected the initiative in March 1984, attacking U.S. Middle East policy as biased toward Israel, the administration withdrew the request for JLP funds.

The failure in Lebanon and the inability of the administration to secure funding for the JLP contributed to a hardening of U.S. policy toward Syria and Iran and an even greater impulse to look for ways to move forward to restore diplomatic relations with Iraq. Following his visit to Baghdad the previous December, Rumsfeld had convinced Shultz to galvanize the bureaucracy to help stop the flow of arms to Iran through the enunciation of a policy that came to be known as "Operation Stanch." Assigning Dick Fairbanks principal responsibility for spearheading Operation Stanch, U.S. diplomacy was aggressively pursuing every report of a possible arms sale to Iran with vigor. This effort helped dissipate lingering suspicions in the Arab world, particularly in Baghdad, that the United States wanted Iraq and Iran to maintain their death grip rather than see either party emerge victorious from the war.

We traveled first to Saudi Arabia. Rumsfeld planned to meet with Minister of Defense and Aviation Prince Sultan to try to persuade him to agree to move forward with joint planning and the pre-positioning of critical equipment, such as tanks and air-defense systems. Such pre-positioning was especially critical early in a crisis, when deployment speed and efficiency could help deter a massing threat before an attack took place. Prince Sultan had rejected previous such suggestions, perhaps out of concern for leaks that might undermine the regime's legitimacy (such as those that facilitated the demise of the JLP) or some fear that the United States might exploit the planning to the disadvantage of Saudi Arabia.

Although the government of Saudi Arabia had created the infrastructure necessary for supporting the influx of the RDF through its ongoing and oversized military construction program, the Saudis understandably wanted to purchase the arms they believed they needed to defend themselves. Riyadh did not want to give the formal impression that it needed to rely on American forces for its defense. Whether contingency planning was conducted or arms were sold, America's Saudi pillar had to believe that Washington would promptly answer calls for assistance. Rumsfeld's goal was to ensure that calls in a crisis situation could be answered promptly so that the United States would be able to protect its vital oil interests. He understood that there was no one else on whom the United States could rely to achieve this goal.

Prior to meeting with Prince Sultan to discuss military matters, Rumsfeld asked to see King Fahd. He wanted to consult him on the post-Lebanon situation, King Hussein's decision to withdraw from the peace process and the current situation in the Iran-Iraq War. Over the course of several visits, Rumsfeld had established a good personal relationship with the king, as illustrated in part by an amusing incident that occurred during one of their meetings.

Arriving at the palace in Riyadh late one night in deference to King Fahd's well-known nocturnal work habits, we were ushered into the king's ornate meeting room and seated on large, comfortable sofas while Fahd sat in his own chair. Each member of the team was served a small brass cup of cardamom coffee, a traditional Saudi Bedouin custom of greeting. King Fahd, who was struggling to lose weight at the time, leaned forward and watched with keen interest as Rumsfeld reached into his pocket for a plastic dispenser containing Equal. Rumsfeld carefully shook two tablets into his hand, dropped them into the cardamom coffee and stirred. Realizing that Fahd was watching him, Rumsfeld started to explain that he was adding the synthetic sweetener made by his company rather than sugar to his coffee. Before Rumsfeld could finish, Fahd, with a grin of delight on his face, reached into his robe, pulled out a small vial, held it up and announced to the group, "I use Equal too!" Madison Avenue would have loved it.

The meetings with Prince Sultan were cordial and somewhat productive, but Saudi Arabia flatly refused to agree to U.S. proposals for joint contingency planning or equipment pre-positioning. Some progress was eventually made through joint command post exercises in the late 1980s. Together with the overbuilding of Saudi infrastructure, these exercises contributed in 1990 to the ability of U.S. forces to deploy to Saudi Arabia to deter an Iraqi advance beyond Kuwait.

Following our visits to Saudi Arabia, Bahrain, Qatar and the YAR, we continued on to Israel for Rumsfeld's penultimate round of discussions with Israeli leaders. Rumsfeld had come increasingly to view Prime Minister Yitzhak Shamir of Israel as a hard-nosed realist who he believed could be relied upon to keep his word. Rumsfeld visited Israel at least once on every trip to the region.

While preparing for this trip, I had been contacted once again by Bechtel representatives with regard to Israeli security guarantees for the Aqaba pipeline. They sought formal political and financial guarantees; however, neither Israel nor the United States (on the financial level) was willing to accommodate Bechtel. For over a year, international efforts had been under way to construct the pipeline, which would add one million barrels of oil per day to the global oil supply. Such a pipeline could have had positive economic and political consequences throughout the region. It would generate substantial revenue for both Iraq and Jordan, while at the same time helping to build confidence regarding the purported nonaggressive intentions of Iraq toward Israel.

Shortly before our arrival in Tel Aviv, I suggested that Rumsfeld discuss this issue with Shamir. Perhaps Rumsfeld could convince Shamir to compromise and provide the United States with some sort of written assurance that might satisfy Baghdad, even if it fell short of the unequivocal guarantee Saddam had demanded. Rumsfeld agreed that a pipeline to Aqaba could reinforce vital U.S. interests, while testing Saddam.

He raised the issue during our meeting with Shamir, who responded surprisingly. Shamir began by noting that the government of Israel had recently concluded that Iran had become a graver threat to Israel than Iraq. Iranian support for Hizbollah and other Islamic fundamentalist factions in Lebanon, coupled with the growing strength of fundamentalism in Jordan and Syria, left Israel convinced that if Iran defeated Iraq, the prospects for further fundamentalist advances toward Israel would dramatically increase. Only Jordan stood between Iraq and Israel, and the Israelis fully realized the limitations of King Hussein's abilities to defend his kingdom against a fundamentalist Iraq under the domination of Khomeini's Iran.

This policy statement by Shamir represented a sea change in Israeli attitudes toward Iraq. Baghdad had been viewed historically as Israel's most implacable, radical adversary. Indeed, Israel's widely criticized decision to bomb Iraq's nuclear reactor in 1981 was motivated by Israel's conviction that if Baghdad developed a nuclear weapon, it would certainly use it against Israel.

Continuing his presentation, Shamir asked us why the United States was persisting in efforts to build a new pipeline. It would take several years to build and would not help the Iraqis in the current circumstances. He then proposed that Baghdad secretly reopen the Trans-Arabian Pipeline, which ran through the Golan Heights to Lebanon and which had been closed during the June 1967 War. The TAPLINE, as it was known, was capable of carrying fifty thousand barrels of oil per day and could start generating modest revenues immediately. He asked us to please pass Israel's offer along to President Saddam Hussein as a message from the government of Israel during Rumsfeld's next visit to Baghdad.

Whether Shamir was genuinely more troubled about Iranian intentions and capabilities or whether he simply wanted to put Iraq to the test and see what developments might emerge was not clear. However, upon reflection it did appear that this was an opportunity to try to open a secret channel of communication which might achieve tangible political and economic benefits, helping to strengthen Iraq in its war with Iran, while also reducing the prospects for a renewal of Arab-Israeli warfare. More significantly, Shamir's offer provided a clear test of Iraq's purported moderation. Arriving in Baghdad several days later, we were advised by Ambassador Eagleton that Saddam would not be able to receive Rumsfeld during this visit. A meeting was, however, scheduled with Tariq Aziz.

The meeting took place at the Iraqi Foreign Ministry several hours later than scheduled. No reason was ever given for such delays, though typically we felt it reflected an attempt simply to make President Reagan's emissary cool his heels. Owing to the extreme sensitivity of the message that Shamir had sent, Rumsfeld asked to meet privately with Aziz before the meeting. The one-on-one was brief, not more than ten minutes. Following this session, the rest of the team was invited in to join the discussion. We spent nearly two hours talking about the status of the fighting in the Gulf. Aziz showed us a videotape made by Iraqi troops which showed an Iranian human wave attacking built-up Iraqi defensive positions. The video showed line after line of advancing Iranian soldiers, many of them clearly young teenage boys, being cut down by machine-gun fire, mortars and land mines, their bodies left hanging limp on barbed wire. It was gruesome and frightening, a vivid reminder of the intensity of the spirit of the Iranians to martyr themselves for what the Ayatollah Khomeini considered a just cause.

Following the meeting, which concluded on friendly terms, I drew Rumsfeld aside and asked what had happened. Tamping down his pipe, Rumsfeld told me he had passed the message exactly as proposed by Shamir. He said that Tariq Aziz had turned pale, looked up at the ceiling, shook his head and then, looking down at the table, responded without equivocation. He asked Rumsfeld to please take back his message. Aziz went on to say that he could not fulfill Rumsfeld's request that he carry the message to his president. He knew how Saddam would respond were Aziz to accept the Israeli message and suggest that he even consider it. He told Rumsfeld that Saddam would execute Aziz on the spot. "That's it?" I asked. "That's it," Rumsfeld replied. "I think we can forget about the Aqaba pipeline."

While I had not expected Saddam Hussein to agree to open a pipeline that flowed through territory occupied by Israel, the manner of Aziz's rejection of the communication from Shamir made manifestly clear the truth about Baghdad's expedient attitude toward the United States and Israel. Deeds are what count when measuring changes in the behavior of states, not rhetoric. Iraq had cleverly moderated its public statements to mask its intentions toward Israel, as well as toward its Arab neighbors. Under the pressure of losing a war with Iran, Iraq had turned to its traditional ideological foes, the Saudis, the Kuwaitis, the Egyptians and the Americans, for the help it needed to survive. Although the rhetoric had changed, the aspirations of Iraq and the bloody tactics of its brutal dictator had not.

Seven years later, in the last days before Desert Shield became Desert Storm, Tariq Aziz met with Secretary of State James Baker in Geneva in a last-ditch effort to avoid a military conflict between the coalition forces and Iraq. Baker carried a letter from George Bush to Saddam Hussein which he reportedly passed to Aziz during the meeting. By his own admission, Aziz studied the letter carefully before handing it back to Baker, telling him that he refused to either accept it or pass it on to Saddam. Did Aziz still believe that Saddam would execute him on the spot if he delivered the letter? Aziz's actions on both occasions spoke volumes about the reality of Iraq.

Unambiguous Instructions

Before returning to the United States, Rumsfeld made one last visit to Lebanon by himself. The rest of the team remained in Tel Aviv for security reasons. Upon our arrival at Ben-Gurion Airport, Dan Kurtzer, a political officer in the American embassy, was waiting with a message from McFarlane instructing me to contact him immediately, using the embassy's secure telephone system. The secure telephone uses an encryption system that scrambles voices so that they cannot be intercepted and deciphered. Assuming the nature of the call would deal with some issue in the Middle East, I asked Phil Dur to join me.

The embassy in Tel Aviv had two secure phones, so we were able to participate jointly in the call. McFarlane greeted us and immediately said that Oliver North was also on the line. Dur and I immediately exchanged surprised glances. North's participation was unusual in that he was not directly involved in Middle East issues, except for counterterrorism.

McFarlane came immediately to the point. He directed me to secretly contact Dave Kimche and propose to him that Israel provide several million dollars of cash assistance to the Nicaraguan contras. "Make clear the urgency of this request and our readiness to find ways of compensating Israel for its assistance. At the same time, do not give Kimche the impression that there will be a quid pro quo for Israel's help. And, Howard, whatever you do, make absolutely certain that Kimche understands that he is not to discuss this matter with anyone in the embassy, including Sam Lewis. He is only to contact you or me with Israel's answer." As we hung up our phones, Dur and I both shook our heads. I was very unhappy at being drawn into any Contra-related issues.

Although it was after eleven P.M., I phoned Kimche at home and told him McFarlane had asked whether he would meet with me to discuss something important, despite the late hour. He agreed, as long as I could come to his home in the Tel Aviv suburbs. An embassy driver had been assigned to take me to the nearby Hilton hotel. Along the way, I directed him to the address and told him to wait for me.

Kimche was gracious, offering me a cigar and cognac as we sat in his living room surrounded by his impressive collection of African masks and art. We first reviewed the status of the situation in Lebanon and Tariq Aziz's response to Shamir's message, then turned to the purpose of my late visit. I carefully delivered McFarlane's message regarding the Contras' needs for cash assistance. Kimche told me that this was a difficult request. Shamir could not undertake such an activity without the cooperation of the finance minister and because it was not an Israeli covert action, it might be difficult to keep secret. Kimche asked me to please tell McFarlane that he agreed to take his request to the prime minister and that he would do his best to convince him to accommodate the United States.

At the end of March, Kimche telephoned me in Washington to advise that Shamir had carefully considered the request but concluded that it was too difficult. He asked me to let McFarlane know that he was sorry Israel could not help. Israel could not make any funds available for the Contras. I walked over to McFarlane's office and reported to him the Israeli decision. McFarlane frowned and expressed his disappointment but promptly went on to another subject.

In late April, the Israeli embassy advised me that Kimche would be in Washington and wanted to meet with McFarlane. I passed the message along, but McFarlane planned to be traveling with Reagan throughout the period of Kimche's visit. He asked me to meet with him and to "clearly communicate my disappointment over Israel's inability to find a way to help the Contras."

On the morning of McFarlane's departure, Wilma Hall dropped by my office with an envelope that McFarlane had directed her to hand-carry to me. Inside the double-sealed envelope was a SECRET memo to me from

McFarlane providing explicit guidance on what he wanted said to Kimche. The memo referred back to McFarlane's March request for aid to the Contras and made unambiguously clear his deep disappointment at Israel's unhelpfulness. The memo was marked NOT FOR THE SYSTEM, meaning that it was a document handled only by the "originator" and the "addressee" without being assigned a control number by the NSC secretariat, the body responsible for NSC paper flow. Moreover, typed on the bottom of the paper were the words DESTROY THIS DOCUMENT. The subject was obviously so sensitive that I was not even supposed to keep the original instruction or a copy in my safe. After returning from the Israeli embassy, where I had met briefly with Kimche, I followed McFarlane's instructions and shredded the document.

Three months later in June, I traveled to Israel to participate in the first Joint Political-Military Group (JPMG) meetings to convene in Israel. Under the chairmanship of director Rear Admiral Jonathan Howe, the JPMG had quickly established the series of working groups envisioned at its creation some eight months earlier. As the meetings drew to a close, Sam Lewis asked me to come by his residence for lunch, where he surprised me by bringing up the secret meeting with Kimche. "Nothing goes on here that I won't find out about," Lewis said. "Please brief me on your side of the story so I have a complete picture."

Shocked that he had learned of my secret meeting, I felt compelled to fill in the details in order to maintain what I considered to be a good working relationship with Lewis. Speaking as a friend, he told me that as careful as I was it was unwise to try to go behind his back in Israel. He said that he was intimately familiar with the CIA purchases of Soviet captured arms, and he was more than willing to help the White House in any way he could. Had he been consulted he would have informed McFarlane that Israel would never be able to provide funds for the Contras and all this embarrassment could have been avoided. Lewis closed the discussion by telling me that he had sent a private message to Shultz when he learned about my talks with Kimche, and Shultz had told him not to do anything about it. In the circumstances, Lewis wanted to make sure that I understood that he wanted to be able to continue working with me in an atmosphere of trust, leading him to tell me what he had learned. I respected and liked Sam Lewis, and I told him I regretted what had happened, but that I had no choice but to follow McFarlane's unambiguous instructions.

In retrospect, my decision to carry out McFarlane's instructions would haunt me for the balance of my government career.

Hamlet of Nations

As a result of the failure of American policy in Lebanon, regional states lost what little confidence they had in U.S. commitments and staying power. The administration's foreign policy goals for the Middle East were to (1) find ways to strengthen our ties with Egypt and the conservative Arab states; (2) bolster Iraq's resistance to repeated Iranian offenses; (3) try to facilitate direct negotiations between Arabs and Israelis; and (4) improve our ability to respond to crises that would affect vital interests in the Gulf. Moreover, in the wake of terrorism's victory in Lebanon, a concerted interagency effort was launched to devise a strategy for combating international terrorism. These were the core issues that I would work on for the balance of my career at the NSC.

When I returned with Rumsfeld from the Middle East in March 1984, McFarlane directed me to draft a strategy paper that analyzed the trends in the region and American options in order to achieve our goals in the Middle East. The paper, entitled "U.S. Policy After Lebanon," gave a lengthy analysis of the changing regional balance of power, changes that resulted from Syria's victory in Lebanon and the abrogation of the May 17 agreement. I proposed that the U.S. focus on restoring the credibility of our military commitments and negotiated agreements, particularly between Egypt and Israel, and on finding ways to engage with West Bank Palestinians in order to maintain some minimum level of peace process activity. I concluded by arguing that the United States had few choices in the Middle East. Vital interests were increasingly threatened by Soviet activism, radical violence and terrorism, while hard-won gains, especially in the peace process, were being eroded. It was essential for the United States to come to grips with its failure and eliminate doubts about American credibility and staying power. Raising false expectations about what the United States might do for Israelis or Arabs would only make matters worse.

With respect to the regional balance of power, Iran had become more dangerous for U.S. interests than Syria. In addition to Tehran's threat to close the Strait of Hormuz, the Iranians posed a genuine military threat to the petroleum infrastructure of the Gulf and the political stability of Arab regimes. Iran was trying to foment instability among Shia Arabs in Bahrain, Saudi Arabia, Iraq and Lebanon. Its successful use of terrorism to support its regional goals increased the potential for popular unrest throughout the entire Moslem world. Were the Iranians to capture the Iraqi city of Basra, or overthrow the regime of Saddam Hussein, it seemed likely that the Gulf Arabs would appease Tehran at American expense. For example, the U.S. risked losing access to military facilities in Bahrain. Iraq's defeat by Khomeini's Iran would have profound negative consequences for America's vital interests in the Gulf. While it was essential that the United States remain skeptical of Iraq's long-term moderation, given Saddam's brutality and hostility to numerous American policies, we had no choice but to work with Iraq in the short term to protect America's vital interests in the Gulf.

McFarlane reviewed the strategy paper and returned it to me with a note saying that he would discuss it with President Reagan. McFarlane also gave a copy to Shultz, who said to me that the paper was the first thing he had seen on the situation in the Middle East and our failure which really took the "bark off the tree." He agreed with the analysis and my proposals for pursuing U.S. interests there. With this as a catalyst, McFarlane directed Kemp and me to "invigorate" the formal interagency study on southwest Asia security strategies.

An intense ground battle had been raging in the Iran-Iraq War since late 1983, and tensions continued to escalate dramatically. Iraq, armed with French-supplied long-range Super Étendard strike aircraft firing anti-ship Exocet missiles, intensified its attacks on oil tankers transiting Iran's Kharg Island oil terminal. Iran retaliated with its own limited antiship capabilities by trying to attack ships bound for Iraq while threatening to blockade the Strait of Hormuz to international shipping. The economic logic of Iraq's military attacks was sound: they would deprive Iran of oil revenue, thereby making it more difficult for Tehran to buy the arms it needed to sustain combat with Iraq. Yet Baghdad's political objective was to try to reduce the world's oil supply, thereby increasing the price of oil. Iraq wanted to increase the pressure on the West to use its "influence" with Iran to bring about an end to the war. This tactic might have been successful had there not been a glut of oil in the international market, minimizing the political concern of Washington and other Western capitals.

In response to Iranian threats to close the Gulf to international shipping, harking back to his corollary to the Carter Doctrine, Reagan cautioned that American forces would take all means necessary to keep the sea-lanes free of interference. In the circumstances, the U.S. statement was clearly directed at Iran and reflected an additional measure of the U.S. tilt to Iraq. While the United States verbally criticized Iraq for its use of mustard gas against the Iranians, no actions followed our diplomatic protests. Indeed, at the end of the year, Reagan received Tariq Aziz in the Oval Office and announced that the United States and Iraq would resume full diplomatic relations.

Quickly exploiting Washington's vulnerability to terrorism, the Iranians and their allies continued to fight the war for the Gulf in Lebanon. Tehran observed that U.S. forces were ready to open fire if unambiguously provoked, such as when Iranian aircraft and patrol boats appeared to threaten the USS *Lawrence* in the Strait of Hormuz in February 1984. Iran figured out how to exact a price from the United States and its allies in a way that minimized the risk of retaliation. To paraphrase Clausewitz, terrorism is an extension of war and politics by other means.

With America's overt tilt to Iraq clearly evident, Iranian-backed terrorists in Lebanon insolently stepped up their use of the Sheikh Abdullah Barracks to train, manage and implement terror operations. They moved their hostages into the barracks. The terrorists knew that the United States had aborted its coordinated strike with the French and calculated that once the hostages were brought to the Sheikh Abdullah Barracks, America would also prevent Israel from striking out of fear of killing the hostages, creating in effect a sanctuary.

On September 20, 1984, Islamic Jihad drove a car bomb into the East Beirut annex of the American embassy, killing two Americans and twelve Lebanese. Ambassador Bartholomew was seriously wounded in the blast. The U.S. government knew that a mock obstacle course similar to the dragon's teeth arrangement in front of the embassy annex had been set up on the grounds of the Sheikh Abdullah barracks and that this was where the suicide driver had trained for his mission. Even such clear-cut evidence as this was insufficient to motivate the United States to act to defend itself. In the NSPG meeting that convened the next day, Weinberger argued against striking the barracks in retaliation. "We don't have evidence which proves that the terrorists who planned the attack will be in the barracks when we strike," Weinberger said. "Let's not kill the wrong people." For their part, the JCS focused on the potential for collateral damage, the prospect of innocent civilians being hurt or killed because they were in the proximity of the terrorist base.

With more Americans and Lebanese dead, President Reagan once again failed to match deeds with words and the terrorists were winning a war being fought under rules defined by Tehran. While the statement issued by the terrorists focused on their desire to force Americans out of Lebanon, it was clear that Tehran was supplying money, the explosives and the guidance. Reinforcing the image of U.S. weakness and indecision, the Iranians hoped to further undermine Arab confidence in Washington's commitments and reduce U.S. influence in the Middle East. Shultz left the NSPG simmering with rage, furious at Weinberger's nonstop obfuscation and manipulation of legalisms. The president, however, deferred to Weinberger's view, and the United States, once again, applied American standards of jurisprudence to states and entities fighting under Hama-like rules.

Expressing the view of many who had expected President Reagan to make terrorists pay a price for waging nonconventional, dirty wars, Shultz tried to stimulate a public debate that would build a consensus for the appropriate use of force in response to terrorism. He argued that the United States might not have the kind of evidence that can stand up in an American court of law, but it could not allow itself to become the "Hamlet of nations, worrying endlessly over whether and how to respond."

Weinberger, an avid debater, met Shultz's challenge some months later, claiming that to "employ our forces almost indiscriminately and as a regular and customary part of our diplomatic efforts would surely plunge us headlong into the sort of domestic turmoil we experienced during the Vietnam War, without accomplishing the goal for which we committed our forces. The commitment of U.S. forces to combat should always be a last resort."

Regardless of the negative consequences for the United States, Weinberger was an unrelenting, blind supporter of the New Never Again Club. He never saw a weapons system he didn't want to buy, but he never saw a situation in which he was prepared to use force to advance U.S. interests. Weinberger's statements were read with delight by the Iranians, who understood that the legacy of Vietnam was alive and well and that the United States had not yet come to grips with the political realities of the Middle East. For better or for worse, it is a fact that the people of the Middle East, Moslems, Jews and Christians alike, are impressed and persuaded by military action. The use of military power translates directly into political influence. Failure to act is almost always seen as weakness rather than restraint born of strength, as Weinberger so firmly believed.

In March, Saudi defense minister Sultan had declined the U.S. offer for joint planning, expressing his confidence that the Saudi Air Force would repel any Iranian attack and that the limited air-defense planning activities that had been under way since 1981 were sufficient. The United States hoped the Saudis would not be tested, however, and braced for Iranian attacks in the wake of an Iraqi escalation. In May 1984, a U.S.-manned-and-operated AWACS plane observed incoming Iranian aircraft and immediately informed the Saudis that an attack appeared imminent in the vicinity of Ras Tanura, Saudi Arabia's massive Persian Gulf oil terminal. The Saudi Air Force, alerted to the threat profile of the attacking Iranian aircraft, scrambled two Saudi F-15s and vectored to a successful intercept of the Iranian F-4s. Despite American trepidation about the Saudis' ability to use the advanced weapons they had purchased in the preceding years, the brief air battle between Saudi and Iranian forces reassured the U.S. government that Riyadh possessed both the capability and will to confront the Iranians when attacked.

As pleased as we were by the Saudis' very effective display of modern military prowess, the fact that a former U.S. ally was attacking a current U.S. ally with American-supplied airplanes and was shot down with the help of the United States was ironic, if not downright pathetic. Yet the administration took a measure of satisfaction in watching U.S. security strategy, based on the AWACS air-defense system and Saudi-flown F-15s, being effectively implemented. Vital Saudi oil resources were accordingly protected. This action would not have been possible in 1979 using un-armed F-15s. Proud of the intercept, the Saudis pointed to this action as justification for their requests for additional armaments. However, Riyadh continued to refuse U.S. appeals to initiate joint planning.

Rat Patrols

In 1984, Qadhafi resumed his campaign of terrorism and subversion, triggering a cycle of Libyan-sponsored attacks and American responses which eventually culminated in the April 1986 U.S. bombing of Libya. Following Libya's ignominious withdrawal from most of Chad due in part to Washington's covert support of Hissein Habre (who successfully employed "rat patrol" guerrilla tactics to wear down the Libyan Army in the wastelands of Chad), Qadhafi resumed his plotting to overthrow President Jaafar Nimeiri of Sudan and his international campaign to assassinate Libyan dissidents. In Chad, the Executive and Congress had cooperated successfully in bolstering Habre.

After the Libyan bombing of Omdurman, Sudan, in March 1984, the U.S. government began to reevaluate how the United States could support dissident groups that might bring down Qadhafi and his regime. Despite the success of U.S. policy in Chad, the nonlethal support for Libyan exiles program was a much more cautious effort, limited to propaganda support, economic assistance and cooperation with Iraq, where the exiles received military training. The exiles attempted a coup in May, but it was immediately crushed, and Qadhafi purged the officer corps of the Libyan Army.

About the same time, the CIA's NIO for the Near East, Graham Fuller, made a strong case for intensifying U.S. efforts against Qadhafi. Fuller's analysis triggered a bureaucratic battle royal. The DOD favored intensifying the pressure on Qadhafi as long as it was not called upon to take any military action. In the State Department's Bureau of Intelligence and Research (INR), a counteranalysis to Fuller's was disseminated which argued that Fuller dramatically exaggerated Qadhafi's vulnerabilities and the opportunities for bringing him down.

The fundamental goal of U.S. policy toward Libya was to encourage Qadhafi to change his behavior, not to destroy him. But as repeated efforts failed to stop his anti-American activities and sponsorship of international terrorism, the frustration level reached the point where most of the bureaucracy agreed that it was necessary to try to remove Qadhafi from power. To Washington's dismay, however, Qadhafi strengthened his regional position in September when he met with King Hassan of Morocco, one of Ronald Reagan's best friends in the Arab world, and signed the Oujda Accords, which created a merger between Morocco and Libya.

These accords had the effect of dramatically undermining Hassan's influence in Washington while reducing Qadhafi's international isolation. Although it was understood that Hassan hoped to use the accords to outmaneuver Algeria, which was providing political and military support for the Polisario Front rebels fighting the Moroccan Army in the Western Sahara, from Washington's perspective Hassan could not have picked a worse ally. Moreover, King Hassan's assurances that he would "tame" Qadhafi through the merger were regarded as simply ludicrous. Following eight months of chilled relations with the United States, Hassan moved away from the Oujda Accords and started to rebuild his badly tarnished image as a reliable regional ally.

Against this backdrop, Qadhafi intervened to support his Iranian ally against Iraq. Although Libya had previously limited its support for Iran to arms supply and rhetoric, most notably long-range SCUD missiles to answer Iraqi missile attacks, in August 1984 the Saudis and the Egyptians discovered mines floating in the Red Sea. Eighteen ships were struck by the mines, which had been rolled off the transom of a Libyan freighter. Qadhafi's goal was to inhibit oil tankers from calling on Saudi Arabia's Red Sea oil terminals from where Iraqi oil was transshipped. The mining scare successfully intimidated international shipping for several weeks, causing a slight increase in the price of oil and Red Sea maritime insurance rates. Intent on confronting America wherever possible, Qadhafi did not limit his intervention to the Middle East or North Africa. He also provided financial and military assistance to the Sandinistas in Nicaragua, including military advisors to help the Nicaraguan Army absorb Soviet equipment and fight the Contras.

Gemayel's formal abrogation of the May 17 agreement in early March was heralded by Moscow as the defeat for American policy in the Middle East and the end of the Camp David process. Moscow was stung by the growing relationship between the United States and Iraq and by U.S. efforts in the Gulf but was bogging down in Afghanistan, finding it necessary to commit more men and matériel. In these circumstances, Soviet air and naval forces began to make regular use of Libyan military facilities in Tripoli and Tobruk in order to increase their ability to monitor the sixth Fleet in the Mediterranean and to perform maintenance work on Soviet ships and planes. In the Red Sea, the Soviets further built up the anchorage of Dahlak Island off the coast of Ethiopia, deploying submarines as well as surface combatants and maritime aircraft, which gave them an "in-theater" capability to interdict shipping in the sea-lanes of the Red Sea and close the Bab el-Mandeb at the mouth of the Indian Ocean. Aden also provided the Soviets with naval anchorages and air bases in the Indian Ocean astride the tanker routes to and from the Gulf.

Weinberger Has Forgotten More Than You Will Ever Know

Israeli elections in the summer of 1984 produced a gridlock, with neither the incumbent Likud bloc nor the Labor party winning enough seats to win control of the Knesset. To break the impasse, Israeli president Chaim Herzog asked Yitzhak Shamir and Shimon Peres, leader of the Labor party, to form a government of national unity (GNU) with a rotating premiership. After weeks of negotiation, the GNU was formed, with Peres as prime minister, Shamir as deputy prime minister and foreign minister, and the Labor party's Yitzhak Rabin as defense minister.

During my June visit to Israel for the JPMG, I had quietly met with Nimrod Novick, Peres's national security affairs advisor, to try to learn what Peres would do with Egypt, Lebanon and the peace process in the event he won the election. I had taken care to coordinate this meeting with Sam Lewis so there would be no repeat of the embarrassing episode with Kimche. Novick and I spoke for several hours about Peres's foreign policy priorities and the expectations of Washington. Complete withdrawal from Lebanon was at the top of Israel's agenda, followed closely

by improving relations with Egypt through completion of the Taba conciliation and arbitration process, in addition to finding a way to stop Israel's
runaway inflation.

With the formation of the GNU, it was more difficult to anticipate
the direction of Israeli foreign policy. Peres and Shamir might have been
in the same coalition, but they viewed the world from opposite directions.
Peres wanted to exchange occupied land for peace with the Arab world,
whereas Shamir hoped to settle the occupied territories and find a political
formula that would leave them forever under Israeli control. It would not
be easy for these two very different leaders to resolve their differences over
such fundamental issues.

Shortly after the Israeli GNU was formed, Weinberger decided to
proceed with a long-scheduled trip to Tunisia, Egypt and Israel. Along
with Bob Pelletreau, who would represent the State Department, I joined
Weinberger in Milan, Italy, where he was attending a Nuclear Planning
Group meeting with NATO defense ministers at Lake Como. The first
stop in the Middle East was Tunisia, where a U.S.-Tunisian joint military
commission (JMC) was convened to review the status of bilateral defense
cooperation and to try to agree on areas where defense ties could be
expanded. Qadhafi had intensified his rhetorical attacks and support for
Tunisian subversives and opposition elements, due to President Habib
Bourguiba's strong support for U.S. policy in the region. A long-time
friend of the United States, Bourguiba had played the leading role in
liberating Tunisia from France and had historically been at the forefront
of political and economic modernization within the Arab world.

During the course of a courtesy call on Bourguiba, the discussion turned
to the prospects for new Israeli policies as a result of the formation of the
GNU. In reply to Bourguiba's question about his views on what might
happen between Egypt and Israel, Weinberger, to my amazement, informed Bourguiba that the United States had decided that it was time to
solve the Taba problem by moving from conciliation to arbitration in
order to eliminate this irritant in the relationship.

This supposed new U.S. policy toward Taba that Weinberger described
was news to me. Egypt had always wanted to go directly to arbitration but
had agreed to work through the conciliation process as laid out in the
peace treaty. The process was still working, and though the United States
did not expect the Egyptians to compromise as Israel hoped, neither the
Egyptians nor the Israelis were complaining. Startled by Weinberger, I
turned to Bob Pelletreau, who was furiously taking notes of the conversation. He caught my eye, looked up from the table, furrowed his brow and

mouthed, "I don't know what he's talking about." As soon as the meeting ended, Pelletreau and I compared notes. Neither of us were aware of any discussions involving Shultz, McFarlane or President Reagan in which the subject of a new U.S. policy toward the Taba conciliation process had been raised.

The negotiation of the Taba compromise by Walter Stoessel, which I had participated in two and a half years before, had resulted from an evenhanded U.S. mediation role, in which Washington carefully avoided siding with either country's preference. While Weinberger was entitled to his opinion about moving on to arbitration, this was not U.S. policy. Pelletreau and I agreed that unilaterally presenting the new GNU with a surprise shift in U.S. policy on Taba would immediately create a policy crisis for the government of Israel. Moreover, such a crisis would strengthen the political hand of Sharon, who had been politically resurrected in the latest election on a platform that attacked the United States as a disloyal ally interested only in currying favor with the Arab world.

As we left the meeting, Pelletreau and I asked Rich Armitage, the assistant secretary for ISA, about Weinberger's remark. Armitage agreed to talk with him about it on the airplane en route to Cairo. Shortly after takeoff, Armitage told Pelletreau and me that "the secretary says that the U.S. should back going to arbitration on Taba now in order to get Israeli-Egyptian relations back on track, pronto!"

I responded that we did not disagree that it would be nice to get to arbitration, especially since none of us believed that conciliation would produce any results. I asked Armitage, "But where does Weinberger get the idea that he can unilaterally change U.S. policy? At a minimum, we should consult with Peres before informing Arab leaders, particularly the Tunisians, who have no stake in the process, that the U.S. has changed its policy." Pelletreau nodded in agreement, but Armitage shrugged and walked back to the front cabin, where Weinberger was talking with his military assistant, Major General Colin Powell.

Upon our arrival in Cairo, Pelletreau and I agreed to contact Washington to find out if, unbeknownst to us, Weinberger might have gotten the president or Shultz's approval to shift the U.S. position on Taba. I called McFarlane at home, where it was nearly midnight. "What!" he exclaimed. "There has been no change in our policy toward Taba. Please inform Cap that he is to desist from asserting that Washington has dropped its neutrality in favor of arbitration." Pelletreau, through Assistant Secretary Richard Murphy, had received the same guidance from Secretary Shultz.

Weinberger was "off the reservation," unilaterally trying to change

U.S. policy because he thought it was the right thing to do. Unfortunately we couldn't see Weinberger, as he was suffering from a bad cold and had retired early. Seeking out Armitage, Pelletreau and I conveyed the identical guidance we had received from Washington and asked him to pass it on to Weinberger first thing in the morning.

The next day included a meeting with Egypt's minister of defense Abu Ghazala followed by the observation of an Egyptian live-fire armor exercise in the desert and a flyover by the Egyptian Air Force flying their newly acquired F-16 aircraft. The status of Taba and prospects for improving Egyptian-Israeli relations was hardly a top priority for a meeting of defense ministers. Yet Weinberger wasted no time raising the Taba issue, once again stating that the United States believed it was time to settle the issue with arbitration. Armitage raised his hands in a gesture that meant "Don't look at me," as Pelletreau and I grimaced at Weinberger's defiance of the clear guidance that he had by now received through Armitage. Abu Ghazala visibly brightened when he heard this news, quite conscious that a change in the U.S. position meant that Washington had decided to drop its neutrality and adopt the Egyptian perspective.

A relatively brief meeting was scheduled for Weinberger and Mubarak before we departed for Israel. I greeted President Mubarak in Arabic, leading him to laugh heartily and wag his finger at me. "My Syrian friend," Mubarak teased, "we must teach you proper Arabic so you can get rid of that Damascus accent." Weinberger saw Mubarak privately before the rest of us joined them. Several topics were covered, including Weinberger's unilateral Taba initiative. Mubarak simply pocketed the new U.S. position, expressing the hope that the matter would be solved quickly and that Peres would be able to control the elements of the GNU that would undoubtedly press for more settlements in order to undermine the prospects for broadening the peace process.

On Weinberger's plane once again, Pelletreau and I requested a meeting with Weinberger before we arrived in Israel. Reemphasizing the instructions we had received from Washington, we once again explained to Armitage that what Weinberger was doing would only play into the hands of his archrival, Sharon. Several minutes later, Armitage came back to our seats, folded his arms and said, "The secretary is not interested in what either of you have to say about this matter. Don't you guys realize that Weinberger has forgotten more about the Middle East than either of you will ever know?"

I could only shake my head in disbelief as Armitage walked away. Regardless of Weinberger's opinion of the NSC staff, and my role in this mission, Pelletreau was a Yale-trained lawyer who had left the law to become a foreign service officer and had been sent to represent the secretary of state. A well-respected Arabist, Pelletreau spoke fluent Arabic and was an accomplished professional. We were both just appalled and soon agreed that our only hope was to corral Sam Lewis immediately upon our arrival in Israel to explain the situation and try to convince him to back Weinberger down. Assuming that Lewis agreed, perhaps his credibility as the U.S. ambassador would rein in the insubordinate secretary of defense.

Lewis was standing by his limousine as the airplane came to a halt on the tarmac. Still under the weather, Weinberger took his time organizing himself before deplaning. Pelletreau and I, however, raced down the steps and briefed Lewis on the Taba issue. His mouth dropping open in surprise, Lewis was shocked. He agreed that if Weinberger unilaterally put forward a new U.S. position arguing for immediate arbitration of the Taba dispute, it would definitely create a crisis for Peres, one that Sharon would exploit. "I can't believe it," Lewis exclaimed as Weinberger started to descend from the plane. He reassured us, "Don't worry, I'll take care of this."

At a dinner reception that evening hosted by Defense Minister Rabin, Lewis took me aside and said that the matter had been settled. Weinberger had grudgingly agreed that he would back off of the arbitration idea and simply ask Peres how he saw the course of Egyptian-Israeli relations in the coming months. Instructions were subsequently cabled to the U.S. ambassadors in Tunis and Cairo to clarify the U.S. position on Taba. Weinberger followed the script when he met with Peres.

Although a potential crisis for the GNU was averted, Weinberger's presumptuous behavior typified the continuing failure of the Reagan National Security Council to work together as a team and Reagan's unwillingness to discipline his principal advisors. Despite explicit instructions from the secretary of state, the Cabinet officer legally charged with the responsibility to conduct American foreign policy, reinforced by the National Security Advisor, Weinberger ignored orders with which he did not agree because they did not suit him. I often wondered how many other instructions, outside of the Middle East arena, Weinberger ignored.

The Truth No Longer Mattered

As the first term of the Reagan administration drew to a close, my NSC colleague Geoff Kemp announced his resignation. Earlier in the summer, McFarlane advised me that Kemp would be leaving and that he planned to promote me to the more senior position of special assistant to the president and senior director for Near East affairs. Several months went by, but McFarlane did not follow up. At the same time, Bob Pelletreau informed me that he was in the running for the position, and if he received it, whoever was the senior player, he looked forward to working together with me as a team, a view which I shared.

One evening, while attending a reception in Washington at the home of the newly appointed Iraqi ambassador Nizar Hamdoon, I saw Pelletreau across the room. I noticed he seemed depressed. I asked him whether anything was wrong. Surprised that I didn't know, he told me that James P. "Jock" Covey, the State Department's deputy executive secretary, would be getting the position, not either of us. I was shocked. Earlier in the day, I had spent nearly three hours with McFarlane during prebriefs with Reagan and subsequent meetings in the Oval Office, where Tariq Aziz and Reagan agreed to resume U.S.-Iraqi diplomatic relations. McFarlane had not mentioned a word of this decision, despite his promise that I would succeed Kemp. In my experience, it was not like him to behave this way.

Upon his arrival at the NSC in early 1985, Covey moved into Kemp's office and assumed the senior position. Immediately, he went out of his way to carve out a highly structured set of "staff responsibilities." This was coincidentally designed to preclude my involvement in many of the issues that I had worked on for nearly four years, particularly the peace process and U.S.-Israeli relations. Covey informed me that from now on he would be responsible for all matters relating to the peace process as well as U.S. relations with Israel, Jordan, Egypt and Syria. The Maghreb, the Gulf and terrorism issues would be my responsibility, while south Asian affairs would be managed by Dr. Shireen Tahir-Kheli, an expert on the Asian subcontinent who formally belonged to the Political-Military Affairs Directorate.

The new arrangement was extremely frustrating. Despite Covey's vision of our mutual responsibilities, both McFarlane and Shultz repeatedly said they wanted me to continue to participate in peace process matters. Nevertheless, on the rationale that these matters were not my direct responsibility, working with his FSO colleagues at State, Covey did his bureaucratic best to minimize my access to papers, cables and meetings. At one point during the TWA 847 hijacking, I attended a meeting in George Shultz's conference room to discuss U.S. policy options early on in the crisis. As the meeting broke up, Shultz asked me to stay behind for a chat. "Howie," Shultz said, "why haven't I seen you in the meetings we have been having on the peace process? I put you on the list of people to invite, but you don't come. Do you have any ideas?" Just as I was about to tell him that I was neither being invited to nor informed of any of these meetings, the door leading into Shultz's office suddenly burst open and Charlie Hill, his personal assistant and the State Department's executive secretary, came rushing in.

Hill was a respected FSO with a balanced view of the Middle East and the Arab-Israeli conflict, and we had known each other for several years. We generally saw eye to eye on most Middle East issues, but he had inexplicably grown cold, almost hostile, toward me over the past six months. His eyes locked on mine, Hill glared at me as he sat down next to Shultz. Regrettably, I did not tell George Shultz what had been going on, not then and not later. As I sat watching Hill glare at me, I suddenly understood that Covey was not acting alone. My relationships with Cabinet officers were clearly not appreciated by some in the foreign service. The foreign service lacked institutional authority over me and the secretary's interest in hearing my views threatened its perogatives. I realized that the foreign service was trying to clip my wings and drive me out of the policy-making process by denying me access to papers, meetings and the secretary of state despite the explicit desires of George Shultz. What I didn't understand was why. What had suddenly soured the relationship? This seemed to go beyond simple bureaucratic rivalry. There is an inside term used by foreign service officers, a term that, in some ways, explains one of the major flaws of the foreign service. FSOs describe a colleague who is doing a particularly good job and whose career is moving in the right direction as a "water walker." By doing my job, had I stepped on the toes of one of the designated water walkers?

Shultz asked me again, on several other occasions, why I wasn't involved, why I wasn't coming to his meetings, but it would have been impolitic to accuse his most trusted advisor, Charlie Hill, of deliberately excluding me because the foreign service wanted to control the turf.

I did not understand at the time what had poisoned our basically solid working relationship. Regardless of the desire of the foreign service to have one of its own assume the senior Middle East position at the NSC, and despite Pelletreau's and my desire for the job, we should all be able to work together collegially on issues of vital concern to the United States. Yet the decision was arrogated to the executive secretary, probably the most powerful bureaucrat therein. While I was very disappointed in not getting the job, I was more than prepared to move on and perform my new responsibilities. This was not to be, however, because something had happened which I did not know about until much later.

It was not until the summer of 1987, during the first hour of George Shultz's Iran-Contra testimony, that I learned what might have happened to sour the relationship and why Covey got the job I had been promised. According to Shultz's testimony, when Ambassador Lewis had learned of my secret solicitation of Israel for funds for the Contras in March 1984, Lewis sent a SECRET/STADIS/NODIS/EYES ONLY FOR THE SECRETARY message (STATE DISTRIBUTION ONLY and NO DISTRIBUTION) to Shultz complaining about the activity that had transpired without his knowledge. Shultz testified that he confronted McFarlane with Lewis's cable, reminding him that the two men had agreed that Israel would not be solicited. Shultz testified that McFarlane replied that he had not instructed me to see Kimche or to make the request, and that I "was acting on my own hook." While McFarlane emphatically denies that he ever said this to Shultz about me, it is clear to me that something happened between the two men.

The foreign service, however, resentful of the independent relationship I had established with Secretary Shultz as well as my position on the NSC staff, used the incident as the lever they needed to neutralize me. Only after the Iran-Contra Affair broke and investigators searched McFarlane's most sensitive files did they discover a copy of the memo that explicitly confirmed that I had been instructed unambiguously to solicit funds from Israel. But by then, it was too late—the truth no longer mattered. Everyone advised me not to take it personally.

Then It Will Be on My Conscience

The fighting in Ethiopia and elsewhere in the Horn of Africa during the 1970s and 1980s claimed many victims. Thousands of people became refugees, victims of war and famine. Among them were many Ethiopian Jews. The Jewish community in Ethiopia dated back over two millennia, yet it found itself increasingly unwelcome and abused by the Marxist regime that had toppled Emperor Haile Selassie. The regime, however, refused to allow the Jewish community to leave Ethiopia. Many thousands of Ethiopian Jews living in the northern province of Gondar simply fled north to the refugee camps of southern Sudan. There Israeli officials and Jewish organizations committed to helping rescue oppressed Jewry, primarily from the Soviet Union but also from Arab countries, stepped in to help the Ethiopian Jews migrate to Israel. Beginning in the late 1970s, a secret rescue operation began to evacuate the Jews from the refugee camps in the Sudan.

As the famine of the early 1980s grew more and more severe, the U.S. government began discreetly to assist in the evacuation process by providing diplomatic support with the government of Sudan and logistic and financial assistance. Typically transported to the Khartoum Airport in small groups and flown to Israel on commercial aircraft via a European transit point, several thousand Ethiopian Jews had by the end of 1984 traveled to Israel.

Throughout 1984, the Reagan administration secretly conducted this quiet campaign to help them. Although public pressure on the U.S. government to move the Ethiopians out of the camps in Sudan en masse grew quite intense by the end of 1984, U.S. officials responsible for humanitarian affairs (HA) at the State Department assured Jewish groups that the United States and Israel were quietly cooperating to rescue the Ethiopian Jews. Elements of the secret rescue began to leak in the press, but the operation was able to continue as long as President Nimeiri could plausibly deny Sudanese involvement. Although Arab leaders had known of the operation for some time, they had not made it a political issue. That situation changed when the leaks became front-page news.

In January 1985 I received a telephone call from Richard Kreeger, the State Department official responsible for the program. Very concerned that the program was in danger, he told me that a reporter at the *Washington Jewish Week*, a weekly newspaper devoted to Jewish affairs, had called him. The reporter had learned about the secret program and was intent on revealing the story further in the forthcoming issue of the paper. Kreeger asked me if I could try to stop him.

Although I did not know the reporter, I tried to persuade him to delay the story, at least until after the remaining fifteen hundred Ethiopian Jews were out of the camps and in Israel. "No," he replied, "I am not going to sit on this so that someone else will publish it first." He argued that the story was generally known, so what difference would it make if it ran in the newspaper?

"You don't get it, do you?" I replied. "Hundreds if not thousands of people are dying of starvation in Africa every day. We have a means, however imperfect, to save some of them from certain death. But political reality dictates that we do it quietly or the program will be turned off and the rest of the Ethiopian Jews who are still in the camp at Gedaref may die along with thousands of others who are suffering from the drought. I have no doubt that the government of Sudan will stop the program if this story is further publicized now. If Ethiopian Jews die it will be on your conscience."

He didn't pause for a second before responding, "Then it will be on my conscience, because I am going with this story." As I hung up the phone, in my mind I saw the refugees trying to cling to their squalid lives in the refugee camps that I had visited in Somalia in December 1980. Conditions were far worse now due to devastating drought. I prayed that Nimeiri would find the courage to let the airlift continue.

The story ran in the *Washington Jewish Week* and the international press, prompting howls of outraged protest throughout the Arab world. Nimeiri acted surprised by the revelations and ordered the Sudanese Security Organization to stop its cooperation with our efforts. The airlift of Ethiopian Jewish refugees was abruptly terminated.

In late February, as international concern for the victims of the African drought grew rapidly (rock stars produced "We Are the World" to raise money for relief organizations), Vice President Bush decided to travel to Africa in order to discuss U.S. humanitarian assistance policies and visit refugee camps to demonstrate America's official concern.

At the same time, with a new counterterrorism policy in place, the United States intensified its pressure on King Hassan to repudiate the Oujda Accords he had signed the preceding year with Muammar Qadhafi. There had been no change in Libya's ongoing support and direction of international terror. Surprised at Washington's continuing displeasure with Morocco, Hassan dispatched Foreign Minister Abdel Latif Filali to the United States to try to resolve the dispute. I met with the Moroccan ambassador to explain to him that it would be of no use for Filali to explain and promise change. The United States would not turn a blind eye to Qadhafi's support for international terrorism despite Hassan's belief that his approach was better than the isolationism promoted by Washington. Unless Morocco chose to annul the accords, it could expect the chill in relations to endure.

Hassan undoubtedly received the message. Filali later explained to Bush and McFarlane that Hassan would find a way to step away from the Oujda Accords, even though they would not be abrogated. The United States should not underestimate King Hassan's friendship for the United States, but Maghreb affairs were not simply a matter of black and white. Although no real progress was made in moving Hassan away from the accords, the tenor of Filali's dialogue with the United States improved, despite concerted congressional efforts to cut Morocco's foreign aid as punishment. The Oujda Accords actually survived until the fall of 1986, when Qadhafi himself abrogated them in anger following the August 1986 visit to Morocco of Israel's Shimon Peres.

At the conclusion of the meeting with Filali, I accompanied McFarlane to his West Wing office in order to discuss something with him, namely a plan to rescue the remaining Ethiopian Jews who were stuck in Gedaref. The number remaining in the camps at the time the rescue program was terminated was around 1,500. "Why not fly a C-5 Galaxy [the Air Force's largest cargo plane] into Gedaref loaded with relief supplies and then fly out at night with the remaining Ethiopian Jews," I suggested. "The vice president will be in Khartoum in two weeks and can raise the matter privately with Nimeiri. If Nimeiri agrees, the United States can save lives while demonstrating that it has the will to undertake politically controversial humanitarian acts."

McFarlane agreed immediately and went to see Bush in order to seek his concurrence. The vice president liked the idea and said he would be pleased to raise the proposal with Nimeiri if Reagan authorized the activity. McFarlane directed me to draft a decision memo for the president, laying out the facts of the earlier program's abrupt termination and the pros and cons of my new idea. On Bush's recommendation, Reagan promptly approved the proposal, and the wheels were set in motion. As planned, during his private meeting with Nimeiri, Bush proposed that the United States fly out the remaining Ethiopian Jews who had been stranded in the Gedaref camp. Publicity having died down, Nimeiri agreed and dispatched the chief of his security organization to Washington to work out the details. After two days of talks, an agreement was reached that the airlift would take place one night in March.

Although Sudan is considered by regional experts to be part of the Middle East, U.S.-Sudanese relations are actually the responsibility of the African Affairs Bureau at the State Department. With the assistant secretary, Chester Crocker, tied up in the "constructive engagement" process with South Africa, Principal DAS Princeton Lyman was assigned the responsibility of overseeing this covert airlift on behalf of State. A respected, knowledgeable career FSO, Lyman had played an important role in the previous Ethiopian airlift. For substantive reasons, he was leery of the United States' undertaking such a dramatic initiative, preferring to wait until the incremental approach could be resumed. However, once Reagan had made his decision and Nimeiri had agreed to the request, Lyman quickly organized a small interagency team composed of State, Defense, CIA and NSC representatives to implement the rescue. Meeting at Lyman's home on a Saturday afternoon, we were joined by the Israeli official responsible for the Ethiopian Jews.

Until this point, the government of Israel had not been informed that the United States intended to go in itself to save those Jews left behind. The Israeli official was very excited when Lyman briefed him on the president's decision and our readiness to act. In the circumstances, no Israeli agents had visited the camps for over one month, and it was not clear whether more Ethiopian Jews had arrived or departed from Gedaref. We agreed that an Israeli "shepherd" would be dispatched to the camp to organize the community for the airlift and update the team on the total number to be evacuated.

Operation Batsheva was scheduled to commence the following Thursday night, March 21. Command of the operation was assigned to CENTCOM, while the Military Airlift Command (MAC) was responsible for the planning and execution of the airlift. Owing to the primitive conditions at the Gedaref airfield, MAC argued against the use of a C-5, and the decision was made to use smaller, propeller-driven C-130 aircraft in their place. The C-130s could accommodate approximately a hundred passengers each, necessitating a staggered schedule of arrivals and departures. Meeting with the CENTCOM and the Air Force commanders of the mission on Tuesday, I briefed them on the people they would be flying out of Sudan. I noted that for most of the Ethiopian Jews this would be their first ride in an airplane. While the shepherds would do their best to maintain sanitary conditions and discipline, they should prepare themselves and their crews for communications difficulties. Special sensitivity would be required to avoid misunderstandings or unnecessary embarrassment.

On Tuesday afternoon, the shepherd and the CENTCOM on-scene commander arrived at Gedaref to set up communications and to organize the refugees for the airlift. Midday in Washington, we were advised that over one thousand Ethiopian Jews had perished, mostly from disease and dehydration, since the airlift had been terminated. Just under five hundred remained alive.

Jim Bishop, the acting assistant secretary of state for African affairs, asked me to come to his office to discuss this disturbing news. When I arrived, he wasted no time coming to the point. "We in State do not believe that the United States should proceed with this operation for only five hundred people," Bishop said. "The risks to our position in Sudan and the region if the story leaks are too great. Please inform the vice president of this recommendation." Looking him squarely in the eye, I said, "Jim, are you sure this is a recommendation that you want to put to the vice president? I will have to tell him that this recommendation comes from you." Bishop did not hesitate. "You can tell him that I don't think it's worth it to the U.S."

Thinking of the one thousand dead and pondering Bishop's comment that saving five hundred lives was not worth the risk, I called Rich Armitage to assess the Pentagon's attitude toward proceeding with the operation. Armitage, to his credit, was unfazed by the bad news from the field. "Look, we're ready to go. The secretary's on board. I don't think our position in the region will be affected if we do this, whether it leaks or not. The damage has already been done with the leaks three months ago."

As I walked down the ornate hallway of the Old Executive Office Building (OEOB) to meet with Don Gregg, Bush's NSC advisor, I couldn't help thinking about America's failure to lift a finger to save European Jewry from Hitler's final solution. Yet here we were, two days away from conducting an operation that would save five hundred people from almost certain death, and a colleague in the State Department argued—out loud—that saving their lives simply wasn't worth the risk.

I briefed Gregg on the situation in the camps and informed him of Jim Bishop's recommendation. He didn't pause. "The vice president is not going to agree to cancel the operation," Gregg replied. "I hope he won't, Don," I answered, "but we have an obligation to inform him of State's opposition." Bush was tied up in another meeting when Gregg asked if he could come in and talk to him. He promised to put the question to him and give me his answer as soon as possible. Less than an hour later Gregg called to say that "the vice president is not interested in State's recommendation that ambiguous political risks outweigh the benefits of saving five hundred lives. Please inform the bureaucracy of his decision to proceed." To his credit, George Bush was determined not to repeat the mistakes of the past, despite the potential political costs.

By coincidence, Dennis Ross, who had since returned to California where he was the director of the Berkeley-Stanford Center for Soviet Affairs, had invited me to give a lecture on U.S. Middle East policy at the University of California, Berkeley, on Friday, March 22. I called the National Military Command Center (NMCC) as soon as I arrived in Berkeley to check on the status of the operation. Sitting with Dennis and Debby Ross in their kitchen with an open phone line while the hours passed, we were all on edge as we waited to see if the rescue operation would succeed.

The NMCC (formerly called the war room) is the nerve center of the

Pentagon, equipped with the most advanced communications technology available. Bishop was in the NMCC monitoring the operation when I called. Through a dedicated satellite channel, a communications line was being kept open to Gedaref in the event something unforeseen happened that required an instant decision. However, there were no problems, and the CENTCOM commander was reporting that people and airplanes were moving almost exactly on schedule. The C-130s started to arrive in Israel Friday morning without mishap, having flown out of Sudan and due north to Israel over the Red Sea.

The first plane of Ethiopian Jewish refugees was greeted by Prime Minister Shimon Peres and Ambassador Sam Lewis, who later described the scene as one of the most emotional events he had ever experienced. "Especially the U.S. Air Force pilots," said Lewis. "One pilot, nearly moved to tears, told me that rescuing these people 'was more worthwhile than anything else I have ever done.' " The U.S. military is often called upon to perform humanitarian missions around the world, typically involving the delivery of food, medicine or other emergency supplies to crisis situations. In this case, they did honor to themselves and to their country. Operation Batsheva represented a welcome departure from the past, as the U.S. government demonstrated that it would not permit bureaucratic hand-wringing and fears of an Arab backlash to prevent America from saving Jewish lives.

Operation Batsheva did not stay secret for long, however. Coincidentally, a journalist for *The Los Angeles Times* happened to be in Gedaref doing a story on the Ethiopian Jews. In preparation for the evening operation, the Sudanese security had sequestered him in his hut for the night without explanation. Although the reporter could hear the C-130s during the night, it was only the following morning that he realized what had happened, when he went back to resume his interviews and found everyone gone. He drove back to Khartoum and filed his story, but was forced to hide in the U.S. embassy once the Sudanese security officials found out.

Some in the U.S. government argue that the subsequent coup that overthrew Nimeiri and ushered in a series of Islamic fundamentalist, anti-American regimes demonstrated that the U.S. opponents of the rescue were correct and that the mistrust Operation Batsheva generated would endure for a long time. But Nimeiri was overthrown by military officers who were fed up with seventeen years of erratic rule and economic chaos. The show trials of Vice President Omar Tayib, the head of the security services and other Sudanese close to Nimeiri resulted from pent-up hostility toward the institutional corruption that had become commonplace in Sudan. Had Operation Batsheva not occurred prior to the April coup, given the nature of the successor regime and the subsequent violence that engulfed southern Sudan, it is safe to say that none of the remaining Ethiopian Jews would have left Gedaref alive, but the Sudan would still have come under the rule of Islamic fundamentalists.

The performance of Vice President Bush during this episode was particularly impressive. When it came time to show political and moral courage, he rose to the occasion, and lives were saved because he acted on the very best of impulses. Looking back, I compare Bush's activism in this episode to the foreign policy role he assumed throughout most of the Reagan presidency. There was never any question that Bush preferred working on foreign policy issues. He was as well informed on substance as any member of the National Security Council. During my five years as a member of the NSC staff, I participated in over seventy meetings with the vice president on issues ranging from crisis management in Lebanon and the Persian Gulf to his regular meetings with foreign dignitaries. We met privately on many occasions for in-depth briefings and discussions of Middle East issues. It was a pleasure to talk with Bush about foreign policy, given his knowledge, experience and genuine interest.

Having served as CIA director, envoy to China and ambassador to the United Nations, Bush had impressive foreign policy credentials. Because of his active involvement in the foreign-policy decision-making process and his frequent overseas travel as vice president, he was fully cognizant of the harm to American influence caused by the polarization of U.S. national security policy. The stalemate between the secretary of defense and the secretary of state damaged America's ability to advance and protect vital interests and would continue to paralyze U.S. policy as long as it was not resolved by the president. Regardless of whose view was correct or what argument made the most substantive or political sense, presidential decisions should have been implemented. Perhaps it was this foreign policy depth that encouraged me to expect that Bush would take more initiative and at least deliver the "bad news" to Reagan about the divisions among his advisors and the need for Reagan to provide determined leadership.

During the Reagan administration, however, very little was ever finally settled or resolved. There were no winners or losers, because endgames could always be played. This was apparent to everyone in the National Security Council, especially to the vice president. Reagan's failure to exert presidential leadership and ensure that his policies were developed and implemented with disciplined coherence damaged the national security of the United States. Bush knew this. But during the course of NSC meetings, where there was almost always dialogue and debate, Bush generally kept silent. The vice president often said publicly that he would not discuss what he told President Reagan in private. Bush was particularly well versed in the intricacies of diplomacy and policy and prided himself on his experience in foreign affairs. He was in a prime position to advise the president. But if he did advise the president in private to settle the differences among his advisors, his advice was not heeded. Whether he weighed in on behalf of Shultz or Weinberger, or whether he simply was resigned to "let Reagan be Reagan," no one knows. The debilitating stalemate continued. Except when we received the hot-line message after the Israeli invasion of Lebanon, when Bush acted assertively to take charge of the situation, the vice president seemed to do little more than carefully follow international events and national security issues, while shrewdly keeping his cards close to his vest. Bush's forthright and courageous action to save the Ethiopian Jews represented a rare exception to his otherwise predictable behavior.

CHAPTER 13

MARRAKECH TO BANGLADESH

---◆---

The Conundrum

My responsibilities for the balance of 1985 and 1986 included managing the interagency process to reach agreement for a southwest Asia security strategy. The strategy needed to protect U.S. interests, create opportunities for expanding American influence throughout that region and cope with the surge in international terrorism. The challenge for the United States in the Persian Gulf was to devise and implement a strategy to defeat the Russians in Afghanistan, and to deal with the ebbs and flows of the Iran-Iraq War, Khomeini's growing frailty and possible Soviet activism in the wake of his death, the direct link between Tehran's most radical elements and the Hizbollah movement in Lebanon, and the proliferating, evolving ties between Baghdad and Washington.

President Reagan's March 1985 decision to broaden the goals and scope of the U.S. covert action program aiding the Afghan Mujahadeen followed a dramatic escalation of Soviet military strategy and tactics in Afghanistan. For over a year, Soviet Spetsnaz (special forces) and armored helicopter gunships had been destroying rebel bases and interdicting supply lines, and had begun to weaken significantly the will of the Mujahadeen to continue their resistance. Among other things, the Mujahadeen lacked the weapons systems and command and control structures that could enable them to rebuff Soviet military operations.

Since the Soviet invasion of Afghanistan during the Carter administration, Congress and the Executive had cooperated to implement a covert action program that raised the cost of Moscow's attempt to consolidate its control of Afghanistan. However, by 1984 the fundamental challenge to U.S. policy was whether and how to counter this Soviet escalation without provoking an expansion of the war into Pakistan or Iran. Were Soviet forces to enter either country, the increased threat to vital

U.S. interests in the Gulf would compel Washington to intervene directly.

Under the direction of Don Fortier and Vince Cannistraro at the NSC, the national security bureaucracy spent nearly one year debating a wide range of policy options before reaching a consensus on a new U.S. policy toward Afghanistan. After a meeting of the NSPG in March 1985, the president signed an NSDD directing the bureaucracy to increase significantly the level of U.S. military assistance to the Mujahadeen in order to enhance the ability of the resistance to defeat the Soviet Union in Afghanistan. In addition to providing larger quantities of sophisticated military hardware, the United States began taking a more direct role in the intelligence, communications and operational planning functions necessary to conduct preemptive strikes against the Spetsnaz and the regular Soviet Army. The new policy was initially successful until the Soviets adapted by modifying their tactical use of MI-24 helicopter gunships. The MI-24 was a fierce weapons system that had been in use by the Soviets since the early days of the war, but was proving decisive when combined with Spetsnaz operations, particularly at night. It was essential to neutralize the MI-24s.

President Reagan had directed that the Mujahadeen be provided with the means to defeat the Soviets. By the summer of 1985, an interagency coalition comprised of the OSD, the State Department, the NSC and several members of Congress argued that the Mujahadeen should be provided with Stinger missiles, which were sophisticated, hand-held surface-to-air missiles capable of bringing down the MI-24 helicopters. The Stinger had only recently been introduced into the U.S. military order of battle. The CIA (except for Casey) and the JCS argued against providing Stingers to the Mujahadeen, even though it had become clear that the older SAMs being employed by the Mujahadeen were not capable of defeating the Soviet helicopter threat. The CIA and JCS argued persuasively that the Stingers might end up in the hands of terrorists, or worse the Iranians, and be used against American interests. The CIA also maintained that providing the Afghan resistance with a weapon that could only have come from the United States would eliminate any semblance of plausible deniability in Washington, and increase the likelihood of Soviet action against Pakistan.

The issue was debated for over a year. However, in June 1986 the Mujahadeen began to receive Stingers and used them effectively against the MI-24s. Coupled with a systematic campaign of well-organized Mujahadeen guerrilla attacks on Soviet command posts, bridges, storage depots and other high-value targets throughout Afghanistan, the Soviet position began to erode as the momentum shifted to the Mujahadeen. Less than two years later, Moscow announced that its forces would withdraw from Afghanistan.

Although we appeared to be winning the Great Game in Afghanistan, the United States seemed to be increasingly under siege throughout the rest of southwest Asia. With the fall of Nimeiri in Sudan in April 1985 and the prompt increase in Libyan influence in Khartoum and threats against Egypt, it initially appeared that Qadhafi's exertions would once again dominate U.S. analysis and action against international terrorism.

But the counterterrorism focus widened significantly, less than two months later, when TWA Flight 847 was seized and held for seventeen days by Hizbollah. Although the operation came under the control of Syria through its Shia ally in Lebanon, Nabih Berri, we soon learned that Tehran held the key to releasing the thirty-nine TWA passengers. In October, the *Achille Lauro* cruise ship was captured by Palestinian terrorists. In November, an Egyptair flight was skyjacked by the Abu Nidal group and sixty people were killed. In late December, Abu Nidal terrorists attempted unsuccessfully to seize airplanes in Rome and Vienna airports, murdering twenty persons and wounding numerous others during the attempt.

As 1985 came to an end, U.S. efforts and international cooperation in combating terrorism were barely in first gear, yet it was increasingly clear that the terrorists and their state sponsors were succeeding. Blustering American rhetoric, absent the willingness to confront the terrorists, would not succeed in deterring attacks against Americans and American interests. The restoration of U.S. military capability to wage conventional war still left America with a highly vulnerable Achilles' heel.

The development of an interagency policy initiative requires the coherent merger of diverse individual perspectives with equally diverse institutional interests and biases. It is a challenging and frequently hazardous undertaking, often characterized by the tendency of discussions and classified papers to be leaked to the media as a means of influencing policy. The purpose of such a process is to (1) get different agencies to agree on the definition of a problem; (2) analyze the current and prospective factors that influence it; (3) identify and analyze a range of factors that might solve a problem; and (4) draft policy guidance that the president can approve and issue to the government. Sometimes the process works and sometimes it doesn't. In the case of the long-studied U.S. security strategy for southwest Asia, the process failed miserably.

Although there were a number of individual initiatives already under way, such as the very successful covert support for the Afghan rebels and the strengthening of regional military infrastructure capable of supporting the rapid deployment of U.S. forces, the U.S. government lacked a comprehensive strategy for protecting American interests and advancing American influence in an evolutionary manner in southwest Asia, an area that stretched from Marrakech in the west to Bangladesh in the east.

During the first half of 1985, I regularly convened meetings with representatives of State, OSD, JCS, CIA, Treasury, Energy and Commerce, who collectively made up the Senior Interdepartmental Group (SIG), to methodically develop a security strategy for southwest Asia. By the spring of 1985, the SIG concluded that given Iran's historic, geostrategic importance, the establishment of a dialogue between the United States and Iran would significantly contribute to America's ability to protect its vital interests throughout southwest Asia. Over time, such a dialogue could lead to a reduction in hostilities between the two countries. No one working in the national security bureaucracy on southwest Asia had any illusions that the government of Iran would suddenly come to view the United States as a friend instead of as the Great Satan. Yet it was clear that it would benefit the United States if means could be devised to alter Iran's hostile attitude and actions and reduce Tehran's substantial support for international terrorism and radical Islamic movements.

Such changes would be difficult to accomplish in the best of circumstances, which these certainly were not. Because of Khomeini's advanced age and poor health, the succession struggle had already begun. Within the SIG, different views emerged from the intelligence community about the prospects for Soviet gains in Iran. The intelligence community was united in its belief that the Soviet Union would try to take advantage of the succession struggle to enhance its influence in Tehran. However, the community was divided over the Soviets' prospects for success. In any case, the SIG had to consider the worst-case scenario. The United States could not afford to be sanguine about the potential for its position in the Gulf to erode as that of the Soviet Union was enhanced. Although the SIG worked efficiently and collegially to draft papers and agree on numerous goals, interests, regional trends, threats and policy options, one issue remained irreconcilable: U.S. policy toward Iran. The members of the group all agreed it would benefit U.S. interests for relations with Iran to improve. Where we disagreed was the price the United States should be willing to pay in order to accomplish that objective.

Don Fortier, the deputy NSC advisor, and I agreed with the position of the NIO for the Middle East, Graham Fuller, that U.S. policy toward Iran needed to change quickly in order to enhance America's ability to protect its vital interests and deal with the vicissitudes of Iranian politics. As clearly evidenced by the history of arms sales in the Middle East, whether to Saudi Arabia, Jordan, Iran, Israel or Egypt, the coin of influence in that part of the world is arms. The United States could not expect to improve relations with revolutionary Iran unless it was prepared to offer the Iranians something of sufficient value to offset the political risks of engaging with Washington. America's vital interests were at stake, involving oil and competition for influence with the Soviet Union. We argued that indirect means of providing low-tech weaponry to Iran were worth exploring in order to establish communications channels and build the stake of the emerging pragmatic factions in improved relations with the West.

The Iranians bitterly resented growing U.S. support for Iraq. Although the United States was officially neutral in the Iran-Iraq War, for several years Iraq had been provided with ever-increasing amounts of tactical and strategic intelligence information in order to prevent an Iranian victory. Furthermore, in order to keep the sea-lanes open in the face of Iranian threats, the United States had deployed naval power to the Gulf, challenging Tehran. Increased state-sponsored terror, in Lebanon and elsewhere, represented Khomeini's response to America's tilt to Iraq.

Under current policy toward Iran, the United States could not move to improve bilateral relations until Tehran agreed to a cease-fire and political solution to the war with Iraq and ended its sponsorship of international terrorism. The potential volatility of the U.S.-Iranian relationship prevented any exploratory movement to try to reduce tension and begin to move toward normal relations. While there was general agreement that the situation was frustrating for U.S. interests, there were no other suggestions on how to break the impasse. Both Murphy and Armitage agreed that weapons could have value in establishing an opening to Iran, but they strongly opposed any initiative that would involve making arms available to Tehran, directly or indirectly.

Following the normalization of relations with Iraq in November 1984, a new U.S.-Iraqi relationship quickly developed. Elements within State, Defense, Commerce and the CIA intensified their respective bureaucratic stakes in U.S. cooperation with Iraq. Operation Stanch, the U.S. effort to stop the flow of weapons to Iran in order to pressure Tehran to agree to a cease-fire, became somewhat of a cottage industry for many in the national security bureaucracy in Washington and overseas. Establishment of an embassy in Baghdad created a plum assignment in the Arab world.

The intelligence community systematically expanded its role in support of Iraq's defensive needs in order to establish a normal liaison relationship with Iraqi counterparts that might provide useful information on the Soviet Union, Syria, Iran and other targets for intelligence collection. In addition, the Pentagon still wanted to acquire a Soviet-manufactured T-72 tank as well as other advanced Soviet military hardware possessed by the Iraqis. But Iraq wanted to maintain its relationship with the Soviet Union due to its reliance on Moscow for military hardware and to play off the superpowers against each other. Baghdad continued to refuse to provide Washington the tank. On the commercial level, the Iraqis rapidly increased their requests for agricultural credits, increasing the stake of American farmers in the U.S.-Iraqi relationship, while U.S. exporters rushed into Iraq in order to compete with the already entrenched Europeans and Japanese.

Recalling the notion of Iraq as a counterweight to Syria and Iran during America's futile efforts in Lebanon, some representatives from State, Defense and Commerce argued that if the Iran-Iraq War could be brought to a peaceful end without victor or vanquished, a rebuilt and prosperous Iraq could assume the role that Iran once played to ensure the security of the Gulf, while cooperating with Saudi Arabia to maintain stability in the world oil markets. In other words, the United States should help Iraq replace Iran as America's pillar in the Gulf.

I strenuously disagreed with the notion that Iraq could serve either as a long-term counterweight to Iran or as a stabilizing force in the Gulf. We all had access to the same information about Iraq's nuclear, biological and chemical weapons programs. We continued to receive reports of Iraq's support for international terrorism, Iraq's 1982 removal from the terrorism list notwithstanding. The use of chemical weapons reinforced my conviction that Saddam Hussein had not changed his goals or personal ruthlessness. Only his masks had changed in order to buy time and gain the political, technical and financial assistance of the West, assistance he needed to survive the war with Iran. I agreed that the United States could not, in the short term, afford to permit Iran to conquer Iraq and establish a militant Islamic regime in Baghdad. But to achieve this limited goal, it was not necessary that the United States bestow "most favored nation" status on Iraq. Iraq or Iran, that was the question.

At the end of April 1985, I advised McFarlane that the interagency process on southwest Asia strategy was deadlocked over the question of policy toward Iran. He encouraged me to keep pushing the bureaucracy to be creative while he discussed the issue with Shultz, Weinberger and Casey. In mid-May, I received a draft Special National Intelligence Estimate (SNIE) from Graham Fuller. Fuller and I often disagreed about U.S. policy in the Middle East, particularly with regard to U.S.-Syrian relations and the Arab-Israeli peace process, although we respected each other's opinions. But he had grown increasingly concerned with the potential for instability in Iran, the prospects for Soviet meddling at U.S. expense and the growing imbalance caused by our tilt toward Iraq. He argued in the SNIE that the United States should assume a more realistic posture in the Gulf to enhance our ability to protect our own interests and not be hobbled by a position defined solely by Iran's attitude toward a cease-fire and support for terrorism. After all, it was Iraq that had invaded Iran in 1980, that had begun to use chemical weapons and that started the tanker war. Other countries, most notably Syria, were well known to support terrorism, yet the United States continued to maintain full diplomatic relations with them. As it had before, Iran still represented the strategic prize in the modern Great Game.

McFarlane agreed with Fuller's analysis and directed Fortier and me to draft an NSDD. The NSDD was based on Fuller's analysis and draft SNIE along with the nearly three years of interagency work that had been accomplished through the SIG. We forwarded a draft NSDD to McFarlane on June 11, 1985, three days before the skyjacking of TWA flight 847. The NSDD argued that in order to improve the U.S. strategic position in the Persian Gulf, the United States should establish a dialogue with Iranian leaders who might be receptive to efforts to improve relations with the United States while enhancing America's ability to influence Tehran to agree to a peaceful settlement of the Iran-Iraq War. The draft proposed several measures to achieve these goals, including a proposal that the United States encourage Western allies and friends to help Iran meet its import requirements so as to reduce the appeal of Soviet assistance and trade offers, while demonstrating the value of correct relations with the West. The proposal included the provision of selected military equipment to Iran as determined on a case-by-case basis.

Fortier was excited by the draft NSDD, confident that McFarlane would be able to convince Shultz and Weinberger to be open-minded about the value of reaching out to Iran. I was less optimistic. Despite the administration's preoccupation with the TWA hijacking, McFarlane distributed the draft to Shultz, Casey and Weinberger on June 17. But by the end of the week the deadlock on a Southwest Asia security strategy endured. Neither Shultz nor Weinberger would countenance any arms to Iran. They were totally opposed. By the end of the month, McFarlane told me to "stand down and file the draft NSDD. I cannot overcome their strenuous opposition to the initiative."

The hijacking of TWA Flight 847 immediately polarized the bureaucracy. Bush, Weinberger, Vessey, Casey and the majority of the foreign service held Israel responsible for the U.S. dilemma, owing to its detention in Atlit prison of hundreds of Lebanese Shias who had been captured during the war in Lebanon. Pressure Israel to release its captives and the TWA passengers would be released, they argued. The terrorists, however, also demanded the release of the Dawa Seventeen held in Kuwait.

By contrast, regardless of their attitude toward Israeli policy toward the Shias, Shultz and McFarlane did not want to reward the terrorists by succumbing to their demands. If the United States could squeeze the Israelis, then it could squeeze the Kuwaitis. Since the United States had not managed to rescue Bill Buckley, the CIA station chief, whom Hizbollah had abducted in March 1984, the Syrian and Iranian mentors of the Lebanese terrorists felt confident that Washington would threaten to act but in the end would not.

The terrorists calculated correctly. The administration had decided not to use force against them, although a range of special military operations had been contemplated to attempt to rescue the hostages and close Beirut International Airport.

With the military options ruled out, several quiet channels of communication were opened to Israel and Kuwait to devise a way to trade hostages for prisoners without admitting to the existence of linkage. Following Israel's unilateral release of thirty-one prisoners, McFarlane instructed me to contact Zvili Ben Moshe, an advisor to Defense Minister Yitzhak Rabin, in order to confirm that as more releases took place, both Jerusalem and Washington would state that there was no linkage between the Israeli actions and the hostage situation in Beirut.

If Only You Were Older

On the fourth day of the crisis, June 18, the president of Tunisia, Habib Bourguiba, visited the White House for an official working visit. The visit had been planned for over six months. In order to convey an impression of business as usual despite the hostage crisis, Bourguiba's visit remained on the schedule. The United States and Tunisia maintained strong political and military ties and shared a growing concern over Libyan hostility toward Tunis. Qadhafi had recently called for "the liberation of Tunisia" and urged the Moslems of Tunis to kill Tunisian Jews. In response, Bourguiba invited the Libyan foreign minister to his office, read him the riot act and then threw him out before giving the Libyan the chance to reply. Reagan planned to assure Bourguiba that the United States would continue to be ready to respond to Tunisian requests for assistance in the face of Libyan threats.

Although eighty-five years old, Bourguiba showed no sign of voluntarily stepping down from the presidency and remained relatively vigorous. In fact, we regularly received reports that, despite his age, Bourguiba continued to maintain a certain fondness for women other than his wife, a situation which led to frequent domestic quarrels and some significant political maneuvering by Madame Bourguiba. In the circumstances and given the state of Tunisian domestic politics, we had reason to believe that Madame Bourguiba was planning to manipulate a social tea hosted by the First Lady, Nancy Reagan, into a "secret White House meeting." I was obliged to include references to the Bourguibas' domestic relations in my briefing memoranda to the President and Mrs. Reagan.

This meeting would be Don Regan's first encounter with a foreign head of state in his new capacity as White House chief of staff, having recently swapped jobs with James Baker. In the Oval Office prebrief at eleven o'clock that morning, Shultz set aside his briefing materials on Tunisia in order to update the president on the TWA Flight 847 hostage situation. Before Shultz could begin, however, Don Regan interrupted. He turned to me and told me I had written a great memo. He then asked whether there were any more details that I could provide about Bourguiba's affections for younger women. Startled by Regan's question, I merely shook my head. Regan and the president praised Bourguiba's robust appetite and then started to tell a series of ribald jokes involving old Irish men. Both the president and the chief of staff were almost overcome by laughter. Shultz gave me a quizzical look and, shaking his head, leaned back in the overstuffed sofa to wait out the comedy routine.

The president met privately in the Oval Office with President Bourguiba for thirty minutes and then joined the rest of the Tunisian and American delegations in the adjoining Cabinet Room for an exchange of views on regional and bilateral issues. The TWA hijacking, Libyan subversion and Tunisia's growing economic and military needs dominated the meeting. The discussions were conducted in both French and English with simultaneous interpretation provided by Sophie Porson, a senior State Department interpreter. Fifteen minutes into the meeting, President

Bourguiba leaned across the table and exclaimed in French to Ms. Porson, "If only you were fifteen years older or I were fifteen years younger, things might happen with us." Stunned by this outburst, Porson was speechless. Reagan and several others who did not understand French turned around to ask Ms. Porson what he had said, while those of us who understood gaped in awe. Porson blushed, mumbled something incomprehensible, and Bourguiba returned to his monologue. However, two other times during the course of the Cabinet Room meeting he made similar comments to Porson, which she was compelled to translate to the embarrassed amusement of the participants. After the third such outburst, Bourguiba's son openly elbowed his father sharply in the chest and harshly whispered that he was humiliating all of them. Reagan, and Porson, took it in stride and the visit ended without further incident. As Bourguiba and his delegation drove away following the departure statements, the president turned to me and said, "Howard, you sure called him right."

TWA Flight 847

On June 25, a week after the Bourguiba visit, the White House spokesman began to drop hints that Reagan's patience in the hijacking had just about run its course and that the use of force was no longer ruled out. Through various means, the United States had detected a high level of Syrian communications back and forth with the Shia leader and the two Iranians directly responsible for Iran's links with Hizbollah, Ambassador Mohtashami-Pur and Mohsen Rafiq-Dust, the leader of the Pasdaran in Lebanon. Nabih Berri was the Amal leader who essentially hijacked the hijackers in order to exploit the media coverage and try to build international sympathy for the plight of the Lebanese Shia community. In the middle of this tense situation, a high-level Iranian delegation led by Speaker of the Iranian Parliament (Majlis) Ali Akbar Hashemi Rafsanjani arrived unexpectedly in Damascus to meet with Assad and Khaddam. Following the meeting, Rafsanjani announced to the international media that Iran would have tried to prevent the hijacking of TWA 847 if the Iranian government had known anything about it.

The terrorists had succeeded in exploiting the international media to the maximum extent possible. Talk show hosts were actually interviewing Nabih Berri on television, while American hostages on the airplane languished in the background. All of us involved in this crisis were besieged by reporters' phone calls looking for leaks and tidbits of information. In light of the apparent impact of this implied U.S. threat to use force and the intense interest of Nabih Berri in using the American media, I suggested to McFarlane that we try to turn the heat up a little further by imposing a "news blackout" on the U.S. government. A news blackout might suggest that perhaps the Reagan administration had finally managed to stop the endless leaks to the press and that some action was imminent. The tactic was approved and Larry Speakes was directed to announce it.

Chris Wallace of NBC News immediately called me to ask what was up. "Absolutely no comment, Chris. Figure it out for yourself." All the networks reported the blackout, speculating that the abrupt silence indicated something ominous. The situation rapidly began to change. It took several more days before the final arrangement to release the hostages into Syrian custody were concluded. The scheduled release was delayed by one day when Hizbollah took back four of the hostages, apparently out of fear that the United States might retaliate against the Shia community.

The Iranians and Syrians spoke with Hizbollah, who demanded a guarantee that there would be no retaliation by the United States. I was in the Situation Room when a cable from Ambassador Eagleton in Damascus arrived asking for a public statement confirming that the United States would not strike at Lebanon once the hostages were released. I drafted a short statement that reaffirmed the U.S. commitment to the security of Lebanon and asked McFarlane to approve its release. It was issued by the State Department at ten P.M. The thirty-nine TWA hostages were released into Syrian custody the following day. The seven others who had been taken at different times by Hizbollah as bargaining chips for the Dawa Seventeen, however, remained in captivity.

Tehran's influence over the Hizbollah was obvious. Syrian involvement was also clear. Assad evidenced concern that the United States might lose patience and act violently against Amal, his principal ally among the Shia of Beirut. I suggested to McFarlane that the Tehran-Damascus axis continued to deserve our attention. Numerous hostages had already been taken and Americans had been killed in this unconventional war being waged against the United States. Despite the renewed commitment to build up our Special Forces, it did not seem likely that the United States would actually use force. Why not try to communicate with pragmatists like Rafsanjani, rather than hope that the radicals would eventually moderate their behavior as a result of U.S. isolation? McFarlane shook his head and told me to just forget about it. Rafsanjani had played a critical role in helping bring the TWA hijacking to an end, yet the notion of finding a way to improve relations with Iran was apparently dead. At least that is what I was led to believe. I decided it was time to take no for an answer.

Achille Lauro

The next terrorist attack came three months later, on October 7, when an Italian cruise ship, the Achille Lauro, was seized by members of the Palestine Liberation Front (PLF). The PLF was a militant PLO faction controlled by Abu Abbas, a long-time comrade of Yasir Arafat and a member of the PLO Executive Council. Taking to heart the lesson that terrorism succeeds when a gun is held to America's head as a means to coerce Israel to take action, the PLF demanded that Israel immediately release fifty convicted PLO terrorists in exchange for releasing the ship.

Admiral Poindexter, then deputy NSC advisor, convened the inter-agency Terrorist Incident Working Group (TIWG) to manage the crisis. The Joint Special Operations Command (JSOC) Delta and SEAL Team Six counterterrorism commandos were instructed to deploy to the region and position themselves to act should an opportunity to free the ship and rescue the hostages arise.

The JSOC forces were commanded by Brigadier General Carl Stiner, with whom I had worked during the McFarlane and Rumsfeld missions. A self-effacing leader, Stiner was the model special-operations warrior. Under fire in Beirut he had remained cool and deliberate even when the windows were shot out of his car in the middle of a bizarre firefight between Phalangist and Druze militias. His leadership style and calm demeanor inspired trust in the soldiers and diplomats who looked to him for advice during battle. Unlike the hostage situations in Beirut, where terrorists were able to take cover behind the innocent to shield themselves from retribution, the Achille Lauro was on the high seas. The chances for a successful rescue operation were better.

While reading the incoming cable traffic through the night, Oliver North and I suddenly realized that the Achille Lauro had stopped using its radio and was maneuvering erratically. With JSOC in the region ready to launch a rescue attempt, the pirated ship had seemingly vanished. Late Tuesday afternoon the terrorists gave themselves away by asking for permission to dock in the Syrian port of Tartus. But Assad wanted nothing to do with pro-Arafat Palestinian terrorists, and permission was denied.

Refusing to take no for an answer, and recalling how Hizbollah's cold-blooded murder of U.S. Navy diver Robert Stethem had successfully intimidated the authorities at Beirut International Airport during the TWA hijacking, the *Achille Lauro* pirates informed Syrian port authorities they would start killing hostages if their demands were not met. At three P.M., Tartus still refusing to grant entry, Leon Klinghoffer, a wheelchair-bound American tourist, was executed and his body thrown overboard. Intercepting the communications between the ship and the port authorities, the U.S. and Israeli services were instantly aware that killing might have begun. JSOC forces were ordered to prepare to assault the ship as it steamed through the night back to Port Said, Egypt, where it had begun its fateful journey.

The government of Egypt negotiated a deal with Yasir Arafat and Abu Abbas to guarantee the terrorists safe passage out of Egypt if the *Achille Lauro*, the passengers and the crew were released unharmed. With a gun barrel to his temple, the captain of the *Achille Lauro* had been forced to state that everybody was in good health, apparently satisfying the Egyptians that U.S. claims of a murder on board ship were incorrect.

The terrorists were taken into custody on Wednesday evening, and the rest of the passengers were set free. At this point the American ambassador in Egypt, Nick Veliotes, found out that the captain had provided his assurances under duress, and that, as we had feared, an American passenger had been murdered. Radioing the news to his staff on shore, Veliotes demanded that the government of Egypt prosecute the "sons of bitches," a well-chosen but rather undiplomatic remark.

Although Egypt was apparently ignorant of the murder of Leon Klinghoffer at the time the deal was cut with Abu Abbas, the following day Mubarak claimed that the terrorists had already left the country when in fact he knew they were then being debriefed by Abu Abbas at an Egyptian military base outside of Cairo. The U.S. government had reason to know that Egypt was not telling the truth but did not think more could be done other than to bring the remaining former American hostages back to the United States.

Everyone was intensely frustrated by the situation until Thursday morning, when NSC staff member Captain James Stark of the U.S. Navy came up with the idea that the United States could try to intercept the Egyptian airplane that would be transporting the *Achille Lauro* pirates from Cairo to Tunis. North called me over to his office to ask for my opinion and asked whether I could arrange a secure channel of communications with the government of Israel to clarify the exact location of the terrorists and the airplane they would be using to fly out of Egypt.

Things began to move very quickly at this point. As North sat at his desk, a telephone at each ear, simultaneously speaking with Poindexter and Admiral Arthur Moreau, assistant to the chairman of the JCS, I called over to General Uri Simhoni, the defense attaché of the Israeli embassy. Simhoni's secretary said she did not expect him in the office for several hours yet, but that I could reach him at home if it was an emergency. I dialed his home number and caught him in the shower. I told him we needed to see him as soon as possible, that the U.S. government would appreciate some Israeli assistance with a tracking problem to Israel's west. Not missing a beat, Simhoni said he would be dressed and at the OEOB within thirty minutes.

With North still on the phone, I briefed Simhoni on the intercept decision and requested that Israel provide the United States with real time information on the terrorists' exact location, destination (in case they decided to travel south to Khartoum instead of west to Tunis), and airplane type and tail number. He called the Israeli embassy to start the process before leaving the OEOB. Within an hour, we had all the information we needed.

In the middle of all this, it was decided that we needed to have a legal rationale for the intercept ready. Fortier told me to call Gayle, who worked at the State Department, and ask her to confer quietly with her boss in the office of the legal advisor, Judge Abraham Sofaer, in order to prepare a legal argument to support the intercept of the aircraft. Sofaer himself called me back shortly thereafter and made the key points of ample legal justification for the action, if legal justification became necessary.

With everything falling into place, Reagan made the decision to try to capture the *Achille Lauro* pirates while he was visiting the Sara Lee Bakery in Chicago. McFarlane was with him and advised him of the pros and cons of the operation, telling him that despite the potential damage to U.S.-Egyptian relations, Shultz strongly favored the operation and that Abe Sofaer had advised that it was legally justified under international law. He also specifically informed the president that Weinberger opposed the operation. Reagan considered the proposal and authorized its execution.

Weinberger was in Ottawa, Canada, when he learned of the president's decision. He ordered the new chairman of the JCS, Admiral William Crowe, to delay the execute order until Weinberger personally confirmed it. The secretary of defense called *Air Force One* to plead with President Reagan to reconsider, but Reagan refused to budge, specifically directing Weinberger to proceed with the operation as instructed. At that point, concerned that Weinberger would again try to find another reason not to proceed, despite the president's unambiguous orders, McFarlane instructed the White House operators not to put through any more calls to the president from Secretary Weinberger that were not first cleared by him personally. Crowe was free to act.

In a matter of hours, U.S. Navy F-14s from the carrier *Saratoga* intercepted the Egyptian aircraft carrying the *Achille Lauro* pirates and diverted it to a NATO airbase at Sigonella on the island of Sicily. Stiner and the bulk of his forces arrived at the base at the same time as the Egyptian aircraft, and U.S. forces quickly surrounded the plane. With a satellite link from the Situation Room direct to Stiner, the NSC staff and representatives of State, Defense, the CIA, the FBI, the FAA and the Justice Department listened silently as Stiner described the unexpected scene on the airport tarmac. Several hundred Italian soldiers had arrived on the base, encircling the U.S. forces to prevent them from taking Abu Abbas and his gunmen back to the United States, where they could stand trial for their acts of terror. At the same time, NSC consultant Michael Ledeen was in the Situation Room's communication center trying to convince Italian prime minister Bettino Craxi, a personal friend of his, to order Italian troops out of the way and permit Stiner to take the terrorists prisoner. Asserting Italian sovereignty and claiming that the matter was for the Italian courts to decide, Craxi refused. He did promise that Italy would prosecute the terrorists. Also on the scene, listening to both conversations, was Victoria Toensing, the Justice Department's principal official responsible for counter-terrorism. She immediately went to work on an extradition request.

In the face of severe domestic opposition, Craxi had demonstrated strong support for the U.S. policy in Lebanon from 1982 through 1984. I had met with him personally on four separate occasions to discuss and coordinate U.S. and Italian policy, and he always expressed a clear determination to resist terrorism, a scourge that had plagued Italy for many years. But following the ignominious U.S. withdrawal in the face of Syrian-and Iranian-sponsored terrorist attacks, Craxi had concluded that the United States lacked the will and endurance to stand up to terrorism. In the face of America's unilateral seizure of the *Achille Lauro* pirates and its uncoordinated use of Italian facilities, Craxi chose the path of least resistance. He minimized the risks of Palestinian and Egyptian retaliation against Italian interests by distancing Italy from the U.S. action. When the extradition request was formally presented to the government of Italy two days later, Rome rejected it on procedural grounds and Abu Abbas was permitted to fly to freedom in Belgrade, Yugoslavia.

The successful intercept of the aircraft carrying the *Achille Lauro* pirates was a tactical operation that dealt with terrorism as a symptom, not as a cause. In order to combat terrorism, the governments of the United States and many other countries had concluded that it was essential to find a way to stop states from sponsoring terrorism in order to advance their radical political goals. In addition to Iran, Syria and Libya, the United States also listed the PDRY and North Korea as state sponsors of terrorism. The United States maintained diplomatic relations only with Syria.

The Line of Death

At the same time that I was working on U.S. policy in the Persian Gulf, Fortier was trying to reinvigorate U.S. opposition to Qadhafi by developing a more aggressive policy toward Libya. Vincent Cannistraro was assigned responsibility to devise new means of increasing pressure on Qadhafi. Cannistraro, a career CIA officer who had served in Libya and had formerly headed the CIA Libya Task Force, was now a member of the NSC staff's Intelligence Directorate. By early 1985, Cannistraro had produced a detailed analysis of Qadhafi's strategies, activities and trends in Libya's behavior and the alarming increase in Libya's value as a Soviet strategic asset. While pointing out Qadhafi's vulnerabilities and the opportunities for U.S. covert action against the Libyan leader, the analysis also highlighted the potential for an escalation in the campaign of Libyan-sponsored terrorism against U.S. citizens and interests.

Cannistraro offered two options. Option one called for the United States to adopt a limited, phased strategy to resume air and naval challenges in the Gulf of Sidra while increasing the restrictions on Americans trying to conduct business in Libya. While joint operations with Egypt were conceivable, military planning would focus on responding to Libyan attacks. Option two provided for a more aggressive strategy, one designed to remove Qadhafi from power. This approach called for military planning with Egypt and Algeria and covert support, to include heretofore banned lethal assistance to Libyan dissidents.

Bush, Shultz, Casey and McFarlane supported the more aggressive approach. Weinberger and the JCS firmly opposed any strategy that required military support on the basis that the goals were not sufficiently clear and that inadequate consideration had been given to likely Soviet defense of Libya. McFarlane decided to try to strengthen the base of support for the policy within the National Security Council.

In mid-August, McFarlane dispatched me to meet privately with Attorney General Edwin Meese and then secretary of the treasury James Baker. I met with each man one-on-one for over an hour, reviewing the analysis and the options in order to prepare them for the forthcoming NSPG meeting, which would address the issue. Both men asked probing but very different questions. Meese questioned the resolve of the Egyptian Army to take on the Libyans to the end, while Baker was primarily concerned with the possible consequences of an anti-American Arab backlash and a disruption of oil supplies. During the late-August NSPG meeting, Meese and Baker joined in support of the more aggressive approach, and President Reagan approved the initiative to work with Egypt. Poindexter, Fortier and a U.S. Army general subsequently traveled to Cairo to propose the plan to Mubarak. The Egyptians were not interested in participating, however, and the initiative was shelved.

Qadhafi and his sponsorship of terrorism continued to be a major problem for the U.S. government. Although there was no evidence of Qadhafi's involvement in the hijacking of TWA flight 847 or in the *Achille Lauro* affair, Libya provided support for the Abu Nidal terrorists who conducted the Egyptair skyjacking and the massacres at the Rome and Vienna airports, which took place on December 27. Evidence of Qadhafi's involvement in Rome and Vienna included Libyan-provided passports, intercepted communications, the existence of terrorist training camps located throughout Libya, and the use of East European–manufactured weapons and explosives that were traceable back to Libya. Although I was on leave, I was summoned back to the office to help coordinate the U.S. response to the airport attacks. Evidence of Libya's involvement in the massacres, which might even hold up in an American court of law, convinced President Reagan that the time had finally come to retaliate.

Weinberger and Shultz once again faced off in a growing stalemate. Weinberger was opposed to retaliating and warned the president that military strikes would endanger the large number of Americans who continued to live and conduct commerce in Libya, possibly creating a hostage nightmare worse than the Carter administration's debacle in Iran. American oil, engineering and construction companies still operated in Libya. Throughout this time, U.S. companies had continued to pump hundreds of thousands of barrels of Libyan oil per day, providing Qadhafi with ample foreign exchange to support all his radical enterprises. Finally, Weinberger argued that the evidence of Libya's direct involvement in the

Rome and Vienna attacks "could not be proved beyond a reasonable doubt," and that it would be wrong to strike at Libya in these circumstances.

Despite Weinberger's opposition, the president had made a decision and the Pentagon immediately began drawing up a list of targets and developing the necessary operational plans. At the same time, the media began reporting details of the plans, including target lists, timing decisions and so forth, receiving the information through a steady stream of leaks from the bureaucracy. Whether or not Reagan had made a decision, the policy could yet be defeated in a properly played endgame. On January 7, 1986, the U.S. government began to lay the groundwork for military action by invoking the International Emergency Economic Powers Act (IEEPA) and warning Qadhafi that further steps would be taken if Libya continued to sponsor international terrorism. Simultaneously, a diplomatic campaign was launched to convince European allies to close ranks behind the United States and isolate Qadhafi by embargoing the sale of arms, halting Libyan oil purchases, closing Libyan People's Bureaus and prohibiting European companies from assuming the functions that had heretofore been performed by U.S. entities. The Europeans listened sympathetically, agreed to increase the exchange of intelligence information on terrorism and urged their companies not to help Libya replace U.S. technicians. But Libyan oil continued to flow, as Libya's sweet crude was always in great demand.

McFarlane had resigned as the president's NSC advisor in December 1985 and was succeeded by his deputy, John Poindexter. Although I had made up my mind that four years at the NSC was sufficient and that it was time to move on to a job in the private sector, Fortier, who had been promoted to the deputy's position, convinced me to stay at the NSC as the senior director for political-military affairs, as Dennis Ross would be returning to Washington to assume the senior Middle East job.

Poindexter was dissatisfied with Covey, and had said so on numerous occasions. Fortier and Poindexter were convinced that Covey was deliberately keeping them in the dark on sensitive issues. The State Department's then executive secretary had refused to provide me with several NODIS cables from our embassy in Damascus which Poindexter directed me to analyze. The staff of the Executive Secretariat told me that "it could wait for Covey to return from his overseas travel," and simply stonewalled when Poindexter requested the cables himself. While Poindexter expressed outrage and wondered what other cables the State Department was keeping from the White House, the executive secretary at the State

Department apparently believed that he was simply performing his duties. Covey was reassigned as DCM to the U.S. embassy in Cairo. Ross planned to join the NSC to work on Middle East issues in early summer. After discussing it at length, it seemed that among the three of us, a team was in place that would make working at the NSC a new and exciting challenge. In the circumstances, and to my profound later regret, I decided not to resign.

Fortier assumed principal responsibility for the development and implementation of U.S. policy toward Libya. He characterized the invocation of IEEPA as a "conditioning process" that would help galvanize the domestic and international debate over what to do about state-sponsored terrorism in general and Libya in particular. Within the NSC staff, I worked with Jim Stark, Vince Cannistraro, Ollie North and Elaine Morton, the latter a State Department detailee who was a member of my directorate, to prepare a strategy of "steadily increasing pressures" and "disproportionate responses" to Libyan provocations that would isolate Qadhafi and help convince him that the price of his radical behavior had become too high.

The military component of this strategy was based on the pattern of exercises established in 1981 when the United States shot down two Libyan jets during a freedom of navigation (FON) challenge in international waters claimed by Libya. In mid-January, the NSPG decided to resume a stair-step set of FON exercises in the Gulf of Sidra to increase the pressure on Qadhafi by demonstrating nonrecognition of Qadhafi's illegal claims and testing his resolve to confront the United States. The first and second exercises would take place just north of the Gulf of Sidra to test the responses of the Libyan air-defense network, without directly challenging Qadhafi's claims to the Gulf of Sidra. Climbing up the stairs, the third exercise, code-named Prairie Fire, was scheduled to begin on March 23 and would involve naval maneuvers by three aircraft-carrier battle groups in and around the Gulf. If Qadhafi chose to ignore the U.S. challenge, there would be no military confrontation. But if U.S. forces were threatened, the rules of engagement, unlike those in Beirut, would permit aggressive self-defense to include the destruction of Libyan targets that displayed hostile intent, even if they had not yet fired at U.S. forces.

Ever eager to shake his fist at the United States and proclaim his readiness for armed struggle, when the exercises were announced Qadhafi drew an imaginary line across the top of the Gulf of Sidra and called it the "Line of Death." He warned America that Libya would respond with force to any challenge. Perhaps Qadhafi doubted our resolve to carry out the exercises or he believed that Libya could inflict a heavy toll on the U.S. Navy. With the Soviet air and naval presence in Libya, Qadhafi might also have convinced himself that Washington would not take military actions that might risk a superpower confrontation. Regardless of Qadhafi's perceptions, to those of us working on Libyan matters on a day-to-day basis, it seemed that a military confrontation with Libya was inevitable. The Line of Death would be crossed and, regrettably, people would die, although nearly all of them would turn out to be Libyan, not exactly what Qadhafi had intended when he dared the United States to act.

What Goes Around Comes Around

In anticipation of a military confrontation, the administration wanted to ensure that our European allies would support our actions, or at least not criticize them. Moreover, Europeans were actually suffering more casualties from Libyan-sponsored attacks than were Americans, suggesting an equal or greater interest in halting Qadhafi's activities. Based on our common experience in Lebanon and the hostility that colored relations between Libya and France, the NSPG decided to pursue cooperation with France in an effort to expand the military pressure to a multilateral level.

Poindexter called General Saulnier, Mitterrand's military advisor, and suggested that the United States and France confer about the possibility of military confrontations with Libya. Mitterrand agreed and invited the United States to dispatch an envoy to Paris for secret consultations. Shultz directed Ambassador Vernon Walters, the U.S. envoy to the United Nations, and me to represent the U.S. government. The goals of the mission were (1) to convince Mitterrand that Qadhafi's policies posed a serious threat to Western interests, a threat that could not be permitted to continue, and (2) to seek his agreement to begin joint military planning for possible confrontation with Libya.

Just prior to the start of the second phase of the stair-step exercises, Walters and I flew to Paris to meet with Mitterrand and Saulnier. Our meeting was scheduled for midafternoon at the Élysée Palace, and we spent the morning reviewing French policy toward the United States and Libya with the DCM at the U.S. Embassy Paris, Jack Maresca. Entering the Élysée Palace grounds through a back entrance to avoid media attention, Walters and I met with Mitterrand in his office for about an hour and a half.

Mitterrand expressed his pleasure that Reagan had sent an emissary to discuss Libya and to confer before anything happened, noting the very great significance that France attached to developments in North Africa and the Mediterranean. Walters and I briefed him on Qadhafi's recent activities and the administration's conclusion that he would continue to escalate his terrorist attacks with ever-increasing deadliness unless he was convinced that the price was too great. As we outlined the analysis, the policy framework and the military activities that were planned for the coming months, Mitterrand sat poker-faced, without asking any questions before presenting France's view.

Mitterrand was less concerned about state-sponsored terrorism than about Qadhafi's growing aggressiveness and subversion throughout Africa. He agreed that it would be useful to stop Qadhafi's support of terrorism, but he questioned whether circumstances would permit the appropriate application of force to the problem. The most grave danger Qadhafi posed was to the stability of North and West Africa. This was the problem with which the United States and France had to deal.

Recalling the failed venture of the MNF in Lebanon, he pointedly noted how the United States had planned joint strikes against the Sheikh Abdullah Barracks in the eastern Mediterranean but then, for reasons that France still did not comprehend, backed out at the last minute. If the United States was now prepared to take *decisive* action against Qadhafi, Mitterrand said, France would be ready to join with America in the venture. But he warned that any action must be serious or it would only enhance Qadhafi's prestige and lead to more problems.

Walters assured Mitterrand that President Reagan intended to escalate the pressure on Qadhafi to force him to change his ways. I added that the United States was no longer short of breath, as we had been in Lebanon. Mitterrand nodded approvingly, and said that France would be supportive and cooperative. He turned to Saulnier and authorized him to open a discreet military planning channel with the United States. I advised Saulnier that General Richard Lawson, commander of the U.S. forces in Europe, would contact him to organize the discussions.

We left Paris the following morning and went directly to the White House to brief Poindexter, Fortier and Stark (who would manage the military planning follow-up) on the results of the meetings. The U.S.-French joint military planning began immediately, with the United States side led by Lieutenant General Richard Burpee, director of operations for the JCS. Several cooperative measures were agreed upon.

Numerous interagency planning meetings were convened in the ensuing weeks, as the U.S. government made the political and military preparations to cross Qadhafi's Line of Death. Fortier was especially concerned that any Libyan fire at U.S. forces should be returned with not only a disproportionate response, but that the U.S. escalation should exact a heavy price on Libyan ships, planes and coastal defense systems. Admiral Crowe supported this doctrine, though Weinberger stated that he did not believe that Qadhafi, faced with the awesome power of three carrier battle groups, would be stupid enough to order his forces to engage in combat with the United States.

In a mid-March meeting in the Situation Room, Rich Armitage reported to Fortier that all the commanders had been fully briefed on the new ROE. Armitage assured the interagency group that U.S. forces would definitely respond but that the DIA had concluded that Libya would not fire first. I asked why the DIA had reached this conclusion. Armitage explained that DIA analysts believed that the Soviets had convinced Qadhafi to lay low, figuring the United States would act harshly if provoked. I took issue with the DIA line, arguing that Qadhafi still doubted American resolve to act and observed that there were deep divisions within the alliance over American policy toward Libya. Moreover, I had yet to see any evidence of Soviet efforts to restrain Qadhafi. Leaning back in his chair with his muscular forearms folded across his chest, Armitage smiled and said, "Howard, I hope you're right, because the U.S. military is ready and will respond disproportionately. Qadhafi will make Cap's day if he is stupid enough to take us on." A major threshold within the national security bureaucracy had clearly been crossed. We were all finally operating as a team.

With all the preparations completed, I traveled with my wife Gayle and three-month-old son Seth to Israel, where I was scheduled to deliver a lecture on U.S. security policy for the Middle East at Tel Aviv University. Fortier was personally supervising the execution of Prairie Fire and encouraged me to proceed with the lecture as cancellation might draw unwanted attention. March 24 was our last full day in Israel and the second day of Prairie Fire. I had arranged for someone from the U.S. embassy to call me if the Libyans responded to the exercise. I received word late in the afternoon that the Libyans had fired long-range, high-altitude SA-5s at U.S. aircraft. I went to the embassy and used Sam Lewis's secure phone to call Fortier for an update.

I reached him in the Situation Room, where he was monitoring all the incoming communications, waiting for a confirmation of a disproportionate U.S. response. He was frustrated. There was still no word of U.S. action. It was up to the on-scene commanders to decide when and how to act. The action belonged to the Pentagon, and Weinberger and Admiral Crowe were expected shortly to brief the president. He promised to call me back within the next several hours, assuming there were any developments to report. Later that evening Fortier reached me at my hotel. Two Libyan patrol boats had been sunk and the SA-5 site at Sirte on the Libyan coast had been destroyed. The exercise over, the carrier battle groups had pulled away from the Line of Death. There were no signs that the Libyans were likely to escalate further.

As our flight from Tel Aviv to London passed over the Mediterranean Sea north of Qadhafi's Line of Death, I couldn't help but think it ironic that I would find myself so close to Tripoli. Looking out the window, the Libyan coastline too distant to see, I believed that the terrorism battle had finally been joined. It was several days later in London when I saw a message that Qadhafi had sent to the Libyan People's Bureaus directing them to prepare to attack U.S. military facilities and Americans in retaliation for Prairie Fire.

On Saturday evening, April 5, 1986, I received a call from the Situation Room informing me that a bomb had just gone off in the La Belle discotheque in West Berlin. There were no casualty reports yet, but Poindexter had called from the West Coast to direct Fortier, North, Stark and me to prepare a memo for him to send to the president first thing the following morning summarizing whatever we learned during the night and outlining potential U.S. options in the event of Libyan involvement.

North was already in the Situation Room by the time I arrived, chewing on a cigar as he talked on one of the secure phones located along the wall. "There it is," he said, shaking his head and pointing to a stack of paper on the conference table, "Muammar's smoking gun." Papers, cables and intelligence reports covered the table. When I finally found the document he wanted me to look at, I understood immediately that Qadhafi had been caught red-handed. It was a garbled transcript of two intercepts from the People's Bureau in East Berlin to the Libyan intelligence headquarters, al-Marafiq, in Tripoli. The first intercept advised that a "joyous event" was imminent. The second intercepted message, transmitted shortly after the bomb exploded in the La Belle discotheque, confirmed that the operation had been successfully executed. The following morning, after he finished reviewing the memo and attachments, President Reagan concluded that Qadhafi was directly responsible for the bombing. He gave the order for the U.S. military to quietly prepare to retaliate against Qadhafi's terrorism infrastructure.

Don Fortier had been experiencing growing pain and fatigue during the preceding months, but had made no change in his regular eighteen-hour workdays, exhilarated by his promotion to deputy NSC advisor and determined to implement a policy that would lead Libya to halt its sponsorship of terrorism. Expressing his skepticism that Weinberger would actually implement the president's orders, Poindexter had Fortier convene daily planning meetings to coordinate the details of the strikes against Libya. Meeting discreetly in the office of NSC executive secretary Rodney B. McDaniel to avoid giving the impression of crisis planning, the group included assistant to the chairman of the JCS Lieutenant General John H. Moellering, Armitage from OSD, Michael Armacost, and Arnold Raphel from State, as well as North, Stark and me. These meetings were productive, giving each agency a full opportunity to understand the others' perspectives. On two issues, however, Poindexter and Crowe locked horns. The first issue involved the targets recommended by the JCS. The second issue involved the selection of weapons. The president had ordered the military to hit the Libyan infrastructure that supported international terrorism. The JCS proposed five targets, including the two barracks where Qadhafi lived and operated from—one in Tripoli, the other in Benghazi. While these and the other military targets that had been selected were appropriate, the institutional nerve center for Qadhafi's sponsorship of terrorism was al-Marafiq. The destruction of al-Marafiq, a large, easily identifiable, oddly shaped building in Tripoli would have done more to disrupt the bureaucracy of Libyan terrorism than any other target. Weinberger and the JCS argued against striking al-Marafiq, because of the high likelihood of collateral damage and civilian casualties owing to its location in a residential neighborhood, across the street from the embassy of France.

"Fine," Poindexter said to Crowe during one meeting. "Then why not use submarine-launched cruise missiles armed with conventional warheads or our F-117 Stealth fighter-bombers? You and I know that these systems are extremely accurate and are more likely to hit their targets and cause less collateral damage than the F-111s dropping laser-guided bombs." Crowe strenuously disagreed with Poindexter's proposal, arguing that the United States should not use its most sophisticated weapons, because we don't want our adversaries to know what kind of capabilities we have, particularly with regard to the supersecret F-117. Instead, the military plan proposed using Vietnam War–era F-111 bombers flying from bases in England, while carrier-based aircraft struck at Libya from off the Libyan shore. At the final NSPG meeting on April 12, the president agreed with Crowe's arguments and approved the mission profile as proposed by the JCS.

Consistent with earlier promises to Mitterrand that there would be consultations in advance of any operation, the administration informed the French president of its plans and requested permission for the F-111s to overfly France en route to Libya. The administration, however, decided not to brief the Congress in advance, choosing instead to disclose the operation to a foreign power before telling the congressional leadership about it. Despite the earlier leaks to the media following the attacks in Rome and Vienna from sources in the Executive Branch who were opposed to holding Libya responsible, the administration continued to maintain that the Congress could not be trusted to keep a secret. But later that same Saturday afternoon, Mitterrand refused Reagan's request. France did not believe that the American operation was decisive and felt it would not halt Libyan aggressiveness and subversion throughout Africa. Nor would it deter Qadhafi from continuing his support of terrorism.

Reading the message from Saulnier, I could only grit my teeth as I remembered my meeting with Walters and Mitterrand two months before. As discussed earlier, in 1983, the United States failed to follow through on the U.S.-French joint operation to bomb the Sheikh Abdullah Barracks in the Bekáa Valley in retaliation for the October 23 destruction of the U.S. Marine and French barracks. By virtue of Weinberger's disobedience, the French had literally been left hanging in the air, unsure and confused over American intentions. Having failed to live up to a commitment that France took dead seriously, the United States left the French pilots to act unilaterally. What goes around comes around, or so the saying goes. If the United States wanted to strike out at Qadhafi and teach him a lesson by bombing some barracks in Libya, rather than decisively solving the problem, Washington would just have to find a way to do it unilaterally.

Everyone was shocked and furious. The United States was left with no other options than for the F-111s to fly out over the Atlantic and then back through the Strait of Gibraltar over the Mediterranean. At the end of that long flight in the middle of the night, the pilots, most of whom had never fired a shot in anger, would then need to lock on to their targets with a laser designator and radar before they could drop their bombs— no easy task in an exercise, let alone a scenario in which Libyan air defenses would presumably light up the sky with fire.

Disproportionate Response

Since the bombing of the La Belle disco, those centrally involved in the planning of the strikes had maintained extraordinary discipline, and little, if any, substantive information leaked out from the core group. Nonetheless, press speculation of U.S. intentions was rampant, fueled primarily by leaks from members of the national security bureaucracy who did not want their media contacts to think they were out of the loop, and from elected officials posturing on Capitol Hill. But by the morning of April 14, the day of the strike, the national media started to report a different line, suggesting that despite the constant rhetoric of striking back at terrorists, it once again appeared that the United States was backing down from the confrontation with Libya.

At five P.M. that evening, the principal spokespersons from the White House, State Department and Defense Department were summoned to the White House and briefed on the plan. Angered at the decision to keep them in the dark until they had a need to know, they were furious when Fortier told them they were to stay in the Situation Room to maintain operational security until the bombs actually started to fall. The strike aircraft were nearly at their targets as we watched the seven P.M. national news broadcasts on the Situation Room television. As Dan Rather began to report that after yet another terrorist attack, it once again appeared that the United States would take no military action, he was suddenly interrupted and told that the CBS correspondent was on the phone calling from his hotel room to report that bombs were falling on Tripoli.

The strike was over in a matter of minutes, and various statements and talking points for the press were completed, enabling us to work quietly in the Situation Room, regularly checking the communications terminals to learn whether all U.S. aircraft had managed to evade the antiaircraft fire and how much damage had been done to Libya. One F-111 did not make it back, crashing into the sea off the Libyan coast, killing the pilot and navigator. In the course of the attack, all five targets had been hit, although the damage to the Libyan terrorism infrastructure was relatively modest, given the amount of bombs and missiles that had been dropped.

The ROE had precluded seven of the nine F-111s from dropping any of their ordnance, although some of the bombs that landed in the Azzaziyah Barracks did do an excellent job of destroying Qadhafi's tennis courts. The collateral damage, however, was very bad, with over forty civilians killed in the neighborhood adjacent to the Azzaziyah Barracks and many more injured. Qadhafi's whereabouts prior to the time of the attack were not known; that he was present in the Azzaziyah Barracks that night was pure serendipity.

Regardless of the extent of the minimal physical damage to the terrorist infrastructure, a political objective of the mission had been achieved. Qadhafi, as well as other state sponsors of terrorism, notably Syria and Iran, could no longer take for granted that the United States would continue to endure terrorist attacks against Americans with impunity. The administration did not expect terrorism to vanish as a result of this strike and braced for retaliation. Neither did anyone anticipate that U.S. forces would retaliate for every terrorist act launched against Americans or American interests. But a major threshold had been crossed, and those who might choose to employ terror in the future to advance their political objectives now understood that the rules of the game had changed.

Having convinced himself that he was invincible, Qadhafi was clearly shaken by the willingness of the United States to target his Tripoli and Benghazi headquarters. Given the widespread tendency throughout the Arab world to perceive events through a fatalistic yet conspiratorial prism, the U.S. attack came as a real shock, and Qadhafi received little support from any other Arab leader. Although the United States was dutifully criticized in public, many Arab diplomats in Washington expressed disappointment that the United States hadn't finished him off. Barely escaping death, Qadhafi hid out in the desert for two months, sponsoring no terrorist attacks, and surfacing in early June to deliver a bizarre, rambling speech in which he tried to mobilize Arab nationalism and mass support to confront the United States. Apparently quiescent, the United States continued to observe Qadhafi, as if under a microscope, looking for any sign of resurgent sponsorship of international terrorism.

Disinformation

Toward the end of July 1986, it appeared that Qadhafi had regained his composure and began to perceive that U.S. pressure was abating. Keen to prevent Qadhafi from reasserting himself, Shultz encouraged President Reagan to turn up the heat by ordering reconnaissance aircraft to overfly Libya and set off sonic booms, rattling windows as well as Qadhafi. The president wanted to see Shultz's ideas more fully developed, and Poindexter directed the NSC staff to convene an interagency group to work out the terms of reference (TOR) for a strategy to increase the pressure on Libya. Don Fortier normally would have supervised this group, but tragically he had recently been diagnosed with terminal liver cancer. In his absence, McDaniel asked the State Department to develop a strategy paper for interagency consideration, which I would thereafter coordinate and turn into a memorandum for the president, in preparation for an NSPG in mid-August.

The State Department proposed a strategy for intensifying the pressure on Qadhafi by keeping him off balance, unsure of the intentions of the United States, European countries and neighboring African states and uncertain over his ability to control the domestic situation within Libya.

To achieve these goals, State devised a psychological warfare campaign that would exploit real and imaginary activities that might lead to the overthrow of Qadhafi, while convincing him that the world would become even more hostile toward Libya if he resumed his sponsorship of international terrorism. One component of this campaign included placing articles in foreign media publications which would be designed to give false and misleading information about the situation in Libya. This disinformation program, which State proposed initiating, had been authorized by the Congress in 1981. It was not a new program, although State recommended that foreign media placements should be intensified. State also recommended that U.S. government officials should increase their backgrounding of the American media with factual information about the situation in Libya, in order to maintain the public consensus in favor of the use of force in response to terrorism. This State Department strategy paper was codrafted by NEA, PM and INR.

The NSC received the paper during the second week of August. McDaniel directed me to review and condense it, circulating it to the other agencies that would attend the NSPG. After giving copies of the strategy paper to my colleagues on the NSC staff, including Ross, Cannistraro, North and Elaine Morton, we met as a group several times to review it. Everyone but Morton agreed that State's paper offered a sound strategy for intensifying the pressure on Qadhafi and that it should serve as the discussion paper and agenda for the principals who would attend the NSPG. Morton strenuously argued that the United States should limit its actions toward Qadhafi to economic sanctions. Further military action or psychological warfare was unjustified in the absence of new acts of terror against Americans and American interests. The rest of the group disagreed with her, taking the position already articulated by the president, the State Department, the Pentagon and the CIA. She held firm, but could not sway the group to adopt her perspective. We agreed to press ahead on the basis of the State paper. I asked Elaine to draft the summary memorandum for the president, inasmuch as she had been a team player during the earlier crisis and I wanted her to experience the sense of professional fulfillment that comes from writing a memorandum to the president of the United States.

I attended the NSPG when it convened several days later. Following an update on Qadhafi, the internal situation in Libya and the emergence of new information linking him to a terrorist attack against the British on the island of Crete and an attempted bombing of the American embassy in the West African country of Togo, the NSPG unanimously agreed to adopt the State Department strategy.

Poindexter volunteered that the NSC staff had already drafted an NSDD in anticipation of a positive decision; the NSDD would be circulated for final concurrence by the principals before the president signed it out. As the meeting was breaking up, the president, always looking for an opportunity for a good joke or to tease a friend, turned to Shultz with mock seriousness and said, "George, I really think we should send Qadhafi to San Francisco." Not realizing that the president was simply playing on their southern California versus northern California rivalry, Shultz started to sputter, asking why we should invite Qadhafi to the United States, let alone to San Francisco. "Come on, George," Reagan replied, "let's give him AIDS."

The members of the National Security Council returned their comments in a matter of days. The president signed the NSDD, which became official U.S. policy. I prepared to go on a long-delayed family vacation to southern California. On my last day in the office, I received a telephone call from John Walcott, national security affairs correspondent of *The Wall Street Journal*. I had met Walcott in April 1983 while participating in Shultz's shuttle between Israel and Lebanon, and we established a dialogue that continued after he left *Newsweek* magazine for the *Journal*.

I had a good relationship with most of the White House press corps and media, including Walcott. I believed that U.S. officials should regularly meet with members of the press, in order to ensure that American policies were clearly understood, as well as to explain the national and foreign context within which policies were devised. Since joining the NSC staff, I had argued consistently that one of the Reagan administration's major weaknesses was its failure to articulate clearly U.S. policies or to maintain good relations with the media. I also believed that the relationship between Congress and the Executive in the area of foreign affairs was divisive and had become distorted by the tendency of some in *each* branch of government to play out policy disputes through leaks to the media. The media in turn both exploited the situation and were exploited by it. I did not believe that the public interest was served by attempts to influence policy-making in this manner.

Walcott said it was "urgent" that he see me. He had learned from "Pentagon sources" earlier in the day that Qadhafi appeared to be up to something. His sources said the United States and Libya, once again, appeared to be on a "collision course." I tried to beg off, explaining that I was busy wrapping up my work so that I could leave early for a two-week vacation on the West Coast. Walcott insisted, however, that he had to see me, assuring me that it wouldn't take long. Given Walcott's persistence and the policy guidance contained in the NSDD to brief reporters factually about Qadhafi and the situation in Libya, I acquiesced and reluctantly agreed to see him for no more than thirty minutes.

Walcott came to my office in the OEOB. He told me that he had learned from "Pentagon sources" that another military operation was under way which would provoke Qadhafi and provide the United States with another pretext for a "disproportionate" military response. He asked me for my comments.

I answered that I had seen unconfirmed reports of a resumption of Libyan involvement in terrorism and said that if Qadhafi was caught red-handed, as he had been in April, I had no doubt that Reagan would order military retaliation. With regard to the claims put forward by Walcott's "Pentagon sources," I categorically stated that "I was not aware of any imminent military action." I questioned whether I would be going on vacation if a military operation was about to start.

I did not give the interview another thought until August 26, while relaxing at Zuma Beach, I read in *The Los Angeles Times* about a lead story in *The Wall Street Journal*, by John Walcott, which alleged that the United States and Libya were *"on a collision course."* Although the facts contained in the article seemed to be otherwise correct, Walcott had evidently chosen to rely on his "Pentagon sources." He wrote that U.S. military action against Libya appeared *"imminent."* I was shocked and called Poindexter to find out whether something was indeed about to happen. He told me there was nothing new, that he thought the article was fine, and that I should just enjoy my vacation.

The day after my return to Washington I participated in a State Department meeting chaired by Under Secretary of State Michael Armacost. One of the NSPG decisions was to send Vernon Walters back to Europe to seek additional political and economic pressures on Libya and to put more pressure on Qadhafi. Armacost distributed talking points, which

State had drafted for Walters to use in his meetings with European leaders. Before the discussion began, Robert Oakley spoke up. Oakley, director of the State Department's Office for Combating Terrorism, complained that *The Wall Street Journal* article had aroused a flurry of speculation at the beginning of the week and damaged U.S. policy by suggesting that military action was imminent when it wasn't. Glaring at me as he spoke, he said, "The White House has got to stop fanning the flames and let us work this issue quietly."

I took issue with Oakley's pointed accusation that the White House was fanning any flames and noted that it was the State Department that had proposed the strategy that would intensify the pressure on Qadhafi. I argued that the goal was to deter Qadhafi from sponsoring terrorism. "The use of force worked. We may have to use force again. What is wrong with stating that in public?" I asked. Armacost agreed with my comment, noting that the president had signed the NSDD that authorized a public campaign to intensify the pressure on Qadhafi, including the forthcoming trip by Walters, and we needed to stop arguing and sort out what Walters would say.

As the meeting drew to a close, Armacost asked if I would accompany Walters and Oakley to Europe. NSC representation would help send a stronger signal of U.S. interest. I agreed to the request and over the course of the next five days, Walters, Oakley and I met with the heads of government or the foreign ministers of West Germany, France, the United Kingdom, Spain, Italy, Belgium, the Netherlands and Canada. In addition to reaffirming the U.S. posture toward international terrorism, we pressed our allies to consider enacting economic sanctions against Libya, particularly to stop importing Libyan oil. Although the trip received widespread international press attention, the allies did little more than listen politely, probe to assess whether military action was indeed imminent and agree to review the status of their respective economic relations with Libya.

Throughout the trip, Walters, Oakley and I debated the pros and cons of the U.S. policy to combat terrorism in general and Libya in particular. Although Oakley and I did not share identical views, our approaches seemed to be not that far apart. When we returned to Andrews Air Force Base, a car picked us up and brought us back to the State Department. Gayle met me. Inasmuch as it was quite late, and Oakley did not have a car, we offered to drive him home. He accepted the ride and we chatted amiably on the drive to his house.

Less than one month later, on October 2, *The Washington Post* published the first of two articles by Bob Woodward which reported that the Reagan administration was engaged in a "disinformation campaign" designed to destabilize Qadhafi. Publishing verbatim excerpts from the State strategy paper, and the memos that Morton and I had drafted, Woodward alleged that this campaign included a deliberate attempt by the U.S. government to lie to and manipulate the American media.

While Woodward might have obtained the State strategy paper from any of a number of sources throughout the government, my paper and the memo to the president drafted by Elaine Morton had not been distributed outside of the White House. Only a very disgruntled individual who disagreed with U.S. policy toward Libya would have chosen to hand over TOP SECRET documents to The Washington Post. In his article Woodward identified me as one of the authors of an NSC memo.

The next day The New York Times reported that "White House, State Department and Pentagon officials almost unanimously pointed the finger at Howard Teicher" as the source of the leak to The Wall Street Journal. As Walcott later confirmed, I was not his source. But the truth no longer mattered. I was particularly saddened that the author of The New York Times article was my old boss, Les Gelb, the former director of the Bureau of Politico-Military Affairs. I was disappointed that Gelb had not checked the story with me first before rushing to file his scoop.

The sharks began to circle as more anonymous sources opposed to U.S. policy toward Libya and bureaucratic adversaries fed journalists disinformation and lies in an effort to undermine U.S. policy while inflicting as much collateral damage on me as possible. In the midst of the furor over President Reagan's Libya policy, I learned the perils of not having an institution to back me. But I had made a series of choices and I was now faced with the consequences. I had relinquished a career job in the civil service when I moved from DOD to State in 1981. Now thirty-one, I had risen through the ranks of the national security bureaucracy relatively quickly. This aroused considerable resentment from some of my colleagues who were compelled by their institutions to move more slowly up the career ladder. Some resented my activism. I never withheld arguing in favor or against a position to serve the institutional interests of my colleagues or superiors. Nor did I skew my analysis to suit others' views. Rather, I vigorously engaged in policy debates on a range of issues pertaining to U.S. interests in the Middle East, such as the use of force; the necessity of protecting vital interests in the Gulf and elsewhere; the danger of small-arms proliferation; the threat to long-term U.S. interests posed by Saddam Hussein; the value of arms sales to America's Arab friends; terrorism; and the value of the U.S.-Israeli relationship. My religion was also a factor that some bureaucratic rivals tried to use against me.

Newsweek magazine claimed I was *"the culprit"* and went on to write that I was known for my ". . . *passionate pro-Israeli views and appetite for self-promotion. Reagan aides [read Don Regan] skeptical of Teicher's explanation suggest he may not survive an internal leak investigation. But he may also be a convenient scapegoat. . . ."*

The media feeding frenzy intensified and the spokesperson of the State Department, Bernard Kalb, resigned over the media's distortion of State's strategy for dealing with Qadhafi. It became evident that a policy designed to destabilize Qadhafi was doing greater damage in Washington.

Poindexter advised the NSC staff that all those involved in the preparation of the Libya documents would be obliged to meet with FBI agents and take a lie detector test. Poindexter, McDaniel, Ross, Cannistraro, Stark, North and I took and passed the test. Elaine Morton, however, refused, as a matter of principle, to submit to a lie detector test. Shultz said he would take one, but then he would resign.

Following Don Fortier's death in September, Alton Keel, a respected physicist with considerable high-level experience in the national security bureaucracy, assumed the position of deputy NSC advisor. Outraged over the distortion of U.S. policy and the damage being inflicted on me personally, Keel arranged for Bob Woodward and me to meet in Keel's office in order to set the record straight. Woodward, whom I had never met, confirmed unequivocally that I was *not* his source, but refused to identify who had given him the TOP SECRET documents. In the middle of all this, John Walcott called me at home to express his regret that I had gotten caught up in such a mess. He also told me that Bob Oakley was one of the anonymous sources making anti-Semitic remarks about me and criticizing U.S. policy toward Libya.

What became known as the Libya disinformation story exposed me to the public eye for the first time in my government career. I found the experience to be quite painful. But in the next month, I would find myself sucked into a whirlwind of such intensity that it would make this episode seem like child's play.

CHAPTER 14

THE IRAN AFFAIR –
TAKING IT PERSONALLY

————— ◆•◆ —————

The Trip

Imagine being pushed out of an airplane at fifty thousand feet, without a parachute, into a shark tank. In November 1986, a Lebanese weekly magazine, *Al Shiraa*, reported that a U.S. delegation, led by former NSC advisor Robert C. McFarlane, had traveled secretly to Iran in May seeking the release of Americans held hostage in Lebanon in return for U.S. weapons. Gayle and I were celebrating her birthday at the elegant Inn at Little Washington when hostage David Jacobsen was released and the story started to break.

Knowing that at least some parts of the *Al Shiraa* story were accurate, because I had been on that secret trip, my heart sank as I foresaw another month of struggle with the media and the bureaucracy to preserve U.S. policy and my reputation. I knew nothing of the covert action to sell arms to Iran until late February 1986, or of the diversion of profits from the arms sales to the Nicaraguan Contras until it was revealed to the nation by Attorney General Meese. What began in early November as another leaked foreign policy dispute became a living hell, as I fought for my life, bare-handed and alone. Washington's sharks began to circle for the kill.

Geoff Kemp, the senior member of the Middle East group, had held the portfolio for Iran issues during the first two years I served at the NSC. Kemp's interest in Iran dated back to a landmark analysis of the U.S.-Iranian military supply relationship he had undertaken for the Senate Foreign Relations Committee in 1975. Throughout his four-year tenure at the NSC, Kemp was responsible for promoting interagency analysis of the changing situation in Iran, the implications for U.S. interests in the Gulf and consideration of policies that might improve U.S.-Iranian relations.

The formal interagency study on southwest Asia security strategy involving State, the DOD, the CIA, Energy, Treasury, the OMB, the NSC and the Office of the Vice President had been under way for several years under Kemp's leadership when he announced his resignation. Upon his departure, I assumed a number of his responsibilities, including matters relating to Iran and the interagency policy review. But when McFarlane directed me to discontinue the interagency effort in late June 1985 because of the opposition of Shultz and Weinberger to the draft NSDD, I abandoned the process and turned most of my attention to the development of a U.S. policy for combating terrorism.

In mid-September 1985, I came across an unclassified news item in the daily Foreign Broadcast Information Service (FBIS) publication, which reported that a plane flying from Spain to Iran had made an emergency landing in Israel. Subsequent press reports alleged that this flight was somehow related to efforts to secure the release of Americans held hostage in Lebanon. My suspicions aroused, I went to discuss the report with North, asking him whether the United States was trading arms to Iran for hostages. He told me he had seen the reports but there was nothing he could tell me about them. Dissatisfied with North's reply, I asked McFarlane the same question. McFarlane replied that "the U.S. is not trading arms for hostages. There is nothing else I can say about this matter." I did not raise the subject again.

The fall of 1985 was a difficult time for my family. Gayle and I were expecting our first child in December, but in late September, her maternal grandmother died, followed by her paternal grandmother in November. Her paternal grandfather died three months later. Still, we behaved like most of the first-time parents-to-be that we knew, and prepared for the birth of our child, shopping for furniture, "oohing and ahing" over baby paraphernalia (although in truth Gayle did more "oohing" than I did) and attending childbirth classes.

In mid-November, I accompanied former president Gerald Ford and Mrs. Ford on an official visit to Oman to represent the United States at the special celebrations commemorating the fifteenth anniversary of Oman's National Day. Although there were a number of substantive meetings with heads of state and foreign ministers, including Sultan Qaboos and his foreign minister, President Mubarak of Egypt, President Zia of Pakistan and Prime Minister Rajiv Gandhi of India, there were also camel races, parties night and day and shopping in the Mutrah *suq*, an open-air market. Mrs. Ford was very impressed when she found out that I had bought a miniature Omani robe, a *dish-desh*, for my unborn child, and made me show her where to buy some for her grandchildren. Flying back to Washington, she and I chatted about children and compared our purchases. Mrs. Ford seemed rather surprised that I could comfortably discuss a number of baby-related subjects, as well as the full range of Middle East issues, and commented that I was definitely a man of a new generation.

I returned to Washington laden with baby clothes from Oman and London. Gayle and I called both sets of parents. Both my mother, Charlotte, and Gayle's mother, Charlene, were always eager to be "briefed," on my trips, especially if they involved state dinners and the like. Unfortunately, the telephone call we had with Charlene was the last time either of us would ever speak with her. On Monday, November 25, she suddenly, and quite unexpectedly, died. Our son Seth Benjamin Teicher was born December 17. The cycle of life had never seemed so real as it did during this bittersweet time.

I had taken two weeks' leave, in order to stay home with my wife and new son. Whether or not I carried a White House badge, I was determined to be an involved, participatory father. My paternity leave was abruptly cut short on December 27, however, when terrorists affiliated with Abu Nidal, using Libyan-supplied passports, committed yet another act of barbarism against innocent civilians in the Rome and Vienna airports. They had planned to hijack El Al flights at both, but had been discovered by alert security agents. In the ensuing gun battles, twenty people were killed, including five Americans.

Admiral Poindexter, now the NSC advisor, had spoken with me several times about my new job and how he viewed the role of the Political-Military Affairs Directorate. Although my office would be directly responsible for all matters involving the use of military force and crisis management, Poindexter told me that North would establish a separate directorate with responsibility for terrorism matters. Additionally, although I was to have primary responsibility for all other security assistance issues, security assistance to Central America, including aid to the Contras, would remain North's responsibility, and my directorate was not to get involved.

I later learned that the reason North's office was also named Political-Military Affairs was due to a bureaucratic turf fight between Shultz and Poindexter over the implementation of NSDD 207, the policy directive on combating terrorism. The NSDD directed that a full-time position be added to the NSC staff and an office established to coordinate all aspects of terrorism policy. The NSDD also established a State Department–chaired Interagency Group on Terrorism, which was to be cochaired by the NSC and the Department of Justice. A Terrorism Incident Working Group (TIWG) chaired by the NSC and cochaired by State, as well as the Operations Sub-Group for coordinating operational aspects of terrorism policy, were also created. Finally, a DCI-chaired Interagency Intelligence Committee on Terrorism (actually chaired by the NIO for terrorism) was established to coordinate intelligence analysis. To avoid offending State by giving the impression that the NSC was responsible for overseeing terrorism policy, Poindexter decided not to name the responsible NSC directorate the "Terrorism Office" and instead named it "Political-Military Affairs." Neither North, nor his subordinates, Robert Earl and Craig Coy, worked for me or were part of the Political-Military Affairs Directorate. The organization charts were mind-boggling, but all that really mattered was that North reported to Poindexter, while I reported to Fortier.

In late February 1986, I had a brief discussion with Tom Twetten, the CIA director for Near East operations. In a friendly, offhand manner, he said that he hoped I was getting plenty of rest, because I was going to be real tired. Suspecting that Twetten was working with North on an activity that might eventually involve me, I checked with North, who said that he was waiting for clearance from Poindexter before he could brief me on the matter to which Twetten had alluded.

Several days later, Fortier called me to his West Wing office, where I found Peter Rodman and North already gathered. Crowded into Fortier's closet-sized office, Rodman and I sat and listened as North briefed us on the outlines of a covert operation that had been in progress for over six months, involving arms sales to Iran, the prospect of a strategic dialogue with senior Iranian officials and efforts to free the hostages in Lebanon. North described how an Iranian intermediary, working on behalf of the government of Israel, had successfully communicated with Rafsanjani during the TWA Flight 847 hijacking to help bring about an end to the episode and particularly the release of four Jewish hostages that Hizbollah had wanted to keep for insurance. North described in general terms how several hundred TOW antitank missiles had been sold to Iran to facilitate more hostage releases. In this context, he said that Iran had used its influence to help secure the release of hostage Benjamin Weir in mid-September 1985. He provided no details on the exact quantities or financing arrangements of the arms shipments.

The most important goal of the program, according to Fortier, was to establish a strategic dialogue with pragmatic elements of the Iranian government, a dialogue that might lead to a thaw in U.S.-Iranian relations. If successful, the thaw would enable the United States to protect

America's regional interests better from Soviet aggression and radical threats. "Remember the draft NSDD that we wrote last year? Circumstances have changed in the region, but the logic still obtains. We might be holding the key to security and stability for the Persian Gulf," Fortier said. Of course, he went on, the United States would engage in this dialogue only if Iran secured the release of hostages, Reagan's fundamental motivation for undertaking such a risky venture.

Noting that the president had signed a covert action finding to legitimize these activities, North told us that the intelligence committees had not been briefed about the finding out of concern for leaks that would jeopardize the lives of the hostages as well as the Iranian interlocutors. I expressed doubts over the failure to notify Congress, inasmuch as I read the law requiring the executive branch to brief a finding within forty-eight hours of its execution. North replied that Meese had reviewed the law and interpreted it to permit the president to defer notification in these circumstances.

Rodman and I learned that North had already established a preliminary dialogue with Iranian officials, meeting with a member of the Iranian prime minister's staff in Frankfurt, Germany, and in Abu Dhabi. As matters now stood, North was advised that Speaker of the Parliament Rafsanjani, Prime Minister Mir Hussein Mousavi and President Sayyed Ali Khameini were prepared to meet secretly in Tehran with a high-level U.S. delegation to begin a dialogue that could lead to an end to the hostility.

North commented that the Iranians had expressed grave concern about the Soviet threat, particularly in western Afghanistan, and what the United States could do about it. I asked North whether he was confident that these officials were prepared to run the political risks inherent in meeting with us. I recalled the fate of Iranian prime minister Mehdi Bazargan, who was ousted from power following a meeting with then NSC advisor Brzezinski in Algiers. Revolutionary politics in Iran were still based on vehement anti-Americanism, which the radicals associated with Hizbollah and the hostages in Lebanon would undoubtedly exploit if the meetings became public. North replied that the Iranian officials had told him that they believed they were strong enough to cope with these pressures, as long as they received something of value for their willingness to meet with American "devils." They nonetheless wanted to keep the matter secret, fearing it could become a dangerous issue that would be difficult to control.

To begin the dialogue, the plan called for the United States and Iran to take parallel but independent steps, which would demonstrate mutual seriousness and commitment, thereby triggering a process that would lead to a restoration of mutual trust. In this context, President Reagan had decided to send McFarlane, now a private businessman, as his emissary to meet secretly with the senior Iranian officials. North explained that McFarlane and his team would arrive in Tehran at the same time the Iranian officials used their influence with Hizbollah to secure the release of the American hostages in Lebanon. He described the complex arrangements he had made with the National Security Agency (NSA) to monitor Iranian communications to ensure that the Iranians were performing the appropriate activities and that the hostages were on their way out. McFarlane and his team would arrive in Tehran and begin discussions with Iranian leaders at the same time a pallet of spare parts for HAWK missiles would be flown into Tehran for delivery to the Iranians.

Smoking a cigar and looking out his window onto the north lawn of the White House, Fortier casually mentioned that I would be "volunteering" to accompany McFarlane to Tehran, along with North and others. Poindexter had decided that it was now necessary for someone with expertise in U.S. Middle East policy and regional affairs to participate in the mission, although I had no knowledge of the events that had transpired to bring the United States and Iran to this point. It is clear that my past relationship with McFarlane was another reason I was now being brought into the operation.

During the mission, my assignment would be to provide substantive staff support for McFarlane, to include note-taking, Middle East analytical expertise as well as expertise on Soviet policy in southwest Asia. In preparation for the trip, Fortier directed Rodman (who was appalled by the entire venture) and me to prepare the terms-of-reference (TOR) draft for McFarlane's discussion with the Iranians. The final TOR would be approved by the president.

Fortier said that Shultz and Weinberger had argued against the initiative every time the subject was discussed, but that Bush and Casey strongly supported it. Poindexter knew that I believed that an initiative toward Iran made sense, not only to counter Soviet opportunism in a post-Khomeini Iran, but also to offset America's exaggerated and potentially harmful tilt to Iraq. Although skeptical that the Iranians could deliver the American hostages as North had been led to believe, under the circumstances, I believed I had no choice but to go or resign. I concluded that the potential for getting the hostages out, as well as the long-term benefits that might accrue from a dialogue with Iran, probably justified taking the risk.

Nearly all of April was dedicated to Libya and the April 15 air strikes, although I worked with Rodman and North to prepare the first two draft TORs. I was told that the revised TORs were being worked on by Fortier and Poindexter and no further input was required from me. My requests to North regarding the status of the Iran initiative were generally met with "no news yet." In response to my probing questions about financial or logistics matters, North told me that I "did not have a need to know." This was, after all, a covert action. On one occasion following the bombing of Libya, Poindexter congratulated me on the NSC's management of the strikes. He went on to say that he hoped the Iran initiative would be managed as well if not better and that "the success of the initiative was very important to the president." At about the same time, Bush asked me whether I thought the attacks against Libya might dampen Iranian interest in the project. I replied that Tehran might complain in public but we would gain greater respect and credibility.

Fortier told me that Shultz had signed off on the TOR and that Weinberger was facilitating the supply of TOW missiles and HAWK spare parts. Furthermore, although I was advised that Bush, Casey, Shultz and Weinberger were fully cognizant of the details of the initiative, I was not informed who on their staffs had been briefed, other than Twetten. I was instructed not to discuss any aspect of this matter outside of the small circle of North, Fortier, Earl, Poindexter, Bush and Reagan.

In March I had briefed Gayle on the general outlines of the Iran initiative and the role I was to play. She was appalled and argued that despite cute semantics, we were doing more than trading arms for hostages. We debated the issue at length, particularly the physical risks of my going to Tehran. She understood, however, that this was a mission authorized by the president which might offer the last hope for getting the American hostages released from Lebanon.

In response to her questions, I told her that North had assured me that "everything had been taken care of" in the event the Iranians tried to detain us. I later learned that the only contingency plan that existed in case any of us were taken hostage rested with North, who brought along lethal pills which some of us might choose to take in order to avoid remaining in captivity. (For many reasons, I wish that I had heeded Reagan's maxim: "Trust, but verify.") Given the circumstances, the trip appeared to be a worthy endeavor that might get the hostages released and could yield significant long-term benefits for United States interests in the Persian Gulf. Gayle remained skeptical but reluctantly supported my decision to go.

On the eve of my departure some weeks later, and fearful that the U.S. government might betray us in the event something went wrong, Gayle asked me to write a note to her which she would keep until my return. At the time, I thought she was being paranoid, but I eventually agreed. The note stated that I had been sent to Tehran on a secret mission on behalf of the U.S. government, together with Robert C. McFarlane and others to secure the release of the American hostages in Lebanon. I shredded the note after I returned to Washington.

In mid-May, North told me that final arrangements had been made for the trip. We were to travel over the Memorial Day weekend. I needed to give Bob Earl a passport photo and a proposed Irish name and identity which a government agency would use to prepare counterfeit passports. I chose the name Timothy McGann of Dingle, Ireland. North asked me whether I thought Amiram Nir, the Israeli prime minister's counterterrorism advisor, should accompany us on the trip. "Absolutely not," I said without hesitation. "We have American equities to protect here. A joint mission with Israel will leave us even more vulnerable if things go wrong. What is the rationale for Israel's participation?" I asked. "Peres wants Nir along to ensure that we try to recover the bodies of Israeli Shin Bet officers being held by Hizbollah in Lebanon," North replied. "We don't need Nir along for that," I said. "Moreover, how can you be sure that he won't try to promote an Israeli agenda that might differ from ours once we get him there?" North acknowledged the point. I learned later that McFarlane had agreed with my opposition. However, the government of Israel decided to make the lease of its cargo airplanes contingent upon the participation of Nir, and the United States acquiesced to Israel's request. "He looks just about as Irish as I do," I told Earl, when we discussed my Irish identity.

Earl was assigned responsibility for coordinating logistics and communications from Washington during the trip, and he told me to report to the Page Aviation Terminal at Dulles Airport on the morning of Friday, May 23, 1986. There I met a CIA officer who coordinated our departure. McFarlane, retired CIA Iran expert George Cave, two CIA communications specialists and I boarded a chartered executive jet for a flight to Rhein Main, Germany, stopping for fuel in Gander, Newfoundland. We arrived at Rhein Main at approximately ten-thirty P.M.

Our jet taxied to a cargo apron and parked next to a 707 cargo plane bathed in bright spotlights. We debarked from our plane to await an Air

Force minivan, which would take us to the bachelor officers' quarters (BOQ) for a rest of several hours before our flying on to Tel Aviv. The Air Force sergeant who drove the minivan nearly caused a disaster, however, when he parked the van fifty feet from the 707 without securing the brakes. As McFarlane, Cave and I milled around on the tarmac, the unattended minivan started to roll forward, picking up speed rapidly as it headed directly toward the 707. McFarlane sprinted after the van, jumped through the open doorway and slammed on the brakes no more than ten feet from the nose gear of the 707. The sergeant, who had been flirting with one of the flight attendants from our executive jet, immediately recovered his van and took us over to the BOQ.

After a two-and-one-half-hour respite, the driver returned to the BOQ and brought us back to where the 707 was parked, still bathed in bright light. As we were approaching the boarding staircase, the area was suddenly blacked out. The lights were out on our vehicle as well and our driver drove past the plane and out into the darkness. We continued driving in darkness for nearly fifteen minutes, the tower and lights of the base barely visible in the distance. Suddenly, the van lurched to a stop at the foot of a ladder that descended from the belly of a St. Lucia Airways 707 cargo plane. Inside the plane were two rows of seats, a pile of mattresses and blankets and a large wooden shipping crate sitting on a pallet wrapped in heavy-duty plastic.

The plane took off around one-thirty A.M. and arrived in a military airfield adjacent to Ben-Gurion Airport at five-thirty A.M. North, who had arrived separately, and Nir came bounding up the stairs to greet us and help load our gear into several waiting cars. Saturday morning at five-thirty is a good time to arrive in Israel if one wants to avoid being noticed. Driving through Tel Aviv's deserted streets, we arrived at the Carleton Hotel just after six A.M. and were hustled up to our rooms via a loading dock and freight elevator. North asked us to "muster" at seven A.M. in one of the rooms, where we met with the crew of the airplane that would take us to Tehran, and much to my surprise, Dick Secord, my former boss at the DOD.

Secord briefed us on the details of the flight plan: fuel load, age of the plane's engines, likely time of arrival and communications arrangements. Secord's briefing was logistically impressive, but he made several remarks that suggested that he would prefer to be going to Tehran himself, rather than staying behind in Tel Aviv to oversee the command, control and communications of the operation. He noted that he knew "better than anyone else how to deal with Iranians." The meeting broke up around eight A.M. and I returned to my room, where I stayed until we all went for lunch at Lura's Romanian Restaurant in Jaffa. Although I wanted to go down to the beach for a swim, Secord asked me not to leave my room. Purported secrecy notwithstanding, that evening the team went out for dinner at the Empire Seafood Restaurant.

We returned to the airport and boarded our plane at eleven P.M. The crew was just about to close the door when one of Nir's associates came running up the stairs with what appeared to be a cake box in his hands. "Ollie," Nir called. "We got it!" I looked over as Nir and North opened the box. In it was a round chocolate cake, fresh from a kosher Tel Aviv bakery that had just reopened after the Sabbath had ended at nine P.M. "It's perfect," North said, laughing as he closed the box and stowed it in the airplane's galley. "It's exactly what Ghorbanifar told us to bring."

The airplane, a vintage 707 cargo plane with relatively new engines, belonged to the Israeli government but had all identifying markings removed. It was painted white. North explained that the tail number had been removed from another 707 cargo plane that he had chartered from an Irish company. The other plane was hidden in a hangar somewhere in Europe while we "borrowed" its identity. As in the St. Lucia plane, there was a row of seats, mattresses, blankets and the ubiquitous box of HAWK spare parts loaded onto a pallet and strapped to mooring rings on the floor. North told me that in fact it was only half of the spares that the Iranians had purchased. North and Secord had decided to keep the other half of the shipment back in Tel Aviv ready to be delivered to Tehran if the Iranians performed and succeeded in bringing about the release of the American hostages.

Taking off from Ben-Gurion International Airport, we flew south over the Red Sea until we reached the Indian Ocean. At that point, in order to mislead any curious air traffic controllers, the pilot banked to the west toward Somalia and then slowly circled back to the east until we were on a flight path that suggested that we were flying from the southeast coast of Africa. To ensure that we weren't identified as an airplane that had originated in Tel Aviv, the pilot answered all queries by reporting that our flight had originated in Mombasa, Kenya.

Aside from a disagreement over our lack of a flight clearance to Tehran with Bandar Abbas air traffic control in eastern Iran, the flight from Israel proved to be uneventful. At 7:20 A.M. on May 25, 1986, we arrived at Mehrhabad Airport in Tehran. (We actually thought it was 8:20, not realizing that the Iranians had reset their clocks.) Prior to landing, North retrieved the cake box, opened it, and with exaggerated comic flourish, placed a brass skeleton key in the middle of the round chocolate cake.

We were surprised when there was no one to meet us and we sat in the plane for half an hour until a staff member in the office of the prime minister showed up and escorted us to the VIP lounge. The reading material in the lounge consisted of quotes from the Ayatollah Khomeini, a history of the Islamic revolution and reprints of classified documents that the Iranians had captured from the U.S. embassy in Tehran during the former hostage crisis.

We waited for another forty-five minutes before another man arrived. North introduced him as Manuchar Ghorbanifar. Ghorbanifar apologized for the delay and the lack of a formal reception. An hour later, a deputy to the prime minister, Mr. Kangerlu, arrived and made polite small talk with McFarlane until he abruptly decided that enough formalities had transpired. Just before leaving the VIP lounge, North walked up to Kangerlu and presented him with the chocolate cake, proclaiming that "this box holds the key to the future of U.S.-Iranian relations." Kangerlu burst into laughter when he looked inside and saw the key on top of the cake, and then proceeded vigorously to embrace North, kissing him on the cheeks four times.

The box of HAWK spare parts remained on the aircraft as we were herded into a Mercedes motorcade and driven through town to the Independence Hotel. We reached the hotel at around eleven A.M. Ghorbanifar told us the deputy prime minister would meet with us at five P.M. After lunch we rested in our rooms until we reconvened at four-fifteen. We had not yet received word whether the hostages had made it out. We made final preparations and received the Iranian delegation at five.

Once the meetings with the Iranians began, I took notes to ensure that a comprehensive record of the exchanges would be available for study once we returned to Washington. (My memoranda of conversations were subsequently turned over to the various bodies investigating the Iran Affair and were declassified and published in their entirety.) In brief, McFarlane carefully hewed to the TOR that President Reagan had approved, laying out the goals, interests and policies of the United States in southwest Asia, emphasizing Washington's desire to find a way to restore a normal relationship with Iran. The Iranians were candid about what they wanted from the United States, notably arms, and questioned why we had only brought a partial shipment of HAWK spare parts. Evidently they had unloaded the box from the plane. No progress was made on the hostages and no progress was made on arms, as it quickly became clear to both sides that Ghorbanifar had misled both Washington and Tehran about each other's expectations and minimal requirements in order to ensure that the meeting took place. Ghorbanifar had obviously hoped that once the parties were together, compromises could be negotiated and a deal concluded.

Outside of McFarlane's room, Kangerlu went up to Ghorbanifar and angrily confronted him with the fact that both sides were aware of his game. Ghorbanifar broke out in a ferocious sweat and tried to rationalize what he had done. Kangerlu was not a nice man. He was a former cobbler's apprentice who had risen to prominence during the revolution when he personally captured several SAVAK agents, tied them to a bangalore torpedo and blew them up. Watching Kangerlu's intense eyes bear down on Ghorbanifar as he cringed with fear, I wondered whether Ghorbanifar would live through the night.

Although Ghorbanifar had behaved true to form, even the Iranians appeared surprised by the depth of his deceit. Innocents abroad, we were in the bazaar but did not know how to behave like a Persian *bazaari*. It appeared that unless we were willing to be very patient, staying on for days if not weeks, bartering in the best Persian tradition, there was no way we would win the hostages' release or meet with Rafsanjani, Mousavi or Khameini.

The days in Tehran were not without their light moments. The Independence Hotel (formerly the Tehran Hilton) tried to maintain the appearance of pre-Revolutionary, first-class service. Our meals were served by a nervous waiter who would arrive at McFarlane's suite at the appointed time in worn black tie. Before each meal, he would formally hand each of us an ornate menu that listed forty or fifty Persian dishes. The menu looked wonderful, but all the kitchen served was kebab, lamb or chicken. Embarrassed by the dismal cuisine, not to mention the truly appalling political situation, Ghorbanifar had his mother prepare a Persian feast that he personally catered.

Then there was that fine Irishman Amiram Nir, code-named "Adam Miller." Nir greeted Kangerlu in the traditional Persian manner on the second morning of the talks. Nir, though, had just completed Israeli Army reserve duty in the Negev desert before we left for Tehran, and had several nasty sun blisters on his lips. Although the blisters did not deter him from kissing Nir, afterward Kangerlu came over to North and me and asked how Adam had gotten such nasty blisters. Without missing a beat, North looked over at Nir and back again at Kangerlu and said, "Herpes. Adam has a bad case of herpes." Not sure what "herpes" meant, Kangerlu walked over to George Cave to ask him to translate. As Cave translated "herpes," we watched all the color drain out of Kangerlu's face. He spent the next two days wiping his mouth continually with a handkerchief in a vain effort to get rid of the herpes virus.

Although we continued to meet for several days and nights, the hostages were still in captivity. An atmosphere of mistrust enveloped the talks. McFarlane believed there was little point in letting the Iranians jerk us around with *bazaari* tactics that might never yield any results. Cave and I tried to explain traditional Persian customs of barter, but to no avail. Bud had made up his mind that enough was enough. Without the promised high-level meetings with Rafsanjani, Mousavi and Khameini, he believed there was no point in staying and told the Iranians that we were leaving.

Intensely disappointed, we left our hotel the morning of May 28 at eight A.M., arriving at the airport and at our aircraft about forty minutes later. Following several last-minute pleas from the Iranians to stay longer, we departed and were airborne by 8:55 A.M. Exhausted, I stretched out on a mattress and immediately went to sleep. I slept nearly all the way to Tel Aviv, where we arrived in midafternoon. The CIA communicator set up the satellite radio system and North and McFarlane spoke with Washington. I walked over to the edge of the tarmac and sat down to enjoy Tel Aviv's warm afternoon sunshine. Secord told us that a chartered Learjet was standing by on the other side of the field to take us back to Washington.

Our first stop was Geneva, where we refueled, changed crews and contacted Washington. Shortly after we arrived in Geneva, a congressional delegation headed by then senator Al Gore, Jr., arrived to observe the ongoing Soviet-U.S. arms control negotiations. Although Gore and McFarlane exchanged greetings, neither the senator nor his associates inquired as to why we were in Geneva. It was just as well. We departed Geneva at dusk, just before the airport closed, and flew on to our next fuel stop at Reykjavik, Iceland. From there we flew on to a remote airport in Quebec to refuel for the last time, finally arriving back at Washington's Dulles Airport around five A.M. on May 29.

At nine-thirty A.M. I accompanied McFarlane and North to brief the president in the Oval Office. Bush, Regan, Poindexter and McDaniel of the NSC staff participated in the meeting. McFarlane summarized the visit, and expressed his opinion that the Iranians would continue to support hostage-taking as a means to secure arms and spare parts from the

United States. Reagan and Bush listened intensely, but had little to say. We reconvened in Poindexter's office at ten A.M., where Poindexter stated that the administration would take no further initiative. It would be up to the Iranians to contact the United States next.

In late July, North asked me to join him to brief the vice president on the status of the Iran initiative in the event that the subject arose during his forthcoming visit to Israel. I explained recent political developments in Israel and Iran, emphasizing that he should not discuss this with anyone but Peres or Nir. North summarized the status of arms deliveries and the prospects for more hostage releases. As the meeting ended, Bush offered to help in any way he could.

This ended my involvement in President Reagan's initiative to Iran. I was not involved again, in any way, until after the *Al Shiraa* story broke, revealing our secret trip to Iran the preceding May. Not yet fully recovered from the stress of the Libya disinformation affair and the long knives, I braced for the policy controversy that doubtless would ensue. What I did not anticipate, however, was that the opening to Iran and the attempt to secure the release of the American hostages would turn out to be a criminal inquiry into a diversion of funds from the Iranians to the Nicaraguan Contras.

Free Fall

For the first few weeks of November, my limited role in the Iran initiative remained secret and I worked diligently to support NSC efforts to find a way to secure the release of more hostages, organized records and helped prepare chronologies for the president. On two occasions, I recommended to Poindexter that he find a way to work with Shultz to try to maintain a dialogue with Iranian officials to see if anything positive could still result. I called Abe Sofaer and, over lunch at the Hay-Adams Hotel, briefed him on the Iran initiative. I urged him to help salvage U.S. policy and prevent further damage to American interests. We couldn't just forget about the hostages now. Sofaer, an ally of mine on several occasions, listened carefully, said he understood what we had been trying to accomplish, but strongly doubted that Shultz would alter his adamant opposition to any further dealings with the Iranians. Sofaer also expressed concern about possible damage to the president.

On November 25, exactly one year after the death of Gayle's mother, the attorney general went on national television to announce that there had been a diversion of profits to the Nicaraguan Contras from the arms sales to Iran. From that moment on, I knew my life and that of my family would never be the same.

Despite the wide media coverage of the emerging scandal, it had not yet been reported that I had been on the trip to Tehran. On Thursday, November 27, however, I received a call, at my home, from a UPI correspondent who was with the president in Santa Barbara. I did not know him and asked how he had gotten my unlisted telephone number. "The senior White House official who told me that you traveled to Iran with McFarlane and North last May and that you were the mastermind of the affair," he replied.

The euphemism "senior White House official" almost certainly meant Don Regan, the chief of staff, or one of his close aides, who were known pejoratively as "the mice." I immediately understood that Regan was trying to divert press attention to me, just as he had done earlier during the Libya disinformation affair. His cowardly "spin control" tactics of shifting the spotlight onto others, in an effort to find a scapegoat while protecting his own hide, were well known throughout Washington. Though we barely knew each other, my participation in the trip to Tehran ensured that Regan would eventually begin throwing his poison darts my way.

Livid, I asked the reporter, "Would you like a statement from me on the record?" "Absolutely," he eagerly replied. "Fine," I said, "I will make your day, on the record, once you tell me who your source is." The reporter audibly gulped and began sputtering, mumbling that he "could not afford to disclose [his] source, he was simply too senior." "Come on," I urged him, gritting my teeth in anger, "you won't be disappointed by what I am prepared to say. I'll give you a comment on the record." He hesitated for several more moments, but said that he simply could not disclose his source. "Okay," I said, "then you can quote me as saying that I see no useful purpose commenting on allegations made by anonymous officials."

Earlier that day in Tehran, Rafsanjani had said that Iran deserved credit for creating a situation in which U.S. politicians were "cutting each other's throats." And to think that I had been concerned about what might happen to the Iranians!

The NSC Is No Different from the FTC

During the first week of December I was subpoenaed to testify before the Senate Select Committee on Intelligence (SSCI) and requested to testify before the House Foreign Affairs Committee about the mission to Iran. I immediately contacted the White House counsel, Peter Wallison, and was referred to his deputy, Jay Stephens (who went on to serve as the U.S. Attorney in Washington, D.C.). A meeting was scheduled in the White House Situation Room with Stephens, Dean McGrath, who worked for Stephens, NSC counsel Commander Paul Thompson, Bob Earl, Craig Coy, NSC deputy executive secretary Bob Pearson and me. Gayle also attended this meeting, after Abe Sofaer authorized her to participate. We were greeted by Stephens, who handed us a copy of government regulations on reimbursement for private legal fees as we walked through the door.

As we sat down at the conference table, we could feel the tension in the air. Stephens opened the meeting by reiterating President Reagan's desire for everyone to "cooperate fully" in the congressional and other inquiries. The president wanted "full disclosure and that everyone should be truthful." He noted that the president was not invoking executive privilege. I asked Stephens what I should do or say or what procedures should be followed in testifying before the Congress or responding to internal and FBI inquiries. In reply to my request for guidance, Stephens directed the group's attention to the federal regulations he had given us on reimbursement for private legal fees.

He announced that neither White House counsel nor NSC counsel would be accompanying us to any hearings, depositions or anything else. I asked him to please explain what we were to do in these truly extraordinary circumstances. Stephens continued with his statement that "he was counsel to the president" and that President Reagan wanted everyone to "cooperate fully with full disclosure, that everyone should be truthful and try to answer questions in a straightforward manner." He said that White House counsel was "institutional counsel."

I asked Stephens about procedures for the disclosure of Special Compartmented Intelligence (SCI) and other sensitive national security information. He thought about that for a moment and said that we "should be careful" not to disclose anything that could "detrimentally affect" national security interests and that I should use my "best judgment." I continued to press Stephens on this issue, pointing out that there were statutes that prohibited me from revealing SCI and other such highly classified information as was involved in the president's initiative to Iran, unless special procedures were followed. I kept emphasizing my concern about the consequences of disclosing very sensitive intelligence sources and methods, inadvertent or otherwise, and I pointed out that I was personally subject to criminal penalties for unauthorized disclosures.

I asked the White House counsel again for guidance as to what could be revealed, particularly with regard to sources and methods. Stephens lamely repeated President Reagan's stated desire for full disclosure but that I "should reveal nothing, except as necessary," that could detrimentally affect the national security of the United States. He offered his opinion that the committees would be "sensitive," but he refused to give specific guidance. Stephens did acknowledge that I faced potential personal liability.

By now everyone else had become quite nervous listening to our increasingly testy exchange. My colleagues started to ask Stephens and Thompson about the various subpoenas and requests to appear before Congress, but both men declined to advise anyone and merely repeated what Stephens had already said while referring us once again to the regulations on reimbursement for private legal fees. They reiterated that neither White House counsel nor NSC counsel could represent or accompany anyone before the committees, although we would all be discussing what had occurred during the course of our official duties.

Gayle had sat quietly, taking notes, but finally interjected with a blunt lawyer's question. Looking Stephens coldly in the eyes, she asked him directly, "Are you telling these men that neither the White House counsel nor the NSC counsel have any fiduciary responsibility to them?" "That is correct," Stephens replied. "There is no attorney-client relationship. *As far as the White House is concerned, the NSC is no different than the FTC* [Federal Trade Commission] *or any other federal agency.*" At that point, Thompson nodded in agreement and looked down at the floor, unwilling to look any of us in the eye.

I became extremely sarcastic at this point and pulled out my White House badge and held it up to Stephens. "This badge reads WHS [White House Staff] and gives me the right to walk into the Oval Office if necessary. And just like you do, I receive my paycheck from the executive office of the president. I cannot believe you would suggest that the institutional relationship between the NSC and the president is no different than the president's relationship to the FTC. Your suggestion that the NSC is no different than the FTC is outrageous. It is inconceivable to me that I would be sent on a dangerous mission at the direction of the president of the United States and then be cut loose to fend for myself without the advice of agency counsel!"

Stephens once again held up the photocopied federal regulations and lamely noted that they provided for reimbursement for legal fees for retention of private counsel. He said, "Unless you are indicted, you should be entitled to reimbursement for your legal fees if you decide to hire a lawyer."

"Great, just great. I was performing my official duties and this is what the White House says?" I asked whether any lawyer from the government could advise me. Stephens said that the Justice Department might be able to provide me with some legal assistance, but he did not know whether it could do so in these circumstances, since Justice was conducting its own investigation of the Iran Affair.

This sorry meeting ended late Friday afternoon, and I began to experience the sensation of free-fall as I grasped for the rip cord on my nonexistent parachute. The White House had made sure that no one on the NSC staff would be provided with a parachute. On the contrary, Stephens had clearly been directed to open the airplane door and push me and my colleagues out into the darkness and over the water. There was no parachute, life raft or any survival aids. This was the measure of appreciation I would receive for ten years of public service.

That evening Gayle and I went to dinner with friends who spent the entire evening telling us that I would be a fool not to hire a lawyer in these circumstances. This was fast becoming a three-ring circus and the truth was irrelevant.

Neither Gayle nor I wanted to believe that the truth did not matter. I had done nothing wrong—why did I need a lawyer? I had nothing to hide and Congress had a right to know what had happened, given Meese's revelations about the diversion of funds to the Contras. Over the course of the weekend every friend we had called us at home to offer their unsolicited opinions that I simply had to hire an attorney to accompany me to the hearings and represent me before the Independent Counsel. By Sunday, it was clear that everyone could not be wrong. A friend, Robert Bauer, put me in touch with Robert Bennett and Carl Rauh, two of Washington's premier white-collar criminal-defense lawyers.

Gayle and I met with Bennett and Rauh in their offices on Monday morning, and they agreed to represent me. We were very upset by the entire situation, bitter over the White House's despicable treatment of those of us who were ready to cooperate with the government investigation and somehow ashamed about the whole situation. Our lawyers understood better than we did what was happening and helped us come to grips with reality. They took matters under their control and reassured us that they would look after my interests with the utmost care.

In the circumstances, I was not yet able to discuss my specific involvement, because they did not have the clearances to be briefed on these matters. They noted that they had received high-level clearances before and would get them renewed promptly. Accordingly, they said they would request a delay in my testimony to give us more time to confer. In the meantime, they urged me in the strongest possible terms to invoke my Fifth Amendment privilege against self-incrimination.

I was aghast. Before I could say anything, however, Gayle injected emphatically, "There is no way Howard is going to take the Fifth." She said that I had done nothing wrong or criminal and that it would certainly ruin my career forever if I invoked Fifth Amendment rights. I told them that I truly had nothing to hide and that I wanted to be forthcoming with the Congress and the Independent Counsel.

Whether or not I believed I had done anything wrong, they warned that I risked serious exposure to charges of perjury or obstruction of justice. They pointed out that I was an analyst who freely gave my opinion, often whether or not I was asked. I had been trained to speculate about what might have taken place. In these circumstances, speculating could get me into big trouble. Bennett pointed to a big trout hanging on his wall and said, "See that trout? He's up there because he couldn't keep his mouth shut." Rauh said he understood how I felt, but that they were obliged to warn me about the potential liability I faced in choosing not to invoke the Fifth Amendment.

Over the course of the next several days, there were various exchanges with the committees. Poindexter and North took the Fifth and a three-ring circus opened for business. The committees accepted Bennett and Rauh's request for a delay until their clearances were granted.

Despite Reagan's professed desire to get all the facts out, and Bush's stated willingness to let the chips fall where they may—even if the truth hurts—senior members of the administration ran for cover to avoid becoming embroiled in the controversy. The essence of Ronald Reagan's decision was that the United States would secretly sell weapons to the Iranian government in exchange for Tehran using its influence to free the American hostages in Lebanon. This would lead to a dialogue between Iranian and American leaders that would enhance the U.S. position in the Gulf.

But after the Iran-Contra scandal erupted, a sudden epidemic of Alzheimer's disease spread through the offices of the president and vice president and the Departments of State and Defense. No one seemed to remember anything, except that the all-powerful yet "mediocre" NSC staff had somehow been secretly running the world behind everyone's backs for many of the preceding years. Controversial national security decisions had apparently been made at a "lower level." No one was in charge. All of the key principals, it seemed, had been out of the loop.

Regan and the White House played dirty, pointing to me as Ollie North's boss and accusing me of being the architect of the Iran initiative. Acting under instructions, Larry Speakes waited days before announcing that I was not North's boss. When he finally confirmed that I wasn't North's boss, the media interest in me dramatically declined. But by then, matters had taken on a life of their own. Television, newspapers and magazines all over the world described me as Teicher, "a 32-year-old Middle East expert," "brilliant," "bold," "imaginative," "devious," "abrasive," "pro-Israel," "Jewish," "self-promoting," "North's boss" and the "architect of the Iran Affair."

The full impact of the media's growing interest in me began to hit home when ABC's Monday Night Football game was briefly interrupted by an announcement that "a man called Teicher will testify tomorrow." After I testified on December 16 before the SSCI, I announced my resignation from the staff of the National Security Council, effective the end of March. Larry Speakes also announced my resignation effective March 31, 1987. Wheel of Fortune was interrupted that night to provide viewers with this news.

I began to comprehend that Admiral Poindexter had betrayed me. It started to sink in that long after someone had decided that it would be a good idea to work with an Iranian intermediary to barter for American hostages and long after someone made the decision to finance the Nicaraguan Contras with the profits from the sale of arms to Iran, Poindexter made the decision to involve me. His contempt for the democratic process, however cumbersome it can be, and his willingness to arrogate to himself the powers and prerogatives of the different branches of government is frightening. Some have called Poindexter's activism a form of leadership. For me, it was no more than the banal and deceitful exploitation of misguided patriotism.

During my testimony before the SSCI and at numerous hearings, depositions and interviews thereafter, I was always asked the one key question of the Iran Affair: Was there really a cake in the shape of a key? In the midst of testifying and the media barrage, my son celebrated his first birthday. A large crowd was in attendance when we brought in his birthday cake to sing him "Happy Birthday." For the record, the only cake in the shape of a key was Seth Benjamin Teicher's first birthday cake, decorated with red, green and white frosting, in honor of the Iranian flag.

Media Terrorism

In mid-November 1986, two *Time* magazine reporters, David Halevy and David Beckwith wrote a story about the "cowboys" at the NSC (Beckwith went on to become Vice President Dan Quayle's press secretary in the Bush administration), I was described as a cowboy "*who craved adventure and seemed to generate controversy.*" In addition to my role in the Libya disinformation campaign, *Time* alleged that I had "*caused another flap five years ago when [I] tried to publish a fictionalized account of Israel's nuclear secrets.*"

The only thing that was fictionalized was the story published by *Time* magazine. I had never written a book about anything, let alone Israel's nuclear secrets, nor had Halevy or Beckwith made any effort to contact me to check the accuracy of this baseless allegation. I immediately called *Time*'s Washington bureau chief, Strobe Talbott, to discuss this matter.

Halevy was the author of another *Time* story which had also turned out to be untrue. *Time* published a story in 1983 which alleged that Ariel Sharon had reportedly discussed the need for the Phalangists to seek revenge for the assassination of Beshir Gemayel. Sharon sued *Time* for libel. The case was heard by then Judge Abraham Sofaer (who later became Shultz's State Department legal advisor). Although the jury ruled on a technicality that *Time* had not libeled Sharon, a statement was issued by the jurors criticizing *Time* and Halevy for negligence and carelessness.

Evidently put out by my call, Talbott arrogantly defended his staff, suggesting that "perhaps you have forgotten about the book you wrote when you lived in Israel." Livid over Talbott's response, I coldly suggested that he check with his staff because "I expect a retraction and an apology." Taken aback when he learned that neither reporter had contacted me, he said he would speak with them.

Less than an hour later Talbott called back to inform me that *Time* had "confused" me with someone else, an Israeli attorney named Eli Teicher. If I wanted to write a letter to set the record straight, they would publish it along with an editor's note "regretting the error." "Thanks a lot, Strobe," I said. "Just put your apology on the cover of *Time* where everyone can read it."

Alton Keel had convinced Frank Carlucci, the new NSC advisor, to agree to permit me to stay through the end of March. I was cooperating with the rapidly proliferating investigative bodies, organizing files for my successor and trying to find a job. However, the day after the release of the *Tower Commission Report* in February, Carlucci reneged, giving me four hours' notice to clear out my desk, turn in my building pass and leave the White House, although I would continue to be paid through the end of March.

One of the most honorable men in Washington, Keel could do little more than stand by and watch as Ken Adelman, Frank Carlucci's hatchet man, and others took every opportunity with the media to belittle almost every member of the NSC staff. The NSC had been designated as the scapegoat of the Iran-Contra affair. The "mediocre" yet all-powerful NSC, which had been secretly running the world behind the back of everyone else in Washington, was no longer a good place to work.

My job search went nowhere, as false and misleading allegations of my role in the Iran initiative and a steady drumbeat of character assassination in the media made me "radioactive" to prospective employers, who feared any possible contamination from the Iran Affair. I was especially disappointed at the behavior of many whom I had always helped and considered to be real, rather than political, friends. Aside from a few individuals and members of my family who stood shoulder to shoulder alongside me, many friends simply failed to return my phone calls. Others expressed sympathy, but simply could not offer me a job or help me in any way. My "presence might be politically embarrassing."

Harry Truman was absolutely right when he said that if you want to have a friend you can count on in Washington, you had better get a dog. In the midst of all the testifying, and as we were squinting into the glare of my unwelcome notoriety, one particular friend called to see how we were doing. Gayle, ever the optimist, started explaining that things were really going as well as could be expected, that we were all healthy and somehow, everything would be all right in the end. Our friend said something that helped us throughout the ordeal. She told us that we had the right attitude: "When you get lemons, make lemonade."

On the strong advice of Bennett and Rauh, my legal "dream team," I declined most interview requests, suggesting that journalists communicate with me through my attorneys to avoid any mistakes and ensure that we maintained an accurate record. The majority of the journalists who tried to reach me were satisfied with this approach. But one, a former *Time* senior correspondent, decided to take a special interest in my situation and repeatedly pestered my attorneys and me for an interview. Now a consultant to *Time*, Murray Gart advised Bennett and Rauh that he had been retained by *Time* for a "special project" and insisted that it was "essential" that he have an opportunity to interview me. He refused, however, to disclose the nature of his special project.

I learned from members of the NSC staff, and others, that Gart seemed to be investigating whether the Iran initiative was all the result of a plot by Israel to somehow suck the United States into selling arms to Iran in order to perpetuate the Iran-Iraq War. According to Jim Stark (a member of my by-now-defunct Political-Military Affairs Directorate, who was authorized to give Gart an interview by the NSC executive secretary), Gart was trying to uncover alleged secret links between Israel and me, "practically going back to the day you were circumcised." Gart's conspiracy theory included my relations with other Jews in the U.S. government, including Gayle and Abe Sofaer, whom he also sought to interview.

It was a dark time to be a Jewish official anywhere in the U.S. government in the wake of the recent spy case of Jonathan Jay Pollard, a Navy intelligence analyst who was caught spying for Israel and subsequently sentenced to life in prison. Pollard severely damaged American national security and helped sow discord in U.S.-Israeli relations. His actions served to reinforce the convictions of some in the national security bureaucracy and elsewhere that American Jews suffer from "dual loyalty" and cannot be trusted to behave as "real" Americans. Together with the stereotypic and false accusation that Jews control the banks and the media, the charge of dual loyalty has become the modern-day siren call of American anti-Semites. For the anti-Semites and self-hating Jews in the Middle East bureaucracy, Washington think tanks and elsewhere, the environment created by the Iran Affair and Pollard presented opportunities that simply could not be passed up. Journalists already intoxicated by whiffs of scandal and conspiracy offered themselves up as willing fodder to be used to help blast me as far from Middle East policy-making as possible.

John Walcott, whose "reliable" Pentagon sources had led him to write that the United States and Libya were on a collision course, proved unable to resist the temptation to play to the gallery in his book *Best Laid Plans*. Although he made a feeble attempt to appear evenhanded, he once again let himself be used. Writing about the murdered CIA chief of station in Beirut, Bill Buckley, Walcott wrote that Buckley would agree to *"brief"* McFarlane *"but not with Teicher present. It'll get right back to the Israelis."*

In fact, I regularly met with Bill Buckley and McFarlane in Lebanon, and Buckley discussed almost every intelligence matter imaginable in my presence. I met with him on almost every occasion I was in Beirut, and the record confirms this. Walcott's allegation is completely false. But who was his source? Buckley was dead and McFarlane denies Buckley ever said anything even remotely like that to him.

Walcott also wrote, *"Teicher was Jewish, a strong supporter of Israel and an ardent foe of Syria. With his dark beard, he bore a physical resemblance to the terrorists he was tilting against. Like most of them, he was young, tireless, committed, and sometimes cocky. He had followed Robert McFarlane from the State Department to the National Security Council staff, and as he rose through the ranks, his religion and his abrasiveness made him a catalyst for the ugly feud between Arabists and supporters of Israel in the U.S. government. Middle East experts in the State Department, the NSC staff, and some Washington think tanks conducted a tireless whispering campaign against him, intimating that he was an Israeli agent. . . . In the absence of any evidence, Teicher was no more guilty of working for the Israelis than his accusers were of working for Syria or the PLO."*

Walcott confirmed that his source was neither Buckley nor McFarlane, but firmly dismissed my protestations. Someone had said it was true, *even if it was not.* His source was "very reliable."

In the meantime, Murray Gart kept trying to interview me. I argued with Bennett and Rauh for nearly six weeks to convince them that an interview could only help clear up what were undoubtedly anti-Semitic attacks on my character promoted by those who wanted to undermine both U.S.-Israeli relations and me. We eventually worked out a compromise to deal with *Time* magazine whereby Gart submitted questions to Bennett and I delivered written answers.

His questions left little to the imagination in trying to surmise where he might be going with his line of questioning. Gart asked me, *inter alia:* Are you a Zionist today as you were in your student days? How does this affect your foreign policy views? Are your views about Israel the same today as when you were a student? Other than the time you were at a kibbutz, have you ever been employed by an Israeli organization? What about your wife? Did she work for any Israeli organizations? Were you aware that your pro-Israeli views were viewed as excessive and that was the reason you were passed over twice for a promotion to the position as director for Middle East policy? Are you a member of the Jewish Institute for National Security Affairs (JINSA)? Are you a member of any other organizations like JINSA? When did you first meet David Kimche? How often did you see Kimche? When was the last time you talked to him? Were your discussions personal or official in nature? Did your wife know Kimche? Was Edward Luttwak your favorite professor in graduate school? Did he give you good grades? What were the circumstances of your meeting Michael Ledeen? How close a friendship did you have with Ledeen and how frequently were you in contact with him? Did you ever consider becoming an Israeli citizen? Did you ever consider emigrating to Israel?

After sending Gart written answers to his questions, neither Bennett, Rauh nor I heard back from him for more than a month, nor did *Time* publish any stories by Gart involving his line of questioning. But the whispering campaign against me intensified in mid-February 1987.

Over lunch, *The New York Times* columnist William Safire asked me what I thought of the article on Qadhafi by the Pulitzer Prize–winning author Seymour Hersh that was scheduled to be published in the forthcoming issue of *The New York Times Sunday Magazine.* When I replied that I didn't know anything about the piece, Safire acted visibly shocked and asked again to make sure that I had not misunderstood him. "No," I answered. "What does Seymour Hersh say?" Shaking his head incredulously, Safire said, "Do you mean to tell me that Hersh did not call you about a major exposé on the April bombing of Libya which comes out this Sunday? Oh boy! You had better read it."

Hersh's lengthy article "Target Qadhafi" appeared in the *Sunday Magazine* and falsely asserted that the primary goal of the April 14 strike was to assassinate Qadhafi. Hersh also wrote, "*At the time of the attack on Libya, North, Poindexter, and Teicher had been deeply involved in the Administration's secret arms dealing with Iran for nearly a year; they also knew that funds from those dealings were being funneled from a Swiss bank account controlled by North to the administration-backed Contras.*" Hersh said that he had reached his conclusions "*after three months of interviews with more than 70 current and former officials in the White House, the State Department, the Central Intelligence Agency, the National Security Agency, and the Pentagon.*" None of Hersh's sources, however, spoke on the record.

I was just outraged. Not only had Seymour Hersh made no effort to ask me for my comments about the Libya strike or about any of the anonymously sourced allegations, but his assertion regarding my knowledge of the diversion of funds was untrue and libelous. I telephoned Hersh, with whom I had never before spoken, after getting his number from the Washington bureau of *The New York Times.*

After angrily informing him who he was talking to, I told him that his story was rife with mistakes, particularly regarding his false allegation that I knew about the diversion of funds to the Contras, and that regardless of the accuracy of the rest of his story, at minimum, he should have had the courtesy to ask me or my lawyers for my comments if he planned to write about me. I said that I expected a retraction from *The New York*

Times and an apology. Outraged himself by my vehemence and unexpected intrusion into his Sunday morning, Hersh lashed out at me shouting "that just because you don't like my version of the truth—" I cut him off and said that I had been in many of the meetings he had written about. I knew the facts, and was not interested in his "version of the truth." Swearing, Hersh hung up on me.

Several days later Bennett called to say that Seymour Hersh had phoned him and wanted to know if he could call me. "Are you ready for this?" Bennett asked me. "He wants to apologize." We spoke later that day and Hersh admitted that the comment about my knowledge of the diversion of funds was wrong, "caused by a mechanical error."

To his credit, he said that he was sorry and that he was sure the *Magazine* editors would agree to publish a retraction and apology. Acknowledging, somewhat ruefully, that he should have contacted me before running the story, Hersh remarked, "At least you're not like all the other dumb schmucks in Washington that let themselves get jerked around by the media."

Somewhat mollified, I asked him why he hadn't called me. "Can I ask you a blunt question?" Hersh asked in a suddenly mysterious and quiet voice. "Will you be straight with me?" "Go ahead and ask," I replied, curious at the sudden change in tone I detected. Hersh asked me, "Is it true that you are being investigated by the FBI on charges that you are an Israeli spy?"

I was stunned. "Ridiculous," I replied, "that's just more anti-Semitic bullshit put out by people who want to ruin my career. I still hold TOP SECRET—CODEWORD clearances, which at a minimum would have been pulled if I was under investigation. Who's telling you this?" I asked. Hersh, however, would say only that it was "a very reliable source" whom he had "no reason to suspect would lie to him." I told him that I appreciated his willingness to apologize but wanted to know who had told him this.

Sitting at the dining room table afterward, the adrenaline still draining, Gayle and I sat together in dazed disbelief. Stricken, her eyes filling with tears, Gayle started talking: "This is like Dreyfus, Howard. It's the Big Lie, you can't unwind it, it has too many strands. It's just McCarthyism. How can you possibly prove that you are not a spy? Somebody is out to destroy you. They've shifted the burden of proof, guilty until proven innocent. How can you defend yourself against anonymous sources? You are being accused because you are a Jew who had the temerity to work on the Middle East! The anti-Semites are coming out of the woodwork. It's right out of history. It's a new blood libel. You were just too uppity and they are making you pay."

Several weeks later during a meeting with Bennett and Rauh, we were discussing that things seemed to be going quite well on the legal front. The official record was proving my innocence and we were relatively pleased, given the circumstances. Gayle agreed, but shook her head. Addressing herself mainly to Rauh, she recalled what Hersh had told me about the alleged FBI investigation. "I can't get it out of my head," she said. "It is such a horrible allegation. It's so scary, it simply terrifies me. I just can't believe Howard has enemies who hate him so much that they would go to such lengths and invent such a horrible lie. It's anti-Semitic intimidation. People who hate Israel are using him to wreck Israel's relationship with the U.S. *What source has that much credibility?*"

Bennett had gone on to other matters, but Rauh looked at Gayle sympathetically and recalled that his father, Joseph Rauh, had stood up to Joe McCarthy in the 1950s. He understood what she was talking about.

The April Surprise

In late March 1987, the U.S. Attorney in Bridgeport, Connecticut, called Bennett to ask if I would agree to testify on behalf of the U.S. government in a criminal case that had been brought against a Pakistani arms dealer, Arif Durrani, for allegedly selling weapons illegally to Iran. Durrani claimed that he and I had met at the Crystal City Marriott in Arlington, Virginia, where I had offered to sell him TOW antitank missiles that he would then deliver to Iran on behalf of the U.S. government. He also had testified that we met in Frankfurt for additional meetings with Iranian officials.

Presumably expecting that I would refuse to testify, just as North and Poindexter had refused, Durrani and his defense lawyer might have hoped that the injection of "Teicher," a White House official, alleged to be the "architect" of the Iran Affair and North's boss, would add an element that would foil the U.S. government's ability to prove him guilty. I appeared as a prosecution witness on April 1, 1987, while en route to Europe. I saw the color drain out of Mr. Durrani's face when I was called to the witness stand. His defense attorney feebly objected that he had not been informed that I would be a prosecution witness. The judge overruled the objection and the Assistant U.S. Attorney, Ms. Holly Fitzsimmons, questioned me under oath about Durrani's testimony.

After establishing that I had served on the NSC staff, she asked me whether I had ever met Mr. Arif Durrani. I said that I had never met the man. Pointing to the defendant, she asked me whether I recognized him. I replied that I had never seen him before in my life. She said that several days ago the defendant claimed that I was his White House handler during the so-called Iran Affair, and that I had met with him secretly at the Crystal City Marriott in northern Virginia, where I offered him TOW antitank missiles. Fitzsimmons asked me whether I had met the defendant at the Crystal City Marriott and offered him TOW antitank missiles. I said that I had never met Mr. Durrani before, nor had I ever been to the Crystal City Marriott or offered to sell him, or anyone else, TOW antitank missiles.

She related that Mr. Durrani claimed that I traveled to Frankfurt, West Germany, where I met him and some Iranians in a hotel for discussions relating to the Iran Affair. "Is that true, Mr. Teicher?" asked Fitzsimmons. Turning to look directly at the jury, I replied, "No, I did not meet with him. In fact, I have never been to the city of Frankfurt except to change planes at the airport." The badly flustered defense attorney tried to question my credibility, but he had no idea who I was or what he should ask. When I repeated under cross-examination that I had never been to Frankfurt, the defense attorney literally threw up his papers as he wailed, "He's never even been to Frankfurt!"

In May, Ms. Fitzsimmons and Steven Arruda wrote to thank me for my cooperation in the case, informing me that "Mr. Durrani was convicted by the jury of all three charges pending against him after deliberating approximately 80 minutes. Your testimony was devastating to the defendant's credibility and crucial to our rebuttal case. We are sure that it contributed significantly to the speed with which the verdict was returned."

Former NSC staff member Gary Sick recently wrote a book entitled *The October Surprise,* which alleges that then candidate Ronald Reagan secretly struck a deal with the government of Iran in October 1980 to ensure that the Americans held hostage in Tehran would not be released prior to the U.S. presidential election. I was amused to learn that Arif Durrani was one of Sick's sources.

Durrani and men of his ilk, like Ghorbanifar, are expert fabricators who thrive on gullible third parties who want to find some deal or a conspiracy. Truth is very relative, as I witnessed in Tehran and in Bridgeport. But while I have no personal knowledge of what might have occurred between the Iranians and Ronald Reagan in October 1980, and I would certainly never presume to speculate, I do know for sure that Arif Durrani was very surprised in April 1987.

Aren't You Dead Yet?

I traveled to Bonn, Germany, the day after I testified in Bridgeport, in order to participate in an international conference on "The Economics of Peacemaking in the Middle East," sponsored by the Sadat Peace Foundation. With the conference scheduled to begin on Sunday evening, I flew first to London for a dinner party in my honor Friday night. Just before dinner was served, the phone rang. It was Bob Bennett.

Bennett apologized for bothering me in London but "a very serious problem has developed involving Murray Gart and *Time*. Gart just called to inform me that his very reliable source has told him about a list of Israeli agents in Washington. He says that the list was given to Bill Casey by the Mossad, Israel's intelligence service, and your name is at the top of the list. Gart said *Time* has already typeset the story. They plan to release it tonight. He is insisting on a face-to-face interview with you or *Time* will go with the story." "Does he know I am in London, Bob?" I asked, feeling my heart begin to pound wildly. "I told him you are out of the country," Bennett replied, "but he said the only way *Time* will hold the story is if you agree to give him an interview." "Let's try to buy some time," I said. "Tell the bastard that he can interview me next week if *Time* holds it. In the meantime I'll try to contact Buck Revell at the FBI. He is in charge of counterintelligence and counterterrorism. If I am under any kind of investigation, or on any kind of list of Israeli agents, Revell will know. He and I are friends and I believe he will tell me whether the allegation is true or not."

"Oh, come off it, Howard," Bennett replied. "I don't care how well you know Revell. The bureau never comments on anything."

"You let me talk to Buck, okay, Bob?" I said. "You just tell Gart to sit tight until I return next week."

Sandy and Lisa Vershbow, dear friends for ten years, having heard my half of the conversation, sat speechless as I recounted what Bennett had said. I immediately called Gayle, who knew that Bennett had called but did not know why. As tough as she is, Gart's slanderous charge was too much and she started to come unglued.

"This is blackmail. *Time* is blackmailing you," she shouted. "Okay. It's okay," she repeated, trying to get hold of herself and calming her rising hysteria. "We have to deal with this, we just have to deal with this, all right?" Breathing deeply several times, she asked, "Do you think it could be true? Do you think the government could really be investigating you? I keep hearing funny things on the phone. What if it's true? Oh my God, what is happening?" she cried. I told her that I did not think I could have kept my codeword clearances if I were being investigated. I said I thought it wasn't true, but that I wanted to call Buck Revell and ask him directly. We simply cried together over the phone, separated by the Atlantic Ocean during one of the worst crises of our lives.

"Well," she said after a while, with a note of defiance in her voice. "Pull yourself together. I'll pull myself together. Even if *Time* publishes this story in black and white, it still won't be true. Just because *Time* says it's true does not make it a fact. We have nothing to be ashamed of. You didn't do anything and no one could prove it even if they allege it. You served your country, you risked your life, you worked your ass off. And no matter what, we're going to be okay because it's not true and we have each other, our son and our health. We will make it through. Call Revell now." I took a moment to thank God that we had each other and said I would call Buck Revell right away.

Unfortunately, Revell was traveling, but his secretary said she would make sure he got my message. That was the longest weekend of our lives. When Gayle and I spoke on the phone, we could hear strange sounds. She was sure the house was being surveilled. Paranoia was settling in.

When I finally reached Revell by telephone the following Monday, I came right to the point, summarized Gart's allegations and asked him point-blank whether any of it was true. "Howard," Revell stated vehemently, "it is absolute horseshit. There is no truth to this story and I would know if there was. It is really regrettable, but you are not the only Jewish official who this is happening to. It is just a crock of shit!"

I felt an overwhelming sense of relief and quickly asked if he would repeat his statement to my attorney. Revell said, "Howard, I'm saying this on the record. I'll gladly repeat it to your lawyer and to the journalist from *Time, on the record*, if they will call me. Just have them call me." I thanked Revell profusely, hung up the phone and immediately called Gayle.

"Thank God," she said breaking down, having been braced for bad news. "Thank God there is a righteous person in Washington. Thank God there is someone honest left in this town." She burst into tears and we laughed and cried together. Imagine: we were relieved to learn from the associate deputy director of the Federal Bureau of Investigation that I was not under investigation for espionage.

Based on Revell's categorical, on-the-record statement, I assumed that Bennett would have dealt with Gart and put an end to *Time*'s threat to run the story if I did not agree to be interviewed. I called Bennett the moment I returned to Washington to get an update. There was good news and bad news. The good news was that Revell had indeed spoken with him and he had confirmed to Bennett that the allegations against me were categorically untrue. He told Bennett that he would state it on the record. Gart also called Revell and had spoken with him. Gart told Bennett that Revell had told him that the story was false, and that Revell was speaking on the record. The bad news was that since Bennett had promised Gart that I would meet with him if *Time* held the story, *Time* still insisted on the meeting, regardless of what Revell had said.

I just couldn't believe it. I phoned Strobe Talbott and asked him whether this had not gone far enough. Wasn't a denial, *on the record*, by the associate deputy director for counterintelligence and counterterrorism of the FBI enough to make *Time* give up and acknowledge that the story was false? Wasn't Revell at least as credible as their "anonymous source"? They were, after all, alleging that I was under investigation for espionage. Wouldn't the FBI know if that were true? Wouldn't my clearances have been pulled if I was at the top of anybody's list? Wouldn't I have been excluded from meetings with Bob Gates or other intelligence officials if I was under investigation for passing TOP SECRET information to a foreign government? And why would the Mossad give the director of the CIA a list of Israeli agents working in the U.S. government? The story made no sense. It was just absurd.

"Sorry, Howard," Talbott said evenly. "Everyone at *Time* holds Murray Gart in very high regard. We really think he is on to something and I am encouraging him to follow it through." As for Revell's on-the-record statements: "Well, what would you expect him to say?" Talbott continued, "Maybe he's trying to protect you. I don't know."

Using the same tone of voice he had used when he had asked me some months back whether I hadn't "forgotten" about the book on Israel's nuclear secrets I had written while living in Israel, Talbott advised me, "Meet with Murray. He thinks that only by meeting with you can he determine the facts."

Bennett and I agreed that I should go ahead and meet with Gart in the hope that I could end this farce once and for all. Bennett had to go out of town, but Rauh would be there to represent me. We met in a conference room next to Rauh's office. Bennett's secretary sat in on the meeting to take notes. Gart showed up with Dave Beckwith (coauthor of the earlier *Time* magazine story about the "cowboys" at the NSC). Beckwith was nervous and fidgeted uncomfortably. Like Talbott, he had relied upon me in the past to help him understand U.S. policy and the situation in the Middle East. Beckwith had even come to my home once, when he really needed my help. At least then I had enough credibility, in Beckwith's view, to be a valuable source.

Sitting next to Beckwith and across the table from Rauh and me, with Bennett's secretary off to one side, Gart repeated the allegation that *Time* had learned from a reliable source that Casey had received a report from a top-level Israeli official during the previous summer, listing U.S. government officials, besides Pollard, who were supplying information to Israel, and that my name was on the top of the list. Gart said that *Time* had planned to run the story and had held it only because I agreed to talk with him. He said that after speaking with Revell, he was persuaded that I had done nothing outside of the law. He admitted that he had never seen the list or any other piece of paper, with or without my name on it. Gart noted that he was not a purveyor of rumor and wondered whether it was possible that he had been set up.

Beckwith left in the middle of the meeting to attend a lunch appointment, but not before he reminded Gart to ask me to pose for a picture.

Rauh interrupted forcefully several times during the meeting in a vain effort to convince Gart to agree that in light of what Revell had told him *Time* should kill the story. Rauh spoke in real anger when he said that this situation was like Joe McCarthy days. "Let's find out who all the Jews are in important positions in government and let's see if we can tie them in with Pollard." Rauh noted that Gart had admitted that he had not seen the report and didn't know for sure whether it existed. He said he had a hard time dealing with the concept that Gart was willing to destroy my life, based on an allegation that did not result in an investigation and for which there was no basis. It was an awful thing to make an allegation when there is no truth to it. Rauh pointed out that just because someone said there was a list, and said that my name was on it, and said that people were being questioned, didn't make it a fact. But we could not prove that it did not happen. *Could we?*

Less than a year later, during a gathering of Middle East specialists and journalists at a prominent Washington think tank, Gart saw me from across the room and walked over. Although *Time* had not run the story, they never would say that they might not yet do so in the future. Extending his hand in a gesture of friendship, as though we were friends that had not met for some time, Murray Gart greeted me. I looked him coldly in the eyes and asked, "Aren't you dead yet?"

I take the Iran Affair very personally.

CHAPTER 15

DESERT STORM

---◆◆◆---

Reflagging

To appease the Arab world, and to ensure that Tehran would harbor no illusions regarding American hostility in the wake of the Iran Affair, the Reagan administration significantly escalated its involvement in the Iran-Iraq War on behalf of Iraq. Desperate to bring an end to the war, Iraqi forces had begun to attack ships going to and from Iran. Tehran retaliated by mining the upper Gulf and attacking international shipping bound for Iraq and Kuwait.

In mid-December 1986, Kuwait asked the United States to reregister its oil tankers as U.S.-flag vessels, hoping thereby to deter Iranian forces from attacking its ships while increasing the pressure on Washington to help end the war. Kuwait asked the Soviet Union to do the same, hoping that Washington would respond to its request from the perspective of traditional American interests in the region: protecting access to Middle Eastern oil while competing for influence with the Soviet Union. The United States agreed to do as the Kuwaitis had requested. Ignoring Kuwait's past relationship with the Soviet Union and its historic antipathy toward U.S. policies in the Middle East, NSC Advisor Carlucci justified the reflagging by announcing that Washington's Arab allies "will be faced with either giving in to Iranian intimidation or accepting Soviet offers of protection, and not just for shipping."

The reflagging began in July 1987, but Iran's mining activities continued to threaten international shipping. In May, Iraqi Exocet missiles struck the U.S. frigate *Stark*, killing thirty-seven American sailors. The United States responded by immediately sending American military officers to Baghdad to establish a liaison relationship with the Iraqi military and ensure that Iraq did not inadvertently strike U.S. warships again.

Whether accidental or deliberate, the net effect of the Iraqi attack on the *Stark* was to bring Washington even closer to Baghdad. Based on policy guidance coordinated by Bob Oakley, who was now responsible for

Middle East affairs on the NSC staff, the military-to-military relationship rapidly evolved, as the United States began providing the Iraqi military with critical intelligence and targeting information, as well as with assistance in planning long-range air attacks against Iran.

Certain that he would forget more about the Gulf than the Congress would ever know, and despite his insistence in 1983 that public support must be guaranteed before committing U.S. forces to battle, Weinberger dispatched special forces to the Gulf, armed for combat with a variety of weapons systems that enabled them to disrupt Iranian mine-laying operations. This was done without informing the Congress. The JCS was directed to apply relaxed rules of engagement to Iranian threats in the Persian Gulf. Accordingly, U.S. forces were permitted to assume a more aggressive posture and preempt Iranian interdiction of international shipping by firing against enemies displaying a hostile intent, rather than waiting to be attacked. These relaxed ROEs had been developed for use against Libyan forces in 1986 for Operation Prairie Fire.

When Senator Sam Nunn asked why the War Powers Act should not be invoked, following the administration's revelation that it had captured an Iranian minelayer in September 1987, the DOD played down the incident, and subsequent U.S. operations were kept secret. The administration did not want the War Powers Act to limit U.S. military operations in support of the reflagging policy.

The Gulf states still refused to permit American forces to use their facilities. Consequently, the United States was forced to construct a large artificial island and anchor it in the waters of the upper Gulf to provide logistics and operational support. The emir of Kuwait refused even to grant American minesweeping helicopters access to Kuwaiti territory. Despite the fact that it was very difficult for American forces to stay over the horizon under these circumstances, Weinberger quietly acquiesced.

The international pressure that Iraq hoped the tanker war would generate, particularly with the United States on its side, failed to convince Iran to agree to a cease-fire, as called for by the U.N. Security Council. Saddam escalated the war in March 1988 and began launching long-range SCUD missiles against major Iranian population centers, hoping to break the will of the Iranian people. But Iran had purchased long-range SCUDs from Libya and retaliated against Iraq with missile strikes of its own against Iraqi population centers, sparking a new phase of hostilities, known as the "War of the Cities."

The United States climbed up another rung on the escalation ladder following the April 1988 explosion of an Iranian mine against the hull of the USS *Samuel Roberts*. Admiral Ace Lyons had developed plans to "drill the Iranians back into the fourth century" when U.S. forces struck back hard four days later, sinking six Iranian warships and destroying two oil rigs. At the same time, the Iraqi Army launched a surprise attack against Iran to recapture the strategic Fao peninsula. Using U.S.-supplied military intelligence and knowing that U.S. strikes against Iranian targets would commence on April 18, the Iraqis launched their only successful ground assault of the war, just before the United States destroyed the Iranian Navy.

During testimony before the House Foreign Affairs Committee in 1987, Weinberger boasted of the extensive assistance the United States was providing to Iraq. But when questioned in late 1991 about the support given to Iraq, prior to its 1990 invasion of Kuwait, Weinberger categorically denied that the United States had helped Iraq in any significant way.

In the midst of a gun battle with Iranian Pasdaran in mid-1988, the USS *Vincennes* mistakenly shot down an IranAir passenger jet, killing 290 innocent civilians. Iran regarded the action of the *Vincennes* as an overt manifestation of Washington's intervention in the war on behalf of Iraq. Two weeks later, however, Tehran announced its acceptance of Security Council Resolution 598, effectively bringing the Iran-Iraq war to an end in August.

How Absurd

U.S. influence and freedom of maneuver increased significantly in early 1988, when Moscow announced its intention to withdraw Soviet forces from Afghanistan. A combination of pressures, notably America's successful covert support for the Afghan Mujahadeen, coupled with the policy of *perestroika* instituted by President Mikhail Gorbachev, contributed to the defeat of the Soviet Union in Afghanistan.

Moscow promptly sent a deputy foreign minister to Tehran to cultivate Iranian support for emerging Soviet policy in the Middle East and to counter Washington's tilt to Baghdad. Given the likelihood for a Soviet withdrawal from Afghanistan, Rafsanjani was ready to deal with Moscow, publicly offering to cooperate against the United States in Afghanistan.

While the prospects for a Soviet-Iranian rapprochement, as suggested by the draft NSDD, might have seemed "absurd" to Weinberger in 1985, they were hard to dispute by the spring of 1988. The pace of improved Iranian-Soviet ties accelerated dramatically following the June 1989 death

of the Ayatollah Khomeini. Less than three weeks later, Rafsanjani traveled to Moscow to meet President Gorbachev. A joint declaration of
principles was issued at the conclusion of Rafsanjani's visit which stated
Moscow's readiness to cooperate with Iran to strengthen its defense capabilities. Soon thereafter, the Soviet Union began to sell modern weapons
systems to Iran, including advanced aircraft. Notwithstanding its continuing role as the principal supplier of military hardware to Iraq, the Soviet
Union managed to establish a strategic foothold in Iran at the same time
it was pulling its forces out of Afghanistan. The Great Game continued.

Flawed Vision

The ink was barely dry on Iran's acceptance of the cease-fire when Saddam
Hussein resumed his campaign to dominate the Persian Gulf. But his first
step was to test the durability of Iraq's strategic ties with the United
States. In the same month that the cease-fire with Iran went into effect,
Saddam Hussein bombed Kurdish villages with chemical weapons, killing
countless numbers of men, women and children. He then sat back to
watch as the Reagan administration successfully resisted congressional
efforts, led by Congressman Howard Berman, to impose trade, finance
and technology transfer sanctions against Iraq. Aside from Secretary
Shultz's harsh criticism of Iraq's abhorrent behavior, no steps were taken
to restrain Baghdad, and political, economic and military ties continued
to develop unabated.

Trade between the United States and Iraq surpassed $2.5 billion in
1988, as the United States imported 500,000 barrels of Iraqi oil per day
while exporting grain, cotton, wool, sugar, tobacco, chemicals, manufacturing equipment, machine tools, computers, airplanes and many advanced technology products that could be used by Iraq for military as well
as civilian purposes. The reconstruction of Iraq, following the devastating
eight-and-a-half-year war with Iran, was viewed as a bonanza for U.S.
commercial interests.

In his inaugural address, President George Bush had extended to Iran
an olive branch in the hope that the two countries could develop a more
normal relationship. But Washington's fear that regional hostilities might
resume, coupled with Iran's rejection, led the Bush administration significantly to increase American support of Iraq in the vain hope that the
goals, aspirations and ruthless behavior of Saddam Hussein would somehow moderate and change for the better.

Angered by the growing relationship between Moscow and Tehran,

Saddam publicly communicated to the Bush administration his readiness to protect America's vital interests in the Gulf. In order to consolidate his leading position among the Gulf states, he demanded that Iraq be extended membership in the GCC. Fearful of Baghdad's historical ambition to dominate the Gulf, GCC leaders rebuffed Saddam. He promptly organized an alternative organization in February 1989 called the Arab Cooperation Council (ACC), composed of Iraq, Egypt, Jordan and the YAR. Saddam used the ACC to advance his strategic ambitions throughout the Middle East, coercing GCC leaders, who suddenly found themselves outflanked by this new alliance, into increasing their financial "assistance" to Baghdad.

King Fahd visited Baghdad in March 1989 where an agreement of noninterference in the internal affairs and the nonuse of force between Iraq and Saudi Arabia was concluded. Riyadh promised to assist in the reconstruction of Basra in return for Iraq's promise of noninterference and nonuse of force to settle disputes between Iraq and Saudi Arabia. Bahrain concluded a comparable agreement with Iraq.

This time, however, the emir of Kuwait refused to give in to Saddam's blandishments and threats. Confident in Iraq's relationship with the United States and no longer deterred by the likelihood that the Soviet Union would aid Kuwait as it had in the past, Saddam reasserted Iraq's "historical" claims to Kuwait. He pressed Kuwait to lease Iraq the strategic islands of Warbah and Bubiyan, pointedly reminding Kuwait that it would be wise to consider the lessons of the Iran-Iraq War, noting that unresolved border disputes remained "a thorn in the flesh" of Iraq. This Iraqi demand was nearly identical to its 1973 treaty proposal, which would have effectively yielded sovereignty of the islands to Baghdad. Surely the emir and others recalled that Iraq had used force before against Kuwait following its rejection of Iraq's demands. But Kuwaitis and others would grasp the full significance of Saddam's threats only eighteen months later when Iraqi forces conquered the emirate.

An interagency review of U.S. policy in the Persian Gulf by the Bush administration culminated in October 1989 with the adoption of National Security Directive 26 (NSD 26). This policy was based on the assumption that Iraq and Saudi Arabia would protect America's vital interests in the Gulf. As a result of the tacit alliance between Baghdad and Washington against Iran and the growing distance between Baghdad and Moscow, NSD 26 directed the national security bureaucracy to strengthen Iraq to ensure that it would be a force for regional stability and a deterrent against

Soviet and Iranian aggression. The tilt was complete. But U.S. forces were still required to remain over the horizon.

Calculating that the Bush administration was preoccupied with the collapse of the Soviet Union and the political changes sweeping across Eastern Europe, and confident that Moscow no longer possessed the power or will to act with force outside its fractured borders, Saddam was emboldened in his belief that he could act with impunity in the Gulf. The administration's desires for a security policy based on the new twin pillars of Iraq and Saudi Arabia, combined with the continued lack of realism by experts in the national security bureaucracy, led the United States to assume that Saddam Hussein would not do to Kuwait, or to Saudi Arabia, what he had tried and failed to do to Iran. They simply refused to take Saddam at his word. Much as they had dismissed Iraqi threats to develop nuclear weapons in the late 1970s, these same Middle East experts discounted Saddam's threats to burn half of Israel in the spring of 1990 or to attack his neighbors as he explicitly threatened he would if he did not get what he wanted from them.

Unable to quench his thirst for hard currency with Iraqi oil exports and unable to convince Gulf leaders to provide him with sufficient financial assistance to compensate for Iraq's cash shortfalls, Saddam took off his mask and revealed his true face. He unambiguously told the U.S. ambassador to Iraq, April Glaspie, that he viewed Kuwait's unwillingness to cooperate with Iraq as military aggression that he would answer in kind.

Saddam had no reason to believe that the United States or any other Western power would forcefully resist his 1990 invasion of Kuwait. On the contrary, the behavior of the West had fueled his ambitions and miscalculations. The United States was not alone in coddling Saddam. Arabs, Europeans, South Americans and East Asians all contributed to Iraq's war machine despite the general knowledge of Saddam's brutal behavior. Very few governments were confused by the facts when it came to making money in Iraq.

Operation Desert Storm succeeded in liberating Kuwait from the grasp of Iraq, but it failed to liberate Iraq from the hold of Saddam Hussein. Until that is accomplished and normal relations are established between Washington and Tehran, America's vital interests in the Middle East will remain at risk.

America's vision in the Middle East has been flawed since the adoption of the Twin Pillars policy during the Nixon administration. While there is no simple solution to the complex ethnic, geographic and security problems that affect American interests in the Middle East, dependence on the region's oil is too great to permit the United States to rely on other countries to protect this vital interest. American policymakers must accept the fundamental importance that power plays in the conduct of international relations and be prepared to use force judiciously when necessary. America's elected officials, the national security bureaucracy and the media must overcome the tendency to analyze and exploit world events through a prism distorted by biases, clientitis and wishful thinking. Notwithstanding the end of the Cold War, presidential leadership, Cabinet discipline and bipartisanship are still lacking in the conduct of American foreign policy. The executive branch and the Congress must set aside the divisive and debilitating struggle to control foreign affairs and must formulate and implement realistic policies that will protect America's interests into the future.

Weakness invites only aggression and isolation breeds only ignorance. The preservation of freedom demands strength, will and realistic knowledge of friend and foe alike. America can afford nothing less.

BIBLIOGRAPHY

Abir, Mordechai. *Saudi Arabia in the Oil Era, Regime and Elites: Conflict and Collaboration.* Boulder, CO: Westview Press, 1988.

———. *Oil, Power and Politics: Conflict in Arabia, the Red Sea and the Gulf.* London: F. Cass, 1974.

Abir, Mordechai, and Yodfat, Aryeh. *In the Direction of the Gulf: The Soviet Union and the Persian Gulf.* London: F. Cass, 1977.

Abrahamian, Ervand. *Iran Between Two Revolutions.* Princeton, NJ: Princeton University Press, 1983.

Adabi, Jacob. *Britain's Withdrawal from the Middle East, 1947–1971: The Economic and Strategic Imperatives.* Princeton, NJ: Kingston Press, 1983.

Ajami, Fouad. *The Arab Predicament: Arab Political Thought and Practice Since 1967.* Cambridge, England: Cambridge University Press, 1992.

———. *The Vanished Imam: Musa al Sadr and the Shia of Lebanon.* Ithaca, NY: Cornell University Press, 1986.

Al-Ebraheem, Hassan Ali. *Kuwait and the Gulf: Small States and the International System.* Washington, DC: Georgetown University Press, 1984.

Allison, Graham T. *Essence of Decision: Explaining the Cuban Missile Crisis.* Boston: Little, Brown, 1971.

Al-Sowayegh, Abdulaziz H. *Arab Petropolitics.* London: Croom Helm, 1984.

Anthony, John Duke. *Historical and Cultural Dictionary of the Sultanate of Oman and the Emirates of Eastern Arabia.* Metuchen, NJ: Scarecrow Press, 1976.

———. *Arab States of the Lower Gulf: People, Politics, Petroleum.* Washington, DC: Middle East Institute, 1975.

———. *The United States and the Middle East: Changing Relationships.* Washington, DC: Middle East Institute, 1975.

———. *North Africa in Regional and International Affairs.* Washington, DC: Middle East Institute, 1974.

———. *The States of the Arabian Peninsula and the Gulf Littoral.* Washington, DC: Middle East Institute, 1973.

Bakhash, Shaul. *The Reign of the Ayatollahs: Iran and the Islamic Revolution.* New York: Basic Books, 1984.

Batatu, Hanna. *The Egyptian, Syrian, and Iraqi Revolutions: Some Observa-

tions on Their Underlying Causes and Social Character. Washington, DC: Georgetown University, 1984.

———. *The Old Social Classes and the Revolutionary Movements of Iraq: A Study of Iraq's Old Landed and Commercial Classes and of Its Communists, Ba'thists, and Free Officers*. Princeton, NJ: Princeton University Press, 1978.

Benard, Cheryl, and Khalilzad, Zalmay. *The Government of God: Iran's Islamic Republic*. New York: Columbia University Press, 1984.

Bethell, Nicholas. *The Palestine Triangle: The Struggle Between the British, the Jews and the Arabs, 1935–48*. London: Steimatzky's Agency Ltd., 1979.

Bill, James A. *Politics in the Middle East*, 3rd ed. Glenview, IL: Scott, Foresman/Little, Brown Higher Education, 1990.

———. *The Eagle and the Lion: The Tragedy of American-Iranian Relations*. New Haven, CT: Yale University Press, 1988.

———. *The Shah, the Ayatollah, and the United States*. New York: Foreign Policy Association, 1988.

Bill, James A., and Hudson, Michael C. *The Precarious Republic: Political Modernization in Lebanon*. Boulder, CO: Westview Press, 1985.

Bill, James A., et al. *The American Media and the Arabs*. Washington, DC: Center for Contemporary Arab Studies, Georgetown University, 1980.

Braun, Aurel, ed. *The Middle East in Global Strategy*. Boulder, CO: Westview Press, 1987.

Broder, David S. *Behind the Front Page: A Candid Look at How the News Is Made*. New York: Simon & Schuster, 1987.

Brzezinski, Zbigniew. *Power and Principle: Memoirs of the National Security Adviser*. New York: Farrar, Straus & Giroux, 1985.

Cannon, Lou. *President Reagan: A Role of a Lifetime*. New York: Simon & Schuster, 1991.

Carter, Jimmy. *The Blood of Abraham*. Boston: Houghton Mifflin, 1985.

Chubin, Shahram. *Iran and Iraq at War*. London: L. B. Tauris, 1988.

———. *The Role of Outside Powers*. Totowa, NJ: International Institute for Strategic Studies, 1982.

Clausewitz, Carl von. *On War*. Baltimore: Penguin Books, 1968.

Cobban, Helena. *The Superpowers and the Syrian-Israeli Conflict: Beyond Crisis Management*. New York: Praeger, 1991.

———. *The Making of Modern Lebanon*. London: Hutchinson, 1985.

———. *The Palestinian Liberation Organization: People, Power, and Politics*. Cambridge, England: Cambridge University Press, 1984.

Cordesman, Anthony H. *After the Storm: The Changing Military Balance in the Middle East*. Boulder, CO: Westview Press; London: Mansell, 1993.

———. *Weapons of Mass Destruction in the Middle East*. London and Washington, DC: Brassey's (UK), 1991.

———. *The Gulf and the West: Strategic Relations and Military Realities*. Boulder, CO: Westview Press, 1988.

———. *The Iran-Iraq War and Western Security, 1984–87: Strategic Implications and Policy Options*. London: Jane's, 1987.

———. *Western Strategic Interests in Saudi Arabia*. London: Croom Helm, 1987.

Dallek, Robert. *American Style of Foreign Policy: Cultural Politics and Foreign Affairs*. New York: Knopf, 1983.

Dawisha, Adeed. *The Arab Radicals*. New York: Council on Foreign Relations, 1986.

Deibel, Terry L. *Presidents, Public Opinion, and Power: The Nixon, Carter, and Reagan Years*. New York: Foreign Policy Association, 1987.

———. *Commitment in American Foreign Policy: A Theoretical Examination for the Post-Vietnam Era*. Washington, DC: National Defense University, Research Directorate, 1980.

Emerson, Steven. *Secret Warriors: Inside the Covert Military Operations of the Reagan Era*. New York: Putnam, 1988.

———. *The American House of Saud: The Secret Petrodollar Connection*. New York: F. Watts, 1985.

Epstein, Joshua M. *Strategy and Force Planning: The Case of the Persian Gulf*. Washington, DC: Brookings Institution, 1987.

Finnie, David H. *Shifting Lines in the Sand: Kuwait's Elusive Frontier with Iraq*. Cambridge, MA: Harvard University Press, 1992.

Frank, Benis M. *U.S. Marines in Lebanon, 1982–1984*. Washington, DC: History and Museums Division, Headquarters, U.S. Marine Corps, 1987.

Freedman, Robert Owen. *The Middle East from the Iran-Contra Affair to the Intifada*. Syracuse, NY: Syracuse University Press, 1991.

———. *Moscow and the Middle East: Soviet Policy Since the Invasion of Afghanistan*. New York: Cambridge University Press, 1991.

———. *Soviet Policy Toward Israel Under Gorbachev*. New York: Praeger, 1991.

———. *The Middle East After the Israeli Invasion of Lebanon*. Syracuse, NY: Syracuse University Press, 1986.

————. *The Middle East Since Camp David*. Boulder, CO: Westview Press, 1984.

————. *Soviet Policy Toward the Middle East Since 1970*, 3rd edition. New York: Praeger, 1982.

Friedman, Thomas L. *From Beirut to Jerusalem*. New York: Anchor Books, 1989.

Fromkin, David. *A Peace to End All Peace: The Fall of the Ottoman Empire and the Creation of the Modern Middle East*. New York: Avon Books, 1989.

Gaddis, John Lewis. *The United States and the Origins of the Cold War, 1941–1947*. New York: Columbia University Press, 1972.

Ghareeb, Edmund. *The Kurdish Question in Iraq*. Syracuse, NY: Syracuse University Press, 1981.

Graebner, Norman A., ed. *An Uncertain Tradition: American Secretaries of State in the Twentieth Century*. New York: McGraw-Hill, 1961.

Graz, Liesl. *The Omanis: Sentinels of the Gulf*. New York: Longman, 1982.

Grummon, Stephen R. *The Iran-Iraq War: Islam Embattled*. Washington, DC: Center for Strategic and International Studies, 1982.

Haber, Eitan. *Menahem Begin: The Legend and the Man*. New York: Delacorte Press, 1978.

Haig, Alexander. *Caveat: Realism, Reagan and Foreign Policy*. New York: Macmillan, 1984.

Halliday, Fred. *Arabia Without Sultans*. New York: Penguin Books, 1974.

Halperin, Morton H., et al. *Bureaucratic Politics & Foreign Policy*. Washington, DC: Brookings Institution, 1974.

Hammond, Paul Y., and Alexander, Sidney S., eds. *Political Dynamics in the Middle East*. New York: American Elsevier, 1972.

Heller, Mark. *The Soviet-American Competition in the Middle East*. Lexington, MA: Lexington Books, 1988.

————. *The Iran-Iraq War: Implications for Third Parties*. Cambridge, MA: The Center for International Affairs, Harvard University, 1984.

Helms, Christine Moss. *Iraq: Eastern Flank of the Arab World*. Washington, DC: Brookings Institution, 1984.

Hiro, Dilip. *Iran Under the Ayatollahs*. London: Routledge & Kegan Paul, 1985.

Hudson, Michael C. *From Lebanon to Irangate: A Review of Recent Middle East Policy*. Washington, DC: Georgetown Center for Contemporary Arab Studies, 1987.

Hunter, Robert E. *U.S. Policy and the Iran-Iraq War*. Washington, DC: Middle East Institute, 1984.

————. *Presidential Control of Foreign Policy: Management or Mishap.* Washington, DC: Center for Strategic and International Studies, Georgetown University; New York: Praeger, 1982.

Hunter, Shireen, ed. *The Gulf Cooperation Council: Problems and Prospects.* Washington, DC: Center for Strategic and International Studies, Georgetown University, 1984.

Hurewitz, J. C. *Middle East Politics: The Military Dimension.* Boulder, CO: Westview Press, 1982.

————. *The Persian Gulf: After Iran's Revolution.* New York: Foreign Policy Association, 1979.

————. *Oil, the Arab-Israeli Dispute, and the Industrial World: Horizons of a Crisis.* Boulder, CO: Westview Press, 1976.

————. *The Persian Gulf: Prospects for Stability.* New York: Foreign Policy Association, 1974.

————. *Middle East Dilemmas: The Background of United States Policy.* New York: Russell & Russell, 1973.

————. *Changing Military Perspectives in the Middle East.* Santa Monica, CA: RAND Corporation, 1970.

Hurewitz, J. C., et al. *Soviet-American Rivalry in the Middle East.* New York: Academy of Political Science, Columbia University, 1969.

Isaacson, Walter. *Kissinger: A Biography.* New York: Simon & Schuster, 1992.

Jabber, Paul, et al. *Great Power Interests in the Persian Gulf.* New York: Council on Foreign Relations, 1989.

————. *Not by War Alone: Security and Arms Control in the Middle East.* Berkeley, CA: University of California Press, 1981.

Jansen, G. H. *Militant Islam.* New York: Harper Colophon Books, 1979.

Kalb, Marvin, and Kalb, Bernard. *Kissinger.* Boston: Little, Brown, 1974.

Karsh, Efraim. *The Iran-Iraq War: A Military Analysis.* London: International Institute for Strategic Studies, 1987.

Katz, Mark. *Russia and Arabia: Soviet Foreign Policy in the Arabian Peninsula.* Baltimore: Johns Hopkins University Press, 1985.

Kelly, J. B. *Arabia, the Gulf and the West.* London: Weidenfeld & Nicolson, 1980.

Kerr, Malcolm H. *Rich and Poor States in the Middle East: Egypt and the New Arab Order.* Boulder, CO: Westview Press, 1982.

————. *America's Middle East Policy: Kissinger, Carter and the Future.* Beirut, Lebanon: Institute for Palestine Studies, 1980.

————. *The Arab Cold War: Gamal 'Abd al-Nasir and His Rivals,*

1958–1970, 3rd ed. London and New York: Published for the Royal Institute of International Affairs by Oxford University Press, 1971.

———. *The Middle East Conflict*. New York: Foreign Policy Association, 1968.

Kerr, Malcolm H., and Becker, Abraham Samuel. *The Economics and Politics of the Middle East*. New York: American Elsevier, 1975.

Kimche, David. *After Nasser, Arafat & Saddam Hussein, the Last Option: The Quest for Peace in the Middle East*. London: Weidenfeld & Nicolson, 1991.

Kissinger, Henry A. *Years of Upheaval*. Boston: Little, Brown, 1982.

———. *White House Years*. Boston: Little, Brown, 1979.

Korany, Bahgat, and Dessouki, Ali E. Hillal. *The Foreign Policies of Arab States*. Boulder, CO: Westview Press, 1984.

Kuniholm, Bruce Robellet. *The Palestinian Problem and United States Policy: A Guide to Issues and References*. Claremont, CA: Regina Books, 1986.

———. *The Origins of the Cold War in the Near East: Great Power Conflict and Diplomacy in Iran, Turkey, and Greece*. Princeton, NJ: Princeton University Press, 1980.

Lacey, Robert. *The Kingdom*. New York: Harcourt Brace Jovanovich, 1981.

Laqueur, Walter, and Rubin, Barry M., eds. *The Israel-Arab Reader: A Documentary History of the Middle East Conflict*. New York: Penguin Books, 1984.

Ledeen, Michael A. *Perilous Statecraft: An Insider's Account of the Iran-Contra Affair*. New York: Scribner's, 1988.

Ledeen, Michael A., and Lewis, William. *Debacle: The American Failure in Iran*. New York: Vintage Books, 1982.

Lenczowski, George. *American Presidents in the Middle East*. Durham, NC: Duke University Press, 1990.

———. *The Middle East in World Affairs*, 4th ed. Ithaca, NY: Cornell University Press, 1980.

———. *Soviet Advances in the Middle East*. Washington, DC: American Enterprise Institute for Public Policy Research, 1972.

———. *Russia and the West in Iran, 1918–1948: A Study in Big Power Rivalry*. New York: Greenwood Press, 1968.

Lewis, Bernard. *The Assassins: A Radical Sect in Islam*. New York: Basic Books, 1968.

Lieber, Robert J. *The Oil Decade: Conflict and Cooperation in the West*. New York: University Press of America, 1986.

Litwak, Robert; Chubin, Shahram; and Plascov, Avi. *Security in the Persian Gulf*, Vols. 1–4. London: International Institute for Strategic Studies, 1982.

Litwak, Robert, et al. *Détente and the Nixon Doctrine: American Foreign Policy and the Pursuit of Stability, 1969–1976*. New York: Cambridge University Press, 1984.

Long, David E. *The Anatomy of Terrorism*. New York: Free Press, 1990.

———. *The Government and Politics of the Middle East and North Africa*, 2nd ed. Boulder, CO: Westview Press, 1986.

———. *The United States and Saudi Arabia: Ambivalent Allies*. Boulder, CO: Westview Press, 1985.

———. *The Persian Gulf: An Introduction to Its Peoples, Politics and Economics*, 2nd ed. Boulder, CO: Westview Press, 1978.

Long, David E., and Shaw, John A. *Saudi Arabian Modernization: The Impact of Change on Stability*. Washington, DC: Center for Strategic and International Studies, Georgetown University, 1982.

Luttwak, Edward. *The Dictionary of Modern War*. New York: HarperCollins, 1991.

———. *Strategy: The Logic of War and Peace*. Cambridge, MA: Belknap Press/Harvard University Press, 1987.

———. *Strategy and History*. New Brunswick, NJ: Transaction Books, 1985.

———. *The Pentagon and the Art of War: The Question of Military Reform*. New York: Simon & Schuster, 1984.

———. *The Grand Strategy of the Soviet Union*. London: Weidenfeld & Nicolson, 1983.

———. *Coup d'Etat: A Practical Handbook*. Cambridge, MA: Harvard University Press, 1979.

Mackey, Sandra. *Lebanon: Death of a Nation*. New York: Anchor Books, 1991.

———. *The Saudis: Inside the Desert Kingdom*. Boston: Houghton Mifflin, 1987.

McNaugher, Thomas L. *Arms and Oil: U.S. Military Strategy and the Persian Gulf*. Washington, DC: Brookings Institution, 1985.

Ma'oz, Moshe. *Asad: The Sphinx of Damascus—A Political Biography*. New York: Weidenfeld & Nicolson, 1988.

Marr, Phebe. *The Modern History of Iraq*. Boulder, CO: Westview Press, 1985.

Martin, David C., and Walcott, John. *Best Laid Plans: The Inside Story of America's War Against Terrorism*. New York: Harper & Row, 1988.

Miller, Judith, and Mylroie, Laurie. *Saddam Hussein and the Crisis in the Gulf*. New York: Times Books, 1990.

Monroe, Elizabeth. *Britain's Moment in the Middle East, 1914–1971*, 2nd ed. Baltimore: Johns Hopkins University Press, 1981.

Moore, Barrington, Jr. *Social Origins of Dictatorship and Democracy: Lord and Peasant in the Making of the Modern World*. Boston: Beacon Press, 1966.

Mortimer, Edward. *Faith & Power: The Politics of Islam*. New York: Vintage Books, 1982.

Mottahedeh, Roy. *The Mantle of the Prophet: Religion and Politics in Iran*. New York: Simon & Schuster, 1985.

Naff, Thomas, ed. *Gulf Security and the Iran-Iraq War*. Washington, DC: National Defense University Press, 1985.

Nakhleh, Emile A. *The Gulf Cooperation Council: Policies, Problems and Prospects*. New York: Praeger, 1986.

———. *The Persian Gulf in American Policy*. New York: Praeger, 1982.

———. *The Arabian Peninsula, Red Sea and Gulf: Strategic Considerations*. Hyattsville, MD: Institute of Middle Eastern and North African Affairs, 1979.

Neff, Donald. *Warriors Against Israel*. Brattleboro, VT: Amana Books, 1988.

———. *Warriors for Jerusalem: The Six Days That Changed the Middle East*. New York: Linden Press/Simon & Schuster, 1984.

———. *Warriors at Suez: Eisenhower Takes America into the Middle East*. New York: Linden Press/Simon & Schuster, 1981.

Niblock, Tim. *Class and Power in Sudan: The Dynamics of Sudanese Politics, 1898–1985*. Albany, NY: State University of New York Press, 1987.

———, ed. *Social and Economic Developments in the Arab Gulf*. New York: St. Martin's Press, 1980.

Niblock, Tim, et al. *Iraq: The Contemporary State*. New York: St. Martin's Press, 1982.

Nixon, Richard. *RN: Memoirs of Richard Nixon*. Touchstone Books/Simon & Schuster, 1990.

Noyes, James H. *The Clouded Lens: Persian Gulf Security and U.S. Policy*, 2nd ed. Stanford, CA: Hoover Institution Press, 1982.

Osama, Abdul Rahman. *The Dilemma of Development in the Arabian Peninsula*. London: Croom Helm, 1987.

Peck, Malcolm C. *The United Arab Emirates: A Venture in Unity*. Boulder, CO: Westview Press, 1986.

Penrose, Edith and E. F. *Iraq: International Relations and National Developments*. Boulder, CO: Westview Press, 1978.

Pipes, Daniel. *Greater Syria: The History of Ambition*. New York: Oxford University Press, 1990.

Prados, John. *Keepers of the Keys: A History of the National Security Council from Truman to Bush*. New York: William Morrow, 1991.

Pranger, Robert J. *American Policy Options in Iran and the Persian Gulf*. Washington, DC: American Enterprise Institute for Public Policy Research, 1979.

Pryer, Melvyn. *A View from the Rimland: An Appraisal of Soviet Interests and Involvement in the Gulf*. Durham, England: Centre for Middle Eastern and Islamic Studies, University of Durham, 1981.

Quandt, William B. *The United States and Egypt: An Essay on Policy for the 1990s*. Washington, DC: Brookings Institution, 1990.

————. *The Middle East: Ten Years After Camp David*. Washington, DC: Brookings Institution, 1988.

————. *Camp David: Peacemaking and Politics*. Washington, DC: Brookings Institution, 1986.

————. *Saudi Arabia in the 1980s: Foreign Policy, Security and Oil*. Washington, DC: Brookings Institution, 1981.

————. *Decade of Decisions: American Policy Toward the Arab-Israeli Conflict, 1967–1976*. Berkeley, CA: University of California Press, 1977.

————. *Palestinian Nationalism: Its Political and Military Dimensions*. Santa Monica, CA: RAND Corporation, 1971.

Rabinovich, Itamar. *The Road Not Taken: Early Arab-Israeli Negotiations*. New York: Oxford University Press, 1991.

————. *Ethnicity, Pluralism and the State in the Middle East*. Ithaca, NY: Cornell University Press, 1988.

————. *The War for Lebanon, 1970–1985*, revised edition. Ithaca, NY: Cornell University Press, 1985.

————. *Syria Under the Ba'th, 1963–1966: The Army Party Symbiosis*. Jerusalem: Israel Universities Press, 1972.

Ramazani, R. K. *Revolutionary Iran: Challenge and Response in the Middle East*. Baltimore: Johns Hopkins University Press, 1986.

Record, Jeffrey. *Determining Future U.S. Tactical Airlift Requirements*. Washington, DC: Pergamon-Brassey's International Defense Publishers, 1987.

————. *U.S. Strategic Airlift: Requirements and Capabilities*. Cambridge, MA: Institute for Foreign Policy Analysis, 1985.

————. *The Rapid Deployment Force and U.S. Military Intervention in the Persian Gulf*, 2nd ed. Cambridge, MA: Institute for Foreign Policy Analysis, 1983.

Regional Surveys of the World. *The Middle East and North Africa (1992)*, 38th ed. London: Europa, 1991.

Roosevelt, Kermit. *Countercoup: The Struggle for the Control of Iran*. New York: McGraw-Hill, 1979.

Ross, Dennis. *Considering Soviet Threats to the Persian Gulf*. Washington, DC: The Wilson Center, 1981.

Rubin, Barry M. *Cauldron of Turmoil: America in the Middle East*. New York: Harcourt Brace Jovanovich, 1992.

————. *Islamic Fundamentalism in Egyptian Politics*. New York: St. Martin's Press, 1990.

————. *Secrets of State: The State Department and the Struggle over U.S. Foreign Policy*. New York: Oxford University Press, 1985.

————. *Paved with Good Intentions: The American Experience and Iran*. New York: Penguin Books, 1981.

Rubinstein, Alvin Z. *Soviet Foreign Policy Since World War II: Imperial and Global*, 4th ed. New York: HarperCollins, 1992.

————. *Moscow's Third World Strategy*. Princeton, NJ: Princeton University Press, 1990.

————. *The Great Game: Rivalry in the Persian Gulf and South Asia*. New York: Praeger, 1983.

————. *Soviet Policy Toward Turkey, Iran and Afghanistan: The Dynamics of Influence*. New York: Praeger, 1982.

Sachar, Howard Morley. *Egypt and Israel*. New York: R. Marek, 1981.

————. *A History of Israel*. 2 vols. New York: Knopf, 1976, 1987.

Safran, Nadav. *Saudi Arabia: The Ceaseless Quest for Security*. Ithaca, NY: Cornell University Press, 1988.

————. *Israel, the Embattled Ally*. Cambridge, MA: Belknap Press/Harvard University Press, 1981.

————. *From War to War: The Arab-Israeli Confrontation, 1948–1967: A Study of the Conflict from the Perspective of Coercion in the Context of Inter-Arab and Big Power Relations*. New York: Pegasus, 1969.

Saivetz, Carol R. *The Soviet Union and the Gulf in the 1980s*. Boulder, CO: Westview Press, 1989.

Schiff, Ze'ev. *October Earthquake: Yom Kippur 1973*. Tel Aviv: University Pub. Projects, 1974.

Schiff, Ze'ev, and Ya'ari, Ehud. *Israel's Lebanon War*. New York: Simon & Schuster, 1984.

Schiff, Ze'ev; Haber, Eitan; and Ya'ari, Ehud. *The Year of the Dove*. New York: Bantam Books, 1979.

Sciolino, Elaine. *The Outlaw State: Saddam Hussein's Quest for Power and the Gulf Crisis*. New York: Wiley, 1991.

Seale, Patrick. *Asad: The Struggle for the Middle East*. Berkeley, CA: University of California Press, 1988.

Segev, Samuel. *The Iranian Triangle: The Untold Story of Israel's Role in the Iran-Contra Affair*. New York: Free Press, 1988.

Sick, Gary. *October Surprise: America's Hostages in Iran and the Election of Ronald Reagan*. New York: Times Books, 1992.

———. *All Fall Down: America's Tragic Encounter with Iran*. New York: Penguin Books, 1986.

Snyder, Jed C. *Defending the Fringe: NATO, the Mediterranean, and the Persian Gulf*. Boulder, CO: Westview Press, 1987.

Spiegel, Steven L. *The Other Arab-Israeli Conflict: Making America's Middle East Policy, from Truman to Reagan*. Chicago: University of Chicago Press, 1985.

Spiegel, Steven L.; Heller, Mark A.; and Goldberg, Jacob. *The Soviet-American Competition in the Middle East*. Lexington, MA: Lexington Books, 1988.

Tahir-Kheli, Shirin, and Shaheen, Ayubi, eds. *The Iran-Iraq War: New Weapons, Old Conflicts*. New York: Praeger, 1983.

Tel Aviv University, Shiloah Institute, Moshe Dayan Center for Middle Eastern and African Studies. *Middle East Contemporary Survey*, Vols. 1–13. Boulder, CO: Westview Press, 1978–1990.

Timmerman, Kenneth R. *The Death Lobby: How the West Armed Iraq*. Boston: Houghton Mifflin, 1991.

Vance, Cyrus. *Hard Choices: Critical Years in America's Foreign Policy*. New York: Simon & Schuster, 1983.

Weinberger, Caspar. *Fighting for Peace*. New York: Time-Warner Books, 1991.

Woodward, Bob. *Veil: Secret Wars of the CIA, 1981–1987*. New York: Simon & Schuster, 1987.

Wright, Robin. *In the Name of God: The Khomeini Decade*. New York: Simon & Schuster, 1989.

———. *Sacred Rage: The Wrath of Militant Islam*. New York: Simon & Schuster, 1980.

Yaniv, Avner. *Deterrence Without the Bomb: The Politics of Israeli Strategy*. Lexington, MA: Lexington Books, 1987.

———. *Dilemmas of Security: Politics, Strategy, and the Israeli Experience in Lebanon*. New York: Oxford University Press, 1987.

———. *Syria Under Assad: Domestic Constraints and Regional Risks*. New York: St. Martin's Press, 1986.

Yarnell, Allen, ed. *The Postwar Epoch: Perspectives on American History Since 1945*. New York: Harper & Row, 1975.

Yergin, Daniel. *The Prize: The Epic Quest for Oil, Money and Power*. New York: Simon & Schuster, 1991.

———. *Shattered Peace: The Origins of the Cold War and the National Security State*. Boston: Houghton Mifflin, 1977.

Yodfat, Aryeh. *The Soviet Union and Revolutionary Iran*. New York: St. Martin's Press, 1984.

———. *PLO Strategy and Politics*. New York: St. Martin's Press, 1981.

INDEX